KARL MARX AND THE
BRITISH LABOUR MOVEMENT

YEARS OF THE FIRST INTERNATIONAL

KARL MARX AND THE BRITISH LABOUR MOVEMENT

Years of the First International

BY

HENRY COLLINS

AND

CHIMEN ABRAMSKY

LONDON

MACMILLAN & CO LTD

NEW YORK · ST MARTIN'S PRESS

1965

Copyright © Henry Collins and Chimen Abramsky 1965

MACMILLAN AND COMPANY LIMITED
St Martin's Street London WC2
also Bombay Calcutta Madras Melbourne

THE MACMILLAN COMPANY OF CANADA LIMITED
70 Bond Street Toronto 2

ST MARTIN'S PRESS INC
175 Fifth Avenue New York 10010 NY

Library of Congress catalogue card no. 65—11940

PRINTED IN GREAT BRITAIN

PREFACE

SEPTEMBER 1964 marks the centenary of the First International. Despite its comparatively short life, that organisation changed the history of the world. It was established in 1864 towards the height of England's mid-Victorian prosperity. The General Council, as its directing body came to be called, included from the beginning a relatively unknown German refugee. It was he who, serving in the modest capacity of Corresponding Secretary for Germany, gave world significance to its activities.

The foundation of the International in London on September 28, 1864 was a turning-point in the history of the European labour movement. Its two predecessors, the Fraternal Democrats of 1846 and the International Association of 1855, remained comparatively feeble and made hardly a ripple either in England or on the Continent. The International was the first working-class organisation to make a decisive impact on European politics. If it helped actively in shaping and moulding the early labour organisations in Europe, this was largely the achievement of one man — Karl Marx.

Marx had come to live in England in 1849. He was soon on friendly terms with leading Chartists, particularly with Ernest Jones and George Julian Harney. But, since Chartism at just that moment was entering its period of disintegration and decline, Marx remained largely unknown in the British labour movement down to 1864. His lasting significance for England derives largely from his activity on the General Council of the International from then until 1872. Though he played no part in founding the International, Marx was co-opted on to the General Council from the beginning and soon established an almost unchallenged intellectual ascendancy. Keeping deliberately in the background, he drafted almost all its statements, addresses, manifestos and general reports.

Both the First International and its General Council in London were hampered throughout their existences by lack of money. The International was hardly the powerful, well administered, smoothly functioning organisation of current legend. But it provided the medium through which the ideas of Marx were transmitted to the young socialist movements of France, Germany, Holland, Belgium, Russia and the U.S.A. as well as, though in smaller measure, to other parts of Europe. In more than a dozen countries the new organisation fired the imagination of the working class. It produced echoes as far afield as India and Australia. Inevitably it also became the bogy of more than one frightened government.

When, during the lifetime of Marx, Socialism became a world force, it was expressed in his terms and armed with his ideas, rather than those of Mazzini, Proudhon or Bakunin. This was almost entirely due to the International and the effective leadership which Marx brought to bear on the labour movements of many countries at a formative stage in their development. But for the International it seems doubtful whether Marx's impact on the future of world Socialism would have been so deep or lasting. It was the International which caused the re-publication of the *Communist Manifesto* in German and other languages. More than any other of Marx's writings, this pamphlet was the means through which his ideas were disseminated.

It seems paradoxical that it was in England, where the General Council of the International was established and where through its work Marx came into contact with so many of the leading trade unionists, that his direct influence was so small. The present book is in part an attempt to explain the paradox. Yet, even at a superficial glance, it is clear that the International made its mark on the British labour movement. For one thing, it was the first political organisation in which trade unions participated as affiliated bodies. For another, industrial and political causes with which the labour movement in Britain was later to identify itself were first raised to prominence on a world scale by the International. The Campaign for the legal eight-hour day was initiated by the International at its Geneva Congress in 1866. A generation later it became the main platform around which the forces of the 'New Unionism' mustered in their struggle to win control of the T.U.C. The second annual Trades Union Congress, meeting at Birmingham in 1869, paid tribute to the achievements of the International and called on its affiliated unions to join it. A few days later the Basle Congress of the International brought a three-year-old controversy to an end, when it included land nationalisation in its programme with the full support of the English trade union delegation headed by Robert Applegarth.

The International also taught the trade unions in Britain to react as organised bodies to international developments. It strengthened the already powerful internationalist currents in the movement against those who wanted the unions to remain insular and to concentrate exclusively on industrial matters. Over the Irish question, Marx and the General Council instructed the labour movement in the first of a long series of 'anti-colonial' campaigns. The International was the first organised labour body to make a definite stand on the question of war in general and it expressed its attitude to a particular war — that between France and Prussia in 1870 — in a memorable address.

If the International made its impact on the working-class movement in Britain, the participation of the British trade unions was decisive for the future of world Socialism. On the Polish question, the eight-hour day, land nationalisation and the participation of workers in politics, it was only through the support of the British unions that 'collectivist' Socialism won its battles with the anarchist trend, at first represented by the French followers of Proudhon. By the late eighteen-sixties the Russian, Mikhail Bakunin, raised the second and much more formidable anarchist challenge to the leadership of Marx. In the year which followed the defeat of the Paris Commune in May 1871 Marx, faced with a growing threat from Bakunin, found himself now without the active support of the British trade unionists. He then took the extraordinary step of transferring the General Council to New York where it died almost unnoticed four years later. For Marx, as for many others, the International had ceased to fulfil a useful political and educational purpose once the first experiment in working-class government had been destroyed. In the circumstances, the International could well be allowed a dignified if inconspicuous funeral in New York.

The present book tries for the first time to assess the International in relation to the industrial and political movement of the British working class. A new analysis has been attempted of the *Inaugural Address*, the first document drafted by Marx for the General Council and of its significance in the development of those ideas which were to find more systematic expression a few years later in *Das Kapital*. New light is thrown on Marx's approach to the British labour movement in an examination of both the *Inaugural Address* and of Marx's subsequent and more spectacular *Civil War in France*. Finally, we have added what we believe to be the most comprehensive bibliography on the First International in existence.

The book has gained greatly, at various stages, from discussion with a great many people who have helped us with criticism and also with advice on the location of documents and with the loan of material. They include in particular Frederick B. Adams Jnr., New York; Bert Andreas, Geneva; Professor Sir Isaiah Berlin; Dr. Werner Blumenberg, Amsterdam; H. L. Beales; Professor Asa Briggs; Hugh Clegg; the late Professor G. D. H. Cole; Dr. Stephen Coltham; Dr. Eric Hobsbawm; Dr. Royden Harrison; Miss M. Hunink, Amsterdam; James Klugmann; Arthur Lehning, Amsterdam; Dr. Paul O'Higgins; Philip McCann; D. N. Pritt, Q.C.; Andrew Rothstein; Professor A. J. C. Rüter, Amsterdam; Marc Tougouchi, Brussels. Our sincere gratitude is due to all of the above who are, however, in no way responsible for the opinions expressed in the book. Our thanks are also due to George Aitken and the office staff of the A.E.U., and to the General Secretaries and office staffs of the A.S.W. and A.U.B.T.W. for their kindness in providing us with access to union records, and to the librarians and staffs of the International Institute of Social History, Amsterdam, the Reading Room and Newspaper Library of the British Museum, the Public Record Office, the London School of Economics, the Goldsmiths' Library and the Bishopsgate Institute, London. Finally, we are most grateful to the Oxford University Delegacy for Extra-Mural Studies for the grant to one of the authors, Henry Collins, of a year's sabbatical leave and to the Trustees of the Arnold and the Cyril Foster essay funds for generous help towards travelling expenses.

We are most grateful for the special advice given by E. H. Carr.

H. C.
C. A.

CONTENTS

PART FOUR
THE WAR AND THE PARIS COMMUNE

PART FIVE
THE LAST PHASE

ABBREVIATIONS

A.B.V.	Arbeiterbildungsverein (German Workers' Educational League)
A.S.C.J.	Amalgamated Society of Carpenters and Joiners
A.S.E.	Amalgamated Society of Engineers
B.F.C.	British Federal Council
Bis.	Bishopsgate Institute, London
G.C.	General Council
I.I.S.G.	International Institute of Social History, Amsterdam
I.L.U.	International Labour Union
I.M.L.	Institute of Marxism-Leninism, Moscow
Int. Her.	International Herald
I.W.M.A.	International Working Men's Association
L.L.L.	Land and Labour League
L.S.E.	London School of Economics and Political Science
L.T.R.A.	Land Tenure Reform Association
L.T.C.	London Trades Council
M.E.S.C. London	Marx-Engels Selected Correspondence, London, 1936
M.E.S.C. Moscow	Marx-Engels Selected Correspondence, Moscow, 1956
M.E.S.W. London	Marx-Engels Selected Works, London, 1942
M.E.S.W. Moscow	Marx-Engels Selected Works, Moscow, 1951
M.E. Soc.	Marx-Engels Sochinenia, Moscow
T.U.C.	Trades Union Congress

Note: There are a number of editions of the correspondence of Marx and Engels. Except where stated, letters can be found in the Marx-Engels Sochinenia, Moscow, volumes XXI-XXIX, under the appropriate dates. Where there is an English edition, volume and page references are also given.

PART ONE

FOUNDATION OF THE INTERNATIONAL

CHAPTER I

Early Attempts at a Labour International

TRADITIONS of internationalism in the British labour movement go back as far as the French Revolution. Internationalism and organised labour alike, however, were effectively crushed during the Revolutionary and Napoleonic Wars. It was not until the 1830s that the reappearance of a labour movement in England and the Continent made possible renewed attempts at an international alliance. From the growth of Chartism in the 1840s there sprang, in the shape of the Fraternal Democrats, the first serious attempt to found a Labour International.

'The first efforts towards international brotherhood', wrote Mark Hovell,[1] 'came from the Chartist leaders, and their methods were studied by the revolutionaries of the Continent and adapted to the conditions of their own lands.' The Fraternal Democrats expired in 1854 and two years later appeared the International Association which led a fitful and flickering existence for some three years. Despite their limited scope, these two societies paved the way for the emergence in 1864 of an International Working Men's Association which was to make a lasting impact on the development of the European labour movement.

THE FRENCH, BELGIAN AND POLISH REVOLUTIONS, 1830–31

The French revolution of July 1830 directly stimulated the revival of democratic activity in England. Together with the Belgian revolution a month later, it saw the end of the Holy Alliance as an effective force in European politics. Formed in 1815 as a union of monarchs to crush 'The Revolution' wherever it might appear, the Alliance had notably failed to protect either the rule of the Bourbons in France or the dominion of the House of Orange over Belgium. The year 1830 was long remembered by English workers. Thirty-four years later, on

[1] *The Chartist Movement*, 1925, p. 312.

the eve of the formation of the First International, a letter in the *Beehive* [1] remarked that the July revolution in France had precipitated both the Polish uprising of 1831 and the movement which culminated in England in the Reform Act of 1832.

The French and Belgian revolutions succeeded. The Polish uprising was crushed and its failure sent a stream of *émigrés* to England where they settled, mostly in London, and made contact with English political circles. While the revolt lasted, moral support for it in England was almost unanimous ; even the *Morning Post* agreeing that theirs was a worthy cause.[2] The National Union of the Working Classes and Others, of which William Lovett, James Bronterre O'Brien and Henry Hetherington were members, was founded in 1831, in part as a response to the events in Europe. Its members used to celebrate the anniversaries of the French revolutions and Polish insurrections while strenuously denouncing the foreign policy of Lord Palmerston which was believed by Radicals to favour Russia.

The National Union of the Working Classes became submerged in the broad stream of movement for political reform which resulted in the Act of 1832. Disappointment with the results of the Reform Act gave new impetus to the drive for independent working-class organisation. For a short time in 1834, Robert Owen inspired some tens of thousands of workers in the Grand National Consolidated Trades Union. The arrival of a Saint-Simonian mission in London in 1832 no doubt helped to stimulate British interest in French revolutionary thought[3] and on June 7 and 14, 1834, James Morrison's *Pioneer* published an exchange of correspondence between a group of workers in Nantes and the Owenite Grand National.

CHARTISM

Owen's apocalyptic experiment collapsed under its own weight. Interest turned from the revolutionary, non-political trade unionism of the Grand National back to independent working class political activity. In June 1836 Lovett founded the London Working Men's Association from which Chartism developed directly. In the same year Henry Hetherington pub-

---

[1] September 17, 1864.
[2] J. H. Gleason, *The Genesis of Russophobia in Great Britain*, 1950, p. 113.
[3] R. Pankhurst, *The Saint Simonians: Mill and Carlyle*, 1957.

lished Buonarroti's *History of Babeuf's Conspiracy for Equality*. Though earlier works by Fourier and Saint-Simon had been translated into English they seem to have made little political impact. Babeuf's book, however, translated and annotated by Bronterre O'Brien, transmitted to the internationally minded section of the Chartist movement the socialist ideas of revolutionary France. From the same source, George Julian Harney, introduced to politics by the *Poor Man's Guardian*, which Hetherington owned and O'Brien edited, obtained his introduction to French radical and socialist thought.

On both wings of the nascent Chartism movement there was intense interest in international contacts. In 1836 Lovett produced for the London Working Men's Association an *Address to the Workers of Belgium*, the first of a series of messages to the European working class. 'If monarchs could unite against the Revolution,' he wrote in one of the earliest of these, 'why should not the "producers of wealth" constitute their own "Holy Alliance"?'[1] Among the signatories of the Address was Robert Hartwell, later manager and editor of the *Beehive* which was to become the first organ of the International.

In 1837 Harney founded his East London Democratic Association, a consciously revolutionary body modelled on the French Jacobin Club. But it was not only French influences which moulded the ideas of the revolutionary wing of Chartism. Harney's associations with the refugee Poles, dating from 1834, profoundly affected his outlook. For forty years, from their arrival in 1832 down to the effective end of the First International in 1872, this group of exiles maintained intimate contact with labour and radical organisations. At a meeting to commemorate the rising of 1830, Carl Schapper, a German revolutionary and himself an *émigré*, said: 'Well, the revolution failed and Poland's sons emigrated, carrying the seeds of freedom with them to Germany, to France, to England'.[2] Much later the Liberal historian, H. A. L. Fisher, was even more specific. The Polish emigration, he declared, 'a cosmopolitan network of conspiracy', was a means of 'bringing into a loose communion the disaffected portions of the European proletariat'.[3]

---

[1] Place Newspaper Collection, set 56, vol. I, fo. 103. Quoted in A. R. Schoyen, *The Chartist Challenge*, 1958, p. 52.

[2] *Northern Star*, December 4, 1847.

[3] *The Republican Tradition in Europe*, 1911, p. 213.

B

With the development and spread of Chartism, international contacts multiplied quickly. Through the Scottish leader, Dr. John Taylor, the Chartists were 'from 1837 to 1840 in communication with the Parisian revolutionists'.[1] The Polish *émigré* leader, Major Beniowski, wrote on the tactics of insurrection for Harney's *London Democrat* in April 1839. The extreme anti-Russian propaganda of David Urquhart, an ex-diplomatic official and a monomaniac on the subject, won a response from some sections of the Chartist movement, notably in Glasgow and Newcastle.[2] The Chartist period also saw the first recorded financial contribution from British workers in support of a foreign strike when a group of English tailors sent a small sum to help their colleagues in Paris.[3]

When the *Northern Star*, the leading Chartist newspaper, moved its offices from Leeds to London in November 1844, there opened a period of much more regular contacts between leading Chartists and foreign refugees. For the first time these contacts included the Germans, whose Arbeiterbildungsverein — Workers' Educational Society — had been established in London in 1840. Its distinctively socialist outlook made it at the time unique among political organisations in England and it was the most important of the foreign societies which later joined the International. It convened a public meeting on September 22, 1844, together with English Owenites and French communists, to welcome the German revolutionary worker, Wilhelm Weitling, to London.[4] At about the same time, through Robert Owen's *New Moral World* and Harney's *Northern Star*, British workers were learning of the existence and activities of Karl Marx, later to play the dominant rôle in the history of the International.[5]

[1] M. Beer, 'The International: its Historical Significance', *Socialist Review*, July-September 1914.

[2] Gleason, *op. cit.*, p. 260, *et seq.*

[3] *L'Atelier*, September 1840, quoted by A. Lehning, 'The International Association, 1855–59', *International Review for Social History*, Amsterdam, 1938, p. 187, n. 1.

[4] A. Lehning, *op. cit.*, pp. 195-6. Lehning points out that this was probably the first political meeting at which workers from different nationalities spoke from the same platform.

[5] *New Moral World*, November 4, 1843; October 5, 1844; December 13, 1844; March 8, 1845. Frederick Engels, author of the articles, was the paper's German correspondent. The series also appeared in the *Northern Star*, beginning November 11, 1843, soon after Engels called on Harney at the *Star's* office in Leeds.

THE FRATERNAL DEMOCRATS

In March 1846 the society known as the Fraternal Democrats was established, largely on Harney's initiative. Though it had no foreign branches, the new society corresponded with the Democratic Association in Brussels and was organised on the basis of one General Secretary for each affiliated nationality — an idea later incorporated in the Statutes of the International. Britain — for which Harney acted as Secretary — Germany, France, Scandinavia, Hungary, Switzerland and Poland were represented on the committee. It is significant that Young Italy, Giuseppe Mazzini's association, did not participate, mainly because 'the egalitarian principles of the Fraternal Democrats precluded any close connection with the great Italian, to whom communism was anathema'.[1]

One of the first activities of the Fraternal Democrats arose out of the crisis in Britain's relations with the United States over the Oregon boundary question. When the Government proposed a Militia Bill, early in 1846, a series of Chartist meetings of protest was held throughout the country to which Harney, then editing the *Northern Star*, gave maximum publicity. The simple slogan of the demonstrators was 'No Vote! No Musket!' and in an *Address to the Working Classes of Great Britain and the United States on the Oregon Question*, Harney rammed home the point. 'When henceforth', he wrote, 'the masses — the impoverished unrepresented masses, are called upon by their rulers to fight for "their country" . . . they will answer. . . . "If you will monopolize all, fight for the country yourselves".' Neither the American nor the British workers had anything to gain in a war for territory.[2]

The formation of the Fraternal Democrats also coincided with the second great Polish insurrection of the nineteenth century, the Cracow rising. Unlike its predecessor of 1830 the Cracow rising attempted a social revolution. Its programme of land reform and the abolition of feudal privilege, though it earned the hostility of the right wing in the Polish national movement, and the disapproval of the London *Times*, won warm support from the Fraternal Democrats and from a Chartist as normally indifferent to international affairs as Fergus O'Connor.

The Cracow insurrection was crushed by Austrian troops

---

[1] Schoyen, *op. cit.*, p. 137.   [2] *Ibid.*, pp. 138-9.

and the old three-power subjugation of Poland was resumed. When in the following year a revolt of the Portuguese Junta against Donna Maria was put down with the help of Britain, France and Spain, the case for a Holy Alliance of labour seemed to Harney to have been underlined. 'People were beginning to understand', he told a meeting of the Fraternal Democrats, 'that foreign as well as domestic questions do affect them; that a blow struck at Liberty on the Tagus is an injury to friends of Freedom on the Thames; that the success of Republicanism in France would be the doom of tyranny in every other land; and the triumph of England's democratic Charter would be the salvation of millions throughout Europe.' Even more explicit was his remark on the second anniversary of the Cracow rising: 'Let the working men of Europe advance together and strike for their rights at one and the same time, and it will be seen that every tyrannical government and usurping class will have enough to do at home without attempting to assist other oppressors'.[1]

Within weeks, Harney's view was vindicated on a spectacular scale. On February 24, two days before his speech was printed in the *Northern Star*, revolution in Paris had forced the abdication of Louis-Philippe. By March 13 the revolution had spread to Vienna and Metternich was in flight. Five days later Berlin rose and soon the triumph of revolution in Bohemia, Hungary and Northern Italy seemed complete.

At a meeting to welcome the revolution in France, from which hundreds had to be turned away, the Fraternal Democrats elected a delegation of three — Harney, Ernest Jones, a recent recruit to Chartism, and Philip McGrath, President of the Chartist executive — to take their congratulations to the Provisional Government in Paris. The three British delegates were accompanied by the Germans, Carl Schapper, Joseph Moll and Heinrich Bauer, all members of the Communist League which, some months earlier, had commissioned Marx and Engels to write the *Communist Manifesto*.

The revolution's honeymoon period was soon over and in June there occurred the first armed clash between a middle-class government and the working class, ending in the workers' defeat. The significance of the June days in England, however, was overshadowed by the Chartist *débâcle* at Kennington

---

[1] *Northern Star*, February 26, 1848. Quoted in T. Rothstein, *From Chartism to Labourism*, 1929, pp. 136-7.

Common on April 10. From then onwards the Fraternal Democrats shared in the general decline of Chartism. But at least for the first two years of its existence, the society's importance in giving organised expression to the idea of proletarian internationalism can hardly be exaggerated. To Harney and the Fraternal Democrats must go much of the credit for the fact that in the 1850s and 1860s the British workers were more responsive to international issues than at any time before or much of the time since.

Nor was its influence confined to England. The Democratic Association of Belgium which corresponded with the English society included Marx among its members. On May 5, 1846, a few weeks after the foundation of the Fraternal Democrats, Marx wrote to Proudhon of his intention to establish an international correspondence committee to keep the socialists in France, Germany and England in touch with each others' ideas. This would be valuable when the 'time for action' arrived. Nothing came of the project, though it shows the lines along which Marx's mind was developing. And on November 29, 1847, at a meeting organised jointly by the Fraternal Democrats and a Polish committee to celebrate the Polish rising of 1830, Marx spoke in public for the first time to an audience of British workers. The speech was reported in the *Northern Star*, which described him as 'a celebrated writer on political economy and social philosophy'. It was during this visit to London that the Communist League commissioned Marx and Engels to write its *Manifesto* — destined to become the most influential single publication in the history of international Socialism.

When the *Communist Manifesto* was published in February 1848, however, its influence was very much a thing of the future. The first publication in English in November 1850 was in the columns of Harney's short-lived *Red Republican*. This first appearance in English passed almost, but not quite, unnoticed. On September 3, 1851 a *Times* editorial drew attention to certain 'Cheap publications containing the wildest and most anarchical doctrines . . . scattered broadcast over the land, in which religion and morality are perverted and scoffed at, and every rule of conduct which experience has sanctioned, and on which the very existence of society depends, openly assailed'. The horrified author was 'not anxious to give it circulation by naming its writers, or the works of which it is composed', but samples printed included two excerpts from the *Red Republican*'s translation of the *Manifesto*. These excerpts from what *The Times* called 'Literature for the Poor' were reprinted by the *Quarterly Review* in November 1851 in a wide-ranging attack on 'Revolutionary Literature'. The authors' worries were premature. 'Judging by everything I see', Engels wrote to Marx on March 18, 1852, 'the Chartists are in . . . a state of complete dissolution and collapse', and Marx found no reason to dissent. He kept up an occasional correspondence with Ernest Jones, the Chartist journalist and poet. Otherwise he held aloof from the squabbles and intrigues of the diminishing Chartist groups.

After the defeat of the 1848 revolutions, Marx had settled permanently in London. He kept alive partly by acting as European correspondent of the radical *New York Daily Tribune*. His articles attracted some attention in England when Ernest Jones reprinted some in his *People's Paper*. More especially, Marx's bitter attacks on Palmerston won the support of Chartists and radicals who blamed the Foreign Secretary for conniving at the defeat of democracy and revolutionary nationalism in Europe. Willingly or otherwise, it was felt — and, Marx thought, willingly — Palmerston's policy was serving the ends of Czarist Russia. These articles brought Marx into touch with the slightly grotesque figure of David Urquhart, a high Tory and a truly original eccentric who shared with him only a common detestation of Palmerston and Russia. Through the efforts of Urquhart and his friends, Marx's writings were widely distributed. A pamphlet containing his articles in the Urquhartite *Free Press* reached a circulation of twenty thousand.

When the Crimean War broke out in March 1854, it was widely greeted as a necessary struggle against the overweaning tyranny and aggressive ambitions of Czarist Russia. Radicals and surviving Chartists alike saw the war as an opportunity for freeing the oppressed nations. There were, of course, exceptions. Cobden, Bright and the Manchester school of Liberals opposed hostilities as bad for trade. Bronterre O'Brien, almost alone among the Chartists, denounced the war as a ruling-class device to distract the workers from their economic grievances.[1] When the allies were joined by Austria, the common oppressor of Hungary, Poland and Italy, Mazzini broke with his fellow *émigrés* and by 1855 was attacking the war with arguments

[1] Cf. *The National Reform Advocate : The War With Russia*, no. 1, n.d. (1854).

similar to those of the Manchester school. But these were aberrations. More typical was the campaign run by Harney and Joseph Cowen in Newcastle, where the Urquhartite 'Foreign Affairs Committee' was influential, denouncing the Government for failing to fight the war with sufficient vigour and single-mindedness. At the same time in London, Jones, in the *People's Paper*, was demanding that the 'War of Shams' be transformed into a 'War of Principles'.[1]

THE INTERNATIONAL ASSOCIATION

Not even a popular cause, however, could revive the waning force of Chartism and in 1854 the Fraternal Democrats faded quietly away. In the following year another attempt was made to found a workers' international. Louis Napoleon's *coup d'état* in December 1851 had sent a further stream of refugees to England where they won the sympathy of politically active workers. Chartists had not forgotten that Napoleon was one of the 150,000 special constables who over-awed their demonstration at Kennington Common on April 10, 1848. After his destruction of Garibaldi's Roman Republic in 1849 and the establishment of a personal dictatorship in France in 1851, he came, in the eyes of English and European democrats, almost to rival the Czar as an object of detestation. When as Emperor, he proposed to visit Britain in 1855, the international committee which had been preparing a welcome for the French revolutionary, Barbès, changed its name to the Welcome and Protest Committee.

Turning in 1856 into the International Association, this body maintained a shadowy existence until 1859. Its story has been reconstructed by Arthur Lehning.[2] The principal English members were Ernest Jones, who saw in it a possible means of reviving Chartism, his Chartist colleague James Finlen, and George Jacob Holyoake, who was to become one of the leading propagandists for co-operation and secularism in the nineteenth century. As in the case of the Fraternal Democrats, Mazzini refused to co-operate in a body with specifically socialist aims. Marx went so far as to attend one of the committee meetings with Ernest Jones in the chair. He was not very impressed with the gathering and when he heard that Alexander Herzen, the

---

[1] April 8, 1854 *et seq.* See John Saville, *Ernest Jones : Chartist*, 1952, p. 56.   [2] *Op. cit.*

Russian revolutionary exile, was to speak at the first public
meeting took no further part in the proceedings. He would
'nowhere and never', he explained to Engels, appear with
Herzen, since he had no wish 'to see old Europe rejuvenated
through Russian blood'. Herzen's speech at the meeting duly
confirmed Marx's forebodings. The salvation of mankind,
Herzen insisted, would come from the Russian peasant commune. On the other hand, 'we revolutionary Russians do not
believe in the vigour, nor in the actual organisation of Europe.
Certainly we do not.' [1]

Formally established with a constitution on August 10, 1856,
the International Association consisted of a few individual
members and four affiliated national groups; the Commune
Révolutionnaire, a French *émigré* organisation of the extreme
left; the German Arbeiterbildungsverein; the English Chartists
and the Polish Socialists. The influence of the Association
remained small and it died almost unnoticed in 1859 — 'rather
a herald of the future than a thing of actual flesh and blood'.[2]
Yet without the experience of the International Association, as
of the Fraternal Democrats, it seems unlikely that an International Working Men's Association could have appeared in the
1860s with such a clear-cut organisational shape. The Fraternal
Democrats had been the first to establish an international
central committee containing representatives of affiliated
national sections. The International Association was the first
society to attempt — though it could never implement — the
idea of a world-wide organisation of labour controlled by a
central council meeting in London. And, as will be seen in
later chapters, many of the men who participated in the
foundation of the First International in 1864 had served their
apprenticeship in the earlier, more limited and doctrinally
much narrower, organisation which had expired five years
earlier.

These two precursors of the First International failed
because the current of the times was against them. The

---

[1] *People's Paper*, March 3, 1855.
[2] Peter Brock, 'Polish Democrats and English Radicals, 1832–62',
Journal of Modern History, June 1953. The English radicals, W. J. Linton,
Joseph Cowen and their friends propagated from the mid-forties a vague
form of Republican Internationalism, in many respects akin to Mazzini's
republicanism. This brought them to co-operate closely with the Russian
Alexander Herzen, the Pole Stanislas Worcel and others. These activities
left their traces on English workers.

Fraternal Democrats were hardly established before Chartism entered its last decline. By 1856, when the International Association was formally constituted, there were no longer any labour political organisations of importance. The trade unions, slowly and painfully finding their feet, were for the most part expressly non-political and there was no soil in which the International Association could take root.

The workers nevertheless maintained, throughout the 1850s, their alert interest in European developments. If few of them joined Chartist organisations, some fifty thousand were reading *Reynolds's Weekly Newspaper* [1] from early in the decade and assimilating from its columns the internationalism if not the communism of the Fraternal Democrats! A series of international developments in Italy, America and Poland, significant not only in themselves but in the order in which they happened, was to produce by 1864 a situation in which the third attempt was to be made to establish an International of labour. If this attempt was to prove immeasurably more successful than either of its predecessors, it was initially because of developments in the world of working-class organisation. These developments, arising out of the strike movement of the London builders during 1859 and 1860, were to make the trade unions, for a time and within limits, responsive to the idea of a Labour International.

[1] George Reynolds, Chartist popular novelist and proprietor of the paper which bore his name — the most widely-read radical weekly of the period — had worked closely with Harney in the late 1840s. Cf. Schoyen, *op. cit.*, pp. 190-1.

CHAPTER II

Origins of the First International

THE First International developed out of the labour revival of the early 1860s. This recovery, which took place in a number of countries, was particularly marked in Britain and France. In Britain the struggle of the London building workers for the nine-hour day led directly to the establishment of new organisations and journals and to the appearance of a new spirit of confidence and initiative. Traditions of internationalism were by then deep-rooted and the new movement responded generously to the struggles for freedom developing in Italy, North America and Poland. Each of the three national movements produced a different kind of response in England. The Italian cause had friends in every section of society; the Northern States of America gradually won the sympathy of radical and labour movements, while enthusiastic support for Poland was almost confined to the working class.

At the same time in France, the Empire had entered its liberal phase with a somewhat greater scope for labour organisation. The workers had recovered from the traumatic experience of 1848 and were ready to take advantage of their new, limited freedom. In both England and France the rising tempo of the labour movement led to renewed demands for working-class representation in Parliament. By 1864 the movements in both countries were ready to come together in a new attempt to establish a workers' international.

THE LONDON BUILDING WORKERS, 1859–62

The lock-out and strike movements among the London builders in the years 1859–62 made the First International possible. The industry during the eighteen-fifties experienced a boom comparable in intensity and irregularity with the railway boom of the forties. Economic crises then had coincided with the peaks of Chartism. The crisis of 1858–9 in the building trade — part of a much wider economic recession — sparked off a tense trade union struggle, but one starting from a higher level of organisation than anything possible in Chartist times.

For one thing, the railway boom of the forties, whose rhythm coincided with the ebb and flow of Chartism, expanded employment mainly among unskilled and largely immigrant navvies.   No doubt it also stimulated organisation in the engineering, metal and mining industries, but these were still largely in the North and Midlands.   Contacts with colonies of revolutionary immigrants which did so much to develop an international outlook among London workers were of relatively minor importance in the Provinces.

Agitation for a nine-hour day among the London builders had started as early as 1853.   The crisis of 1858, with its ensuing unemployment, seemed to strengthen the case for a shorter working day.   'The Nine Hours' Movement', wrote the bricklayers' leader, George Howell, 'was the starting-point for other movements, some of which have left their mark on the political, as well as the industrial history of the country.' [1] These other movements included the setting up in 1860 of the London Trades Council, the establishment by the bricklayers of a monthly journal in September 1861 and the founding, a month later, of the weekly *Beehive*, in its time the most influential newspaper of the labour movement.   The London Trades Council was to participate officially in the foundation meeting of the International; its Secretary, George Odger, became the first — and only — President of the International, on whose central leadership other members of the London Trades Council were to serve.   The *Operative Bricklayers' Society's Trade Circular and General Reporter* was conducted by George Howell, C. Shearman, H. Noble and E. Coulson. All four men later served on the General Council of the International.   The first manager of the *Beehive* was George Potter who came into prominence as chief spokesman of the building workers in 1860.   His paper was to be the International's first official organ.   When the International was founded in 1864, twenty-seven Englishmen were elected to its first General Council.   At least eleven of them were from the building trade.[2]

---

[1] G. Howell, *Labour Legislation, Labour Movements and Labour Leaders*, 1902, pp. 128-9.

[2] The list of the first General Council, published in the *Beehive*, October 1, 1864, is complete except for the omission of Odger and Dell.   Those

The prolonged and stubborn strike movement of building craftsmen, located in an area traditionally responsive to international issues, had other distinctive features which help to explain its importance in giving rise to the First International. When the employers insisted that the men sign the 'Document', disavowing trade union membership, before being allowed back to work, sympathy with the workers was strengthened among sections of the liberal middle class. Frederic Harrison, a lawyer and a leading Positivist, wrote that while there were usually two sides to every quarrel, 'I do firmly believe that in this particular struggle the men were *all* right and the masters were *all* wrong'.[1] This view was common among Positivists and Christian Socialists, many of whose leaders came for the first time into regular contact with trade union delegates and Secretaries, notably with Cremer, Howell, Robert Applegarth and Henry Broadhurst — the first three of whom were to serve at various times on the General Council. Among such contacts those with the Positivists [2] were of particular importance in influencing trade union attitudes to international affairs.

In July 1861 the Government intervened in the dispute by sending troops to work at Chelsea Barracks. Benjamin Lucraft, like Howell a former Chartist and later to feature prominently on the General Council and in the wider labour movement, was at hand to point the moral. The Chelsea affair, he urged, in a letter to *Reynolds's* on July 28, was a new and powerful argument for a working-class franchise. 'I should hope', he wrote, 'that the operative builders are by this time convinced that political power has something to do with the social conditions of the people.' In December the journal of the Operative Bricklayers drew the same conclusion from the affair, declaring that trade unions should 'watch over the welfare of their members, politically as well as socially', while adding that this view was still strongly opposed in trade union circles. The new tendency was strengthened by the emergence in 1860 of the Amalgamated Society of Carpenters and Joiners. From the beginning the new

from the building trade were: plasterers, Nieass, Osborne; bricklayers, Noble, Howell, Shearman; joiners, Lucraft, Trimlett; painters, Shaw, Facey; carpenter, Cremer; mason, Gray.

[1] *Autobiographic Memoirs*, 1911, vol. I, p. 253.

[2] Followers of the French philosopher, Comte, the Positivists felt a special affinity with France both as the source of their creed and as the country of the great Revolution. In shaping the society of the future, they attached special importance to the working class as a source of co-operative values against bourgeois individualism.

Society made a point of encouraging political interest and discussion among its members [1] — a tendency which was strengthened when two years later Robert Applegarth became its first Secretary.

Though foreign labour was not apparently used by the building employers in their attempts to break the strike, its use was certainly threatened.[2] A few weeks before the builders' lock-out, a strike of London gas workers had been broken partly by the introduction of 'a number of German sugar bakers, who as men accustomed to intense heat, could be made available'.[3] When five years later the International was established, the most important single motive impelling unions to affiliate was the desire to prevent strike-breaking through the use of foreign labour. It seems certain that the building strike played its part in focussing attention on the need to strengthen their bargaining power against such contingencies.

Finally, and still more important, some financial help reached the building workers from France through contacts established by the Positivists. It was a modest sum, amounting only to £5 : 18 : 0,[4] but its political importance was considerable. The *Bricklayers' Trade Circular* remarked in October 1861. 'We hope again to hear from our brother toilers, the French workmen, and that some steps will be taken to keep up a correspondence not only between France and England, but also with the workmen of Italy, Belgium, Holland, Hungary, Poland and indeed the whole of continental Europe.' The contribution was again referred to by Odger when, two months before the foundation of the International, the bronze workers of Limoges appealed to the London Trades Council for help during a strike.[5] The building workers' dispute, in fact, aroused unprecedented interest abroad throughout continental Europe, including Russia, and as far afield as the United States.[6]

THE RISORGIMENTO, 1859–64

The movement among the building workers, meeting as it did with a considerable measure of success, increased the

[1] Professor E. S. Beesly, *Fortnightly Review*, March 1867.
[2] *Daily Telegraph*, June 24, and comment in *Workman*, July 5, 1861 ; *Westminster Review*, October 1861, and comment in *Bookbinders' Trade Circular*, January 21, 1862.   [3] *Leader*, August 6, 1859.
[4] London Trades Council *Minutes*, Annual Report, March 1862.
[5] *Beehive*, July 16, 1864.
[6] G. Howell, *Nineteenth Century*, July 1878; D. Ryazanoff, *Marx-Engels Archiv*, 1927, vol. I, pp. 138-9.

international awareness of the labour movement in London. By a coincidence, it began at a moment when the Italian Risorgimento was winning enthusiastic support from public opinion throughout the country. Mazzini was something of a public hero, while Garibaldi had been a legend since his heroic defence of the Roman Republic in 1849.

While the cause of Italian independence had a natural and spontaneous appeal to liberal sentiment in mid-Victorian England, there was also a feeling that the working class, in particular, had a special responsibility for helping on the movement. To some extent, the idea arose directly out of those currents in Chartism tending to favour a Holy Alliance of labour. As early as September 27, 1856 Jones's *People's Paper* had published an appeal from the Genovese to the English workers for a collection in aid of Italian emancipation. The same sentiment found expression in the institution of a 'Garibaldian Penny Fund' in 1860. Moreover, the personal influence of Mazzini was becoming significant among just that section which at the time of the builders' strike was rising to positions of control in the labour movement. William Randal Cremer was by the early sixties 'already on terms of intimacy with Mazzini',[1] and Howell was to write that in this period 'Mazzini was known personally to many of us; Garibaldi soon became an idol'.[2]

The idea that the workers had a distinctive contribution to make in the development of a foreign policy based on morality and justice, which was to be forcibly expressed by George Odger at the foundation meeting of the International, was a commonplace in the writings of Mazzini. More specifically, Mazzini rejected the approach of conventional diplomacy and the foreign policy of Palmerston, calling instead for an alliance of the subject peoples — Italians, Hungarians and Poles — against both Austria and Russia.[3] That the idea was sympathetically received by workers, not only in political but also in trade union circles, may be seen from the *Bricklayers' Trade Circular*, which stated forthrightly in October 1861 that: 'We

[1] Howard Evans, *Sir Randal Cremer : His Life and Work*, 1909, p. 41. Cremer, a building worker, who prepared the first Trade Union Directory, became the first Secretary of the International. Later devoted all his considerable talents and energies to the promotion of peace. Was knighted and received Nobel Prize for Peace.
[2] *Op. cit.*, p. 140.
[3] See 'Two Letters on the Crimean War, printed for the Working Men of England', *Life and Writings of Mazzini, 1846–70*, vol. VI, pp. 309-35.

would rather be allied to a free Poland, a free Hungary, a free Italy, than to any German despotism or Russian autocracy'. The Neapolitan workers' organisation, strong under Mazzini's influence, corresponded with the London Trades Council in the early part of 1862 and received from Howell, at that time its Secretary, a letter of encouragement and advice.[1]

Robert Hartwell who had signed Lovett's *Address to the Workers of Belgium* in 1836 became Secretary to the new Trades Garibaldian Demonstration Committee in 1862 when a visit from the celebrated Italian was awaited. When Garibaldi arrived in April 1864, London turned out in force. Writing soon after the event, Herzen described how 'workmen and clerks, lords and sempstresses, bankers and High-church clergymen; the feudal wreck, Lord Derby, and the relic of the February revolution, the republican of 1848; Queen Victoria's eldest son and the barefoot swiper born without father or mother, vie with one another in trying to capture a hand-shake, a glance, a word'.[2]

Garibaldi's abrupt departure from England before he could start on his projected provincial tour, gave rise to protests, particularly in labour circles. No one believed the story that he had left for health reasons and there was widespread suspicion of Court and Government intrigue. The *Beehive* complained on April 23, that not only was the visit suspiciously short, but that in the few days it lasted Garibaldi had been monopolised by a clique and kept away from his real friends among the people. Herzen made the same point.[3] From the political right came the protest that, on the contrary, it was the trade unionists who treated Garibaldi as a mascot and made out of his visit a plebeian festival. 'Publicola', of the *Weekly Dispatch*, found it 'impossible not to recognise the "fine Roman hand" of the Potters, Cremers, Odgerses, Hartwells, and the *Beehive* gentry in this Working Men's Reception Committee' and thought it incongruous that there should be any real feeling for Italy among 'men who were never out of Wapping and Brick Lane'.[4]

---

[1] *Reynolds's*, April 20, 1862. See also London Trades Council *Minutes*, May 1862. For Mazzini's influence in British radical circles, see H. M. Hyndman, *Record of an Adventurous Life*, 1911, p. 32, and E. Gryzanovski, 'On the International Workingmen's Association, its origin, doctrines and ethics', *North American Review*, Boston, 1872.

[2] *My Past and Thoughts*, 1926, vol. 5, p. 34.　　[3] *Op. cit.*, p. 53.

[4] April 24, 1864. 'Publicola' was the pen name of Sydney Smith, main propagandist for the employers during the engineering lock-out of 1852.

THE AMERICAN CIVIL WAR

Incongruous or not, both sides were at least agreed on the fact that labour regarded Italy's cause as its own. On the other hand it was equally clear that, with few exceptions, the whole nation was pro-Italian and that labour was making a special but not an exclusive affirmation. But by another coincidence, a new international issue arising at about the same time precipitated a different alignment of class forces. The American Civil War which broke out in 1861 eventually saw the Whig and Tory establishment supporting the rebel South, while an uneasy coalition of labour and Bright radicals adhered to the North.

Admittedly, things were not at first so clear-cut; until Lincoln made the abolition of slavery an issue in the war English workers showed little interest in its progress. What interest they did show was often unfavourable to the North and both *Reynolds's* and the *Beehive* supported the South in its fight to secede from the American Union.[1] What roused feeling among the workers, however, was not so much the war itself as the inadequacy of public relief for the unemployed victims of the cotton famine which resulted from the Yankee blockade of Southern ports. The Lancashire manufacturers were widely believed to be niggardly with their contributions and even to be using their influence on relief committees to discriminate against trade unionists.

Here, it was felt, was yet another issue on which the workers must act for themselves. The London Trades Council set up a Working Men's Central Committee to administer relief independently of the official Mansion House Committee. Applegarth, the newly elected leader of the Carpenters and Joiners, was its Secretary. By February 1863 Professor Beesly had become convinced that independent workers' action was necessary on relief committees since the manufacturers had 'proved themselves unworthy of our confidence'.[2] At the same time he wrote to the London Trades Council suggesting a public meeting in support of the North with trade union participation. The suggestion was well received.

Lincoln's proclamation abolishing slavery in all territory

[1] Cf. Dr. Royden Harrison, 'British Labour and the Confederacy', *International Review of Social History*, Amsterdam, vol. II, Part 1, 1957.
[2] *Beehive*, February 28, 1863.

under Federal control was decisive in rallying labour support
to the North. While at first, wrote Howell, 'there were a few
waverers who still stressed the South's right to secede, once it
became clear that slavery was the issue the workers rallied to
the North with almost singular unanimity'.[1]

The *Beehive*, in the direction of which both London's
leading trade unionists and the Positivists, Beesly and Harrison,
now played a considerable part, demonstrated the change with
dramatic suddenness. On January 17, 1863, without warning
and without even a formal acknowledgement of its pro-Southern
past, it published a powerful article by Hartwell (under the
pseudonym 'Scourge') against the 'attempt . . . now being
made by the slaveowners and slavebreeders of the South to
overthrow the glorious American republic', which must have
startled its readers.

A trade union meeting chaired by John Bright took place
at St. James's Hall on March 25. Apart from Bright, all the
speakers were trade unionists, including Howell, Odger and
Cremer. Marx, at the time in almost complete retirement
from public life, made an exception and attended the meeting.
In a letter to Engels on April 9 he described how every reference to the republican institutions of the United States was
greeted with applause. 'The workers themselves', he added,
'spoke *excellently*, with a complete absence of bourgeois rhetoric
and without in the least concealing their opposition to the
capitalists (whom Father Bright, by the way, also attacked)'.
Much the same impression of the meeting was reported in the
radical *Morning Star* on March 27 and by Henry Adams, son
and secretary to the United States ambassador, who saw in the
occasion a tremendous 'demonstration of democratic strength'.[2]
Afterwards it seemed natural for *The Times* to declare : 'The
members of Trades Unions would have a natural bias towards
the North ; other classes have insensibly acquired a leaning
towards the South'.

THE POLISH INSURRECTION

The alliance between Bright and the unions, for which Beesly
had worked assiduously, seemed to have been consummated.

[1] *Op. cit.*, p. 41.
[2] Charles I. Glicksberg, 'Henry Adams Reports on a Trades-Union
Meeting', *New England Quarterly*, December 1942, and E. D. Adams,
Great Britain and the American Civil War, p. 293.

C

Before the honeymoon had fairly got going, however, the re-emergence of an old quarrel subjected it to severe strain. When Russia moved in to crush the Hungarians in 1849, Bright's colleague, Richard Cobden, had incurred Harney's wrath by proposing merely diplomatic and financial action in support of Hungary. Only war against Russia, Harney insisted, would be of any use, and Cobden's pacifism was 'moonshine'.[1] Cobden's opposition to the Crimean War had caused an even bigger rift with the labour movement.

These were differences, not merely of political assessment, but of moral and social values. To a Chartist, such as Charles Murray, the cold economic calculations of the Manchester school seemed sordid. 'It appears', he wrote in 1854,[2] 'that Russia is a better customer to England than Turkey. . . . It would appear from Mr. Cobden's speech that he calculates the worthiness of a people for National independence to depend on the amount of manufactured goods they are able to take of England.'

The Polish insurrection which broke out in January 1863 once again brought these differences into the open. Bright's pacifist views were promptly repudiated in the *Beehive*, which wrote as early as January 31 that 'the pure and simple doctrine of non-intervention does not apply to the case of Poland'. A meeting on April 28, which called for full diplomatic and financial support for the Poles and which was chaired by Beesly, was even more distinctively trade union in character than the American meeting of the previous month.[3] A deputation to Palmerston was elected which included, besides Beesly and the *Beehive*'s manager, Potter, five future members of the International — Cremer, Murray, Nieass, Applegarth and Facey. The deputation conveyed the demand of the meeting for war against Russia as a last resort. Palmerston's attitude to the deputation, though studiously non-committal, was friendly and respectful. The working class was coming—four years before the Reform Act of 1867 — to be accepted as a political force.

THE FRENCH LABOUR MOVEMENT

The campaign for Poland marked yet another stage in the growth of labour internationalism. While Italy had evoked

---

[1] Schoyen, *op. cit.*, p. 191.
[2] *A Letter to Mr. George Jacob Holyoake*, p. 11.
[3] See the advertisement in *Morning Star*, April 24, 1863.

the broadest measure of support, the American Civil War had divided left from right. The flaking process was taken a stage further by the Polish rising which separated the unions from their former allies among the Bright radicals. It left them, however, still with the significant support of the Positivists. Among other things, the Positivists favoured a French orientation and in fact, for nearly six months before the Polish events, contacts of the utmost importance had been developing between English workers and a newly awakening labour movement in France.

Stunned by their defeat in June 1848 and further demoralised by Louis Napoleon's *coup d'état* and the severe repression of political activity, the French workers had confined themselves during the 1850s to establishing friendly and co-operative societies. Socialism as a movement disintegrated, with the Fourierists fading away, the Saint-Simonians supporting Napoleon, while deep underground Blanqui and his followers kept alive the conspiratorial traditions of Babeuf and Buonarroti. In these conditions the ideas of Pierre Joseph Proudhon made considerable headway. Proudhon preached a version of anarchism which eschewed politics and looked to the 'free exchange' of products between independent artisans and co-operatives as the means of emancipating the small producer. There was no place in his scheme for the State to participate in economic affairs. All forms of coercion, whether by the State or by associations of employers or even of workers should be opposed as incompatible with freedom. The small-scale production he envisaged was to be made viable by cheap credit from a 'people's bank' whose interest charges would cover only its running costs. It is easy to see the attractions of such a theory in France of the eighteen-fifties and sixties where the State was associated with a tyrannical kind of centralisation and where large-scale industry was beginning to advance at the expense of the independent producer.

In the early 1860s Napoleon himself, seeking a counterweight to the liberal opposition, began making overtures to the workers. In 1862 he sponsored — to the accompaniment of some head-shaking on the part of his Prefect of Police in Paris [1] — an elected delegation of French workers to the London Exhibition.

---

[1] E. E. Fribourg, *L'Association Internationale des Travailleurs*, Paris, 1871, p. 149.

Soon after the Frenchmen arrived they were invited to a
tea-party and soirée by the committee of the *Working Man*.
This was a monthly journal founded in the previous year and
devoted to the progress of co-operative societies.[1] The meeting
took place under the most respectable auspices with letters and
donations from Lords Shaftesbury and Palmerston. The
speeches were for the most part innocuous and some writers have
denied a connection between this occasion and the appearance
two years later of the International.[2]

In fact there can be little doubt that the International did
spring from this harmless looking gathering. Three of the
French visitors, Tolain, Fribourg and the refugee Talandier,
subsequently joined the International, as did the British representatives, G. E. Harris and Charles Murray.[3] Both Harris
and Murray were members of the *Working Man*'s board of
management and both were followers of Bronterre O'Brien.
Before the meeting dispersed, Bocquet,[4] a French refugee and
later a foundation member of the International, proposed that
'a corresponding committee should be formed in London for
the purpose of interchanging ideas with the workmen of
France'. Even so, such a proposal could well have come to
nothing but for the Polish revolt which broke out five months
later.

FRENCH LABOUR AND THE POLISH CAMPAIGN

Correspondence was kept up between the English and
French workers. By July 1863 petitions to Napoleon III were
circulating in French workshops calling for armed intervention
against Russia. A mass meeting at St. James' Hall on July 22
was attended by a five-man delegation from the Paris Working
Men's Polish Committee; three of the Frenchmen, Tolain, a
metal carver who had been a visitor to the Anglo-French tea-
party of the year before, Perrachon, a bronze fitter, and Murat,
a wire worker, were to figure prominently in the French

[1] Its original title had been the *Workman*. In 1866 G. J. Holyoake
edited a weekly paper published by Cassell which was also called 'The
Working Man'.
[2] E. G. G. Howell, *Nineteenth Century*, July 1878: D. Ryazanoff,
op. cit.
[3] Harris and Talandier had been closely connected with the earlier
International Association. Charles Murray and his brother James lived to
help Hyndman found the Social Democratic Federation in 1883.
[4] The report in the *Working Man* mistakenly called him 'M. Picque'.

section of the International.   Next day the English and French workers met at the Bell Inn, where the *Beehive* had its office, and agreed to conduct a joint campaign on behalf of Poland.

The idea that the workers, as a class, were particularly identified with the Polish cause gained further ground with the formation on August 5 of the National League for the Independence of Poland under the chairmanship of the radical barrister Edmond Beales.   Membership cards were priced at sixpence, 'so as to bring them within the reach of all working men'.[1]   On August 24 *The Times* referred scathingly to 'the totally uneducated portion of the British population' which had 'long made up its mind that the Poles are a democratic people who are fighting for liberty, equality and fraternity', a view which *The Times* found surprising in view of the nature of Polish society and politics.   This was a fair point, and the Polish leader, Prince Adam Czartoryski, went out of his way to assure a largely working-class audience that the workers of Poland would receive 'full political equality' if the revolt succeeded.[2]

The manifestly working-class character of the Polish agitation also attracted unfavourable notice in the *Daily Telegraph*. In a comment on the Czartoryski meeting it said that 'the cause of Poland is not fortunate in its friends' and thought that so momentous an issue could hardly be left in the hands of nonentities like 'Facey and company'.[3]   Facey, however, as the *Beehive* retorted next day, was perhaps better known to the editor of the *Telegraph* than he cared to remember, having been one of the leaders of the builders' strike in 1859–60 whom 'the Telegraph then misrepresented and calumniated'.

Five trade union leaders — Facey, Odger, Cremer, Goddard and Eglinton — who had been elected at the Anglo-French meeting at the Bell Inn on July 23, signed an address of the English to the French workers which appeared in the *Beehive* on December 5.   The document had been drafted by Odger.[4] It was 'reproduced in almost every European country' and

[1] *Beehive*, August 8, 1863.

[2] *Beehive*, October 24, 1863.

[3] October 23, 1863.   Facey was Vice-President of the new National League for the Independence of Poland.

[4] See Odger's statement in a speech reported in *The Times*, June 29, 1871; also his obituary notice in the shoemakers' journal, *St. Crispin*, March 10, 1877.   For further details of Odger's career see Ph.D. Thesis by D. R. Moberg, University of London, 1953.

established its author as the man more responsible than any other single person for the foundation of the International.[1] The address called for 'a gathering together of representatives from France, Italy, Germany, Poland, England and all countries, where there exists a will to co-operate for the good of mankind'. Read out at the foundation meeting of the International almost a year later, Odger's statement presented the clearest picture of the motives and ideals in the minds of the British trade unionists who established the first effective workers' International.[2]

AN ANGLO-FRENCH ENTENTE

Since the delegation to the London Exhibition of 1862 there had been some important developments in the French labour movement. In 1863 the first workers' candidates had run, though with little success, against middle-class republicans. On February 17, 1864 there appeared the 'Manifesto of the Sixty', a landmark in the revival of the labour movement which stated bluntly that there was a conflict of interests between capital and labour. The sixty signatories included Tolain and Murat.

In April a deputation of workers arrived from Paris and met the English Working Men's Garibaldi Committee. The deputation formally proposed a 'congress of Continental and English workmen' to be held in London. The proposal was well received and a provisional committee was constituted to prepare for the Congress. Links between the labour movements of Britain and France were further strengthened after a strike of porcelain workers in Limoges. A financial appeal appeared in the *Beehive* on June 18, and in the following month Talandier, Le Lubez, a French republican from Jersey, and Luigi Wolf, Mazzini's secretary, attended a meeting of the London Trades Council to explain the position of the strikers. Talandier referred to Odger's Address, with its call for a 'grand fraternity of peoples' and on a motion of Daniel Guile, the Ironfounders' Secretary, the Council agreed to launch a campaign for assistance. In conclusion, Odger recalled the French contribution to the builders' strike fund in 1860.[3]

[1] Howell, *Nineteenth Century*, July 1878.
[2] For a detailed analysis of the Address, see Chapter IV.
[3] *Beehive*, July 16, 1864.

THE WORKERS' FRANCHISE

All currents were flowing the same way and the general heightening of political interest which had followed from the builders' strike culminated in a revived demand for a working-class franchise.   On two occasions during that dispute the Government had intervened against the unions. First troops were used to replace workers on strike at Chelsea Barracks. Shortly afterwards in November 1862 the Admiralty discharged workers on strike at Chatham docks, and although no building workers were involved in this instance, the strikers' dismissal reinforced in the minds of trade unionists the impression of Government hostility.   This gave an old Chartist like Hartwell another telling argument : 'those unions', he wrote, as 'Scourge' in the *Beehive*,[1] 'or most of them, can go on repeating "we have nothing to do with politics".   Politics, however, replies, "We have a great deal to do with you, and when we think proper can help your employers to defeat your demands".' The same issue of the *Beehive* reported the formation of a Trades Unionists' Manhood Suffrage and Vote by Ballot Association with Facey as Secretary and Odger as Chairman.   Almost simultaneously there were discussions on the franchise at the London Trades Council [2] but it was another year before the reform movement became really popular with large meetings addressed by Bright and Cobden in the provinces by the end of 1863.

The publication of Odger's Address in December 1863 was therefore perfectly timed.   It led almost at once to a curious attempt at founding a Labour International in the form of a Universal League for the Elevation of the Industrious Classes under the aegis of the Marquis of Townsend.   The Marquis had declared himself immensely impressed by Odger's Address and his objects included not only shorter hours but also 'a fraternal communication with the industrial populations of all other countries' for joint action in the interests of labour.   A number of prominent trade unionists, including Odger, Potter, Howell, Applegarth and Guile, attended a conference of the league on May 30, 1864 to campaign for improvements in trade union law.   Less than a month later the League added manhood suffrage to its list of objectives.[3]

[1] November 22, 1862.
[2] L.T.C. *Minutes*, October 30 and December 17, 1862.
[3] George Howell's *Diary* (MSS.), June 20, 1864.

The Liberal leader Gladstone responded to the rising current of working-class feeling. On May 11, 1864 he demanded a wide extension of the franchise. On June 22 there was a 'Grand Demonstration of the Middle and Working Classes' at the Freemason's Hall where the Anglo-French tea-party had been held two years before. The meeting was publicly advertised by Facey ;[1] Beales of the Polish League was Chairman and among those moving resolutions were J. A. Nicholay, who had taken the chair at the 1862 tea-party, and Leno, Howell, Worley, Weston and Longmaid—all five of whom were to be elected three months later to the first General Council of the International.

On August 27 the *Beehive* published a letter from Le Lubez announcing an international meeting to be held on September 28. On September 3 the paper gave the project its editorial blessing. The London Trades Council, normally careful to avoid becoming involved with outside political organisations, elected an official delegation. Even the Marquis's Universal League sent a donation and a delegation.

On September 28 at a crowded meeting in St. Martin's Hall, Long Acre, the International Working Men's Association was formally established. Its two predecessors, the Fraternal Democrats and the International Association, had been created by sects, exiles and doctrinaires. This was the first association to arise directly out of the co-operation of workers' societies in England and France. Its initiator and president was George Odger, Secretary of the London Trades Council, itself the direct outcome of the builders' strikes. While the idea of a workers' International had been in the air since the tea-party in 1862, the International which emerged stood for an idea unacceptable to Lord Palmerston, to Napoleon III and even to the Marquis of Townsend — the idea of a world-wide union of workers to serve their own interests and led by men of their own class.

That this was possible by 1864 was due not only to the general labour revival accompanied by three highly challenging international issues, but to the order in which those issues appeared and to the progressively narrower social appeal of the Italian, American and Polish movements. By 1864 the workers were almost isolated from their allies in other classes with the notable exception of the Positivists. But it was precisely the

[1] *Beehive*, June 18, 25, 1864.

Positivists who for philosophical reasons encouraged the workers to develop their independent standpoint and activities, while themselves remaining deliberately — and for other philosophical reasons — outside the workers' organisations. The Bright radicals saw the workers as suitable and preferably docile allies in the fight for political reform. The Positivists saw in them a new class with its own distinctive values, destined to play a leading part in 'moralising' the harsh, anti-social tendencies of capitalism. The Polish campaign, therefore, which put the workers in opposition to the Bright radicals while strengthening their relations with the Positivists, was the decisive factor in the development of a labour international.

There was, finally, a scholarly German refugee who had played no part in establishing the International but who was invited along with other 'distinguished exiles and friends of the people'[1] to attend its foundation meeting. He was to play a decisive part in its affairs, though his social philosophy was very different from that of his hosts. On most immediate issues, however, his views coincided remarkably with theirs. He saw at once that the International could provide him with the means of influencing the British, and through that the emerging European labour movement. Marx was, therefore, present as a 'mute figure'[2] on the platform at the foundation meeting. He soon rose to a dominating position in the counsels of the International and his political objectives, mostly unknown to his colleagues, were to govern its main lines of development for the next eight years.

[1] *Beehive*, September 3, 1864.
[2] Marx to Engels, November 4, 1864.

CHAPTER III

Karl Marx and the Foundation of the International

MARX had played no part in the preparations for the meeting of September 28. That he was there at all was something of an accident, yet Max Beer was right in claiming, on the meeting's fiftieth anniversary, that 'but for this accident the International would not have left any deeper mark on the history of Socialism and Labour politics than the previous attempts at an understanding between the workmen of various nationalities'.[1]

THE LEGEND

Because of the part he was later to play in directing the International, a good deal of legend has accumulated about Marx's part in its foundation. In his speech at Marx's grave-side in 1883 Engels referred to him as the 'founder' of the International. Marx's American biographer, John Spargo, went much further in exaggerating his rôle, making Marx responsible for the main Polish and American demonstrations of 1863.[2] Similarly, Applegarth's biographer attributed to Marx the idea of the Anglo-French tea-party in 1862. 'Marx', he wrote, 'was very friendly with Odger and other leaders of the working-class movement in England, and he suggested the entertainment of the visitors.'[3] This story, however, had no more foundation than the claims of Spargo.

MARX AND THE BRITISH LABOUR MOVEMENT

So far from being friendly with Odger and other labour leaders, Marx, for at least two years before the formation of the

[1] M. Beer, 'The International: Its Historical Significance', *Socialist Review*, July-September 1914.
[2] John Spargo, *Karl Marx*, New York, 1910, pp. 224-5, 228.
[3] A. W. Humphrey, *Robert Applegarth : Trade Unionist, Educationist, Reformer*, 1914, p. 85.

International, was living in comparative isolation, often ill and spending all his available time in the reading-room of the British Museum. He had published nothing since December 4, 1862.[1] His private correspondence was sparse, and apart from what he wrote to Engels, only nine of his letters written between January 1863 and September 1864 have been found. None of them mentions the labour movement in Britain. Such a period of quiescence was without precedent in Marx's career. Presumably it was the time he worked on *Capital* with greatest intensity. But whatever the full explanation, Marx was not at that time the *éminence grise* directing the labour movement towards the establishment of the First International. He probably did not even know of the decision to found an International until a week or so before the St. Martin's Hall meeting. But while Spargo and Humphrey wrongly show Marx as deeply involved in international movements for two years up to September 1864, E. H. Carr comments that the 'origin of the momentous decision to invite Marx — a decision which determined the whole course of the International from its inception to its death —is wrapped in strange obscurity'.[2]

Yet despite his two years of self-imposed isolation, Marx was by no means unknown among the Englishmen who attended the foundation meeting. Chartists such as Hartwell, Lucraft and Leno may well have remembered his articles in the *People's Paper* during the 1850s. His speeches at the Chartist meeting on Poland in 1847 and on the anniversary of the *People's Paper* in 1855 may also have been recalled, as may his writings in Collet's *Free Press* which had attracted attention and approval through their spirited attacks on Palmerston. No doubt a number of Englishmen knew of his contributions to the *New York Daily Tribune*. It is not, therefore, surprising that Marx was one of the 'distinguished exiles and friends of the people' whom it would naturally occur to the organisers of the meeting to invite.

A 'STRANGE OBSCURITY'

There still remains some conflict of evidence as to how Marx came to be involved. It is most commonly assumed that the organisers approached him through the German

---

[1] *Die Presse*, Vienna, *Marx-Engels Sochinenia*, XII/2, Moscow, 1933.
[2] *Karl Marx : A Study in Fanaticism*, 1934, p. 184.

Arbeiterbildungsverein.[1] This is the version given by Friedrich Lessner in his autobiographical *Sixty Years in the Social Democratic Movement* [2] who claims that he was delegated by the A.B.V. at the request of the English organisers to invite Marx to the foundation meeting. But Lessner's account was written nearly forty years after the event. Moreover, he was not co-opted on to the General Council until November 1, 1864 on the proposal of Marx himself, more than a month after it was established. It is a mistake to treat Lessner's version as reliable. Marx's own statement, on the other hand, was written a few weeks later and is otherwise quite compatible with the rest of the direct evidence.

In his letter to Engels of November 4, 1864, already quoted, Marx explained the background to the meeting in the contacts between the French and British workers in support of Poland. He continued: 'A public meeting in St. Martin's Hall was summoned for September 28th, 1864 by Odger (shoemaker, President of the Council here of all London Trades' Unions and also especially of the Trades Union Suffrage Agitation Society, which is connected with Bright), and Cremer, mason and secretary of the Mason's Union'. He ended with an account of how he came to be involved. 'A certain Le Lubez was sent to ask me if I would supply a German worker to speak at the meeting etc. I provided them with Eccarius, who came off splendidly, and ditto was present myself as a mute figure on the platform.' Though he had been refusing for some years to take part in political activity, Marx added that this was something different. 'I knew that this time real "powers" were involved both on the London and Paris sides and therefore decided to waive my usual standing rule to decline any such invitations.'

The letter shows among other things how out of touch Marx — and, *a fortiori*, Engels — were with British workers' organisations. Odger was Secretary, not President, of the London Trades Council, while Cremer was a carpenter and neither a mason nor a trade union Secretary. But as an account of Marx's initiation it seems valid and is confirmed by a letter from Eccarius to Marx on September 26. Eccarius, a tailor from Thuringia and an old comrade of Marx in the Communist League, complained that he was 'supposed to speak in a public

[1] *E.g.* G. D. H. Cole, *A History of Socialist Thought*, 1954, vol. II, p. 90.
[2] 1907, pp. 33-4.

meeting about a programme whose contents I do not know, whose language I do not understand. Last night (after 11 o'clock) Odger could tell me only that it deals with the Press, with a congress, a credit bank, mutual aid while travelling, etc.' Odger must have told Eccarius, perhaps none too clearly, about the programme of the Paris delegation. Mention of a 'credit bank' and the term 'mutual aid' — which does not seem to have been used in England at the time — strongly suggest the Proudhonist preoccupations of the Parisians. 'Perhaps', Eccarius added, 'if the Frenchmen were at your house and you know the contents of the programme, let me know where and how some hints can be gotten. If I must remain in the dark until I hear it read tomorrow evening in the meeting, I shall certainly be able to say very little about it.' [1] This last remark of Eccarius only strengthens the impression that the meeting was organised by the English and French, with the Germans participating as guests. Le Lubez, who was acting as liaison officer between the French and English representatives, must have introduced the Frenchmen at their request to Marx. He was asked by them to 'supply a German worker', since the French followers of Proudhon were adamant — as they were soon to make much clearer — that a workers' organisation should be run by workers with intellectuals excluded as far as possible.

The conduct of the meeting on September 28 reinforces this impression of its origins. While Eccarius spoke, his speech was not reported and was probably only a formal address of welcome to the French. Apart from that, the German contribution was limited to songs from the A.B.V. choir. Of the thirty-four members elected to the first General Council, Marx and Eccarius were the only Germans.

If Lessner was drawing on his memories after a lapse of forty years, the picture which emerges from the letters of Eccarius and Marx is quite clear. Despite his period of inactivity, Marx was fairly well known in old Chartist and refugee circles in London. Le Lubez has possibly heard of him, directly or indirectly, from Harney during the latter's prolonged stay in Jersey. Marx was in any case known in France since the appearance of his *Misère de la philosophie* in 1847. He was also friendly with at least one member of the 1848

[1] *Founding of the First International*, Marx-Engels-Lenin Institute, Moscow, 1939, p. 56.

Provisional Government, the Fourierist, Flocon. And even if the Parisians remembered Marx's scathing attack on their teacher, Proudhon, seventeen years earlier, they would still be interested to meet the most distinguished among the socialist exiles in London. Nevertheless, it is clear that Marx was drawn into the proceedings from the periphery. Had he not been, the International might soon have shared the fate of its two predecessors.

The Foundation Meeting

Half an hour before the meeting was due to start, a committee met in St. Martin's Hall to finalise the arrangements. Cremer had invited Marx to attend almost literally at the last minute; from the formality of the letter, it was probably the first he had addressed to Marx.[1] No doubt it was this committee which arranged that Richard Butler, the compositors' delegate on the London Trades Council, should propose Professor Beesly as Chairman.

The meeting was crowded and enthusiastic.[2] Tolain in his report to *L'Opinion Nationale* estimated the audience as at least two thousand. This was a respectable figure for an indoor meeting; John Bright's demonstration on the American Civil War eighteen months earlier had drawn about three thousand.[3] In his presidential speech, Beesly expressed the hope that 'the results of the meeting would be to create a co-operative and fraternal feeling between the workingmen of England and all the other countries', but he made no organisational proposals, nor did he refer to the proposed formation of a permanent international association. As a Positivist, he believed strongly that the workers had their own independent contribution to make to society; intellectuals from other classes should give sympathy and advice, while avoiding direct participation. As a Positivist he also saw France as the embodiment of human progress and he made a point of calling for an Anglo-French alliance 'to secure and maintain the liberties of the world'. As things stood, British foreign and colonial policies were at least as bad as those of the continental autocracies. 'England wrongfully held possession of Gibraltar from Spain, and her

---

[1] Cremer to Marx, September 28, 1864, quoted in *Founding of the First International*, p. 57.   [2] Howell's *Diary*, September 28, 1864.
[3] Charles T. Glicksberg, *op. cit.*

conduct in China, Japan, India and elsewhere was cowardly and unprincipled.' Beesly included Britain's policy towards Ireland in his indictment, a fact which was omitted in the *Beehive* report.[1]

After a contribution from the German choir Odger read the *Address to the Workmen of France* which he had written in the previous December. As the first comprehensive statement on foreign policy representative of trade union opinion, it is worth some detailed attention.

Up to a point Odger's Address covered the same ground as Beesly's speech from the chair. The occasion of the meeting he pointed out was the decision by English and French workers to protest jointly against the 'insults and cruelties' inflicted on Poland. It was appropriate, he felt with Beesly, that the French, who led the world in the arts of civilisation, should have proposed the bringing together of those who produced the world's wealth. Odger's approach was not only Mazzinian in content, but was shot through with phrases taken straight from the orotund, lofty and vague writings of the Italian leader. Foreign policy must be based on such concepts as 'duties', 'reason and moral right' and 'dignity',[2] by means of which 'the power of the despots will be weakened'.

The statement contained no suggestion of Socialism or any radical change in property relations. It did not even go so far as the Positivists in assigning a leading place to the workers in establishing the new society. The task of the working class was rather to 'clear the way for honourable men with comprehensive minds' — another characteristically Mazzinian touch — 'to come forth and legislate for the rights of the many, and not the privileges of the few'.

If Odger's ideas on social reform and on foreign affairs were vaguely benevolent, his views on trade union problems were more precise. The other main aim of the 'fraternity of peoples' must be to strengthen the bargaining power of labour. As things stood, the workers' attempts to reduce hours and raise wages were met with threats from the employers to bring in 'Frenchmen, Germans, Belgians and others to do our work

---

[1] *Beehive*, October 1, 1864. The reference to Ireland was reported by Le Lubez and appeared in *Le Phare de la Loire*, on October 2, 1864 — see Ryazanoff, *op. cit.* The *Beehive*'s omission may be significant. When, in 1870, the International finally broke with the paper, it was partly because of its suppression of the General Council's resolutions on Ireland.

[2] Cf. Joseph Mazzini, *The Duties of Man*, Everyman edition, p. 7, *et seq.*

at a reduced rate of wages'. This happened, not through the malevolence of foreign workers, 'but through a want of regular and systematic communication between the industrious classes of all countries', which it was one of the main objects of the meeting to bring about.

CONFLICTING VOICES

If Odger's Address dealt exclusively with political and trade union matters, the main French reply was concerned overwhelmingly with economics. Delivered by Henri Louis Tolain, Paris engraver and later a Senator, it was a straightforward essay in Proudhonism. There was no reference to trade unions or strikes, either because strikes were still illegal in France or because Proudhon opposed unions as inherently coercive [1] — perhaps for both reasons. Exactly four sentences were devoted to the rights of oppressed nationalities, one of which in passing mentioned Poland. Even this was probably no more than a formal approval of the ostensible purpose of the meeting. Proudhon had expressed strong hostility to Poland; [2] his followers, including Tolain, were later to oppose all attempts to involve the International in the Polish question.

In contrast, Proudhon was desperately concerned with the impoverishment and destruction of the small farmer and artisan by the competition of big capital. This was also Tolain's preoccupation. Under the existing social system both 'free trade' and 'the laws of supply and demand' were reducing the workman to the status of 'a manufactured article'. The only tolerable solution in Tolain's view was through a system of 'free exchange' in which the small peasant or artisan could receive a price on the market corresponding to the labour embodied in his product.

In emphasis, in approach and in the social philosophy underlying both, there were vast differences between the speeches of Tolain and Odger. Such differences passed unnoticed in the glow of the foundation meeting. Le Lubez, who followed Tolain, confined himself to an outline of the French plan for organising the Association. There was to be a central commission in London representing all the affiliated national

[1] P. J. Proudhon, *De la capacité politique des classes ouvrières*, Paris, 1865, p. 428.
[2] P. J. Proudhon, *La Guerre et la paix*, Brussels, 1862, p. 448.

sections.   This would appoint sub-commissions in every European capital to correspond with it.   Such correspondence would culminate in agreement on a common policy for the international labour movement.   The Association should hold its first Congress in Brussels in the following year to confirm the rules and statutes.

Le Lubez then read in translation a speech by Henri Lefort, French radical republican and one of the founders of the International.   Like so many pronouncements of the French radical left, the speech was highly abstract, full of such phrases as 'What is indeed liberty without equality?   What is equality without liberty?' and of references to 'the great revolution of 1792 . . . 1830 and 1848.'   Whereas Tolain had carefully avoided mentioning the political régime in France, Lefort spoke of the French people as being 'shut up in the narrow prison' of 'arbitrary power'.   On the other hand, while Tolain had dealt at length with the oppression of labour by capital, Lefort made no reference whatever to class conflicts.

An English trade unionist, George Wheeler, formally moved the establishment of an international association, and the election of a committee with powers of co-option to draw up the rules on the basis of Le Lubez's proposals.   Another Englishman, William Dell, who later became the International's treasurer, seconded, and the first General Council was duly elected.   It consisted of twenty-seven Englishmen, three Frenchmen, two Germans and two Italians.   The Frenchmen, Le Lubez, Bocquet and Jules Denoual, the Germans, Marx and Eccarius, and the Italians, Major Luigi Wolf and Dr. Domenico Lama.   All lived in London and the General Council remained throughout a London organisation.

The International emerged from its foundation meeting without name, programme or rules.   The *Beehive* became its first official organ.   In a warm and rather undiscriminating editorial the *Beehive* welcomed the new Association stressing both its humane international and social aims and that the rights of labour were to be 'advanced and protected without unduly interfering with the legitimate rights of capital'.

Neither the *Beehive* nor anyone else perceived in the proceedings the seeds of future dissension.   Tolain's speech was praised as a masterly exposition of the relations between capital and labour.   The ominous contrasts in tone and content between the speeches of Tolain and Lefort went unnoticed.

D

Within months the two French sections were to be at each others' throats. The winning faction, largely Proudhonist in outlook, was to quarrel with the English trade unionists on every major issue of domestic and foreign policy. The Italians, led by Luigi Wolf,[1] could not remain long in a body which did not conform in ideology and organisation to the principles of Mazzini. In the absence of Marx, the International's chances of survival would have been slight. He gave the organisation a cohesion and a sense of purpose which kept it going at a surprisingly high level of effectiveness through innumerable splits and schisms. His object in doing this was revolutionary. He approved of the struggles of the British workers to build up their trade societies, to win political rights and to force through social reforms. But Marx did not view such achievements as ends in themselves. He assessed them, as he assessed everything, solely in relation to the European revolution for which he ceaselessly worked. He did not delude himself that the English workers were revolutionary or could quickly or easily become so. But at least it seemed to Marx they might emerge again, as in the days of the Chartists, as an independent political force fighting for an independent class programme. If this force could be re-created and then welded into an international organisation led by conscious revolutionaries, it could play an indispensable part in securing the success of the next round of European revolutions. Marx left the foundation meeting confident that an important step had been taken towards the realisation of his life's work.

---

[1] Documents published under the Paris Commune in 1871 showed him to have been a spy of Napoleon III.

CHAPTER IV

Marx's Conception of the International

MARX'S task was to reconcile the irreconcilable. The International at its inception had five affiliated national groups — English, French, Italian, German and Polish. The Poles were concerned exclusively with Poland and played no independent part in the development of the International. Each of the other four groups saw in the new Association a projection of itself on a world scale. The four images were of course different and, beyond a certain point, incompatible. For a brief period, however, all were agreed on the basic aim of establishing a workers' international. This gave Marx a platform and an opportunity.

FOUR NATIONAL GROUPS

The English view, expressed at its clearest in Odger's Address, was the least complicated. Trade unionism had begun to sink roots in England, at least among the skilled workers. This was not yet true of the Continent. There, for the most part, the right of collective bargaining was not recognised and workers' associations took the form of friendly and co-operative societies. Continental wages were substantially lower than English and such leaders as Cremer, Howell, Applegarth and Odger saw in this a double threat to their own standards. Firstly, there was the competition of goods produced by low-wage industries; secondly, and intermittently, there was the threat to replace English workers on strike by Europeans. In the International such leaders saw a grand opportunity of meeting both threats at the same time. Liaison with the European workers could be the means both of preventing the import of foreigners during strikes and of spreading the principles of British trade unionism on the Continent.

To do them justice, English workers did not join the International only for parochial or selfish reasons. They had, as we have seen, a genuine sympathy with movements for democracy and national independence in other countries. Many influences had combined to stimulate this feeling. The idea that a victory for the people in another country strengthened the popular cause at home was deep rooted and went back at least as far as the French Revolution. The conception of a Holy Alliance of labour owed much to the writings of Lovett, Harney and Reynolds during the Chartist period. While Mazzini was living in London he undoubtedly influenced such leaders as Howell and Cremer and it would be surprising if Odger were not included in their number. Positivist influence tended in the same direction and reinforced the view that existing foreign policies were not only mistaken but immoral. The rise of the workers, according to Beesly and Harrison, would 'moralise' not only social but also international relations.[1]

In France the workers' movement, largely influenced as it was by Proudhon, was growing up along radically different lines. To complicate the position further a section of the French working class followed the lead of the middle-class republican opposition. With Lefort and Le Lubez, they thought the workers' cause best served by the overthrow of Napoleon and the restoration of republican democracy. Leaders of this school viewed with suspicion the evolution of an independent workers' movement following the 'Manifesto of the Sixty'. Such a movement seemed designed to split the republican opposition and willy-nilly to strengthen the Bonapartist régime. Was it accidental, they asked themselves, that Napoleon had financed the visit of the delegation to the London exhibition in 1862? Was it not strange to find men like Tolain standing for parliament in opposition to other republicans while preaching the gospel of salvation through economic organisation, not political change? Before long the antagonism between the two French sections came to a head, leading to the first but by no means the last split in the International Working Men's Association.

The Italians were represented on the first General Council by Mazzini's secretary, Luigi Wolf, and by Domenico Lama, Chairman of the Italian Working Men's 'Associazione di Mutuo Progresso' in London. This Association had been established

---

[1] For a detailed discussion of the influence of Positivist ideas on labour, see the thesis by Dr. Royden Harrison, *English Positivists and Labour Movements, 1859–1885*, Oxford, 1955.

in July 1864. Its programme was based on the 'Brotherly Agreement' adopted by the Tenth Congress of Workers' Organisations at Parma in 1863. The Brotherly Agreement was a Mazzinian document. It provided for a union of workers' societies with three sections catering respectively for the moral, intellectual and economic progress of their class. Mutual self-help was the keynote of their programme which provided for the establishment of libraries, schools and co-operatives. There was no mention of wage struggles or of politics except for a general clause about the need for the workers to 'make known to the government in legal manner their conditions, their desires, and their wants. . .' . Well-intentioned and innocuous, the Mazzinists were the least radical of the groups affiliated to the International.

Most radical were the Germans. The Arbeiterbildungsverein had been revolutionary socialist since its foundation in 1840. By 1864 Lassalle's agitation, abruptly ended by his death in August, had resulted in the formation of the General Association of German Workers which was to gain ground in succeeding years. In South Germany the movement of Bebel and Liebknecht — the latter already strongly influenced by Marx — was just beginning. The rapid advance of Socialism, which led to the founding of the German Social Democratic Party in 1869, confirmed the members of the A.B.V. in their revolutionary views. Throughout the history of the International, the Germans provided Marx with his most consistent support. Eccarius for a number of years, and Lessner throughout, were his most reliable adherents on the General Council.

THE GENERAL COUNCIL: WESTON, WOLF AND LE LUBEZ

With such a heterogeneous mixture it is hardly surprising that the General Council made heavy weather from its first meeting on October 5. Odger was elected Chairman and Cremer General Secretary. When it came to discussing the programme it was found that after a 'very long and animated discussion' no agreement could be reached. Weston, an old Owenite whom everyone liked but whom most people found it difficult to listen to, and Luigi Wolf were deputed to submit draft programmes for consideration.

Marx, who was suffering from one of his frequent bouts of illness, missed the Council meeting at which the two drafts were discussed. Both were referred back to a sub-committee for reconsideration. Though the *Minutes* are not very explicit it seems certain that Eccarius had a hand in the reference back. He did not like the way things were going and it seemed to him that with the vagueness of the English on matters of theory almost anything could happen. At the same meeting on October 11 a proposal was actually made to merge the International in the Marquis of Townsend's Universal League. Eccarius was largely instrumental in killing the suggestion.

It was in some alarm that he wrote to Marx the next day begging him to attend future meetings. Weston's draft was dreadful — 'a sentimental declamatory editorial'. Cremer had remarked privately that Weston should have nothing more to do with the document. It should be handed over to a commission of three 'which could make use of the available material or not as they saw fit'. Odger and a number of others had agreed, adding that 'The right man in the right place' will undoubtedly be Dr. Marx'.[1]

Despite the warning, Marx missed the sub-committee meeting on October 15, having been told of the rendezvous too late. In his absence Le Lubez was instructed to draft a composite of Weston's document and Wolf's translation of the rules of the Italian Workingmen's Association. Le Lubez submitted his draft to the full Council on October 18. What happened next was described by Marx in his letter to Engels on November 4. 'As Eccarius had written to me that delay would be dangerous I appeared and was really frightened when I heard the worthy Le Lubez read out an appallingly wordy, badly written and utterly indigestible preamble, pretending to be a declaration of principles, in which Mazzini could be detected everywhere, the whole being crusted over with the vaguest tags of French socialism.' To make matters worse, the Italian statutes providing for a centralised control over the entire European labour movement, which Marx regarded as 'utterly impossible', had been incorporated. He and Eccarius succeeded in getting the draft referred back once again to the sub-committee.

Marx, in the course of a very brief contact with the English, had clearly made a deep impression on them. He combined to an unusual degree enormous erudition, powers of creative thought and political acumen. This acumen, which had

---

[1] Eccarius to Marx, October 12, 1864. *Founding of the First International*, pp. 64-5.

enabled him to see at once that the projected International could be of major importance, stood him in good stead at the critical sub-committee meeting on October 20. It was held in his house and he succeeded in keeping the discussion going until 1 a.m., by which time his weary colleagues were only too glad to accept his offer to incorporate the drafts of Wolf and Le Lubez in a new document, while preserving the sense of the originals. Marx saw at once, he told Engels, 'that it was impossible to make anything out of the stuff. In order to justify the extremely strange way in which I intended to present the "sentiments" already "voted for", I wrote *An Address to the Working Classes* (which was not in the original plan; a sort of review of the adventures of the working classes since 1845) . . . I altered the whole preamble, threw out the declaration of principles and finally replaced the forty rules by ten. *In so far as international politics come into the address, I speak of countries, not of nationalities,* and denounce Russia, not the lesser nations. My proposals were all accepted by the sub-committee.' The spirit of Mazzini, however, was not to be quite extinguished and Marx 'was obliged to insert two phrases about "duty" and "right" into the preamble to the statutes, ditto "truth, morality and justice", but these are placed in such a way that they can do no harm'.

Marx's draft was submitted to the General Council on November 1. At the same meeting, his position was strengthened by the co-option of three new members who were to figure prominently in the future history of the International. Hermann Jung, a Swiss watchmaker, Friedrich Lessner, a German tailor, and Eugène Dupont, a French musical instrument maker, were all *émigrés* living in London and all strongly under Marx's influence. Even so, Marx was forced to make one more concession. Wheeler, who had tried to merge the International in the Universal League, and Worley, a printer who had already objected to the statement 'that the capitalists were opposed to the labourer', demanded the removal of the phrase 'profit mongers' from a passage denouncing the opponents of the Ten Hours' Bill in 1847. They succeeded by eleven votes to ten, but apart from that and the addition of one explanatory footnote, Marx's *Address* was adopted as it stood.[1] It became the International's provisional and, after the Geneva Congress

---

[1] G.C. *Minutes*, October 11, 18, November 1, 1864. *Founding of the First International*, pp. 22-6.

in 1866, the definitive statement of aims. In every way a re-markable document, it repays detailed examination.

CHARACTER OF THE INAUGURAL ADDRESS

The *Address*, like all the other documents which Marx wrote for the General Council (except for his subsequent attack on the Bakuninists), was in English and was directed primarily to the English working class. As such it was signifi-cantly different from the *Communist Manifesto* which he had written with Engels sixteen years earlier. The first two sections of the *Manifesto* were built on broad, sweeping generalisations with the minimum of supporting fact. Its main theme was the historical destiny of the proletariat, its seizure of power followed by the forcible destruction of capitalist property relations. The *Address*, by contrast, was specific, detailed and circumspect. Marx knew very well that the English workers were not interested in generalising about society or in speculating about the historical destiny of the proletariat. They were concerned with raising wages, reducing hours, winning the vote and reforming trade union legislation. They were more interested in repealing the Master and Servant Act so winning for the wage earner equality before the law than they were in the nature of the social system or in possible alternatives to it. The Co-operative movement appealed to them as a practical way of keeping down the cost of living; few paid more than lip-service to the ideal of a co-operative commonwealth. And as they were more than ready to work with liberal-minded employers in replacing strikes by arbitra-tion, so they demanded, politically, little more than democratic rights and a little social legislation from liberal-minded poli-ticians. Marx knew all about the political limitations of the men who had invited him to help build an International of labour. But he also knew of the solid and unique organisational strength of the movement which they led. If it was possible to harness such a movement to the task of a European revolution, Marx would achieve this. The *Inaugural Address* was designed for just this end.

The document was ready on October 27.[1] Remarkable from a literary as from a political point of view, it is at first sight

[1] Cremer to Marx, October 27, 1864, *Founding of First International*, p. 68.

surprising that even so indefatigable a worker as Marx could have written it in less than a week. He did it by incorporating some of the data he had already collected for the first volume of *Capital* which was to be published three years later. Almost all the economic material reappeared in *Capital*, often in the same words. In the *Inaugural Address* it was deliberately and skilfully adapted to a British trade union audience. 'It was very difficult', he explained to Engels on November 4, 'to frame things so that our view should appear in a form accept-able from the present standpoint of the workers' movement. In a few weeks the same people will be holding meetings for the franchise with Bright and Cobden. It will take time before the reawakened movement allows the old boldness of speech. It will be necessary to be *fortiter in re, suaviter in modo*.' Marx's unfamiliarity with the audience he was address-ing made his achievement all the more remarkable.

ECONOMIC CONDITIONS

The *Communist Manifesto* in its first section had dealt with the rise and character of capitalism and of the class conflicts it engendered. The *Inaugural Address* began with a description of economic conditions in Britain. Despite unprecedented technical progress in the sixteen years since 1848, the misery of the working people had not diminished. Marx quoted from a Blue Book of 1863 dealing with the conditions of those under-going transportation and penal servitude. It showed that 'the worst of the convicted criminals, the penal serfs of England and Scotland, toiled much less and fared far better than the agri-cultural labourers of England and Scotland'.[1] A physician investigating the diet of Lancashire operatives during the cotton famine of the early 1860s had found it barely above starvation level,[2] while many categories of unskilled workers were getting even less. Conditions among farm workers were so depressed that cleanliness was only possible at the price of additional hunger.[3]

In general, the poverty of large sections of the working class was so appalling that it constituted a source of physical and moral degeneration and Marx quoted the 1863 Report of the Children's Employment Commissioners to show how the health

---

[1] Cf. *Capital*, vol. I, London, 1946, p. 698.
[2] *Ibid.*, p. 671.   [3] *Ibid.*, p. 673.

of future generations was being impaired.[1]   Inadequate diet
was made even worse by frequent adulteration as shown in
Tremenheere's Blue Book on the *Grievances Complained of by
the Journeymen Bakers*.[2]

In spite of all this, Gladstone, as Chancellor of the Ex-
chequer, had boasted of the country's increasing wealth, while
admitting that 'this intoxicating augmentation of wealth and
power is entirely confined to classes of property'.[3]

For Marx, England constituted the model for capitalist development throughout the whole of Europe.   He explained
that if the *Inaugural Address* concentrated exclusively on
English conditions, this was because England 'heads the Europe
of commerce and industry'.   For the rest, 'with local colours
changed, and on a scale somewhat contracted, the English facts
reproduce themselves in all the industrious and progressive
countries of the Continent'.   This was a dangerous over-
simplification for which Marx was to pay dearly.   Capitalism
was to develop in the several countries of Europe in very
different political and social contexts and against a background
of very varying national traditions.   Even in its early stages
capitalism did not repeat elsewhere the English pattern, nor
was its impact on communities of peasants and craftsmen the
same in Europe as it had been in Britain.   It was to anarchism
that the early victims of capitalism were to turn in many parts
of Switzerland, Russia, Spain, Italy and France.   Probably
through this error of analysis these later developments were to
take Marx completely by surprise and to cause him to take
desperate measures which would involve the destruction of the
International.   In Europe outside Germany, Marxism, by contrast, did not strike roots until the 1880s and 1890s, finding
expression in a new and very different International.

When in the *Inaugural Address* Marx turned to a more
detailed examination of capitalism's economic prospects in
England, his conclusions were more ambiguous.   While conceding that in the period under review a minority of the workers had
succeeded in raising real wages, the majority was 'sinking down
to a lower depth, at the same rate at least that those above them
were rising in the social scale'.   Marx ended his description

---

[1] Cf. *Capital*, vol. I, London, 1946, p. 229.   [2] *Ibid.*, p. 153, n. 3.
[3] *Ibid.*, p. 668.   This quotation from Gladstone led the German economist, Luigi Brentano, to accuse Marx of falsification and to a long, acrimonious controversy.   See Engels's preface to the fourth German edition of
Capital, 1890, and Engels, *In Sachen Brentano Contra Marx*, Hamburg, 1891.

of economic conditions with the prediction that no palliatives would alleviate the workers' plight, that 'no improvement of machinery, no appliances of science to production, no contrivances of communication, no new colonies, no emigration, no opening of markets, no free trade, nor all these things put together, will do away with the miseries of the industrious masses ; but that, on the present false base, every fresh development of the productive powers of labour must tend to deepen social contrasts and point social antagonisms'. This was in some ways an echo of the view expressed in the *Manifesto* that the worker under capitalism 'instead of rising with the progress of industry, sinks deeper and deeper below the conditions of existence of his own class. He becomes a pauper, and pauperism develops more rapidly than population and wealth.'

Yet taken literally, the prediction in the *Inaugural Address* is a shade more guarded. Here Marx did not commit himself without qualification to the inevitable and absolute impoverishment of the workers. He said rather that no economic changes under the existing social system could do away with the misery of the masses or prevent the antagonism between capital and labour from increasing, through the deepening of 'social contrasts'. Inseparable from Marx's model was the relative impoverishment of the workers through a growing disparity between productivity and real wages. If Marx was right, the felt poverty of the workers would increase, whatever might happen to the absolute level of consumption, since wages would decline in relation to the wealth of society and the ruling class.

Whatever may be the final verdict of economic historians on the validity of Marx's model for his own day and for some generations to follow, Marx in the 1860s could cite a good deal of empirical evidence to support his view that the triumphs of science and technology had brought no corresponding benefit in the living conditions of the masses. But even in his own day Marx recognised that a limited number of skilled workers had improved their standard of life. He could draw one of two conclusions from the success of the craftsmen, strongly organised in exclusive unions in raising their level of wages. One was that such success could only be temporary, since the simplification of production resulting from new machinery would undermine the craftsman's position, facilitating his replacement by female and child labour. The alternative hypothesis was that trade unionism would spread from the craftsmen to the unskilled giving rise to the possibility that the entire working class might eventually benefit from concessions wrung out of the employers.

In the *Address*, as previously in the *Manifesto*, Marx adopted the first alternative which reinforced his revolutionary conclusions. Two years later he became aware of the need to organise the unskilled. He drew the attention of the craft unions to this problem in the *Instructions* which he wrote for the General Council's delegation to the Geneva Congress of the International in 1866. However, he felt that trade union organisation was mainly of importance in strengthening the class consciousness and fighting spirit of the workers. While local and temporary successes in raising wages were not excluded, the growth of technological unemployment, which he believed to be innate in capitalism, would continually throw the workers back to a subsistence level of existence.[1]

The validity of Marx's analysis of capitalism falls outside the scope of this study. What is immediately relevant is the fact that in the lifetime of the First International efforts to organise the unskilled majority of the working class failed almost completely. The organised minority, under conditions of prolonged mid-Victorian boom and industrial expansion, was able, as Marx recognised, to improve its standard of life. Paradoxically, the men who allied themselves with Marx in the period of the International came from this privileged stratum of the working class. For seven years, with occasional signs of stress, the strange alliance lasted. For different and conflicting reasons each needed the other. But Marx knew well enough that his trade union allies if forced to the point would rather ally with the Liberals than try to develop the workers as an independent political force. Nor did Marx for his part succeed in creating the party of communists which had been projected in 1848. All of this was to play its part in Marx's final decision to abandon the International and transfer his hopes once again to the rising socialist movement in Germany.

THE CONQUEST OF POLITICAL POWER

In the political field Marx recognised that the European workers had not recovered from their defeat in 1848. For this

[1] See Chapter VIII for Marx's speech to the General Council on the effects of machinery, July 1868.

defeat 'the diplomacy of the English government, acting then as now in fraternal solidarity with the Cabinet of St. Petersburg' had been responsible.[1] The events of 1848, reflected in the collapse of Chartism, 'unmanned the English working classes and broke their faith in their own cause', while 'it restored to the landlord and money lord their somewhat shaken confidence. They insolently withdrew concessions already advertised'.[2]

Even under such adverse conditions the English workers had not been completely crushed. Two encouraging developments had taken place in the previous twenty years. The first, the passing of the Ten Hours' Bill in 1847 had resulted in 'immense physical, moral and intellectual benefits', though the orthodox economists 'had predicted, and to their hearts' content proved, that any legal restriction of the hours of labour must sound the death knell of British industry, which vampire-like could but live by sucking blood, and children's blood too.[3] The Ten Hours' Act had not only yielded direct benefits; it was also the victory of a principle; it was the first time that in broad daylight the political economy of the middle class succumbed to the political economy of the working class.' This victory of the workers, secured through their taking advantage of divisions within the ruling class, had also been noted in the *Manifesto*, though in much less fulsome terms. Despite its limited character, Marx considered the Ten Hours' Act as an example of social control over economic relations; as such it pointed the way, however modestly, to the future victory of the working class. In this respect he was more flexible than other revolutionary thinkers such as Bakunin. For Marx the State was an instrument of oppression in the hands of the propertied class. Nevertheless it could be made, in certain circumstances, a means by which the workers could extract concessions and reforms from their employers.

More, even, than the Ten Hours' Act, the growth of the co-operative movement represented 'a still greater victory of the political economy of labour over the political economy of property', since it showed in practice that large-scale enterprise could be conducted 'without the existence of a class of

---

[1] This was an old idea of Marx, first expressed in his pamphlet, *Wage-Labour and Capital* in 1847. See also *Neue Rheinische Zeitung*, February 14, 15, 1849. It was the crux of his persistent attacks on Palmerston's foreign policy.

[2] Cf. *Capital*, p. 272.   [3] *Ibid.*, pp. 285-6.

masters employing a class of hands'.   From this experience
the workers might be helped to realise that 'like slave labour,
like serf labour, hired labour is but a transitory and inferior
form, destined to disappear before associated labour plying its
toil with a willing hand, ready mind, and a joyous heart'.
This was the only part of the *Address* in which Marx made
reference to his theory of history and to his belief that capitalist property relations were destined to give way to collective
ownership.   The belief in Socialism was there for anyone
who chose to read the passage carefully enough.   But it was
guarded and unobtrusive in contrast to the uncompromising call in the *Manifesto* for the forcible expropriation of
the capitalist employers by a revolutionary working class.
Marx was here deliberately vague about the way in which
Socialism would be achieved.   He paid glowing tribute to
Robert Owen for sowing 'the seeds of the co-operative system'.
At this point his readers might conclude that he had nothing
more revolutionary in mind than the gradual and peaceful
expansion of co-operative societies.   He went on immediately,
however, to make it clear that the capitalists would not allow
themselves to be supplanted so easily, since they could always
be counted on to 'use their political privileges for the defence
and perpetuation of their economical monopolies'.

From all of this, Marx, in contrast to both Odger and
Tolain, drew the conclusion that 'to conquer political power
has therefore become the great duty of the working classes'.
Odger saw the International as a pressure group to force a more
moral foreign policy on governments and to co-ordinate international action during strikes.   Tolain wanted the International to work out schemes for saving the poor from the
pressure of big business by means of economic associations for
the promotion of free credit and free exchange.   Only Marx
proposed that the workers should organise internationally to
win political power and use it to change the social system.
His tactics throughout the history of the International can only
be understood in the light of his overriding aim, an aim which
few of his English associates shared or even understood.

George Howell thirty-eight years later wrote of the International in this period that 'no doctrine was broached or
proposal made which could not have been publicly stated on
any English platform'.[1]   And of Marx himself he could say, in

[1] *Op. cit.*, pp. 150-1.

blissful innocence: 'Some of the theories connected with his name were not then known to his colleagues, and I am not sure that they had at that date been even propounded'.

A STRANGE OMISSION

There was one peculiar omission in Marx's survey of working-class progress since the 1840s. For the first time the workers had established stable trade unions, though admittedly on a narrow basis. Yet it was from these footholds that they advanced to secure a measure of political influence in 1867. From the passing of the Reform Act of that year they became a powerful pressure group and exerted influence on legislation for the rest of the century. Industrial organisation was to spread from the craftsmen to the unskilled and to lay the foundation a generation later for an independent party of the working class. Yet the development of trade unionism was not even mentioned in the *Inaugural Address*.

Later Marx was to give some attention to the achievements and limitations of trade unions. The *Communist Manifesto* had described their appearance as a necessary stage in the 'organisation of the proletarians into a class'. In his Instructions for the Geneva Congress of the International in 1866 he described them in similar terms, as 'organising centres of the working class in the broad interest of its complete emancipation', destined to do for the workers what the 'medieval municipalities and communes did for the middle class'.[1]

Marx was at least as conscious of the limitations of English trade unionism from a revolutionary point of view. In a debate at the London Conference of the International in September 1871 he was to dwell on their shortcomings. They constituted only 'an aristocratic minority', excluding the unskilled and enrolling, in the East End of London, one worker in ten. Whatever their uses, the unions could not exercise leadership over the working class as a whole, being non-political according to their own rules. To unite the entire class a political leadership was needed and this it was the function of the International to provide.[2]

[1] For the text of this draft see the *Working Man*, March 1, April 6, 1867. For Marx's authorship see his letter to his daughter, Jenny, on September 5, 1866.

[2] *Londonskaya Conferentsia Pervovo Internationala*, 1871, Moscow, 1936, pp. 38-55 and 154-7.

Marx, then, saw in trade unions an indispensable school for the class struggle, a useful auxiliary in the broad movement of labour towards Socialism, but essentially subordinate to the political aims which the workers were destined to acquire. In a number of European countries developments did in fact follow some such course. But in England the trade unions remained the dominant and formative influence in the labour movement. They never accepted the subordinate rôle Marx had projected for them. For all its tactical skill, perspicacity and depth, therefore, the *Inaugural Address* goes some way towards explaining the ineffectiveness of Marx's ideas in England, the country in which he lived most of his life and from whose economic development he drew the main data for his major work. He neither anticipated nor would have approved the main lines of development which the British labour movement was to follow.

INTERNATIONAL AFFAIRS

The final section of the *Address* was devoted to international affairs. In noticeable contrast to Odger's statement less than a tenth of the *Address* was concerned with foreign policy. Many a revolutionary *émigré* drafting such a document would have reversed the proportions. But Marx was determined to use the occasion to express as much of his underlying social philosophy as could be made acceptable to English trade unionists. In his last paragraph he insisted that since 'the emancipation of the working classes requires their fraternal concurrence' they could hardly 'fulfil that great mission with a criminal foreign policy playing upon national prejudices, and squandering in piratical wars the people's blood and treasure'.

In every respect but one Marx expressed the same approach to foreign politics as Odger in his earlier *Address*. Like Odger, Marx appealed to the workers in Mazzinian terms to 'vindicate the simple laws of morals and justice which ought to govern the relations of private individuals, as the rules paramount of the intercourse of nations'. But while Odger had praised 'the achievements of the Italian liberators, when led by one of their own class' and lauded the heroism of 'the greatest of all modern chiefs, Garibaldi', the *Inaugural Address* made no reference to Italy or Garibaldi. The ruling classes, said Marx, in supporting the slave owners during the American Civil War and in conniving at the suppression of Caucasians and Poles by 'that barbarous power, whose head is in St. Petersburg, and whose hands are in every cabinet of Europe', had proved once again their unfitness to govern. On the Risorgimento, however, Marx was silent. Both he and Engels had mixed feelings about the movement. They were afraid that it could lend itself to exploitation by Napoleonic France and Czarist Russia and they cannot have lost sight of the fact that, unlike the Polish and American issues, it did not divide left from right in English politics. While the lack of all reference to the New Model unions was due to an inadequate understanding of the British labour scene, the omission of Italy was probably deliberate. Deprecating what he later described to Engels as the 'old Mazzinism of Odger, Howell, Cremer, etc.',[1] he saw no reason to encourage it in his *Address*. The omission passed quite unnoticed.

PROVISIONAL RULES

After the *Address* there followed the *Provisional Rules* beginning with the preamble 'That the emancipation of the working classes must be conquered by the working classes themselves'. Emancipation was defined as 'the abolition of all class rule'. Since this might well be taken by English trade unionists to mean merely the extension of the franchise to the working class, Marx went on to explain that 'the economical subjection of the man of labour to the monopoliser of the means of labour, that is the sources of life, lies at the bottom of servitude in all its forms, of all social misery, mental degradation and political dependence', from which it followed that 'the economical emancipation of the working classes is therefore the great end to which every political movement ought to be subordinated as a means'.[2]

Marx had already made clear in the *Address* that economic emancipation implied the organisation of 'production on a large scale . . . without the existence of a class of masters employing a class of hands'. He deliberately left open the question of how the future society would be organised. The

---

[1] Marx to Engels, March 24, 1866.
[2] The first French translation of the *Rules* omitted the phrase 'as a means', giving the passage a different and decidedly Proudhonist tone. See below.

Communist Manifesto had spoken of the need 'to centralise all instruments of production in the hands of the State'. Here Marx not only omitted those revolutionary demands which would have alienated the English. He was also obliged, in deference to the French followers of Proudhon, to omit all reference to State centralisation as the form which socialist society would take.

After listing the reasons for the formation of the International, Marx made his greatest verbal concession to those who shared Mazzini's outlook on society. Members of the International, he declared, 'will acknowledge truth, justice and morality, as the bases of their conduct towards each other'. The next paragraph went further in asserting, with what must have been a deliberate imitation of Mazzini's style, that 'They hold it the duty of a man to claim the rights of a man and a citizen, not only for himself, but for every man who does his duty. No rights without duties, no duties without rights.' This juxtaposition of the concepts, duty and right, had occurred in Odger's *Address* and would be familiar to any reader of Mazzini.

The ten provisional rules with which the document ended were concise. They laid down as the main function of the General Council the co-ordination of international action in defence of working-class conditions and of international peace. A project of which much was subsequently heard but of which nothing came was for an international enquiry into social and economic conditions in all countries in which the Association had sections. Rule seven provided for the co-ordination of separate local societies in each country under 'central national organs', adding carefully that the application of the rule would depend on 'the peculiar laws of each country, and that apart from legal obstacles, no independent local society shall be precluded from directly corresponding with the London General Council'. This rule, which gave the General Council considerable powers of intervening in the affairs of national sections, was later to prove invaluable to Marx in his life-and-death struggle with Bakunin.

Rule eight devolved on the provisional General Council the dual function of directing affairs internationally while enlisting members in the United Kingdom. For the future the first Congress of the International would be empowered to ratify the rules and elect a new General Council. Rule nine undertook, as the Fraternal Democrats and International Association had both done, to provide 'fraternal support' from the local sections to any member moving to a foreign country. Rule ten gave the International its federal structure by providing that affiliated societies should 'preserve their existent organisations intact'.

THE BASIS OF AN ALLIANCE

The *Inaugural Address* made little impact on the Press at the time of its publication. The *Beehive* [1] and the *Miner and Workman's Advocate* [2] published it in full, while the General Council issued it as a pamphlet in a print of a thousand.[3] Otherwise, for the general public, its appearance passed practically unnoticed.

The controversies implicit in the speeches of Odger, Tolain and Lefort at the foundation meeting were soon to be waged in the open. Of the three points of view represented — English trade unionist, French Proudhonist and French radical republican — the *Address* was closest to the first. In his struggles with the Proudhonists and later with Bakunin and his followers, Marx could rely almost to the end on the support of the English. The basis for this alliance was laid in the drafting of the *Address*.

[1] November 5 and 12, 1864.   [2] December 10, 1864.
[3] *General Council Minutes*, November 15, 1864. The first edition was published by the *Beehive*; the second by the Westminster Publishing Co. — J. B. Leno — appeared in 1866. This edition was reproduced by the Socialist International in 1924 to celebrate the sixtieth anniversary of the International's foundation.

PART TWO

THE INTERNATIONAL IN ENGLAND, 1864–9

The International in England.
Progress : 1864-7

IF Marx was optimistic about the prospects of the International, Engels was — and remained for nearly two years — unimpressed. To Marx's long and enthusiastic letter of November 4 he returned a guarded answer. It was good, he wrote three days later, to be in touch once more with real representatives of the working class. Perhaps, at last, the influence of 'the worthy Giuseppe' on the Italian workers might be undermined. But so far as England was concerned, the International must end in a split between the 'theoretical bourgeois and theoretical proletarian elements'. Though Engels was sent a copy of the *Inaugural Address* he made no comment on it, nor was he to show much interest in the International during the first year and a half of its existence. He urged Marx not to be distracted from his theoretical work and clearly regarded the new Association as of marginal importance.

One of the first public acts of the International was the statement drafted by Marx congratulating Lincoln on his re-election as President of the United States. The tone was unwontedly rhetorical and was no doubt concerned in part to emphasise labour's unqualified support for the North in contrast to the divisions and ambiguities of the period 1861-2. It claimed that 'as the American War of Independence initiated a new era of ascendancy for the middle class, so the American anti-slavery war will do for the working classes'. Lincoln was addressed as 'the single-minded son of the working class' who was 'to lead the country through the matchless struggle for the rescue of an enchained race and the reconstruction of a social world'. Although the *Address to Abraham Lincoln*, with its overblown rhetoric and exaggerated hopes, was not one of Marx's most memorable productions, it attracted early and favourable publicity for the International when Lincoln returned a warm and friendly letter of thanks. 'You can imagine how much good this does our people', Marx wrote to Engels on February 10, 1865 in another fruitless attempt to interest his friend.[1]   And, indeed, the International, after its first few months of life, looked reasonably thriving.

THE FIRST RESPONSE

The Italian Working Men's Association and the London Germans were the first societies to affiliate, each with its characteristic manifesto.   The Italians wanted to replace 'inequalities, compulsory ignorance, the present wages system' by 'equal duties and rights for all, true national education and the association system for producing and consuming'.[2]   The Germans recalled the revolutionary traditions of the Arbeiterbildungsverein since its formation in 1840 and its close relations with 'the Socialists and Chartists of this country', including the Fraternal Democrats.   In contrast to the Italians, the Germans explicitly attacked 'the rule of the capitalists'.

The first English trade union to affiliate was the Operative Society of Bricklayers.[3]   A local branch of the International was set up in Greenwich on January 15, 1865 and anyone attending the Association's first soirée in the Cambridge Hall off Oxford Street on the following day must have received the impression of a vigorous and flourishing society.   The *Beehive* reported about a thousand present.[4]   Speeches from Odger, Le Lubez, Eccarius, Beales, Jung, Cremer and Fox [5] were interspersed with entertainment from the Italian band and

[1] The *Address to Abraham Lincoln* was printed in the *Beehive*, January 7, 1865; Lincoln's reply in *The Times*, February 6, 1865.   See Marx and Engels, *The Civil War in the United States*, New York, 1940, which also prints the International's *Address to President Johnson* after Lincoln's assassination — see pp. 279-85.

[2] G.C. *Minutes*, December 13, 1864 and January 3, 1865.   *Beehive*, January 7, 1865.

[3] The decision to affiliate had been taken before the end of 1864, though the formal application was made in the following February.   Cf. Marx to Engels, December 10; *Bricklayers' Trade Circular*, October 1, 1864; G.C. *Minutes*, February 28; *Bricklayers' Trade Circular*, March 1, 1865. For the Bricklayers' certificate of affiliation, see Appendix to this Chapter.

[4] January 21, 1865.

[5] An English journalist, publisher of the secularist *National Reformer*. At first, a Positivist, Fox later came under Marx's influence through his work on the General Council.

German choir. Only Howell does not seem to have enjoyed himself.[1]

In March came the affiliation of the Amalgamated Cordwainers with about five thousand members, while the Bricklayers strengthened their links with the General Council by appointing their Secretary, Coulson, to represent them along with Howell.[2] Towards the end of April the International received its first request for assistance from abroad. The Leipzig compositors were on strike and Wilhelm Liebknecht forwarded from Berlin their request for help. The General Council at once made contact with the London compositors and from this and other sources collected a certain amount of money for the strike.[3] A month later the tulle makers of Lyons reported a wage cut on the pretext that their employers were being ruined by English competition. The workers were sceptical and asked for details of the state of the trade in England — production and transport costs, taxes and retail prices. In this instance the General Council, with still very limited trade union connections, failed to get anything of value.[4]

Nevertheless, the fame of the International was gradually spreading during the spring and summer of 1865. On April 1 the Chelsea Branch of the Amalgamated Society of Carpenters and Joiners asked for a deputation from the General Council to visit them and 'explain the principles' of the International. The Branch, which had shown an active interest in politics since the Chelsea Barracks affair during the London building strike, was later to secure the affiliation of its Society to the International. The *Bricklayers' Trade Circular* for July 1 carried a letter from some strikers in Wolverhampton. They were afraid that as in the past foreign labour would be brought in to break their strike and they warned their representatives on the General Council of the International to be prepared for such developments. It is noticeable, however, that the perceptible if slow spread of interest in the International was still confined to the building trade, aroused by the London strike movement,

---

[1] He wrote in his *Diary* on January 16, 1865: 'In evening went to International Soirée. Plenty of company but great disorder.' Perhaps he was annoyed at not being asked to speak.

[2] G.C. *Minutes*, March 28, 1865.

[3] *Beehive*, April 29, 1865.

[4] *Beehive*, April 29, May 27; *Miner and Workman's Advocate*, June 3; G.C. *Minutes*, July 25, 1865.

and to the shoemakers, whose interest in politics was as notorious as it was exceptional.[1]

POTTER AND THE JUNTA

The progress of the International in the trade union field suffered a temporary check from August 12, 1865 when the *Beehive* abruptly ceased to report its activities. It seems certain that the Association was caught up in the ferocious struggle between George Potter and the leading trade unionists in London whom the Webbs christened the 'Junta' and who were prominent alike in the International and on the London Trades Council. The dispute, which had started with Potter's support for the South in the American Civil War, widened into a major battle over trade union strategy and tactics.[2] Potter was violently opposed both to the structure and the policies of the narrowly based New Model unions of skilled craftsmen which the members of the Junta were painfully building, mostly from their London offices. Potter considered the Junta bureaucratic and over-cautious; they regarded him as irresponsible and disruptive.

Things came to a head in 1865 when Potter bitterly attacked the Junta's support for arbitration in connection with the iron workers' dispute in Staffordshire. Potter demanded uncompromising support for the strikers and called a trades delegate meeting in London to mobilise support for his policy. This was taken as a grave affront by the London Trades Council which issued a two-page leaflet attacking him.[3]

The establishment of the Reform League in April provided a new arena for the conflict. A group of middle-class radicals, led by Edmund Beales, combined with six workers to form a standing committee of this society which revived the old Chartist demand for universal manhood suffrage. The six workers, including Odger and Eccarius, were all members of the General Council; Eccarius being the first foreigner ever to hold office in a workers' movement concerned with purely English aims. Odger was a member of the 'Junta', and the other workers supported it against Potter and his irrepressible

[1] Howell, *Labour Legislation* . . ., p. 140.
[2] See the thesis by Dr. S. Coltham, *George Potter and the Beehive Newspaper*, Oxford, 1956. For the dispute on the London Trades Council, see L.T.C. *Minutes*, November 22, 1864.
[3] L.T.C. *Minutes*, March 29 and *Annual Report*, July 1865.

'strike jobbing'. Potter tried hard to win control of the
League and failed. The *Beehive* then launched an attack on
the Reform League expressing its pained surprise that such an
estimable man as Beales should have such a bunch of scalliwags
as colleagues.[1]

Meanwhile, Marx had tried to win control of the *Beehive*,
by persuading Engels to buy up a majority of the shares, but
this failed too. On the subject of Potter, about whose rôle in
the trade union movement there has been a good deal of subsequent controversy, Marx accepted uncritically the views of
the Junta.[2] Potter, he told Engels on May 9, was 'a rat of a
man', who derived his influence 'from the fact that he is
presently the manager of *Beehive*, the official organ of the trade
unions, though he uses it against the *official* council of these
unions, which is in our hands'. Marx was probably repeating
what he had been told by Odger and Cremer. Potter, for his
part, must have regarded the International, like the London
Trades Council, as a creature of the Junta. From August 12,
1865 to July 13, 1867 the *Beehive* ceased to publish regular
reports of the General Council's proceedings.

THE REFORM LEAGUE

On the other hand the foundation of the Reform League
seemed to Marx an important success for the International.
For six months he had been trying without success to influence
Engels in its affairs. With the affiliation of the Bricklayers
and the Cordwainers, both sizeable unions, Marx could point
proudly to the fact that the International had an affiliated
membership of twelve thousand.[3] Less than three weeks later
he was writing in triumph: 'The great success of the International Association is this: the League is our work'.[4] For
once Engels showed a flicker of interest. It was good, he
replied, that the International was now concerning itself with
English affairs. Perhaps, after all, something might come
of it.

Superficially, Marx's optimism was justified. With six
members of the General Council on the League's standing

---

[1] *Beehive*, August 5, 1865 and August 12 for Beales's reply.
[2] As did the Webbs — see B. C. Roberts, *The Trades Union Congress,
1868–1921*, 1958, pp. 31, n. 3 and 64, n. 1.
[3] Marx to Engels, April 14, 1865.   [4] Marx to Engels, May 1, 1865.

committee and seven out of a total of ten on its executive [1] it seemed as if the International would control the new, broader organisation. Howell, the Reform League's Secretary, was a member of the General Council and had been among the first of the leading trade unionists to welcome the International. Edmund Beales, the League's president, actually applied for membership of the International, but Marx thought that this would be too much of a good thing. He told Le Lubez that though Beales was undoubtedly 'honest and sincere', his admission would be followed by the entry of other middle-class radicals and the working-class character of the International destroyed. [2]

Prior to its formation, the Reform League's policy had been discussed on the General Council. Cremer, Howell and other trade unionists were under heavy pressure to come in behind the middle-class National Reform Union, led by Bright and Cobden, with its more modest demand for ratepayers' suffrage. Discussions on the General Council were largely instrumental in stiffening the resistance of the workers to these blandishments and bringing about the formation of the largely, though not exclusively, working-class Reform League. [3]

Once launched, however, the League went its own way and there was little sign that its development was in any way influenced by the International. On the contrary, the Reform League's campaign seems actually to have weakened the International as an organisation. It was originally intended to hold the first Congress of the International at Brussels in 1865. When the time came it was decided to postpone the Congress for a year, largely because the preoccupation of active workers with the reform struggle had 'retarded the maturity of the association'. [4] Instead, a Conference was arranged in London for September 1865 to assess progress and to agree an agenda for the full Congress in the following year.

Before the London Conference assembled, the General

---

[1] For details, see Reform League *Minute Book*, April 21, May 24, 1865.

[2] Marx to Le Lubez, February 15, 1865. Quoted in I. Tchernoff, *Le Parti républicain au coup d'état et sous le Second Empire*, Paris, 1906, pp. 456-7.

[3] G.C. *Minutes*, February 21, March 21, 1865. See also: *Report of Proceedings at the National Reform Conference held in Free Trade Hall, Manchester, May 15 and 16, 1865, George Wilson chairman*, quoted by F. E. Gillespie, *Labour and Politics in England, 1850–1867*, North Carolina, 1927, p. 254.

[4] *Beehive*, July 29, 1865.

Council had secured another organ in place of the *Beehive*.   In his fight with the Junta, Potter drew his main support from the older and small trade societies, but he also reached an understanding with Alexander Macdonald, Secretary of the National Miners' Union.   Towers, a political adventurer who had been fighting Macdonald for control over the miners' organisation — though not himself a miner — had started the *Miner and Workman's Advocate*, mainly to combat Macdonald's influence. Since Macdonald was Potter's ally, Towers was his enemy and his paper was the enemy of the *Beehive*.   Seeking a replacement for the *Beehive* the General Council made contact with Towers and took over his ailing journal, re-naming it the *Workman's Advocate* and appointing a multi-national board of directors. Among the English representatives were Odger, Cremer, Coulson, Facey, Weston and Applegarth — who was later to join the General Council.   There were three Germans — Marx, Eccarius and Lessner.   Jung represented the Swiss and Le Lubez the French.   The paper's declared policy was extremely radical, covering manhood suffrage, direct taxation, the shorter working week, land nationalisation and 'the development of co-operative self-employment to national dimensions'.[1]

PRECARIOUS FINANCES

The acquisition of a weekly paper did little to improve the fortunes of the Association.   The International was the first political organisation in England to enrol trade unions as affiliates and in the early months they were exceedingly slow to respond.   The idea of English trade unions paying money to outside bodies was new and unattractive.   This was even truer of the Continent.   Karl Kautsky was to write that 'the payment of regular contributions was a thing to which the workers had first to grow accustomed.   On the Continent at first it would have been easier to get up a riot than to get them to pay affiliated contributions'.[2]   Even in England, the Reform League, which had considerable working-class support, would have been in dire straits but for 'handsome subscriptions . . . from rich Radicals'.[3]   And when Odger succeeded Howell as

[1] *Workman's Advocate*, September 16, 1865.
[2] *The International, 1864–1924 (Souvenir)*, p. 4.   Published by the Labour and Socialist International, 1924.
[3] S. Maccoby, *English Radicalism, 1853–1886*, 1938, p. 88.

Secretary of the London Trades Council in 1862 his salary
was half a crown a week.[1]

The General Council's difficulties were increased by
Cremer's inadequacies as Secretary due partly to his preoccupation with the Reform League. In October he proposed
the adjournment of the General Council for a month as there
were 'too many movements in hand'.[2] No minutes were kept
or cards stamped between November 28 and December 19 and
on the latter date Cremer announced his resignation. He was
persuaded to remain in office until the first Congress planned
for May 1866. But it was already clear that what Engels had
termed 'the naive fraternity in the International Association'[3]
was under strain.

EARLY QUARRELS: THE GERMANS AND MAZZINI

For one thing the *Inaugural Address*, though acceptable to
everyone as a broad statement of principles, concealed the
enormous gulf which separated the English from the German
approach to international issues. To the English Mazzini was
a hero. To the Germans and to most of the French he was a
reactionary opponent of Socialism. One incident, trivial in
itself, revealed the extent of the gulf. The radical M.P., P. A.
Taylor, asked Howell, as Secretary of the Reform League, to
raise a subscription in honour of Mazzini. Howell thought the
International the appropriate body to launch the project and
was completely taken aback by the vehemence with which it
was opposed. He had to explain a little shamefacedly to Taylor
that though the formal proposal of Cremer and Odger had
been carried against opposition from 'a large number of our
Continental delegates . . . those to whose care it was committed completely killed it'.[4]

Soon afterwards the *Workman's Advocate* was renamed
Commonwealth and Eccarius appointed editor. This raised
another storm on the General Council, in which the personality
of Eccarius no doubt played its part. An old friend of Marx
from the 1840s, the self-educated German tailor was a talented
but tactless and over-sensitive man. A stalwart defender of

[1] G. Howell, *The Conflicts of Capital and Labour*, 1878, p. 426.
[2] G.C. *Minutes*, October 10, 1865.
[3] Engels to Marx, April 12, 1865.
[4] Howell to P. A. Taylor, M.P., Reform League, *Secretary's Letter Book*,
November 18, 1865.

Marx's views on the Council but lacking his master's diplomacy, Eccarius was fairly consistently unpopular with the English, against whom Marx had frequently to defend him.   Moreover, Le Lubez, like most of the French radical republicans a strong admirer of Mazzini, had not forgotten the fracas over the proposed subscription and was determined to 'undermine German influence' on the General Council.[1] Under heavy pressure Marx agreed to drop Eccarius and replace him by Odger with Fox acting as assistant editor.   Marx felt, as he told Engels on April 4, that it was more important 'to maintain good agreement with the English than to satisfy the personal ambitions of Eccarius'.

Relations with Odger and Cremer were in any case becoming difficult enough.   The dispute over Mazzini was only a minor irritant, the English maintaining an attitude of puzzled incomprehension over the doctrinal disputes of their continental colleagues.   More serious differences were beginning to emerge over English politics when the Liberal Government introduced its Reform Bill in 1866.   The Bill would have enfranchised only part of the working class and stopped a long way short of the Reform League's demands.   But the opposition of the Conservatives and a section of the Liberals convinced a majority of the Reform League's executive, including Odger, that the Bill should be supported as an interim measure.[2] This was for Marx a disillusioning experience.   Once again, he wrote bitterly to Engels, 'the cursed traditional character of all English movements' had appeared.   Concessions, dismissed at first as completely inadequate, had come to be regarded as victories, merely 'Because the Tories cry: guard'.[3]   This seemed to Marx not only cowardice but ingratitude.   Exaggerating, as he was prone to do, the influence of the International, he complained that 'the London English leaders . . . after we have made their position, have become very *cold* towards our more narrow movement'.[4] Doubting now his ability to control the English, Marx was heartily relieved when the General Council agreed to postpone the first Congress from May until September, to give the Geneva branch more time to prepare.[5]

---

[1] Marx to Engels, March 24 ; cf. G.C. *Minutes*, March 6, 1866.
[2] Reform League *Minute Book*, March 20, 1866.
[3] Marx to Engels, April 2, 1866.   [4] Marx to Engels, April 6, 1866.
[5] *Commonwealth*, May 5, 1866.   See also Engels to Marx, April 10, 1866.

THE TURNING POINT

Suddenly things took a turn for the better. The British members of the General Council produced a leaflet appealing for trade union support in connection with the forthcoming Congress at Geneva. The appeal was notable for a complete lack of reference to the social and political aims of the International. The Association was presented solely as a means of preventing international blacklegging during strikes. The leaflet was probably written by Odger, since the argument was strikingly similar to that used in his Address to the French workers.[1]

It was perhaps in response to this appeal that the Coventry ribbon weavers affiliated in April. Their industry was undergoing a severe crisis during the 1860s. Chinese silk, the raw material on which their trade depended, was becoming scarcer and dearer from the effects of the Taiping rebellion. Increasing competition from the ribbon manufacturers of France — more intense since the Free Trade Treaty of 1860 — and from German Switzerland was causing the spread of unemployment and some replacement of adult males by women and juveniles.[2] It was no doubt these conditions which made the Union, with its membership of about one thousand[3] susceptible to the International's appeal.

In the same month the General Council gave help to the London wire workers who were on strike by dissuading other wire workers from taking on new work while the dispute was on.[4] More important was the strike of the London Amalgamated Tailors who were worried about the possible introduction of blacklegs from Europe. For the first time the

[1] *An Appeal from the British Members of the General Council to their fellow working men of the United Kingdom.* The leaflet is undated but seems to have been issued shortly before the decision to postpone the Geneva Congress, that is to say some time around March, 1866. There were twenty-eight signatories, including Odger, Cremer, Howell, Coulson, Lucraft, Shearman, Leno and Weston.

[2] Report of R. Baker, Royal Inspector of Factories, 1865, p. 64; Children's Employment Commission (1862) Fifth Report (1866), pp. 114-15. Quoted by Dona Torr. *Tom Mann and his Times*, vol. I, 1956, p. 306: 'a Basle ribbon sold in London at 3/6 the piece, could not be made in Coventry under 6/- or 7/-'. *Ibid.*

[3] G.C. *Minutes*, April 3, 1866.

[4] G.C. *Minutes*, April 24; *Commonwealth*, April 28, 1866. The London wire workers thanked the General Council but did not make good their undertaking to join.

International made an important contribution to the success of an English strike. The significance of the occasion was remarked by *Reynolds's* on April 15 in an article which recalled that while the foundation meeting of the International had been 'almost ignored by every newspaper save *Reynolds's*,[1] this small and unnoticed gathering realised important results'. Through the medium of the International the London Tailors had been able to communicate with 'trade organisations abroad' so that the attempts by the West End employers to recruit foreign labour had been completely frustrated — in marked contrast to previous strikes in the trade.

Now, for the first time, the potentialities of the International as an asset in trade disputes began to be widely recognised. *The Times*, while careful not to mention the International by name, explained the failure of the master tailors to recruit European labour by the fact of 'the Continental workmen having been informed by telegraph from the operatives' committee of the state of affairs in London'.[2] The tailors, however, having secured 'a very considerable addition to their weekly wages',[3] realised very clearly to whom they owed their success. 'It was, beyond a doubt', said their representative, Barry, to the General Council, 'through the influence and agency of the International Association that the master tailors had failed to procure men on the Continent.' His Society accordingly affiliated. A month later the London example was followed by the Amalgamated Tailors of Darlington, expressing to the General Council their 'strong gratitude for its exercises' and bringing with them the Amalgamated Cordwainers of the same town.[4]

The outbreak of a second tailors' strike in the middle of the year extending this time to many parts of England and to Scotland was accompanied by renewed threats from the employers to import cheap labour from Germany. The German members of the General Council were particularly energetic in responding to the threat and appeals appeared in two London German papers, the *Hermann* and the *London Anzeiger*. Marx himself wrote a notice for the *Mitteldeutsche Volkszeitung* and letters were sent to many towns in Germany, to Copenhagen

[1] It had been almost ignored by *Reynolds's* as well. *Ibid.*, October 3, 1864. Not so the *Beehive*, — see Chapter III.

[2] *The Times*, April 3, 1866.   [3] *The Times*, April 6, 1866.

[4] G.C. *Minutes*, April 10; *Reynolds's*, April 22; *Commonwealth*, May 12, 1866.

F

and to Christiana in Norway. The General Council sent two representatives to Edinburgh in connection with the appeal and once again the tailors expressed their gratitude to the International.[1]

This burst of activity was followed by the affiliation of the Amalgamated Cordwainers, the West-End Cabinet Makers and the Hand in Hand Society of Coopers.[2] In August they were joined by the Packing-Case Makers and the Day-Working Bookbinders, a small society which had broken away from the larger Journeymen Bookbinders in 1850.[3]

These five affiliations were all of small societies, with an aggregate membership of only a few hundred, but they were straws which showed a rising current, and August saw a still greater triumph for the Association. The Sheffield Conference of Trades Delegates, a precursor of the meeting in 1868 which is conventionally regarded as the first Trades Union Congress, officially recommended the unions to join the International. The resolution, proposed by J. Constantine of Halifax, had been seconded by W. Harry of the Amalgamated Society of Carpenters and Joiners' Chelsea Branch, a future Joint Secretary of his union and a man who had come vigorously into working-class politics immediately after the Chelsea Barracks affair.

Despite this recognition of its efforts at the highest trade union level, the International was severely rebuffed when it tried to enrol the Amalgamated Society of Engineers. William Allan, the Engineers' General Secretary, refused even to receive a deputation from the General Council. Throughout its history the International's trade union support was to come largely from building unions and from such relatively backward industries as tailoring, clothing, shoemaking and cabinet making. In mining, engineering and in heavy industry generally, its strength was to remain small or non-existent.

CONTINUED ADVANCE

So far the General Council had confined its trade union recruitment to craft societies of skilled tradesmen. In August it gave help to the Excavators' Society by persuading a number

---

[1] G.C. *Minutes*, May 15; *Commonwealth*, June 23, August 11, 1866.
[2] *Commonwealth*, July 17, 24, 1866.
[3] See Ellic Howe and John Child, *The Society of London Bookbinders*, *1780–1951*, 1952, p. 160.

of Belgian blacklegs brought over by Waring Bros. to join the union.[1] The Excavators affiliated and their Secretary, James Lee, became the only representative of unskilled labour ever to sit on the General Council.

On the eve of the International's first Congress two further affiliations provided some welcome financial relief. The Cigar Makers contributed £5 and the Saddlers and Harness Makers £4 towards Congress expenses. By the time the delegates assembled in Geneva, seventeen unions had affiliated and another thirteen were negotiating.[2] Though the Congress received little notice in the English Press, the International had clearly established itself as a body with a recognised function in the labour movement. It represented, as Cremer told the delegates at Geneva, societies with a total membership of 25,173.[3] With the unions which were considering enrolment, membership should soon reach fifty thousand. The 'moral effect of the International Association', he concluded, 'had been very great throughout Britain'.

After the Congress, at the General Council meeting of September 25, Marx himself was proposed for the position of President by Lawrence of the tailors and Carter of the journeymen hairdressers. He declined the offer on the grounds that a manual worker should occupy the post and proposed Odger who was duly elected. With his bitter experience of the Reform League still rankling, Marx was by this time convinced that 'Cremer and Odger . . . have already entered on to the road of compromise with the bourgeoisie'.[4] But he clearly recognised the importance of keeping the Secretary of the London Trades Council as President of the International, especially as the latter post was largely nominal. In the case of Cremer, a man of some prominence in the peace movement but of much less importance in trade union affairs, Marx had already decided to replace him by Fox.[5] In the election for a new Secretary Fox defeated Cremer by thirteen to four. Though Marx proposed a testimonial to the late Secretary for his two years of 'almost entirely gratuitous' services, Cremer

---

[1] *Commonwealth*, September 1, 1866. Waring Bros. were sufficiently alarmed by the mood of the English navvies to ask the Home Office for police and even military help. H.O. 45 O.S. 7853, August 1866.

[2] *The Times*, September 8, 1866.

[3] *Commonwealth*, September 8, 1866.

[4] Marx to J. P. Becker, August 31, 1866.

[5] G.C. *Minutes*, September 25, 1866.

ceased to attend meetings of the General Council soon after his defeat.

For the rest of the year the International continued to make headway in trade union matters. An agreement which the London Hairdressers had secured on Saturday early closing was being violated by a number of employers with the help of foreign labour. Carter, the hairdressers' representative on the General Council, secured the publication of an 'Appeal of the English Journeymen Hairdressers to their Continental Fellow-Workmen', authorised by the General Council.[1]

It was among the tailors, however, that efforts at developing international contacts had most success. Matthew Lawrence, a former Secretary of the Glasgow Trades Council and now President of the London Operative Tailors, had attended the Geneva Congress as a member of the General Council's delegation. On his return he wrote a report of the Congress in *The Tailor*.[2] Like almost all English statements on the International, the article dealt mainly with the question of continental blacklegs and included a comment on the wretched condition of the German and Danish tailors 'who had been deceived and decoyed to Edinburgh during the late lock out'. After the Geneva Congress, Lawrence was sure that there could be no more question of the master tailors 'being able to intimidate their workmen by the importation of foreign labour'. Lawrence had spoken at a mass meeting of Geneva tailors on September 5 advising them not to accept advertised vacancies in Britain during a strike.

Stimulated by contact with the International, the London Tailors established close relations with their colleagues in Europe. The *Tailor* printed correspondence between members of the trade in England, France and Germany. Mutual support in strikes, it was declared, constituted an implicit repudiation of 'this modern version of the true political economy, the sole condition of which is to reduce the worker to the rôle of a soulless machine, to be used or thrust aside according to the masters' whim'.[3] In a little over three months both French and English tailors were again engaged in strikes; both found

[1] *Commonwealth*, October 13, 1866. See also *Vorbote*, November 1866, p. 176.

[2] October 6, 1866. *The Tailor* — later the *Tailor and Cutter* — was at that time a trade union journal. Lawrence's article was signed 'Thistle'.

[3] *Tailor*, October 6, 1866. See also *Tailor*, December 1, 1866.

the contacts established through the International standing them in good stead.

At the beginning of November the International received its first political affiliation from an English society. The National Reform League, founded by Bronterre O'Brien in 1850, was still carrying on propaganda for his ideas. Throughout the existence of the General Council in London, old Chartists such as Hartwell, Howell, Leno, Lucraft, Mottershead, Charles Murray and Walton were at one time or another to be found active among its members. It was not therefore surprising that at a time when its prestige stood high in the labour movement, the International should receive an application from the sole surviving Chartist organisation. The National Reform League was the only society in Britain to maintain, in the period between the decline of Chartism and the socialist revival of the 1880s, a consistent propaganda in favour of Socialism, albeit of the O'Brienite variety. 'It is the land and money laws of a country', O'Brien had written in 1850, 'that must ever mainly determine the social condition of its people'.¹ Land, banks and communications, in the view of the O'Brienites, should be brought under public ownership, and there was much emphasis on the need for currency reform as a method of preventing economic crises. Unlike most other socialists the O'Brienites did not intend to nationalise the means of production other than land. When the League's application was received on October 30 there was some doubt whether, as a political body, it was eligible for affiliation. On November 6, however, it was decided that it should join on the same terms as a trade union.²

John Hales, who had joined at the beginning of 1866, brought in his small union, the Elastic Web Weavers' Society of London on November 13. At the same time the General Council won further credit from the help it gave to the Basket Makers, whose employers had already imported twelve Belgians to work at cut rates and were proposing to bring in a good many more. The Belgians had been put to work in Bermondsey, where they were 'as strictly guarded against coming

¹ *Reynolds's Political Instructor* — the precursor of *Reynolds's Weekly Newspaper* — April 13, 1850. Reprinted in O'Brien's posthumously published *The Rise, Progress, and Phases of Human Slavery : How it came into the World, and how it shall be made to go out*, 1885, p. 105.
² G.C. *Minutes*, September 14, 1867.

into contact with the outside public as a kidnapped girl in a monastery'.[1] The General Council sent friends, one of whom spoke Flemish, into the workshop, masquerading as potential employees. After getting permission to look round, they made contact with the Belgians who, once they understood the situation — and the fact that the union would pay for their accommodation and passage home — agreed to leave by the next boat. The Basket Makers affiliated immediately.

Two Rebuffs

Amidst many such small successes, a much greater prize eluded the International. Marx had set his heart on securing the affiliation of the London Trades Council. 'If that is done', he told his friend Kugelmann, 'then in a certain sense we shall have control of the working class here, and we can push on the movement very much.'[2] On December 19 a deputation consisting of Jung, Lessner and Hales attended the Trades Council. There was a long discussion, with Harry, Allan, Applegarth, Howell and others taking part. Finally it was agreed to adjourn the debate for a month, while a statement was drawn up defining the relations between the two bodies.[3] By January a compromise decision was reached. The London Trades Council recognising the need of regular international communication by workers 'for the purpose of regulating the hours of labour and assimilating wages' decided merely to co-operate with the International 'for the furtherance of all questions affecting the interests of labour, at the same time continuing the London Trades Council as a distinct and independent body as before'.

If this was disappointing to Marx who had hoped that the London Trades Council would 'call itself the British Section of the International Association', it was for other reasons a source of concern to *The Times* [4] which reported the resolution in full. In an editorial comment *The Times*, still avoiding mentioning the International by name, deplored the Trades Council's view that 'the real remedy . . . is a general combination of working men against their employers all over the world'.

[1] From the Third Annual Report of the General Council, written by George Eccarius, and printed in the *Beehive*, September 14, 1867.

[2] Marx to Kugelmann, October 13, 1866.

[3] L.T.C. *Minutes*.   [4] January 16, 1867.

While there was still little publicity for the International in the general Press, slow progress with trade union affiliations went on throughout 1867. In January the Blockmakers joined in the course of a strike which the employers were trying to break with French labour. There were further adhesions of small societies but a renewed attempt to interest the Amalgamated Society of Engineers was a complete failure. Two deputations from the General Council had to be abandoned when Odger, the President, failed to appear. Fox, the new Secretary, then wrote personally to Allan, but had to report an 'evasive' reply.

THE LIMITS OF EXPANSION IN ENGLAND

The blow was softened by two notable successes, the first of considerable importance. The Amalgamated Society of Carpenters and Joiners, second largest of the 'New Model' unions and itself the product of the builders' strike, joined in the course of the year. Continual prodding by Harry and the Chelsea branch produced a sympathetic response from the leadership but no action. Finally, Chelsea moved a formal resolution calling on the executive to affiliate, which it did at the end of 1867.[1] This was the most important union ever to subscribe to the International and its Secretary, Robert Applegarth, was for two years to figure prominently on the General Council.

The second success, which came in the middle of the year, was the development of friendly relations with John Kane's Society of Malleable Ironworkers which subsequently affiliated. This union, whose headquarters were in Darlington, was the first and only representative of heavy industry ever to appear on the General Council. A possible explanation may be found in the contact which was established in 1867 between the General Council and the National Labor Union of America whose Secretary, William Sylvis, also led the Ironmolders' Union in the United States. The 1860s was a decade in which British ironmoulders emigrated in large numbers to America and close relations grew up between Sylvis and Kane.[2] It is, perhaps, reasonable to suppose that Sylvis, a pioneer of labour

[1] A.S.C.J. Monthly Report, November 1866, September 1867. S. Higginbottam, *Our Society's History*, Manchester, 1939, pp. 104-5.
[2] Clifton K. Yearley Jr., *Britons in American Labor*, Baltimore, 1957, pp. 57-9.

organisation in the United States and a keen advocate of international solidarity, drew Kane's attention to the Association, to which the Darlington Tailors were already affiliated.

This solitary exception only serves to draw attention to the nature and limits of the International's progress in the trade union field. Outside the building trade, the list of affiliated unions [1] consisted largely of trades — cabinet makers, bookbinders, harness makers, packing-case makers — whose techniques had been affected little or not at all by the Industrial Revolution. Other trades, such as the ribbon weavers, had special problems which have already been touched on, while trade unions of tailors and cordwainers were finding themselves in an exceptionally difficult position through the advance of mechanisation. Here the new industrial processes were undermining traditional crafts, a position not reached to a comparable extent in engineering until the 1890s. This created problems with which the unions were failing to cope. The tailors, for example, 'had succeeded neither in controlling the new machine industry, nor in upholding the standard earnings of the handworkers' and after the merging of local societies into the Amalgamated Society of Tailors in 1866, the new Society 'included only a small proportion of those at work in the trade'.[2]

In shoemaking, the 1860s was a period of growing tension between the hand-sewn shoe workers and the new and growing class of 'riveters' and 'finishers' in the machine-made boot and shoe trade, a tension resulting in the secession of the riveters and finishers and the formation of the National Union of Boot and Shoe Operatives in 1874. Kendal, where the riveters' and finishers' sections were expelled by the Amalgamated Cordwainers in 1867,[3] was one of the three provincial branches of the Cordwainers to join the International.

Among the larger craft unions, however, the Engineers and Ironfounders showed no inclination to join though both were ready on occasions to help continental strikes with encouragement and even money. The failure of the International to win the support of unions in heavy industry, for example in coal and cotton, was intensified by the fact that the General Council

---

[1] See Appendix 3 to this Chapter.
[2] S. and B. Webb, *History of Trade Unionism*, 1920, pp. 436-7.
[3] Alan Fox, *A History of the National Union of Boot and Shoe Operatives, 1874–1957*, 1958, p. 3.

met in London.   The main centres of industrial development
were in the North and Midlands, but few provincial unions
joined the Association.   Those which did were mainly societies
or branches in building, shoemaking and tailoring which merely
followed the example set for them in London.   Because of its
cosmopolitan character and traditions, London was the obvious
centre for a workers' International.   At the same time it was
geographically remote from the main and growing centres of
heavy industry.   On the other hand both Allan of the Engineers
and Guile of the Ironfounders served on the London Trades
Council.   If this body could be persuaded to affiliate, the
International would have broken through to a position of major
importance in the labour movement.   Its failure in this respect
was, therefore, crucial.   Marx realised the importance of the
London Trades Council which before the establishment of the
Conference of Amalgamated Trades and the Trades Union
Congress was the key labour organisation in the country.
Though he was disappointed by the decision of the Council in
January to continue as 'a distinct and independent body as
before', he may not have realised the full extent of the setback.

This refusal of the engineering workers to join the International was a reflection of the very technological superiority
which had made the British workers the most highly organised
in the world.   While tailors, basket makers and even bricklayers might have reason to fear replacement by foreign workers
in the course of — or even, as with the basket makers, without
the excuse of — a strike, the engineers were confident that
there were too few skilled workers outside Britain to make this
a serious possibility.

Even in the building trade, where its main strength lay, the
International never succeeded in enlisting the Stonemasons.
This exclusive union, which ran its own strike organisation
separate from the rest of the trade in the dispute of 1859–60,
may have felt confident that its members' knowledge of local
stone would prevent them being replaced by European masons.

By 1867, in short, the International had almost reached the
limit of its expansion in England.   Few new trade societies
affiliated after the Lausanne Congress [1] and a stagnation set in
which was to lead to some restiveness on the part of the English
members.   For the time being, however, Marx was reasonably

---

[1] See article in *The Times*, October 27, 1871, presumably by Eccarius,
its usual correspondent.

well pleased. 'Things are moving,' he told Engels, on the morrow of the Lausanne Congress, 'and in the next revolution, which is perhaps nearer than it appears, *we* (you and I) will have this powerful engine *in our hands*. Compare this with the results of Mazzini's etc. operations during the last thirty years! And without any financial means, moreover. With the intrigues of the Proudhonists in Paris, of Mazzini in Italy, of the jealous Odger, Cremer, and Potter in London, with the Schulze-Delitzsches and Lassalleans in Germany! We can be very well content.'[1] Marx's disillusionment was slow, but when it finally came it was, almost literally, shattering.

[1] Marx to Engels, September 11, 1867.

CHAPTER V: APPENDIX I

An early document of the International

INTERNATIONAL
WORKING MEN'S
ASSOCIATION.

Central Council, 18 Greek Street, London, W.
Founded on 28th September, 1864 at a
Public Meeting held at St. Martin's Hall, London.

The Address and statutes issued by the Provisional Central Council fully explain the Association's objects and aspirations, which, however, may be summed up in a few words. It aims at the protection, advancement, and complete emancipation, economic and political, of the Working Classes. As a means to this great end it will promote the establishment of solidarity between the manifold divisions of labour in *Each Country*, and the co-operation of the Working Classes of *Different Countries*.

Its organisation with a Central Medium in London and numerous affiliated branches in *Europe* and *America*, will assist in *uniting* the Working Classes of all Countries in a perpetual bond of *fraternal co-operation*. Annual Congresses of Delegates elected by the affiliated Working Men themselves, will create for the Working Classes a public and powerful European representation.

The Executive Council on behalf of the . . . Operative Bricklayers' Society . . . assembled at the . . . 25 Hatfield Street, Blackfriars, London having subscribed to the principles, and applied to enter the fraternal bond, are hereby admitted as an affiliated branch of the Association.

Dated the . . . 21st of April, 1865.

G. Odger, President of Council
G. W. Wheeler, Honorary Treasurer.

E. Dupont Corresponding Sec. for France
K. Marx   do.   Germany
E. Holtorp   do.   Poland
H. Jung   Corresponding Sec. for Switzerland
L. Lewis   do.   America
W. R. Cremer, Honorary General Secretary.

(Original in two colours, about 2½ ft. × 2 ft., is in the office of the Amalgamated Union of Building Trade Workers, Clapham.)

Copy of Balance Sheet of the International for the period March 29th, 1865 to April 28th, 1866

Receipts	£	s.	d.
Balance in hand, Mar. 28, 1865	6	3	8½
Declaration of Enrolment		10	-
Annual Subscription of Arbeiter Bildungs	1	-	-
Greenwich Branch per M. Le Lubez		10	-
Marigney, 1/6, Kaub, loan £6.10.-			
Jung do: £1.5,-			
Paris Administration	7	16	6
Lyons do: £8 — Caen do: £1	4	-	-
Germany do: per Dr. Marx	9	-	-
Voluntary Contributions for the Soirée of 1865	3	1	6
Operative Tailors' Contribution	3	-	-
Shoemakers West End Ladies	1	-	-
Members Subscriptions	8	3	9
Addresses and Rules sold 13 months		4	3
80 Do: from April 28th to Sept. 1st 1866		11	-
0 Total	48	-	8½
Members subscriptions and rules	3	3	6
Declarations of Enrolment	1	6	-
Fees given to Deputations, presented to the Assoc.			
Societies Subscriptions for Geneva Congress	51	15	5
Subscribed by members of the Council do:	1	14	6
4 months Total £57.19.5d	£106	-	1½

	L.	S.	D.
Liabilities			
Printing Leno	9	8	-
do: Member cards	5	-	-
Postage & Stationery Le Lubez	1	-	9
Loan bal. due to Kaub	6	10	-

Audited and found correct
Sept. 1st, 1866.   Signed, James Buckley.

(The balance sheet is in the Howell Collection, Bishopsgate Institute, London.)

Expenditure	£	s.	d.
Changing money — commission		1	6
Share of expenses meeting at Cleveland Hall		12	-
Writing address to President Johnson		10	-
Rent of 18 Greek St., Soho	6	7	-
Mounting declaration of enrolment	1	18	6
Painting & Engrossing	4	7	-
Delegations to Reform Conference Manchester	5	5	11
Postage & Miscellaneous Items	7	17	-
Board & lodging of Delegates		3	6
Van to remove chairs from Adelphi		18	-
Refreshment to Delegates at Conference		5	-
Loss on Sept. Soirée	11	17	-
13 months March 29th 1865 to April 28th 1866. Total	46	18	8
Do: April 28th to Sept. 1, 1866			
Postage of appeals of Painters Societies		4	-
Rent of office 1 quarter	1	5	6
Printing Mr. Kenny	2	2	-
Do: Mr. Leno	2	-	-
Ads. 6/6 Postage Cremer 19/6	1	6	-
Secretary's Salary. Mr. Cremer	7	15	-
Paid to Treasurers' s/c		14	10
Delegates to Geneva Congress	42	12	1

Total amount 4 months to Sept. 1st.

Assets in hands of Treasurer   £1. 1. 1. —   Repaid balance of loan, Jung, £1. 5. -   Total: £2. 6. 1.

£57 19 5

CHAPTER V: APPENDIX 3

Societies in England affiliated to the I.W.M.A. in September, 1867

From General Council's Third Annual Report.
Beehive, Sept. 14, 1867.

	Gifts and Entrance Fees 1866			Contributions 1867		
	£	s	d	£	s	d
London Arbeiter Bildungsverein	2	0	0	0	1	4
London French Branch	0	0	0	0	4	9
Central Section of Polish Exiles	0	0	0	0	4	10
Operative Bricklayers' Executive	0	0	0	1	0	0
No. 1 Lodge of Operative Bricklayers	0	8	0	0	0	0
Alliance Cabinet-Makers' Society	10	0	0	1	13	4
West-End Cabinet-Makers' Society	5	0	0	1	7	0
Day-working Bookbinders' Society	0	8	6	0	17	6
Hand-in-hand Coopers' Society	6	0	0	0	5	0
London Cigar Makers' Executive	5	0	0	1	9	0
Amalgamated Cordwainers' Executive	5	0	0	0	0	0
Darlington section of ditto.	0	5	0	0	0	0
Nottingham section of ditto.	0	5	0	0	2	1
Coventry and Warwickshire Ribbon Weavers	0	5	0	1	13	4
Packing-case Makers	1	5	4	0	0	0
Saddlers and Harness Makers	4	0	0	0	0	0
Kendal Shoemakers' Society	0	5	0	0	1	8
West-end Ladies' Bootmakers	6	0	0	0	10	0
London Operative Tailors	3	0	0	0	0	0
Darlington Section of Amalgamated Tailors	0	5	0	0	1	8

Societies affiliated since Sept. 1866.

	£	s	d	£	s	d
London Basket-makers' Society	0	5	0	0	7	6
Block-printers of Lancashire	0	5	0	2	1	8
London Coach Builders	0	5	0	0	0	0
Coach Trimmers (The Globe)	0	5	0	0	1	10½
Coach Trimmers (The Crown)	0	5	0	0	5	0
Elastic Web Weavers	0	5	0	0	5	0
United Excavators	0	5	0	0	0	0
French Polishers	0	5	0	0	0	0
Organ Builders	0	5	0	0	2	1
Pattern Drawers and Block Cutters	0	5	0	0	0	0
Carpenters' and Joiners' Executive	0	0	0	2	0	0
United Society of Journeymen Curriers (joined August 27)	0	0	0	0	0	0
National Reform League	0	5	0			

Paid for Congress Fund.

	£	s	d
West-end Ladies' Bootmakers	4	10	0
London Cigar Makers	1	1	0
Elastic Web Weavers	0	10	0
Basket Makers	0	12	6

CHAPTER VI

The International in England.
Stagnation : 1867–9

ALTHOUGH in England the International had almost ceased to grow by 1867, there were still apparently good reasons for Marx's optimism. On the Continent of Europe the Association was entering on its period of maximum activity and influence. Strikes followed each other in quick succession and the General Council found itself fully occupied in developing the new spirit of international solidarity. Considering the immature state of labour organisation it had remarkable success and by the time of the Basle Congress in September 1869 it was a force in Europe. Although progress on the Continent took place almost independently of the General Council's efforts, it was impressive enough and helped to distract the attention of friends and enemies alike from the fact that the Association in England was stagnant.

THE PARIS BRONZE WORKERS. A TURNING POINT IN FRANCE

When the workers of Western Europe began to develop the strike weapon on a significant scale, they found the General Council in a position to give useful service. Not much could be done for the Belgian miners, a number of whom were killed by troops during a strike in February, except to issue an appeal to British miners and ironworkers for financial and moral support.[1] There seems to have been little response, but there was a very different result in the case of the Paris bronze workers, locked out for refusing a reduction in wages. The tailors' strike in 1866 had marked a turning point in the fortunes of the International in England, and the bronze workers' lock-out in 1867 was to produce similar results in France.

Eugène Dupont, who reported on the situation to the General Council, said that while financial aid was already

[1] G.C. *Minutes*, February 26 and *Working Man*, April 6, 1867.

coming in from the other trades in Paris, the moral effect of aid from London would be considerable.[1] The London Trades Council at once honoured its undertaking to co-operate and unanimously agreed to give the International credentials 'to appeal to the trades' societies for assistance'.[2] The visit of the French representatives to England was long remembered on both sides of the Channel. Beesly wrote of it more than three years later. According to his account the Frenchmen visited the executives of about twenty unions.[3] The fact that the French employers were insisting on the dissolution of the union helped to rally English support for the strike.[4] The International was largely responsible for the success of the mission and its French branch in London was one of the organisations visited. Loans from English unions included one of £10 from the Bricklayers [5] — duly repaid two years later.

The bronze workers' success acted as a tonic throughout the French labour movement. Marx wrote jubilantly to Engels on April 27: 'Our International celebrated a great victory. For the Paris bronze workers . . . we have succeeded in getting financial support from the English trade unionists. Seeing this, the masters immediately gave way. This has created a lot of noise in the French papers and now we are in France a recognised force.'

The Paris and London Tailors

At about the same time the value of the International was further demonstrated in connection with the tailors' strikes which broke out in Paris in March and London in April. The new Secretary of the London Operative Tailors, Druitt, who served on the General Council, went over to Paris with Blissert,

[1] *Commonwealth*, March 9, 1867.
[2] London Trades Council *Minutes*, March 4, 1867.
[3] *Fortnightly Review*, November 1870. The unions included the Gilders, Compositors, Engineers, Carpenters, Cabinet Makers, French Polishers, Coach Makers, Curriers, Tinplate Workers, Masons, Excavators, Hatters, Shoemakers and Iron Moulders.
[4] G.C. *Minutes*, March 4 (probably an error for March 5), 12, 19, 26, April 2, 9; *Commonwealth*, March 9; *Bricklayers' Trade Circular*, April 1, 1867.
[5] See letter to Jung from E. Coulson, March 15, enclosing £10; also from George Dodshon of the Amalgamated Cordwainers, March 20, enclosing £5 and expressing 'delight' at 'the awakening spirit of trades unions in France', March 20. See also letters of apology from Guile of the iron-founders, March 22 and Allan of the engineers, April 4, 1867. I.I.S.G.

a member of his Executive. Both spoke at a public meeting in support of the strike, paying tribute to the help they had themselves received from the International in the previous year. Their visit had a tonic effect on the Parisian tailors and contributed something to the success of their strike.[1]

Soon afterwards, the London tailors were themselves on strike again. They held a crowded meeting at the Alhambra Palace in Leicester Square. According to *Reynolds's* on April 28 there were seven thousand at the meeting and another two thousand outside in the Square. Two representatives of the General Council, the Swiss, Hermann Jung, and Joseph Collet, the French refugee, were on the platform. Jung reminded the meeting of the International's contribution to the success of the previous year and translated, to the accompaniment of 'loud cheers', a letter of support from the tailors of Brussels who were also on strike. Collet foresaw on the basis of such mutual support the growth of an international labour alliance which could put an end to wars.

At the same time the London tailors sent a gift of £200 to the Parisians with the assurance that 'no London house would be allowed to execute work for Paris houses'.[2] The Brussels and Paris strikes were won. The London strike, lasting until September, was defeated largely through an adverse legal decision affecting the right to picket.

The 'Great Lever'

In the year following the Geneva Congress of September 1866 the General Council had established itself as an international trade union liaison committee, the first of its kind and, for the period, surprisingly successful. Paradoxically, but accurately enough, Howell wrote of the same period that 'meetings were scantily attended, funds were low, disputes frequent, and complaints general'.[3] Trade unionists were ready to give general support to the International, in some cases to affiliate and in others to listen to it respectfully as the representative of workers overseas. But they were not ready at a time of other pressing preoccupations to attend meetings

---

[1] *Tailor*, April 13, 20, 1867.

[2] *International Courier*, April 24, 1867. This paper appeared in an English and French edition. Like the *Working Man* it was published by Joseph Collet.

[3] George Howell's summary of the G.C. *Minutes*, Bishopsgate.

of the General Council.   Cremer was always casual about his
duties as Secretary, and on his replacement by Fox there was
considerable difficulty in obtaining the accounts from him.[1]
Odger's attendances were irregular. Signs of frustration began
to appear and there seemed some point in the suggestion of
John Hales, a recent recruit and representative of the Elastic
Web Weavers, that the International should set up its own
branches, on the model of the Reform League.[2]

Marx was strongly opposed to the idea and remained so for
another five years for reasons which he later explained in a
confidential circular to the members of the International.
English branches would involve in his view an English regional
council.   But in England, although 'the organisation of the
working class through the trade unions had acquired a certain
degree of maturity and universality', the labour movement was
totally lacking in 'the spirit of generalisation and revolutionary
ardour. It is only the General Council', he added optimistically,
'which can supply this deficiency.' Infused with socialist
theory and a revolutionary temper, the British trade unions
would become 'a great lever of the proletarian revolution'.[3]
Left to themselves they would remain bodies with limited
industrial objects, politically tied to the advanced wing of the
Liberal Party.

Marx's position was based on two assumptions ; that the
International could win the support of a decisive section of the
British trade union movement and that when the next revolution broke out in Europe the General Council could use its
position in control of the 'lever' to swing the movement into
support. Pending such developments, however, the position
of the General Council remained difficult. For one thing, the
subscriptions which it was possible to collect from trade unions
were strictly limited. Smaller societies and local branches
usually contributed at the rate of $\frac{1}{2}$d. a member — the London
Cigar Makers, for instance, paying £1 : 10 : 0 a year for seven
hundred members, and the West-End Cabinet Makers £1 : 2 : 0
for five hundred. Among the larger unions, such as the Bricklayers and Carpenters, only the Executive Committees affiliated,
leaving it to the local branches to join or not as they wished.

---

[1] G.C. *Minutes*, December 4, 1866 and January 1, 1867.
[2] G.C. *Minutes*, November 20, 1866.
[3] The confidential circular of January 16, 1870 is reproduced in Marx's
Letters to Dr. Kugelmann, n.d. pp. 102-9.

G

The Bricklayers' Executive usually paid £1 a year, and the Carpenters £2. Special collections were made to pay delegates' expenses to Congresses and conferences. Between these occasions it was often difficult to pay the rent. By the middle of 1867 the General Council had been evicted from its normal meeting place at 18 Bouverie Street owing £6 in arrears. The offer of Maurice, a member of the Council who kept a café at 16 Castle Street, to allow the use of his premises for the ensuing quarter, was gratefully accepted.[1]

'But actually we cannot act', complained Marx, '*by want of funds* and also *of men*, as all the English are taken up with the movement on behalf of reform.'[2] He might argue later, in the confidential circular already quoted, that it was unnecessary to establish local branches in England since the General Council could set up political organisations as necessary, but such bodies as the Reform League could only succeed by draining the life blood from the parent body.

Early in 1867 the franchise agitation was reaching its height. The Reform League called a demonstration on February 11 and Howell issued a special appeal for trade union support. The response was impressive. Engineers, Ironfounders, Carpenters, Cordwainers, Bricklayers all participated, as did the General Council itself.[3] The demonstration was huge, provoked lively comment in the Press and certainly made an impact on public opinion. Yet two of the four General Council meetings in February adjourned after reading the *Minutes* on account of the small attendance.

Besides the Reform agitation there were other cogent reasons preventing the unions from paying full attention to the International. Early in 1867 the judgement in the case of Hornby *v.* Close threatened the legal security of trade union funds and strengthened the demand for a change in the law which would be favourable to the unions. The 'Sheffield Outrages' of 1866, however, had given rise to much unfavourable comment on trade unions as a whole, and in March 1867 a Royal Commission began enquiring into their affairs. Many of the working-class leaders feared with reason that if the enquiry went the wrong way there might even be adverse changes in their legal position.

[1] G.C. *Minutes*, June 25 and *Working Man*, August 3, 1867.
[2] Marx to Engels, December 17, 1867.
[3] *Commonwealth*, January 12 and G.C. *Minutes*, February 5, 1867.

Allan of the Engineers had the opportunity of explaining to the Royal Commission why his Society held aloof from the International. Lord Elcho asked him whether his union had taken any part in the Geneva Congress of the preceding year. They had been asked to go, explained Allan in reply, but had refused as 'they believed that the best thing the foreigners could do would be to organize themselves into trade societies similar to ours, and then we could begin to discuss questions with them'. For the Engineers' Secretary, complacent in the knowledge of Britain's technical superiority, it would clearly be some years before the Continentals caught up and threatened serious competition. By that time trade unions would no doubt have spread to France and Belgium, where they would 'have the tendency of raising the wages and thereby remove that fear of competition that our English friends are so much alarmed about'.[1] In the meantime there was nothing to worry about and no reason for the Engineers to rub shoulders with lesser unions in an International Association. The alarm which 'our English friends' were beginning to express[2] was in Allan's view unwarranted.

More serious for the International was the fact that those unions which had affiliated were too preoccupied with the Reform campaign and the Royal Commission to give time to the General Council.

'What our party lacks is money'

In one respect only, the Royal Commission and the issues connected with it brought benefit to the Council. From lack of money it was impossible to continue the publication of *Commonwealth* and the last issue of the paper appeared on July 20, 1867. On the other hand, the threat to trade unionism caused Potter and the Junta to sink their differences and draw together in a common campaign to improve the legal status of the unions. The *Beehive* began once again to publish regular reports of the International and to function in a sense as its organ.

[1] *Organisation and Rules of Trades Unions : First Report*. British Parliamentary Papers, XXXII, 1867, Paras 995-6.

[2] Cf. Editorial in *The Times*, January 15, 1867, on the lack of trade unionism in the continental iron industries; also editorial in *Reynolds's*, December 23, 1866, on 'Trade Unions and Foreign Competition'. The writer was particularly worried by the fact that 'France and Belgium now construct locomotives for British railways . . .'.

As a result the International was again brought regularly to the attention of trade unionists. After the Lausanne Congress at the beginning of September 1867 trade union affiliations continued to come in. Recruiting was still apparently easiest in the building trade, and the Liverpool Plasterers and Birmingham House Painters joined at the first meeting of the General Council after Lausanne. For reasons which are not clear, the Amalgamated Cordwainers had withdrawn from membership before the Congress,[1] but trade union membership remained considerable. The financial position, however, was still as bad as ever. After its move to Castle Street, the General Council was threatened by its former landlord with legal action for the recovery of £3 : 10 : 0. The sum was not large, yet the General Council was in such straits that it had to buy time with an interim payment of ten shillings.[2]

'What our party lacks is money', wrote Marx in some bitterness to Engels on October 19. 'But for this deficiency we should still, despite our great and irreplaceable losses, be the strongest party today, as we were in 1848.' But lack of money was only a symptom of the larger fact that the International had failed to break through to the widest sections of the British labour movement. Of the hundreds of thousands of organised workers in the country, some fifty thousand were represented on the General Council. Yet even that figure was in a sense illusory. The Carpenters and Joiners with over nine thousand members contributed only two or three pounds a year. While for individual members of whom there were some hundred and sixty the annual subscription was a shilling a year, societies were asked to affiliate on a basis of ½d. a year for each member. But this was never insisted on and it had been agreed on the General Council as early as November 22, 1864 that contributions from workers' organisations would be 'left to their means and discretion'.[3]

With such casual financial arrangements — and with overseas contributions coming in even more haphazardly than the English — it is hardly surprising that the General Council spent its days in want. The lack of money of which Marx complained was in one way an illustration of his own dialectical

---

[1] General Council: Third Annual Report, presented to the Lausanne Congress. *Beehive*, September 14, 1867.

[2] G.C. *Minutes*, October 8, 1867.

[3] See income from members' subscriptions in balance sheet, Chapter V, Appendix 2, above.

principles.   The relative technical advancement of British
industry which made the British workers the most organised
in the world made them also — except for the industries
already noted, and these not the most advanced — comparatively
unresponsive to the appeal of the International.

THE GENEVA BUILDING WORKERS

Yet, run on a shoestring as it was, the General Council
could be exceedingly effective.   The help given to the London
tailors in 1866 and to the Paris bronze workers in 1867 had
already brought the International into the public eye.   The
lock-out of the building workers in Geneva in 1868 put the
Council once again to the test and once again it emerged
triumphantly.   The building workers had applied for a wage
increase of twenty per cent and a reduction in the working day
from twelve to ten hours.   The employers refused and were
horrified when the workers appealed to the Geneva branch of
the International to conduct the struggle on their behalf.   'The
relations between employers and workers', they told the men,
'have been cordial in the past.   It seems useless to interpose
between them the action of a society which, like yours, draws
its principles and methods from abroad.' [1]

The Genevese workers applied at once to the General
Council for aid pointing out how contact between the English
and European workers through the medium of the International
had 'had the effect of accelerating the formation of trades'
unions on the continent and quickened their course of action'.[2]
Aid was soon promised from the International's centres in
London, Paris and Brussels.   The employers, as in Paris the
year before, took fright and gave concessions.   The workers
won a wage increase of ten per cent and reduction in the
working day from twelve to eleven hours.   The victory was
vividly remembered more than twenty years later [3] and the
prestige of the International soared.

[1] Antony Babel, 'La Première Internationale, ses débuts et son activité
à Genève de 1864 à 1870', in *Mélanges d'études économiques et sociales*, ed.
W. E. Rappard, Geneva, 1949, p. 312.

[2] *Beehive*, April 14, 1868.

[3] See the account by Vera Zasulich, after talking to J. P. Becker and
other participants in the dispute in Geneva. *Ocherk Istorii Mezhdunarodnovo
Obshchestva Rabochich*, Geneva, 1889, reprinted in her *Sbornik Statei*, St.
Petersburg, 1906, pp. 245-318.

The English trade unions which were members of the International had responded well to the appeal. The sums received included loans of £20 from the Carpenters and Joiners, and £10 from the Day-Working Bookbinders, together with gifts of £5 from the Elastic Web Weavers, £2 from the Shoemakers, £3 : 4 : 0 from the Amalgamated Cordwainers — despite their having left the International — and £1 : 10 : 0 from the London French branch.[1] It was no doubt to be expected that such a success would expose the International in England to attack as an organisation for fomenting strikes. Eccarius, who had succeeded Fox as General Secretary on the latter's move to Vienna in 1867, and Shaw, as Chairman of the General Council, wrote to explain the position. The General Council had neither the power nor the wish to call strikes. If they occurred, however, and if the General Council were appealed to, it would certainly use its influence 'to prevent the workmen of one country being used as industrial mercenaries against the workmen of another' and to raise money for the strikers. But at Congresses of the International both producers' co-operation and industrial arbitration had also been considered as means for furthering the interests of the working class and there was no particular emphasis placed on the use of the strike weapon.[2]

This was inevitably the view of a General Council on which leading members of the Junta served. Howell was still a member though he had long ceased to attend. Odger, however, appeared intermittently and Robert Applegarth, who had been sympathetic for some time, became an active member of the Council after the Brussels Congress in September 1868. As a group the Junta was more interested in arbitration than in strikes, and 'strike jobber' was a term of abuse which they used against Potter. Marx, though he attached more importance to strikes than did his trade union colleagues, regarding them as useful training operations in the class struggle, was not inclined to question the Junta's approach to English industrial matters or their assessment of Potter. What worried him about the Junta was its attachment to Liberal politics and he expressed a certain sombre satisfaction when the working-class candidates who stood in the General Election of 1868 — including Howell and Cremer — were badly beaten. He wrote

[1] *Beehive*, May 2, 1868. The 'Shoemakers' were presumably the West-End Ladies' Bootmakers — Odger's union.   [2] *Beehive*, April 11, 1868.

to Engels on November 18 about the 'highly *amusing upshot* of the elections' and told him that the General Council, meeting the previous evening, had attributed the *débâcle* to the 'false policy of the Reform League' in co-operating with middle-class Liberals.[1]

ODGER, LUCRAFT, APPLEGARTH

On political questions a majority of the General Council followed Marx in opposing identification with Gladstonian Liberalism. This caused some embarrassment to Odger who intended to stand as candidate for Chelsea, though he withdrew before the Election. He had been anxious to secure a message of support from the General Council and Marx drafted an appropriate address.[2] Before this could be endorsed by the Council, however, Lucraft drew attention to a statement by Odger at a meeting in Chelsea that if elected he would act as an 'unflinching supporter of the Great Liberal Party'. Before he could secure the Council's support, Odger was obliged to explain that his declaration of support applied only to Gladstone's policy on Irish Disestablishment.[3]

So far as politics went, Applegarth's outlook was at least as flexible as Odger's. He could co-operate as easily with Mundella as with Marx.[4] On the other hand, as Secretary of one of the largest unions in the country and as a man of unusually wide interests, he was considerably impressed by the International's success in spreading trade unionism on the Continent. In the period of internationally depressed trade which opened in 1867 it seemed to Applegarth more than ever essential that the experiences of British trade unionism should be conveyed to the European working class. He had maintained friendly relations with the General Council since early in 1867, and it was in May of that year that he was instrumental in establishing a branch of the International in King's Lynn.[5] For more than a year after the Brussels Congress in September 1868 he attended

---

[1] Both the Russian and German editions of the Marx-Engels correspondence wrongly date the letter October 18.

[2] No copy of this address has so far been found.

[3] G.C. *Minutes*, October 6 and Marx to Engels, October 10, 1868.

[4] Cf. Asa Briggs, *Victorian People*, 1954, p. 206. Applegarth was keenly interested in Mundella's schemes for industrial arbitration.

[5] It is not clear whether this was a local branch of the International or, more probably, a branch of the A.S.C.J. which affiliated. See G.C. *Minutes*, May 14, 1867.

fairly regularly at meetings of the General Council and became one of its most enthusiastic supporters.

ROUEN, BASLE AND THE BELGIAN MASSACRES

There was evidence from both Austria and Germany that trade unionism was spreading as a direct result of the International's influence.[1] As Chairman at a meeting of the General Council on January 5, 1869, Applegarth heard a report from Germany which pointed out that the unions of that country, numbering a hundred and ten thousand members, were developing 'on the model of the English ones' and that they had been considerably influenced by the resolutions on trade union policy adopted at Congresses of the International.[2] At the same meeting an appeal was received from the cotton workers of Rouen. There the employers had demanded wage reductions on the plea that they were necessary to meet English competition. After an appeal from the International, the London Trades Council on January 23 called for the 'sympathy and support' of all British unions. However, the trade depression with its heavy drain on trade union funds was making it increasingly difficult to raise money. In response to a request from Marx, Applegarth readily agreed to transfer the £20 loan, which the Paris bronze workers had just repaid, to the cotton spinners of Rouen. His Society regarded the money, he explained, as a loan to the International.

The Rouen strike was over with the men defeated before much help could be received from abroad. At about the same time the dyers and ribbon weavers of Basle were locked out by their employers and deputations were sent by the General Council to a number of unions. Again, the response was disappointing. Even the small sums received, however, were sufficient to frighten the Swiss employers who sent a representative to London to ask Applegarth whether the International was behind the dispute. As in Rouen, the workers acknowledged defeat and returned to work on their employers' terms.[3]

The next appeal to reach the General Council was from

---

[1] See the appreciative message from 'The Viennese Workmen to the English Workmen', *Social Economist*, September 1868.

[2] G.C. *Minutes*, January 5, and *Beehive*, January 16, 1869.

[3] G.C. *Minutes*, February 2, 16, March 23, 30; *Beehive*, February 6, 13, 20, April 3, 1869. For the effects of the trade depression on English support for foreign strikes, see Marx to Engels, January 13, 1869.

the Belgian iron workers, whose strike at Seraing near Liège had been repressed with considerable brutality. Almost exactly a year before, some miners on strike at Charleroi had been shot dead by the Belgian police. Belgium was a country which combined a considerable amount of political toleration with the practice of savage repression in industrial disputes. In an address which he drafted for the General Council, Marx pointed the contrast in searing phrases.[1] Strikes in other countries, he wrote, were on the increase and were usually settled peacefully. The outstanding exception was Belgium, that 'model state of continental constitutionalism, the snug, well-hedged little paradise of the landlord, the capitalist, and the priest. The earth performs not more surely its yearly revolution than the Belgian Government its yearly Working Men's massacre. . . .' The address ended with an appeal for funds to provide legal defence and aid for the victims' dependants.[2] Under prevailing conditions there was little response to the appeal, although a few pounds were contributed by the Carpenters and Joiners, the Cabinet Makers and the West-End Bootclosers, while Applegarth personally collected individual subscriptions.[3]

THE POLITICS OF TRADE UNIONISM

During the period in which he worked with Marx on the General Council, Applegarth came increasingly under his influence. He declared himself enormously impressed by Marx's address on the Belgian massacres.[4] His interest in the International, however, remained primarily industrial. He was stirred by the Rouen cotton spinners' strike because he knew that the employers' 'avowed object . . . was to enable the French cotton manufacturers to compete with the English manufacturers in our home markets' and that this had already produced repercussions in Preston where the cotton employers were likewise demanding a ten per cent cut in wages.[5] Politically, Marx's influence was largely responsible for Applegarth's

---

[1] 'To the Workmen of Europe and the United States on the Belgian Massacres', see G.C. Minutes, April 20, 27, 1869. Marx's address was printed as a leaflet on May 4; a copy is in the Howell Collection, Bishopsgate. It is the first item published for the International by E. Truelove, the leading Positivist and radical.   [2] Beehive, May 8, 1869.

[3] G.C. Minutes, May 25, June 1; Beehive, June 12, 1869.

[4] Beehive, May 8, 1869.

[5] Amalgamated Society of Carpenters and Joiners, Ninth Annual Report, December 1867–December 1868.

support of land nationalisation at the Basle Congress later in the year. Possibly it was his close contact with Marx which caused Applegarth to move much further to the left than any other member of the Junta.

Though Applegarth might develop, under Marx's influence, towards a socialist outlook, he never adopted Marx's views on the class struggle and this duality of outlook was characteristic of other members of his union. J. D. Prior, a future General Secretary of the A.S.C.J. and at that time Secretary of its Islington branch, presided at the branch's anniversary dinner in 1869 and proposed a toast of 'Success and Prosperity' to the International. His wholehearted tribute to the success of the International in discouraging the importation of blacklegs was followed by a speech from Hermann Jung, one of the earliest members, who described the achievements of the International in spreading trade unionism on the Continent. After this, without any sense of incongruity, the branch members at the dinner unanimously approved a motion wishing 'Health and Prosperity to our Employers'.[1]

When the Royal Commission, which had been investigating trade unions, produced an unexpectedly favourable report, working-class energy became concentrated in a drive to improve the legal position of the unions. The Positivists, Beesly and Crompton, had drafted a Bill to strengthen the rights of combination, provide security for trade union funds and secure a more satisfactory position with regard to such matters as conspiracy and intimidation. An unusual degree of unity was for the moment maintained. The unions which had participated in the Trades Union Congress at Sheffield in 1866, the London Trades Council and Potter's London Workingmen's Association had agreed on a joint campaign, and Marx wrote to Engels on September 26, 1868 about the new spirit of unity which was replacing the old divisions in the trade union movement.

The International participated in a meeting in London on October 14 to discuss the draft of Beesly and Crompton's Bill. In addition to the two drafters and a number of trade union representatives, Lloyd Jones, the prominent co-operator and Christian socialist, Hartwell from the *Beehive*, Howell from the Reform League and Marx and Jung from the International

[1] A.S.C.J. *Monthly Report*, July 1869.

were present.[1]   The conference endorsed a Bill which was presented in the Commons by Mundella and by Hughes, the Christian socialist.   Weston, a prominent disciple of Robert Owen, represented the International on a deputation to the Home Secretary.   The labour movement, immeasurably strengthened by the 1867 Reform Act — to which Marx, judging from his correspondence, attached little importance — was embarking on a new round of activity in a spirit of vigour and confidence.   Within the next six years it was to secure nearly all its main objectives.

Like the earlier campaign of the Reform League, however, these developments consumed time and energy in ways which did nothing to strengthen the International as an organisation. Further, though the Reform League had been wound up early in 1869,[2] there was a demand for an organisation which could take advantage of the Reform Act to promote labour representation in the Commons.   The electoral fiasco of 1868 it was felt was due largely to lack of organisation.   To meet this deficiency, the Labour Representation League was set up in September 1869.   Its first Secretary was Lloyd Jones and ten other members of its executive — Applegarth, Coulson, Dodshon, Druitt, Hales, Howell, Mottershead, J. Osborne, Dixon Stainsby and A. A. Walton — were past, present or future members of the General Council.[3]

The following month saw the establishment of the National Education League, with Applegarth and Lloyd Jones again figuring prominently among the founders.   The League stood for free, compulsory and secular education which conformed fully with the programme of the International.   But in the National Education League trade unionists co-operated harmoniously with Randal Cremer, who had become a liberal pacifist, and with the radical Joseph Chamberlain, later to become a liberal imperialist.   Independent labour representation in fact was desired not for a policy of class struggle against capitalism but for the furtherance of political reforms within the existing social order.

If the unions were friendly to the International, then, it was strictly on their own terms.   But the friendship, while it lasted, was real enough.   In August 1869, a few days before

---

[1] *Beehive*, October 17, 24, 1868.
[2] Some branches — *e.g.* in Holborn — maintained an independent existence.   [3] B. C. Roberts, *op. cit.*, p. 56.

the decisive Basle Congress of the International, the second
Trades Union Congress met in Birmingham. It represented
about two hundred and fifty thousand workers. The delegates
included John Kane, W. Harry, A. A. Walton, the O'Brienite
and advocate of producers' co-operation, Odger, Cremer and
Howell.[1] Though Cremer had scarcely attended a meeting of
the General Council since the Geneva Congress in 1866, he
moved a resolution calling on all workers and workers' organisations to affiliate to the International. Under conditions of free
trade and unrestricted international competition, it was pointed
out, the interests of labour would inevitably be lost sight of.
Within the labour movement, local organisation was giving way
to national and the process should culminate in the establishment of a workers' International. This would not only serve
the economic interests of labour but 'would also conduce to
lasting peace between the nations'. The resolution was
seconded by a member of the A.S.C.J. from Birmingham and
carried unanimously.[2]

STAGNATION OF THE INTERNATIONAL IN ENGLAND

Superficially, the Basle Congress, which opened on September 5, 1869, registered a further growth in the influence of
the International in England. For the first time the Secretary
of a powerful union played a leading part at a Congress;
Applegarth, moreover, supported the policy of land nationalisation in a critical debate, as did the joiner, Lucraft, and the
nephew of Lord Carnarvon, Cowell Stepney. With the unanimous support of the T.U.C. it seemed as though the International was firmly established in the world of labour. Yet
there were dangerous features about the position which seem
to have been ignored. The International had ceased to grow.
There had been only three trade union affiliations since the
end of 1867 — the small societies of Trunk and Portmanteau
Makers having joined on the eve of the Brussels Congress in
1868 and the West-End Bootclosers six months later.[3] For
reasons already discussed, the International had made no headway in the basic industries of coal, engineering and ironfounding

---

[1] R. S. Kirk, *The Second Annual Congress of Trade Unions* (*August 23-28,
1869*), MSS. No pagination.   [2] *Ibid.* and *Beehive*, September 4, 1869.
[3] G.C. *Minutes*, August 18, 25, 1868. *Beehive*, March 20, 1869. Even
these small gains were partially offset by the unexplained withdrawal of
the Birmingham House Painters, *ibid*.

and in the whole field of heavy industry the Malleable Ironworkers stood out as a solitary exception.

By the time of the Basle Congress, the International in
England had been virtually stagnant for two years. This
stagnation was reflected in the finances of the General Council,
which were in an even worse state than usual. To some extent
the financial depression which has lasted from 1866 to 1869
contributed to the general *malaise*. The drain of the depression
on the funds of such firmly established unions as the A.S.C.J.
and the A.S.E. made them reluctant to respond to financial appeals.[1] For many of the smaller unions the effects of the slump
must have been worse. It was a relief when the Bricklayers, on
being repaid their loan of £10 by the Paris bronze workers, gave
half of it to the International, 'knowing the usefulness of that
Association' [2] to help meet the expenses of the Basle Congress.

The contrast between political life in England and the
Continent was now becoming marked. While in England
trade unions were struggling for political reforms, in Europe
they were fighting for their bare existence. English employers
were coming to accept strikes as an inevitable if odious part of
the social scene. In Switzerland the employers of Geneva
building workers and Basle ribbon weavers convinced themselves that strikes could only be the result of an international
conspiracy. In Belgium the striking miners of Charleroi and
the iron workers of Seraing were shot down by soldiers. In
France, where political associations were prohibited, the correspondence between Dupont, for the General Council, and
local branches of the International, was regularly intercepted by
the police. In January and again in May 1868 the leading
members of the Paris section were tried and sentenced to fines
and imprisonment.[3] The instability of the French Empire was
not a secret and 'Gracchus', writing in *Reynolds's* on August 30,
1868, had predicted that 'an unsuccessful war would assuredly
end in the dethronement of Louis Napoleon'. In South
Germany the labour movement was virtually founded by Bebel

---

[1] See 9th Annual Report to the A.S.C.J. by Applegarth, *Reynolds's*,
April 18, and the address by Allan to the A.S.E., *ibid.*, July 11, 1869.

[2] *Operative Bricklayers' Society's Trade Circular*, September 1869. See
also letter from E. Coulson to Jung, August 27, 1869.

[3] *Procès de l'Association Internationale des Travailleurs*, Paris, 1870, 2nd
edition, see especially pp. 42-3, 104-5 and 144-65. See also Marx to Engels,
January 11, G.C. *Minutes*, January 21, March 30: *Beehive*, January 4,
April 4, June 20, 1868.

and Liebknecht, both disciples of Marx. Shortly before the Basle Congress the Marxist and Lassallean parties in Germany had fused at Eisenach to form a Social Democratic Party with a substantial membership.

By contrast, the English workers, particularly since 1867, were beginning to feel themselves part of society — a society no doubt riddled with oppression and injustice, but one which they could hope to change peacefully. In Europe the workers' organisation existed on sufferance. French and Prussian workers owed their political rights, such as they were, to the whim of an Emperor and the tactical calculations of Bismarck. Applegarth, after listening to the reports from continental delegates at Basle, realised more acutely than before the unique situation of labour in Britain. 'I have a somewhat different account to give', he told the Congress, 'to those we have heard today. Fortunately, in England, we have no need of creeping into holes and corners lest a policeman should see us.' [1]

Marx also realised the limitations, from his point of view, of the labour movement in England. As early as 1858 Engels had written to him that 'the English proletariat is becoming more and more bourgeois, so that this most bourgeois of all nations is apparently aiming at the possession of a bourgeois aristocracy and a bourgeois proletariat *as well as* a bourgeoisie'. The explanation, he was sure, lay in England's industrial supremacy and her domination of the world market.[2] But Marx was confident that this would be a passing phase. The English workers were the most highly organised in the world. Their political deficiencies could be remedied through the influence of the International. With all its weaknesses, the International was at least firmly established. 'And in the next revolution', Marx had assured Engels after the Lausanne Congress, 'which is perhaps nearer than it appears, *we* (*i.e.* you and I) will have this powerful engine *in our hands.*' [3]

Marx accordingly kept the engine oiled against the day when it could be used in support of the revolution. In 1871 the revolution he was expecting duly arrived. His tragedy lay in the fact that it was the unsuccessful revolution and that by the time it came the engine had grown rusty.

[1] *Reynolds's*, September 19, 1869, and *Report of the Fourth Annual Congress of the International Working Men's Association*, p. 18.
[2] Engels to Marx, October 7, 1858.
[3] Marx to Engels, September 11, 1867.

PART THREE

CONFLICT OF IDEAS IN THE
INTERNATIONAL, 1864–9

CHAPTER VII

London and Geneva

In the development of ideas the direct influence of the International in England was small. By contrast, the influence of England on the International was decisive. When Marx drafted the *Inaugural Address* he produced a document which, while studiously moderate in tone, committed the International to the task of leading the workers to political power. The *Address* was soon to play a part in the bitter struggle which broke out between the two French sections of the Association.

THE LEFORT CASE AND MAZZINI

The radical republicans, the party to which Le Lubez and Lefort belonged, stood for the overthrow of the Empire and the restoration of parliamentary democracy. Th ugh in principle approving of economic and social reforms, their propaganda was devoted almost exclusively to the advocacy of political change. Conversely the Proudhonists, represented by Tolain and Murat, were republican in theory while in practice they concentrated on the economic emancipation of the workers through the establishment of co-operative production financed by a people's bank. While at first sight the differences might seem merely to be one of emphasis, the Proudhonists came increasingly to oppose the participation of working-class societies in politics.

Both sections had contributed, though independently, to the foundation of the International. But the latent antagonism came to the surface as soon as the two sections got down to the work of establishing the Association in France. The Proudhonists published the first French edition of the *Provisional Rules* in which the sentence declaring 'That the economical emancipation of the working classes is therefore the great end to which every political movement ought to be subordinate' appeared shorn of the concluding phrase 'as a means'. The omission made it look as though the International was asserting the primacy of economic over political struggles. According to this version, wrote Lefort in disgust, it appeared that 'we are putting aside the political question and that we think it possible to achieve economic progress independently of politics . . . It is Bonapartism, it is Imperial Democracy.' [1]

At once the darkest suspicions were aroused. The republicans had resented the running of independent workers' candidates in the election of 1863. It was bound, they considered, to benefit the Government by splitting the republican front. Was it an accident, they began to ask, that the Emperor himself had financed the workers' delegation to the London Exhibition of 1862? At this point Moses Hess, Paris correspondent of the German *Sozial-Demokrat*, picked up some gossip and wrote to his paper that the workers' leaders were Bonapartist agents.[2]

Marx was worried by the turn things were taking. Both sections had played an important part in founding the International and both in his view should remain in membership. When Hess's story appeared, Tolain was only with difficulty dissuaded from resigning. Marx and Engels wrote to the *Sozial-Demokrat* repudiating the story.[3] In Paris Lefort was acting as the International's Press agent and Fribourg, Tolain's principal colleague, was enrolling members. It would be a good thing, Marx told Engels on February 10, if the two men could continue performing those functions.

The Proudhonists forced matters to a crisis. Only workers, they insisted, should fill posts in a workers' society. Lefort, who was not a worker, should be dismissed from his post. The English were frankly bewildered by the dispute and the decision rested in the hands of Marx. It was not an easy choice. 'But in Paris', he told Engels on February 25, 'on one side stands *Lefort* (a literary man and also a man of means and so a "Bourgeois" but the purest of men and as regards la belle France the real founder of our society) and on the other side, *Tolain, Fribourg, Limousin*, etc., the workers.' The General Council decided to send Le Lubez to Paris to investigate.[4] His report

---

[1] Lefort to Le Lubez, February 4, 1865. Quoted by Tchernoff, *op. cit.*, p. 453.

[2] Tolain to Le Lubez, February 10, 1865. Tchernoff, *op. cit.*, pp. 455-6.

[3] See Marx to Engels, February 6, 1865.

[4] G.C. *Minutes*, February 14, 21, 1865.

was strongly favourable to Lefort and at the end of February Tolain and Fribourg arrived in London.[1] The English were in a dilemma. They were not impressed by the arguments against Lefort. But they were impressed by Tolain's threat to resign and to take with him the most authentic representatives of the Paris workers.

The decisive meeting of the Council took place on March 7 and lasted till midnight. Le Lubez was 'completely overwhelmed'. It was all 'very painful, stormy, and created, particularly on the English the impression that the Frenchmen stand really in need of a Bonaparte'.[2] Inevitably, when forced to choose, Marx and the Council sided with the workers and Tolain was asked to reconsider his many offers of resignation. Lefort was removed from his post and the Council paid him generous tribute as 'one of the initiators' of the International. At the same time it emphatically refused to 'sanction the principle that none but an *ouvrier* is admissible as an official in our society'.[3]

The matter could not rest there and Lefort's dismissal was followed by the resignation of Le Lubez and Denoual among the French — Eugène Dupont, who replaced Le Lubez as secretary for France, was strongly under Marx's influence — together with the Italians, Wolf, Lama and Fontana. In their approach to politics, labour and the national question, the French radical republicans were close to Mazzini, and Marx had no doubt at all that the 'distinguished Italian Patriot' had made use of the Lefort case to bring his followers out of the International. Mazzini's brand of republicanism, Marx told a Belgian correspondent, based as it was on a denial of the class struggle, could only produce 'another form of bourgeois despotism'.[4] In the debate on the *Inaugural Address*, Mazzini had instructed his followers 'to cut out . . . all hostile references to the bourgeoisie'. Years later, describing the episode to another correspondent, Marx wrote that after the rejection of Wolf's version of the Rules, of which Mazzini was the real author, 'Mazzini . . . induced his partisans to secede from the General Council and remained, from that time to his death, the

---

[1] Fribourg, *op. cit.*, pp. 26-7.
[2] Marx to Engels, March 13, 1865.
[3] Marx to Engels, *ibid.*, and G.C. *Minutes*, March 7, 1865.
[4] Marx to Léon Fontaine, April 15, 1865. Marx had been elected Corresponding Secretary for Belgium.

most irreconcilable enemy of the International'.[1] Though the
Italians withdrew six months after the rejection of Wolf's
Address and on another issue, Marx was probably right in
dating Mazzini's antagonism from that event.

Engels, still in his sceptical phase, saw a stormy future
ahead for the International. 'The thing', he told Marx on
April 12, 'will be repeated many times through the same
phases' and warned Marx that it would cost him a good deal
of his time. The prognosis was to prove only too accurate.
Though the Mazzinists proper had now dropped out of the
International, the quarrel with the French persisted and in the
orgy of mutual recrimination which was to follow the overthrow of the Commune it acted as a time fuse, contributing
powerfully to the International's disintegration.

VALUE, PRICE AND PROFIT

It was characteristic of the English that the first subject
which they debated on their own initiative was not the relative
merits of continental ideologies, but whether trade union
pressure for wage increases could raise the standard of living.
Weston, an Owenite, proposed the question for discussion on
April 4, 1865. He believed that not only could such pressure
bring no benefit to the workers directly involved but that it
would also 'operate prejudicially to the other sections of
industry'.

Weston was bringing on to the General Council a view he
had been advocating for some time in the correspondence
columns of the *Beehive*. In 1864 a series of articles began to
appear, almost certainly by Weston[2] and continued intermittently until May 6, 1865. A vigorous controversy had
developed and many of the views on both sides of what has
become a perennial controversy were forcefully expressed.[3]

---

[1] Unpublished letter to an unknown correspondent, dated July 14, 1875.
The letter was sold at Sotheby's on February 6, 1952. For Mazzini's views
on Marx and the International, see his article in the *Roma del Popolo*,
appearing after the Paris Commune and translated, after Mazzini's death,
in the *Contemporary Review*, July 1872.

[2] The articles were signed 'W' and the writer's views on co-operation
and religion as well as on wages policy were those of the Owenite school to
which Weston belonged. The title of the series, 'Sparks from the Workshop', also suggests Weston's authorship — he had been a carpenter and
handrail manufacturer since 1863.

[3] See especially *Beehive*, April 29, 1865.

Both Marx and Weston read papers to the General Council.[1] While the debate was not recorded in the *Minutes*, Marx's contribution was found by his daughter Eleanor among Engels's papers and published in 1898 as the pamphlet *Value, Price and Profit*. Weston, who believed in producers' co-operation as the only salvation for the working class, had claimed that increased wages would normally be offset by higher prices both because wages determined the price of commodities — a version of the now current theory of 'cost inflation' — and because of the effect on prices of a higher level of working-class demand. Marx replied by insisting that higher wages would change the structure of demand, that the production of wage goods would expand relative to the production of luxuries and capital goods, and that working-class standards would benefit accordingly.

Marx qualified this view by adding that the bargaining power of labour in a capitalist society must be inadequate unless supplemented by political pressure. The most outstanding example of such pressure successfully applied was the Ten Hours' Act of 1847. Such legislative interference was necessary because 'in its merely economic action capital is the stronger side'.

Trade union pressure for wage increases, therefore, though far from useless, would be insufficient unless supplemented by political action. On this Marx's views were entirely in accord with those of his English trade union colleagues. They also, no doubt, listened in agreement when he added the warning that trade unions 'fail generally from limiting themselves to a guerilla war against the effects of the existing system, instead of simultaneously trying to change it, instead of using their organised forces as a lever for the final emancipation of the working class, that is to say, the ultimate abolition of the wages system'. This had been said already in the *Inaugural Address* and in the same general terms. In his dealings with the English, Marx continued to expound that part of his creed for which he could count on their support. This support became all the more necessary as the International embarked on its first major ideological battle — a battle which was to determine the future development of international Socialism.

[1] See Marx to Engels, May 20 and June 24, 1865. Marx gave his friend a full summary of Weston's views and of his own paper together with his own reservations with regard to publication.

THE PROUDHONISTS AND THE POLISH QUESTION

The first Conference of the International opened in London on Monday, September 25, 1865. Its object was the preparation of an agenda for the Congress to be held in Geneva a year later. The main questions debated in London were Poland and religion. The English delegation included Weston, Odger, Cremer, Howell, Shaw and a number of representatives from affiliated organisations.[1] The battle was opened unobtrusively by Tolain who reported that 'In France they were paying particular attention to social questions which he considered more important just now under the present regime and likely to produce the most important political results'.

This was too vaguely worded to provoke opposition, but the Proudhonists did not confine themselves to advocating the priority of social over political aims. They insisted that at Congresses all members of the International should have the right to speak and vote, a point of view which astounded the English. To restrict rights to elected delegates, argued Tolain, would be a denial of that 'perfect equality' for which the International stood. After vehement opposition from Cremer and Howell the French were overwhelmingly defeated. No doubt their suggestion was based on an exaggerated anti-authoritarianism combined with an awareness of the precarious legal position of workers' societies in their own country. To the English trade unionists, accustomed to electing their committees and sending delegates to conferences and trades councils, the French position must have seemed incomprehensible.

More significant of the differences developing within the International was the controversy over Poland. This was the issue which had first brought the English and French workers together to found the Association and in Marx's mind it was crucial. The Polish movement, he believed, was not just another instance of a nation struggling for independence. It was uniquely important because the Russian Empire was uniquely important. This semi-Asiatic autocracy, with its feebly developed capitalism and without a labour movement, was the bulwark of European reaction. Any revolution on the Continent stood a good chance of being strangled by Russian military intervention combined with financial pressure from England. Reaction was therefore being maintained by the

[1] *Workman's Advocate*, September 30, 1865.

most backward and the most advanced of the great nations. Each, however, had its Achilles' heel in the form of an oppressed nation struggling for freedom. Consequently, the Polish and Irish national struggles were of supreme importance, tending to undermine the twin pillars of European reaction.

When the General Council was first set up it was inevitably Poland which loomed largest in the minds of its members. The subject had come up for discussion on the General Council before the end of 1864. Closely linked to it was the question of France about which there had been some controversy even before the foundation of the International. The common view among trade unionists and ex-Chartists was that Louis Napoleon was the murderer of democracy in France and that his régime was reactionary in home and foreign politics alike. The Chartists had made their first political contact with Napoleon when he signed on as one of the army of special constables who helped to overawe their demonstration at Kennington Common in 1848. Their next news of him, when he suppressed Garibaldi's Roman Republic in 1849, did not cause them to revise their impressions. These views were considerably reinforced by the arrival of French democratic refugees from his *coup d'état* in the early 1850s.[1] Marx fully shared this attitude.

For the Positivists, on the other hand, the hope of progress in the world rested on an alliance between England and France, while Napoleon III was 'the representative, however unsatisfactory, of the European revolution'.[2] This Positivist view of France as the fountain-head of progress had found expression in a policy statement on Poland drafted by Fox for the General Council in December 1864. France, he maintained, had been traditionally the friend of Poland and a democratic foreign policy for Britain implied a pro-French orientation.[3] On January 3, 1865 Marx replied at length in a detailed statement — the most elaborate he had prepared for the Council since the *Inaugural Address*.[4] Fox had traced the pro-Polish,

---

[1] For a typical old Chartist reaction, see J. B. Leno, *The Aftermath*, 1892, pp. 82-4. See also, *Letter of the Jersey Exiles to the Queen of England*, an offprint from the *People's Paper*, October 1855, published by E. Truelove. Reprinted, without signatures, in *Labour Monthly*, August 1952.

[2] E. S. Beesly, *Beehive*, April 25, 1863. For a criticism of this view, see editorials in *Beehive*, August 15 and November 28, and Beesly's reply, December 5, 1863.   [3] Marx's summary to Engels, December 10, 1864.

[4] Marx's reply has been printed, from the MSS., for the International Institute of Social History, Amsterdam. See Karl Marx, *Manuskripte über die polnische Frage (1863-1864)*, Amsterdam, 1961, pp. 165-96.

anti-Russian policy of France back to the sixteenth and seventeenth centuries. But at that time, Marx pointed out, 'Poland was still a powerful State' while 'Russia, in the modern sense of the word, did not yet exist. There existed then a Grand Duchy of Muscovy, but there existed not yet a Russian Empire.' French policy, in that period, had been of the ordinary, dynastic kind, directed primarily against the Holy Roman Empire. He went on to examine in some detail the development of French foreign policy in the reigns of Louis XIV and XV, a policy tending towards the dismemberment and impoverishment of Germany and even providing the Czar Alexander II with a model on which to base his own handling of foreign relations.

After Marx had finished what must have been an impressive display of erudition, the Council decided, since Fox's statement was 'not borne out by historical facts, that it be amended so as to accord with the truths of history'. No doubt Marx failed to win Fox from his Francophilia since he was billed to speak on three successive Sundays in August on the fiftieth anniversary of peace with France for the short-lived Greenwich and Deptford branch of the International.[1] But the position of intellectual leadership which Marx secured in the first few months of the General Council's existence he maintained unchallenged for the next eight years.

It was to stand him in good stead. At the London Conference of the International, a resolution in the name of the General Council called attention to 'The Muscovite invasion of Europe' and the need to re-establish 'an independent and integral Poland'. It was formally moved by the Pole, Bobczynski, seconded by Wheeler and supported by the Frenchman, Talbot, who as the delegate from Calvados, did not share the position of his Parisian colleagues.[2]

Opposition came first from Le Lubez who argued that since every people had the right to self-government there was no need to lay special emphasis on Poland.[3] A much more radical criticism was made by César de Paepe, from Belgium, and next to Marx the most outstandingly original thinker in the International. A follower of Baron de Colins, de Paepe

---

[1] Poster in the International Institute of Social History, Amsterdam.

[2] *Workman's Advocate*, September 30; *Reynolds's*, October 1, 1865.

[3] Fribourg's statement in *L'Association Internationale des Travailleurs*, p. 45, that Le Lubez supported Marx on Poland at the London Conference, is certainly wrong.

developed a distinctive approach to Socialism which combined State ownership of the land and other means of production with a considerable amount of decentralised control through the medium of local communes. His debt to Colins is well known. What has not been appreciated is the extent to which his early development was influenced by Russian revolutionary thinkers of the school of Zemlya i Volya — 'Land and Liberty' — from which the Russian Narodnik or Populist brand of Socialism also took root. Serno-Solovievitch, one of the founders of Zemlya i Volya, had visited Herzen in Brussels in 1862 and it is more than likely that de Paepe met and was influenced by the Russians. Only twenty at the time, he was already active in socialist propaganda.[1]

For the workers, de Paepe insisted — as Rosa Luxembourg was later to do — the real struggle was between classes, not nations. In Poland, as in Russia, the enemy of the peasant was his 'own' landlord. He told the Conference that 'it was not the Russian government or people that blotted out Polish freedom. The Russian peasants strove for "Land and Liberty". The Polish peasants should do likewise. The French government was as dangerous to liberty as the Russian.'[2]

To Wheeler, as to most of the English, the issue was simple. 'Russian despotism', he argued, 'was the most blighting in the world. . . . He denounced despotism everywhere; but Russian was the most dangerous and cruel in Europe.' When the vote was taken it was decided by an overwhelming majority to put Polish independence on the agenda for the forthcoming Congress.

The struggle was soon to be resumed, but Marx's position on the General Council was strong. With the exception of Weston, the English members supported him. Among the French, he had a firm and effective adherent in Eugène Dupont and among the Poles his position had been strengthened by the

---

[1] De Paepe collaborated in a translation of Chernishevsky's *Political Economy in the Light of Science* in 1874 — G. D. H. Cole, *Marxism and Anarchism*, 1954, p. 49. He also translated *What is to be Done?* by the same author, in 1888 — *Commonweal*, November 16, 1889. See also V. I. Romanenko, *Mirovozzrenie M. A. Serno-Solovievitcha*, Moscow, 1954, p. 24, *et seq.*, and Louis Bertrand, *Histoire de la démocratie et du socialisme en Belgique*, Brussels, 1909, vol. II, p. 44 and his *César de Paepe, sa vie, son œuvre*, Brussels, 1909, p. 14, *et seq.*

[2] *Workman's Advocate*, September 30, 1865. (The word 'Not' was omitted in the text, clearly in error.) The phrase 'Land and Liberty' suggests that de Paepe regarded himself as an adherent of Zemlya i Volya.

resignation of Holtorp, a Mazzinist, over the Lefort case, and his replacement by Bobczynski. Marx's position was more sophisticated than that of the English, though it amounted to much the same thing. De Paepe was against supporting the Polish cause and the Proudhonists were against supporting any political cause because both, for somewhat different reasons, urged the primacy of economic issues. Radical republicans like Le Lubez followed Mazzini in supporting the equal right to independence of all nationalities without preference or distinction.[1] For Marx it was exclusively a question of power. Czarism, while its strength was unshaken, was an insuperable obstacle to the European revolution. The English, for their part, had learned from Harney that a victory for democracy on the Tagus — or on the Vistula — was a victory for democracy on the Thames. With their help, and against the opposition of the Belgian and both French sections, Marx kept the International on its original lines with regard to Poland. On another question, however, the issues were at first sight less clear-cut.

THE 'RELIGIOUS IDEA'

Writing in the *Nineteenth Century* for July 1878,[2] George Howell said that 'the introduction of the "Religious Idea" by a German "doctor" named Karl Marx had sown the seeds of discord and decay' at the London Conference. Marx at once sent a reply to the *Nineteenth Century*. The editor refused to publish it[3] and it appeared in the *Secular Chronicle*[4] a month later. 'The programme of the General Council', he claimed, 'contained not one syllable on "Religion".' The subject had been introduced 'at the instance of the Paris delegates' and was then 'left in their keeping. In point of fact they dropped it at the Geneva Congress of 1866, and no one else picked it up.'

[1] Alone among the English, Weston supported this view. He seems to have been close, personally, to the London French branch which was to be a cause of much embarrassment in the bitter quarrels which marred the last years of the International — see Chapters XIV and XV.

[2] Interest in the then defunct International had been revived by the attempted assassination of the German Emperor, which provided the pretext for Bismarck's anti-socialist legislation of that year.

[3] James Knowles to Marx, I.I.S.G., July 21, 1878. Knowles considered Marx's corrections, which were numerous, insufficiently important to justify publication.

[4] The magazine was edited by Harriet Law, a member of the General Council since June 18, 1867, and later an energetic rationalist. Marx's article was reprinted in *Labour Monthly*, September 1954.

After all this, it is a little surprising to read in the *Workman's Advocate* for October 1, 1865, reporting the London Conference, that 'Dr. Marx proposed, and Le Lubez seconded, the following question for the Congress. "The religious idea : its relations to the social, political, and intellectual development of the people." ' The resolution was supported not only by the Parisians, Fribourg and Tolain, but also by the Belgian, de Paepe, the Pole, Holtorp and, strangest of all, by the Englishman, Howell! Nor was Howell's support in any way ambiguous. While he would not countenance any attack on 'men's religious opinions', they must sooner or later attempt a rational assessment of religion 'as an ethical and philosophical principle interwoven with every social and political movement'. The English habit of avoiding discussions on fundamental principles was 'one reason of our slow progress'. The other Englishmen did in fact oppose the inclusion of this item on the agenda as tending, in Weston's words, 'to destroy the association'. Marx made no intervention, beyond formally introducing the motion and it was finally adopted by only a small majority.

On balance, the evidence supports Marx's account. Howell's memory after a lapse of thirteen years was certainly patchy. The draft agenda submitted to the Conference by the General Council contained, as Marx said, no mention of religion.[1] Nor did any subsequent policy statement or programme issued by the General Council. On the other hand, a draft programme drawn up in France some weeks before the London Conference contained the question : 'Is morality derived from religion?'[2] While Marx's part in the proceedings is at first sight puzzling, there seems no doubt about the French origin of the proposal. On no other occasion did Marx attempt — as did Bakunin — to introduce religion into working-class politics. It seems likely that on this occasion he agreed to propose the motion formally, as a conciliatory gesture towards the Parisians who shared Proudhon's conviction that religion and the church should be attacked as inimical to the working class.

[1] See G. Del Bo's Bibliography, *La Premierè Internationale, Imprimés 1864–1876*, Paris, 1961, Nos. 5 and 6.

[2] *Avenir National*, July 18, 1865, quoted by J. L. Puech, *Le Proudhonisme dans l'Association Internationale des Travailleurs*, Paris, 1907, pp. 95-6. See also *Congrès Ouvrier*, edited by M. Fribourg, Paris, 1865, p. 3. The proposal came originally in an agenda sent by the Paris branch and signed by Fribourg and Ch. Limousin. In this and other respects, the Paris programme was completely Proudhonist.

No official report of the London Conference appeared.[1] After some unofficial reports had been published in the French Press, Marx suggested that for this reason the official report should be postponed until May of the following year. As a pretext for postponement, this was flimsy and nothing more was heard of the matter. In fact a good deal went on at the London Conference that never found its way into the Press. 'The real business of the Conference', Marx wrote later, 'was transacted in private sittings, not at the semi-public meetings in Adelphi Terrace.'[2] Perhaps nothing could be published about the private sittings without embarrassing one or the other — or both — of the French sections which had joined battle over the Lefort case. Possibly, too, a full account of the debates might have caused legal difficulties for the delegates returning to France. But it is clear from the published accounts that the London Conference marked the beginning of a controversy that reached one climax with the defeat of the Proudhonists at the Brussels Congress in 1868 and a second and fatal climax with the expulsion of the Bakuninists at the Hague in 1872.

THE POLISH QUESTION AGAIN

Almost as soon as the Conference dispersed, the controversy over Poland was resumed. Vésinier[3] wrote an attack on the Polish decision in the *Écho de Verviers* and Jung was instructed by the General Council to reply.[4] Luigi Wolf suddenly reappeared on the Council to protest against Jung's article and also to defend the general political position of Mazzini. Mazzini's social ideas, he argued, were appropriate for Italy where 'there were no Socialists . . . in the French sense of the word'.[5] Afterwards Marx complained that 'The old Mazzinism of Odger, Howell, Cremer, etc., found an outlet. Le Lubez heated the flames',[6] and the General Council repudiated Jung's article.

Marx carefully prepared his counter-attack. By accident

[1] Marx wrote an account of the Conference. The manuscript is in the Institute of Marxism-Leninism, Moscow and has now been published. See *Karl Marx, Chronik seines Lebens*, Moscow, 1934, p. 246.

[2] *Secular Chronicle*, August 1878.

[3] A republican journalist, at one time secretary to Eugène Sue and later author of a history of the Paris Commune.

[4] G.C. *Minutes*, January 9, 1866.   [5] G.C. *Minutes*, March 6, 1866.

[6] Marx to Engels, March 24, 1866.

or design all six Corresponding Secretaries — Marx himself
for Belgium, Dupont for France, Jung for Switzerland, Longuet
for Italy, Lafargue for Spain and Bobczynski for Poland —
were of the same mind. The next meeting of the General
Council was carefully prepared. First, the previous meeting
was declared invalid, since Wolf was no longer a member and
had no right to attend.[1] Then Cesare Orsini [2] was produced to
convince the English — for the second time [3] — that Mazzini
was repudiated by the advanced socialist workers on the Continent. It all worked perfectly and the English members
agreed to withdraw their repudiation of Jung. The Mazzinists,
outmanœuvred, retired once again and this time permanently
from the General Council.

For Marx, however, it was not sufficient to defeat his
opponents by good caucus tactics. They must also be conquered intellectually. Vésinier, now in Belgium, was preaching
the pure gospel of de Paepe in the *Écho de Verviers*. Why, he
demanded, should the forthcoming Geneva Congress of the
International concern itself with Poland when 'the serfs of
Russia and Poland have just been freed by Russia, while the
Polish nobility and priesthood have always refused to give
freedom to their own'. The International, he concluded, was
in danger of 'degenerating into a committee of nationalities'
and so serving the aims of 'Bonapartism'.[4]

On the General Council Vésinier was defended not only by
Le Lubez but also by Weston who attacked the Council for
'not having discussed a single social question'.[5] It was time,
Marx felt, for a reply to be made in the English organ of
the International and he appealed to Engels to deal with
the matter. Engels replied in a series of three articles in the
Commonwealth, making at the same time his first public appearance in connection with the International.

In his first article [6] Engels recalled the activities of the
Chartists and Fraternal Democrats on behalf of Poland. The
German workers had an even greater interest in Polish

[1] Le Lubez, who had resigned with Wolf, returned to the General
Council for a time as representative of the Greenwich and Deptford branch.
[2] Brother of Felice Orsini, executed for his attempt on the life of Napoleon
III in 1858.   [3] For the first occasion, see Chapter V.
[4] Quoted in Marx to Engels, January 15, 1866.
[5] G.C. *Minutes*, January 9, 1866.
[6] Engels. 'What have the Working Classes to do with Poland?' *Commonwealth*, March 24, 1866.

independence. Prussia's share in the partition of Poland had strengthened reaction in Germany by tying its leading State to Russian policy. Russia was not merely, like Austria or Prussia, a country saddled with a reactionary government. Lacking a labour movement she was a reactionary nation. This state of affairs would not last, since 'whenever the working classes of Russia form a political programme, and their programme contains the liberation of Poland, then, but not till then, Russia as a nation will be out of court too, and the Government of the Czar will remain alone under indictment'. In the meantime the entire European working class was concerned to secure Poland's independence.

If German emancipation required freedom for Poland, it also required freedom for Italy. Vésinier had argued that in supporting the independence of the various nationalities, the International was playing into the hands of Napoleon III who made use of the disruptive tendencies of nationalism to further his own imperial aims. Engels replied by drawing a clear distinction between nationalities and nations, a distinction which Mazzini, who tended to support national movements indiscriminately, never made. In many countries, Engels argued, there were nationalities such as the Highland Scots, the Welsh and the Bretons, but 'nobody will give to these remnants of peoples long gone by the title of nations . . .'. Nor was language by itself an adequate criterion of nationhood. German speakers in Switzerland and Alsace did not want to be part of Germany and French speakers in Belgium and Switzerland did not want to be part of France. The definition of a nation must include territorial, economic and cultural factors.

Here then, Engels claimed, lay the difference between 'the principle of nationalities' which could be misused by a Bonaparte to disrupt rival nations and 'the old democratic and working class tenet as to the right of the great European nations to separate and independent existence'. Such nations were historically constituted entities of proved viability. Many nationalities, on the other hand, which had 'figured for a longer or shorter period on the stage of history were finally absorbed as integral portions into one or the other of these more powerful nations whose greater vitality enabled them to overcome greater obstacles'.[1]

[1] *Commonwealth*, March 31, 1866. Like Marx, Engels thought that the Slav peoples in the Austrian Empire were just such nationalities, destined

After Engels's articles had appeared the controversy continued on the General Council. Paul Lafargue, Marx's future son-in-law, but still strongly under the influence of Proudhon, expressed the view that nationalities and nations alike were obsolete. These arguments, however, were only preparations for the full-scale attack which the French were preparing for the forthcoming Congress at Geneva, an attack which included the Polish question while ranging much wider.

THE GENEVA CONGRESS: PRELIMINARY SKIRMISHING

In preparation for the clash, Marx wrote a series of *Instructions* for the General Council's delegation to Geneva. He did not attend this Congress or any other except the last at the Hague, in 1872. But he devoted, as he told his friend Kugelmann on August 23, 'a great deal of time to the preparations for Geneva', and his *Instructions* laid down with the greatest clarity the line which the Council's delegation was to follow.[1] Without this guide it seems likely that the General Council delegates, lacking any very firm ideological position from which to operate, would have allowed the Parisian Proudhonists to dominate the proceedings. Even as it was, they left their mark on the decisions to an extent that Marx found disturbing.

The ten Parisians — a much larger delegation than at London the year before — were voluble, and as Eccarius suggested,[2] their lack of experience 'in the transaction of business at public deliberative gatherings' may help to explain their strange behaviour. They objected unsuccessfully to the election of a standing committee to settle the order of business 'as

to be absorbed by the Germans. Apart from this, his views on what constituted a nation were identical with those later expressed by Lenin in his controversy with Liebman (Hersch) and Stalin in his controversy with Otto Bauer and the Bund. See V. I. Lenin, *Critical Remarks on the National Question*, October–December 1913, Moscow, 1951, and J. V. Stalin, *Marxism and the National Question*, 1913. Reprinted in *Marxism and the National and Colonial Question*, 1936. Engels's *Commonwealth* articles, however, were only republished by Ryazanoff in 1916.

[1] The *Instructions* were written by Marx at the end of August 1866. They were published some time after the Geneva Congress in the *Working Man*, March 1 and April 6, 1867, together with a fairly full report of the Congress proceedings, and in Collet's two other papers, *Le Courrier International* and *The International Courier*, beginning February 16 and 20 respectively. For Marx's authorship, see his letter to his daughter, Jenny, on September 5, 1866. Lafargue translated the *Instructions* into French for the Congress, see *Soc.* vol. XXV, p. 447.

[2] *Commonwealth*, September 8, 1866.

a resignation of their sovereign right to dispose of themselves'. This was anti-authoritarianism with a vengeance. The coercion of individuals by the collective had been anathema to Proudhon and the Parisians were more than ever under his posthumous sway. 'At the inception of the movement, a few years earlier', wrote J. L. Puech, 'although a small number of workers had read a negligible portion of the works of Proudhon, it would be truer to say that the ideas of the proletariat were coming to coincide involuntarily with those of the Socialist thinker in his declining years, rather than that they had undergone his direct influence. But in 1866 the similarity of opinion was conscious and the Mutualists of Paris knew themselves to be Proudhonists.' [1]

The French made a renewed attempt to allow 'every well-meaning individual' to participate fully in Congresses; as at the London Conference, the English insistence on delegates being fully accredited won the day. The French then raised yet again the demand that only 'productive labourers' should be admitted to the International. As a compromise it was agreed that each national section should decide on its own rules of admission.

TRADE UNIONS AND STRIKES

The first theoretical dispute at the Congress concerned the attitude to be taken towards trade unions and strikes. Here the English were clear enough and their case, which was that of the whole General Council, had been put with masterly brevity by Marx in his sixth instruction. This dealt with 'the past, present and future' of trade unions. It stressed the inherent inequality of bargaining power between capital and labour. The workers could only offset this disadvantage, to a certain extent, by organisation. Beginning as spontaneous attempts of the workers to limit competition among themselves, trade unions were developing into 'centres of organisation of the working class, as the medieval municipalities and communes did for the middle class'. Starting as agencies of a scattered, guerrilla warfare, the unions must develop into 'organising centres of the working class in the broad interest of its complete emancipation. They must aid every social and political movement tending in that direction'. Finally, in a tactful reference to the craft narrowness of the New Model unions,

[1] *Op. cit.*, p. 120.

Marx urged the organised workers to 'look carefully after the interests of the worst paid trades, such as the agricultural labourers, rendered powerless by exceptional circumstances'. Trade Unions, in short, 'must convince the world at large that their efforts, far from being narrow and selfish, aim at the emancipation of the downtrodden millions'.

So far had Marx developed from his position of having completely ignored trade unions in the *Inaugural Address*. For him, as for the English, trade union struggle represented a necessary phase through which the workers must pass on the road to full emancipation. For the French they were a barbaric expedient, necessary perhaps, as a last resort in particular circumstances, but contributing nothing of value to the movement. In a memorandum read to the Congress by Chemalé the Mutualists condemned the prospect of 'strike against strike . . . war between masters and men . . . to the detriment of all.' 'Capital', they added, 'is as necessary to production as labour; the causes of conflict lie entirely in their present relations which it is essential to transform. We must establish exchange based on reciprocity.' [1]

Odger, Eccarius and Cremer presented the British case, with Cremer referring once again to the decisive builders' strike and the employers' threat to introduce foreign labour. A powerful case was made by Dupont who claimed that through strikes and the degree of organisation they entailed, the English trade unions had attained a level 'of compact organisation' which 'no other European country' could show. By comparison, the French policy of developing producers' co-operation would prove ineffective because of the limited resources available to the workers.[2]

The issue was settled by a compromise which, while conceding that strikes were sometimes necessary under existing conditions, commended to the workers the 'more elevated aim' of replacing the wage system by an economy 'based on justice and reciprocity'. With this explanatory resolution, Marx's

---

[1] *Mémoire des délégués français au Congrès de Genève.* Quoted by Fribourg, *op. cit.*, p. 76. Cf. Proudhon's comment on the Act of 1864 which legalised trade unions in France. 'I especially object to the new law: association for the purpose of increasing or lowering wages is entirely the same as association for the purpose of increasing or lowering the prices of food and other commodities.' *De la capacité politique des classes ouvrières*, Paris, 1865, p. 428.

[2] *The Working Man*, June 1, 1867. A similar argument had been used against Weston in the *Beehive*, April 29, 1865.

I

instruction on trade unionism was endorsed.[1]

Congress passed unanimously and without debate Marx's instruction calling for an international collection of statistics on labour conditions in very considerable detail, including wages, the incidence of piece and night work, working hours, health conditions and the state of trade. Though the resolution was to be passed unanimously on many subsequent occasions, it was never implemented. The labour movement was to lack for a long time the organisation and equipment for carrying through so ambitious a project.[2]

THE LEGAL EIGHT-HOUR DAY

The next controversial item was the instruction proposing the legal limitation of the working day to eight hours. This was the first occasion on which the issue was raised internationally. It was to become the slogan of the Second International on its foundation in 1889 and also the main issue of trade union policy around which the battle between the 'New' and 'Old' Unionism was to be waged in England. When Marx raised the question it must have been meant as a deliberate challenge to the Proudhonists who rejected State intervention in all spheres, including labour relations. 'In enforcing such laws', Marx insisted, 'the working class do not fortify governmental power. On the contrary, they transform that power now used against them, into their own agency.' This served as yet another bond between Marx and the British workers' representatives.

As might have been anticipated, Fribourg opposed the resolution 'in the name of freedom of contract and of the contracting parties'.[3] Odger defended the instruction and quoted 'Robert Owen, the famous communist', to the effect that, in a properly organised society, three hours' work a day would suffice. Cremer also spoke in support citing the decision of the recently formed National Labor Union in the United States to begin a movement for the eight-hour day.[4] While on

[1] *Working Man*, June 1, 1867.

[2] Marx was to revive this project in the *Questionnaire* which he wrote for the French Socialist Party in 1881, but it was still to remain a paper project until after the end of the First World War.

[3] Fribourg, *op. cit.*, p. 88.

[4] The N.L.U. was successful in persuading Congress to limit the hours of federal employees to eight in 1868.

other issues the Proudhonists could rally some support outside Paris, on this they found themselves isolated. The resolution was carried with only the ten Parisians voting against.

FEMALE AND CHILD LABOUR. STANDING ARMIES

In opposing the next resolution on female and child labour, the Proudhonists won much more support. Marx's instruction had stated baldly that child labour was a 'sound and legitimate tendency' since productive work was beneficial to the full development of the personality and even adults should 'work not only with the brain but with the hands too' — a view he was to express in more detail in his *Critique of the Gotha Programme* in 1875.[1] While this was consistent with Marx's general outlook on the progressive nature of industrialisation, even under capitalism and on the need to eliminate the distinction between mental and manual work as well as the contrasts between town and country, it inevitably aroused a good deal of opposition. What was wrong, explained the instruction, was not child labour itself but the excessive amount of it imposed by capitalism. Hours should be strictly limited. Education, moreover, must be mental, physical and technical. Like child labour, women's labour was also beneficial, subject to suitable legal restrictions safeguarding their health.

It was the support given to female labour which aroused the hostility of most of the Proudhonists. Women, they maintained, 'are not made to work hard; their place is at the family fireside'. Varlin of the Paris Book-binders, however, broke with his fellow-mutualists on this issue.[2] While he was against exploitation he thought that the opportunity of doing paid work was essential for the emancipation of women. Matthew Lawrence of the London Tailors, a former Secretary of the Glasgow Trades Council, said that the Congress should 'aim at being practical rather than utopian'. The word 'utopian' was used in its Marxian sense, for Lawrence went on to urge the need for 'gaining a comprehension of the social movement and not to think of imposing upon it our personal

[1] London, n.d., pp. 14 and 33.
[2] Together with Bourdon he had submitted a minority report on education and the family opposing the memorandum drawn up by his colleagues. Fribourg, *op. cit.*, pp. 66-7.

sentiments and theories'.[1] In terms of a later jargon, Lawrence
was advancing a 'historicist' and opposing an 'open' view of
society. The laws of 'social movement', he implied, were to
be understood and made use of, but they set limits to what
could be achieved. If the laws of historical development drew
women into industry, breaking down in the process the established pattern of family life, this had to be faced and it would
be of more use to humanise than to deplore the process. It is
possible that Lawrence acquired this still not very familiar point
of view and mode of expression from Marx. If so, the Scottish
tailor proved more receptive to Marx's philosophy than any of
his English colleagues on the General Council. Despite his
arguments, however, the Council's resolution was adopted only
with an amendment prohibiting female labour.

There was more general agreement on the attitude to be
adopted towards standing armies. Marx's instruction on this
dealt with the economic cost of militarism. Instead of standing
armies there should be a 'universal arming of the people and
universal teaching of the use of arms'. As a temporary expedient, standing armies might be reduced in size and each
citizen would serve for a short time so as to receive the rudi-
ments of military training. This instruction brought out, quite
deliberately, the General Council's opposition to pacifism as
well as to militarism. Nor was there any expression of pacifist
ideas at the Congress — such as those of the League of Peace
and Freedom, founded only a year later with Cremer's help.
Marx's instruction was passed unanimously, together with a
French amendment urging the arming of the people and a
German resolution recommending military training for the
workers.

The 'Religious Idea' Again

The course of the next debate on 'The Religious Idea'
tended to confirm Marx's subsequent account of the episode
as against Howell's. On only two items — 'The Religious
Idea' and 'International Credit' — did Marx's instructions say
merely that 'the initiative should be given to the French'. No
member of the General Council took part in the discussion on

---

[1] Cf. *Communist Manifesto*. The Communists 'do not set up any
sectarian principles of their own, by which to shape and mould the proletarian movement'. M.E.S.W., vol. 1, p. 44.

religion. Six Swiss, one Pole and Tolain from Paris spoke to the motion after which a curiously phrased resolution was passed, stating that 'the members of the Congress were unanimous in favour of ridding the human race of every variety of religious prejudices. It desired that note be taken of this unanimity and therefore it passed to the next question.' The resolution could be interpreted as opposing religion or as merely deploring 'religious prejudices'. It was not a statement of policy but of opinion, of which 'note' was formally taken. It could mean much or little according to taste and it is clear that the General Council, wishing to get the question disposed of with as little fuss as possible, did not oppose the resolution but accepted a form of words which would render it harmless. Marx's statement that the question was introduced 'at the instance of the Paris delegates' was no doubt true. Hostility to religion was kept out of the programme of the Association, though it was to feature prominently in the platform of the Bakuninist Alliance where it did a certain amount of harm to the International.

POLAND: A COMPROMISE DECISION

The London Conference, against strong opposition from France and Belgium had put the Polish question on the agenda for Geneva. Marx prepared a careful statement in his *Instructions*, covering the Polish issue. He knew that while de Paepe and Vésinier had opposed the Polish insurrection, the French would confine themselves to claiming that it was not the concern of a workers' international. Marx, therefore, set himself to answer more succinctly the question which Engels had dealt with in his *Commonwealth* articles on *What have the Working Classes to do with Poland?* Poland, he explained, was a workers' cause because the enemies of the working class, the 'aristocrats and bourgeois, look upon the dark Asiatic power in the background as a last resource against the advancing tide of working-class ascendancy'. Russian power could be broken 'only . . . by the restoration of Poland upon a democratic basis'. Until that happened, the working-class movement would find itself 'continuously interrupted, checked and retarded'.[1]

[1] *Working Man*, March 8, 1867.

At Geneva the Polish resolution was moved by Card [1] and seconded by the German-Swiss, Johann Philipp Becker. It embodied the substance of Marx's draft. The French, who opposed the resolution as 'purely political', submitted a remarkable draft of their own. While Proudhon in his last years had been pro-Russian and anti-Polish,[2] his French followers condemned Russia wholeheartedly, not only for what it was, but for what it might give rise to. Their draft read: 'We, partisans of freedom, protest against despotisms; we condemn and emphatically denounce the organisation and the social tendencies of Russian despotism, as leading inevitably to the most brutalising form of communism; but, as delegates at an economic congress, we consider that we have nothing to say about the political reconstruction of Poland'.[3]

As a concession to the French, Becker produced a compromise resolution declaring that since, with the development of the international labour movement, all despotisms would disappear, the democratic reconstruction of Poland would then follow as a matter of course.[4] Becker's amendment, which conceded the substance of the French case, was carried. This was a serious defeat for Marx, though he could derive some consolation from the fact that the English delegates, at least, had given him unanimous and consistent support.[5]

ORGANISATIONAL MATTERS

After the Congress had finished its political discussions it turned to organisational matters. First came the question of block fees from affiliated organisations. It had been agreed that individual members were to pay a shilling for their card and a subsequent annual contribution of a halfpenny. It was suggested by the General Council that trade unions should affiliate at special rates to be fixed by themselves. The French inevitably opposed. The fact that in their own country they were only allowed to collect money from individuals no doubt helped to influence their decision. But they argued that any

---

[1] Pseudonym for Cwierciakiewicz, editor of the short-lived Zürich paper, *Der Weisse Adler*.

[2] P. J. Proudhon, *La Guerre et la paix*, Brussels, 1862, vol. II, p. 448 and *Du principe fédératif*, Paris, 1863, p. 286.

[3] Fribourg, *op. cit.*, p. 85.

[4] *Working Man*, June 29, 1867.

[5] Cf. Oscar Testut, *L'Internationale*, 3rd edition, Paris, 1871, p. 127.

reduction of the rate for organisations would savour of privilege and violate the principle of equal rights and obligations for all. Matthew Lawrence warned the Congress that this would simply frighten away the unions whose affiliation was so clearly desirable. After a long wrangle the French proposed, as an exceptional measure for the current year, an initial contribution from affiliated bodies of 3d. a head. The compromise, which deliberately postponed a final solution, was gratefully accepted.[1]

The French did not understand, and did not want to understand, the special problems of trade unions in Britain. Next they treated the Congress to an outbreak of 'ouvrierisme'. The London Conference had declared, against strenuous French opposition, that non-manual workers could be members of the International. Towards the end of the Geneva Congress, Tolain, no doubt preoccupied by the bitter aftermath of the Lefort case, proposed that in future only workers should be eligible as delegates to Congresses of the International. Believing, as they did, that existing society generated a class struggle, they saw the only solution in the growth of producers' organisations, eschewing politics and building the new society from the ground upwards. Such a movement, in their view, would be better without the help of doctors, lawyers, middle-class journalists and *savants*.

The English were strongly opposed to this suggestion. Not only because of their experience with Positivists and Christian Socialists but because of the impression which Marx had made on them, they thought that the policy of exclusion was monstrous. Cremer regretted that the 'invidious question' had been raised. The movement in Britain, he pointed out, owed much to members of the General Council who were not manual workers. 'Among those members I will mention one only, Citizen Marx, who has devoted all his life to the triumph of the working classes.' Carter, the hairdresser, added that Marx had deliberately stayed away from Geneva so that the first Congress at least should be purely working class, but that this should not be taken as a precedent. 'The middle class', he reminded the delegates, 'only triumphed when it allied itself with men of Science.' The workers also have much to

---

[1] It was ignored by the General Council, on Cremer's advice. G.C. *Minutes*, October 2 and 9, 1866. Had it been operated, the Bricklayers would have been asked to contribute about £50, the Carpenters and Joiners over £90.

gain from such men, particularly those who could expose 'the fallacies of middle class political economy'. The French amendment was narrowly lost by twenty-five votes to twenty.

A month later Marx confessed to Kugelmann that he had entertained 'great fears for the first Congress at Geneva. On the whole, however, it turned out better than I expected.' But the strength of Proudhonism was disturbing. Proudhon's 'anti-authoritarian individualism' had attracted support from students and, through them, from workers, 'particularly those of Paris who, as workers in luxury trades, are strongly attached, without knowing it, to the old muck'.

Geneva was a half-way house. The Congress had committed itself to support for the legal eight-hour day. On other issues — Poland, strikes, female and child labour — the strength of the Proudhonists had been sufficient to prevent clear-cut decisions. The debates must have constituted a political education for many of the delegates, particularly the English who, however experienced in trade unionism and radical politics, were newcomers in the field of ideological disputes. In retrospect, Geneva appears as the first tentative encounter in the conflict between centralism and anti-authoritarianism which deepened in intensity throughout the history of the International and dominated its closing years.

CHAPTER VIII

From Geneva to Brussels

THE Geneva Congress had little impact in England. *The Times* printed only the briefest report and did not use the detailed accounts which Eccarius had sent from Geneva.[1] A significant exception was the Positivist *Fortnightly Review* which published on December 1, 1866 an article from its editor, George Henry Lewes, who regarded the Congress as a landmark in European history. Almost unnoticed by the Press, he wrote, the Geneva Congress would be regarded by historians as the most important event of the year. It marked the entry of a new class into the social arena and so was comparable to the rise of the Communes in the twelfth century and to the meeting of the States General in Paris in 1789. 'The Third Estate was formed when citizens began to combine', wrote Lewes. 'The artisans are now beginning to combine, and their enormous power, were it only the power of brute force, will soon be felt if it be directed by organisation.'

Lewes noted that the main conflict at Geneva had been between the practical, cautious English, striving through trade union pressure to improve their standard of life within the existing system, and the visionary, revolutionary-minded French, whose intention was 'nothing less than that of removing Industry from its present conditions of Capital and Labour, and substituting universal co-operation'. A similar contrast between English practicality and French doctrinaire revolutionism was drawn by the Christian Socialists, J. M. Ludlow and Lloyd Jones, in *The Progress of the Working Class, 1832–1867* appearing in the following year.[2]

To the French journalists it looked very different. J. Alaux, writing in *Revue Contemporaine*,[3] remarked that while the English and Germans favoured the alien doctrine of State intervention, it was a healthy sign that the French emphasis

---

[1] G.C. *Minutes*, September 18, 1866.   [2] 1867, p. 208.
[3] October 15, 1866.

had all been on 'individual initiative'. The real issue at
Geneva, he concluded, was whether what was clearly a new
force in the world would develop as an aberration from, or
along the lines of, the French Revolution. More forcefully,
Louis Reybaud, in *Revue des Deux Mondes*,[1] contrasted the
innocuous French programme of peaceful co-operation with the
'brutal English formula of the strike'. On this, as on the eight-
hour day, the English had been the evil geniuses of the Congress. The infection of the class struggle, generated by English
trade unions, could spread to France, 'in as much as our neigh-
bours show themselves concerned to send us over the germ'.[2]

Despite such tributes to the French section, Napoleon's
Government became increasingly hostile after Geneva. The
danger of infection to which Reybaud pointed impressed the
authorities rather more than did the anti-political and anti-
strike arguments which the French delegates had put to the
Congress. Jules Gottraux, returning from Geneva, was arrested
on the frontier and his papers were confiscated. Odger reported this to a meeting of the General Council on September
18. On their way home from Geneva he and Cremer had
intended staying in Paris for a while to make contact with the
French workers. In view of the changed attitude of the French
Government, however, they had cut short their visit and returned to England. The General Council, which had lost
some of its property when Gottraux's papers were confiscated,
later received it back from France after intervention by the
British Foreign Office.

THE LEAGUE OF PEACE AND FREEDOM

By the time of the Lausanne Congress in September 1867,
another international body, the League of Peace and Freedom,
had been set up with strong support from the Reform League.
Its first Conference was scheduled to meet in Geneva at about
the time that the International was to hold its second Congress
in Lausanne. Odger and Cremer were going to Geneva as
delegates from the Reform League and though Cremer was no
longer Secretary to the General Council, Odger was still its

---

[1] November 1, 1866. Reybaud was the author of a well-known account
of socialist doctrines, *Études sur les réformateurs contemporains*, Paris, 1842.
[2] Swiss employers were also afraid that their workers might learn the
habits of trade unionism from the turbulent English — see Chapter VI.

President and relations between the two international bodies assumed a certain delicacy. Marx was against the League because of its heterogeneous character and semi-pacifist leanings. At the same time it was hardly politic to denounce it outright and he suggested to the General Council that there could be no objection to the International's delegates attending the Geneva gathering as individuals. But it would be wrong, he insisted, to send an official delegation from Lausanne. Wars would only cease through the 'union of the working classes of the different countries' and this formed no part of the League's programme.

Marx went on to give an account of the causes of war. One of the main factors since 1848 he believed was the development of large standing armies. These 'were not kept up for international warfare, but to keep down the working classes'. Once formed, however, they constituted in themselves a potent cause of tension leading to war.[1]

Apparently the *Beehive's* report of Marx's speech was not completely accurate.[2] Nevertheless, it is clear that Marx did not lay special stress on economic factors as a major cause of wars. He tended to see their origins in militarism arising, as here, from the exigencies of the class struggle or, as later in the Franco-Prussian War, out of dynastic ambitions or, finally, from the struggle of subjugated nations for independence and unification. Whatever its causes, however, every war and every international policy must be judged by its effect on the power of Russia and Marx concluded his speech with an attack on the 'peace at any price party' which would be strongly represented at Geneva and whose policy would 'leave Russia alone in the possession of the means to make war upon the rest of Europe'.[3]

The International considered its relations with the League on the first day of the Lausanne Congress, September 2, 1867. The General Council's case was presented most forcefully by de Paepe. Peace, to which the League paid lip-service, was impossible without a fundamental 'reorganisation of society'. He went on to stress the economic causes of war and to oppose

---

[1] *Beehive*, August 17, 1867. For the view that the crushing weight of European armaments, while partly due to military ambitions, was also due in part to the danger of revolution, see *The Times*, September 9, 1867, in an editorial criticising the Geneva Conference of the League of Peace and Freedom.

[2] Marx to Engels, September 4, 1867.

[3] *Beehive*, August 17, 1867.

the liberal views prevailing at Geneva. 'War is not only the fruit of monarchical ambition; for example, in the Mexican expedition the real causes of war were the interests of a few capitalists: war results from a disequilibrium in economic and political affairs.' [1]   The view that wars are inevitable under capitalism because of economic disequilibria which force capitalists to seek sources of profit overseas is now exceedingly familiar.   It was incorporated into the Marxist canon by Lenin after gaining ground in socialist circles since the 1890s. But it formed no part of Marx's doctrine and was first given formal expression in the International by César de Paepe at its Lausanne Congress.

Tolain, for once on the side of the General Council, proposed that co-operation should be conditional on the League agreeing to the social emancipation of the working class. Carter of the London hairdressers supported the Council's position from a standpoint of anti-clerical radicalism.   Wars would persist, he prophesied, 'as long as there exist ignorance, nationalities, religion and a clergy . . . Let us fight the priesthood and replace the religion of the clergy by the religion of God and science.'   The main support for the idea of co-operating with the League came from the Swiss.   No English delegate spoke in favour, though there was considerable support for the Peace Conference from members of the Reform League.[2] Tolain's conditions, which were certainly and intentionally unacceptable to the Peace Conference, were endorsed by thirty-two votes to fourteen.[3]

MUTUAL CREDIT AND LAND NATIONALISATION

The Geneva Congress had been mainly concerned with political and industrial questions.   At Lausanne the emphasis was economic and the economics were those of Proudhon. Though the Proudhonists and O'Brienites might differ on land nationalisation, they were in substantial agreement on co-operation and monetary policy.   A committee of the Congress,

---

[1] Cf. the very similar view of Proudhon from whom de Paepe learned a great deal. *La Guerre et la paix*, Brussels, 1862, vol. II, pp. 163-4.

[2] See 'A Voice from the Reform League of England to the Peoples of Europe', *Reynolds's*, June 16, 1867.

[3] *Procès-Verbaux du Congrès de l'Association Internationale des Travailleurs, réunis à Lausanne de 2 au 8 septembre*, 1867, pp. 21-5, and *Beehive*, September 4, 1867.

chaired by Longuet, presented a report on the desirability of
co-operation financed by mutual credit. A. A. Walton of
Brecon, a member of the National Reform League and later
prominent in the T.U.C., had the main hand in drawing up the
report.[1] It recommended a State bank, issuing free credit to
finance production and trade by 'corporations or individuals'.

The resolution was carried. De Paepe, who supported the
Proudhonist position on credit, had himself chaired a commission on the future of co-operation which had reported on
similar lines. Unity was shattered, however, when de Paepe
introduced an amendment recommending land nationalisation
as a subject of study by the movement. This was more than
any of the Proudhonists could accept, though they had mostly
moved away from Proudhon's sweeping rejection of State
ownership. No doubt the increased hostility of the French
Government after Geneva and the strike of the Paris bronze
workers had caused the Proudhonists to re-think some of their
earlier attitudes towards the State. Tolain, who spoke for the
group, now agreed that some kinds of property, including
mines, canals and railways, should be collectively owned. But
others, notably land, 'by their nature must remain individual'.
De Paepe insisted that, as a 'mutualist', he wanted not only
'that the cultivator should be guaranteed by society the full
product of his toil', but also that society in its turn should have
some control over what was produced. Social ownership must
be extended to the land as the most fundamental of all means
of production. After strong opposition from the Swiss, the
amendment was lost by twenty-seven votes to eleven, but de Paepe
managed to raise the matter again at the end of the Congress.
This time he was opposed by Longuet who argued on orthodox
Proudhonist lines that a strong class of independent peasant
proprietors was a necessary safeguard against the power of
the State.

Finally, the Proudhonists carried a resolution affirming the
moral basis of society adding that codes of justice and morality
must be based on human needs and not on superhuman
injunctions.

Marx viewed the results of Lausanne with resignation. So
far, he told Engels, on September 11, he had not been inclined

---

[1] Cf. Walton's pamphlet of 1848, *An Appeal to All Trade Societies on
the necessity for a National Organisation of Trades for the Industrial, Social
and Political Emancipation of Labour.*

to interfere directly in the International's controversies 'until my book was published [1] and our Association had struck roots'. Now the Association had struck roots. Next year at Brussels he would settle accounts with the Proudhonists. Engels, who wrote to Marx on the same day, had independently reached the same conclusions. 'This time', he wrote, 'the French, apparently, have carried the Congress, the number of Proudhonist resolutions is rather large. It is well that the next Congress will be in Belgium, and by that time it may be possible to do something in North Germany, and then with the help of the English to dam this flood.' And, as a good party tactician, Engels was careful to add: 'At the same time these resolutions have no value as long as the General Council remains in London'.

In the year since Geneva the International had made notable headway. 'The Geneva Congress of 1866 had been ignored by the London papers. But the labour question had come to the front in 1867, and *The Times* had lengthy reports of the proceedings at Lausanne.' [2] *The Times* also published an editorial on September 16 which compared the debates at Lausanne with those of the National Labor Congress at Baltimore in 1866 and Chicago in 1867. All three Congresses, it complained, had shown the same shameful ignorance of the laws of political economy. The workers were not, apparently, prepared to recognise that capital originated in 'industry and thrift' or that supply and demand constituted the 'only possible law' governing the relations between capital and labour.

The reactions of Liberal papers were more sympathetic. The *Star* [3] considered Lausanne more important because it was more representative of working-class thought and attitudes than the Peace Conference at Geneva. The *Examiner* saw in the Congress a sign that 'the working class had arrived at the consciousness of its weight and importance in society'. [4]

THE GENERAL COUNCIL

Eccarius's reports in *The Times*, though Marx considered

---

[1] Marx finished correcting the proofs of the first volume of *Capital* seventeen days before the Congress opened at Lausanne.

[2] E. S. Beesly, *Fortnightly Review*, November 1870.

[3] September 10, 1867.

[4] September 7, 1867. Brief notices of Lausanne appeared in a number of other papers, including the *Newcastle Weekly Chronicle*, September 7, and *Glasgow Sentinel*, September 14, 1867.

them useful publicity, got him into serious trouble with his colleagues. Either through his own wording or through a twist imparted by *The Times*, his reports from Lausanne appeared in a tone of condescension and mild derision which infuriated the members of the General Council. Fox, who distrusted what he considered to be 'German dictatorship',[1] called for Eccarius's resignation and Carter withdrew from the Council when this was refused. Marx, by no means for the last time, defended Eccarius against his English critics and the affair subsided.

Such squabbles were still comparatively rare and unimportant. From the modest post of German Secretary Marx was able to exercise effective control over the Council's decisions. Eccarius, the Secretary, and Shaw, the Treasurer, almost always supported him and he had a majority among the other Corresponding Secretaries, consisting of Dupont, Zabicki, Jung and Lafargue.[2] Marx realised a long-cherished wish when he secured the removal of Odger from his post by having the office of President abolished.[3] Marx had not forgotten the willingness of Odger and Cremer to compromise over the Reform Bill agitation. Now, with both removed from office, there were no important differences over policy, whatever personal frictions might occasionally mar the proceedings.

THE IRISH QUESTION

The International had been brought into existence by the Polish insurrection of 1863. Over four years later, within a few months of the passing of the 1867 Reform Act, the radical and labour movement was again confronted by the national question, this time on its own doorstep. On September 18 a group of armed Fenians attacked a prison van and killed a policeman in an attempt to release some of their number who were being taken to Manchester prison. A large number of arrests were made and although the identity of the killer was never established, three of the prisoners were sentenced to death. There was an impression of arbitrariness about the proceedings which resulted in widespread protests and demands

[1] G.C. *Minutes*, October 8 and Marx to Engels, October 4, 1867.
[2] For France, Poland, Switzerland and Spain respectively.
[3] Marx to Engels, October 4, 1867. According to the *Minutes* of the General Council, September 24, 1867, the proposal was formally moved by Hales, but Marx's influence on Hales was already considerable, and remained so for another four years.

for the commutation of the death sentences. Both the International and the Reform League participated in the campaign and the *Beehive*, though it later turned strongly anti-Fenian, then wrote of Fenianism as 'the offspring of injustice and misery'.[1]

A rancorous debate broke out in the Reform League, over a letter in which its President, Beales, while approving the objects of the Fenians, had condemned their tactics. He was attacked on the Council of the League, and most strongly by those of its members who also sat on the General Council of the International — Lucraft, Odger and Weston. The Irish, they maintained, had every right to use force, since force was used to deny them their freedom.

There followed a widespread attack in the Press on the Reform League and on Lucraft and Odger in particular, for encouraging Fenian assassins. Marx was delighted. 'The trial of the Fenians', he told Engels on November 2, 'passed as was expected. You will see what a scandal "ours" have created in the Reform League. I have tried hard to provoke this demonstration by English workers on behalf of Fenianism.'

Beales sent a letter to the League, explaining that he was not opposed to force in all circumstances — not, for example, in Italy — but that in the particular case of Ireland he thought that other methods should be tried first. Odger defended his original standpoint while protesting that he had explained the conditions in which force came to be used rather than advocated its use — an explanation which seems in no way to have appeased his critics. Whatever the differences on the Council of the Reform League — and Baxter-Langley, the Chairman, had difficulty on occasions in making himself heard — all united in denouncing the death sentences and Marx described 'a great demonstration . . . on behalf of the Fenians at which Colonel Dickson, Charles Bradlaugh, Weston, Fox and Cremer had spoken'.[2]

When the question was debated on the General Council, all the speakers seem to have been of one mind. Jung stated that he was 'no abbettor of physical force movements' but that the Irish had no other way of impressing their rulers. Lessner said that Ireland had been denuded of its population and — as if to confute prevailing Malthusian views of which

---

[1] October 19, 1867.   [2] Marx to Engels, November 7, 1867.

Bradlaugh, for one, was a staunch partisan — added that 'no country can be prosperous with a declining population . . . The Irish have a right to revolt against those who drive them out of their country.' Dupont gave clearest expression to the social and political issues involved in Irish independence. He claimed that the Fenians 'affirm the republican form of government, liberty of conscience, no state religion, the produce of labour to the labourer, and the possession of the soil to the people. . . . The English working men who blame the Fenians commit more than a fault . . . they have the same enemy to defeat — the territorial aristocracy and the capitalists.' Weston insisted that in England there was no need for physical force but that in Ireland it was justified. England's crime in 'starving the Irish was far greater than the accidental killing of one man in trying to rescue the Fenian prisoners. . . .'.[1] Finally, a resolution was carried expressing strong sympathy with the Fenians and equally strong condemnation of British policy in Ireland.[2]

On a motion of Marx the discussion was adjourned to the following day, November 20, when a memorandum to Gathorne Hardy, the Home Secretary, was unanimously adopted asking for the sentences to be commuted as 'an act not only of justice but of political wisdom' since the execution of the prisoners would 'greatly impair the moral influence of England on the Continent'. The memorandum, with its liberal sounding phraseology was drafted by Marx.[3]

Apart from drafting the memorandum, Marx had taken little if any part in the debate. His attitude to Fenianism was complex and, as he told Engels in a letter on November 28, required some 'diplomacy' in expression. Neither he nor Engels approved of Fenian tactics, which Engels described as the sort of 'foolishness which is to be found in every conspiracy'.[4]

The General Council resumed its discussion on November 26 when Marx proposed another adjournment. He had not yet clarified his ideas and, to help himself do so, he wrote to Engels

---

[1] *Reynolds's*, November 24, 1867.

[2] *Beehive*, November 23, 1867. Though publishing this summary of the resolution, the *Beehive*, compared with *Reynolds's*, a very cursory account of the discussion on Fenianism. When the final break came between the International and the *Beehive* it came over the paper's handling of the Irish question.

[3] *Soc.* XIII/1, pp. 261-2. The full text is in the G.C. *Minutes*, November 20, and appeared in *Beehive*, November 23, 1867.

[4] Engels to Marx, November 30, 1867.

K

an account of the Irish question which seems to have been substantially the one he gave to the General Council on December 17.[1]

Recent Irish history, thought Marx, could be divided into three phases. The first, from 1783 to 1801, had seen the beginning of Irish industrialisation. The second period, from the Act of Union to the repeal of the Corn Laws in 1846, had seen the destruction of Ireland's infant industries. The third period, following the repeal, had seen the sacrifice of her agriculture in the interests of sheep, cattle and pig-breeding. The English workers must therefore demand the repeal of the Act of Union. Possibly, after separation, a voluntary union between the two countries might develop. But in the meantime the Irish needed self-government, followed by agrarian reform and protective tariffs to encourage the re-development of Irish industry, for which 'the little bit of linen is in no way a substitute'. 'Once the Irish are independent,' concluded Marx, 'necessity will turn them into protectionists, as it did Canada, Australia, etc.' [2] With this letter Marx completed an important stage in his re-assessment of the Irish question. Previously he had considered Ireland's separation from England impossible. Now he thought it 'inevitable although after the separation there may come *federation*'.[3] In this analysis Marx presented the germ of much subsequent socialist thinking on colonialism, under-development and the drive to industrialisation which would follow the political liberation of subject agrarian nations.

Despite the public campaign for reprieve — which included a mass meeting at Clerkenwell Green, addressed by Finlen, Bradlaugh and Weston, with an audience of twenty thousand [4] — the prisoners were executed. Members of the General Council, particularly Odger, Hales and Weston continued to argue Ireland's case on the Council of the Reform League. Odger and Harry carried a resolution calling for

---

[1] Cf. L. E. Golman, 'The Irish Question and the Struggle for Proletarian Internationalism' in *Iz Istorii Borby Marksa i Engelsa za Proletarskuyu Partiyu*, Moscow, 1955, pp. 520-6, based on a draft which Eccarius made of Marx's statement, now in the Institute of Marxism-Leninism, Moscow. The draft includes the sentence: 'The Irish question is not simply a national question, it is a question of land and a question of survival'. Golman gives the date, wrongly, as December 16.

[2] Marx to Engels, November 30, 1867.

[3] Marx to Engels, November 2, 1867.   [4] *Beehive*, November 23, 1867.

manhood suffrage in Ireland. This was not to the liking of
the middle-class members of the League who were still more
disturbed when Mudge and Harry, with the support of Weston,
secured a resolution demanding that the land in Ireland should
be nationalised and leased in lots of from five to thirty acres [1] —
the first demand for land nationalisation in Ireland to come
from an English organisation.

William Gilliver, Chairman of the Birmingham Trades
Council and member of the Cordwainers' Society, who was at
that time corresponding with the General Council with a view
to affiliation,[2] expressed a view common among working-class
radicals when he suggested that the cost of repressing the
Fenians would accentuate the economic depression in England.
He added that Fenianism was being used as a pretext for
opposing Ireland's just claims in the same way that the 'Sheffield
Outrages' were being used against trade unionism in England.[3]
But the anti-Irish prejudices of many workers were strengthened
when on December 13 Fenian sympathisers blew in the wall of
Clerkenwell prison, killing seven people and injuring over a
hundred.

TRIALS IN PARIS. THE LONDON FRENCH

More strictly international issues were also preoccupying
the General Council during the early months of 1868. The
French occupation of Rome at the end of 1867 and the con-
sequent expulsion of Garibaldi from the city led to a protest
meeting organised by the Reform League at which the London
French branch of the International was represented.

The French Government, which was certainly watching the
activities of the London French, began a series of house searches
and arrests among members of the International in Paris. The
French police had seized a number of letters, some of them
from Eugène Dupont, to the Paris section of the International.
Dupont, Corresponding Secretary for France on the General

---

[1] Reform League *Minutes*, January 8, February 21, 1868. George
Howell disapproved strongly of Odger's support for the Irish — see Howell's
Diary, January 8, 16, February 26, 1868.

[2] *Birmingham Daily Post*, December 6, 1867, quoted by F. E. Gillespie.
Labor and Politics in England, 1850–1867. North Carolina, 1927, p. 225.
Gillespie is wrong, however, in her impression that the Birmingham Trades
Council did not affiliate — see Chapter XI.

[3] *Beehive*, January 25, 1868.

Council, 'wrote carelessly about the Fenians to his Paris correspondents, and Bonaparte, dancing on his hind legs before the English government, sent them on to Downing Street'.[1]

Dupont's letters were used against the leading members of the Paris section who were put on trial early in 1868 on a charge of belonging to a political society. The sentences were surprisingly light — thirty days' imprisonment or 100 francs fine. 'It is possible', wrote 'Onslow Yorke' in his *Secret History of the International*,[2] 'that Napoleon was dreaming still of an alliance with these serious artisans, who were, in truth, the only men in Paris whom a Throne, supported by an army like the French, had cause to fear.' The sentences were clearly intended as a warning to Tolain, Murat, Chemalé, Camélinat, Varlin and the others to keep away from politics.

Both the Paris defendants and the General Council were embarrassed by the folly of the International's London French branch which had deteriorated since the days of the Lefort case in 1865. Harbouring a permanent grudge against the General Council for having sided with the Proudhonists, the branch had lived on its grievances and on the more or less intoxicating oratory of such adventurers as Félix Pyat.[3] Though not a member of the International, Pyat had attended an 1848 anniversary dinner of the London French branch in February 1868 where he seems to have proposed the assassination of Napoleon III.[4]

The Brussels section was worried. Its members had assured the General Council that it would be possible to hold the third Congress of the International in their city. But they did not want to be identified with Félix Pyat. They wrote to Marx with a report of Pyat's indiscretions which had appeared in a local newspaper. Marx moved a resolution on the General Council on July 7, clearly stating that Pyat was in no way con-

[1] Marx to Engels, January 11, 1868. Dupont's letters, which for the most part, merely urged the French sections to organise more vigorously on behalf of the International's various solidarity campaigns, are reproduced in the *procès de l'Association Internationale des Travailleurs*, Paris, 1870, 2nd ed., pp. 42-3, 104-5.

[2] 1872, p. 112.

[3] In opposition to the Parisians, the London French gave strong support to the Polish cause — see Leaflet advertising tea-party and public meeting in commemoration of 1863 uprising, January 22, 1867. This, with other leaflets of the London French branch, is in the I.I.S.G.

[4] 'Bold, however, as Pyat was in his writings, he was physically a coward.' Ernest A. Vizetelly, *My Adventures in the Commune*, 1914, p. 120. Cf. G. D. H. Cole, *op. cit.*, p. 149.

nected with the International. The London French branch
came in for some scathing attacks in the discussion, and relations, which had been cool, became frigid.

THE BRUSSELS AGENDA

By now the time of the Council was increasingly taken up
with preparing the agenda for the third Congress.   By July
this had been completed with five items selected for discussion.
These topics — credit, machinery, education, land and strikes
— were largely those suggested by the King's Lynn branch
which Applegarth had founded the year before.   Two of the
subjects were then debated on the General Council.   At a
formative and fluid stage in the growth of the labour movement,
the Council was serving as an important forum for discussions
on principles.   Its debates reflected and may to some extent
have influenced the development of working-class thought in
England.

A significant discussion on the effects of machinery was
opened by Marx [1] who treated the subject with characteristic
power and sweep against its historical background.   So far
from alleviating the burden of labour, machinery had at first
resulted in an inhuman prolongation of the working day.   Only
in the last few decades had the hours of labour begun to be
reduced and the capitalists had replied to this both by improving machinery and by increasing the intensity of labour.
As a result of overwork it would 'soon be necessary to limit
the working day to eight hours'.   Another effect of machinery
had been to draw women and children into the factory system
with results that were in the long term beneficial but immediately 'abominable'.

Some would argue that the hardships caused by machinery
were temporary and that, by widening markets, employment
must eventually increase.   Marx did not hold this view.
Mechanisation was a continuous process and 'if it attracts and
gives employment to large numbers at one time it continually
throws large numbers out of employment.   There is a continual surplus of displaced population, not as the Malthusian
asserts a surplus population in relation to the produce of the
country, but a surplus where labour has been superseded by more
productive agencies.'   Mechanisation in farming produced

[1] *Beehive*, March 7, 1868.

a rural surplus which flocked into the towns, exercising 'a wage-lowering pressure upon the labour market. The state of the East of London is one of the phenomena it produces.' Machinery, in fact, did not only hurt those workers directly displaced; its worst victims were to be found in non-mechanised occupations. However, machinery was not only disastrous but also revolutionary in its social effects, leading 'on the one hand to associated, organised labour, on the other to the disintegration of all formerly existing social and family relations'.[1]

The case against Marx was put once again by Weston. Marx, he maintained, had drawn all his examples from the textile industry; had he considered others, for example building, a different picture would have emerged. When 'a man with a machine could do in ten hours what required ten days if done by hand, this would not diminish the aggregate demand for labour'. This was consistent with Weston's earlier argument on wages which had been based on an implied wages fund theory. If there is a fixed wages fund, the total demand for labour will remain unaffected by increases in productivity.

Weston had argued that 'if it rained hats from heaven for people to wear for nothing that would not diminish the aggregate demand for labour'. A tailor drew attention to the problem of frictional unemployment. 'If it rains clothes from heaven', he asked, 'and the money now spent for clothes be devoted to the building of houses, the carpenters' and the masons' work done by machinery, how many superseded tailors would find employment in the building trade?'

Hales supported Marx, making use of the concept of demand inelasticity. Machinery, the effects of which he had experienced since childhood, reduced prices and admittedly increased demand, but rarely enough to employ fully the labour displaced. This was especially true since, with machinery 'the labour of grown men was constantly displaced by that of women and children'. Hales did not condemn machinery as such — only its effects under the existing social system. After Eccarius had made a powerful speech in support, Marx carried a resolution stating that while machinery in the hands of the capitalist class had proved a most powerful instrument of despotism and extortion, its development also created the

---

[1] *Beehive*, August 1, 1868; reprinted in *Labour Monthly*, July 1956. In this speech Marx gave the General Council a popular précis of the main historical theme in *Capital*, vol. I.

material conditions necessary for replacing the wages system by a truly social system of production.[1]

Eccarius then opened a discussion on the reduction of the working day.[2] Taking his examples from the conditions of women in tailoring, he argued for reduced hours and increased factory inspection. Excessive hours were detrimental to health and Eccarius cited cases in which the death rate had fallen during periods of unemployment caused by the cotton famine in Lancashire and trade depression in East London. Reduced hours, he thought, would increase the demand for labour. Weston, the Owenite, had opposed the resolution on the effects of machinery and Milner, the O'Brienite, representing the National Reform League, opposed the agitation for a shorter working day on the grounds that it would reduce the amount of wealth produced. A demand for higher wages would be more effective, he thought, in improving conditions.

On one point Marx disagreed with both Milner and Eccarius.[3] Where working hours had been reduced, usually in the most mechanised industries, the result had been to stimulate further mechanisation with resulting increases both in productivity and technological unemployment. The case for reduced hours should be based not on its effect on unemployment but on the workers' need for health, education and culture.

The discussions on the General Council were followed almost at once by the Brussels Congress which assembled on September 6 and dispersed on the 15th. It was the longest Congress ever held by the International. It was also unusually well attended, with ninety-nine delegates, including twelve from Britain. The twelve comprised Dupont, Eccarius, Jung, Shaw, Cohn, Lucraft, Cowell Stepney, Lessner and four delegates who played little part in the International before, after, or for that matter, during the Congress.[4] The unusual size of the General Council's delegation probably reflected

[1] *Beehive*, August 1, 8 and G.C. *Minutes*, August 11, 1868.

[2] This was a special interest of his — he published a pamphlet on the *Hours of Labour* in 1872, see Chapter XV.

[3] *Beehive*, August 22, 1868, printed in G.C. *Minutes* with a correction in ink.

[4] *Troisième Congrès de l'Association Internationale des Travailleurs, Compte Rendu Officiel*, Brussels, 1868, pp. 52-3. The last four delegates were: Philippe Matens, a French engineer from London; Frederick Dean, a blacksmith; John Foster, senior, a carpenter; and John Foster, junior, an engineer. An interested observer at the Congress was Auguste Blanqui

Marx's determination to inflict a decisive defeat on the Proudhonists, a task made easier by the presence of fifty-five delegates
from Belgium.

ATTITUDE TO WAR

The first debate dealt with the attitude of the labour movement to war. Henri, from Paris, denounced the French expedition to Mexico as an example of the evils of autocracy. De
Paepe elaborated what was to become the standard socialist
view. The cause of war, he insisted, was not to be found in
'the individuality of kings and princes. . . . It lay in the
economic institutions of society.' The way to end wars was
for the workers, internationally, to refuse to make supplies.

The final resolution, carried with only three dissentients,
was a straightforward amalgam of the conflicting views, though
it ended by endorsing de Paepe's proposal. The basic causes
of war were economic, but arbitrary force resulting 'from
centralisation and from despotism' was an important con-
tributory factor. Finally, since any future 'war between the
peoples . . . could not be considered anything else than a
civil war [1] . . . since it would be waged between the producers. . . . The Congress urges the workers to cease work
should war break out in their respective countries. . . .'

Despite the qualifications, the resolution was a triumph for
de Paepe and his Belgian followers who had originated the idea
of a general strike against war. The English, though they
voted for the resolution, do not seem to have taken it very
seriously and Marx regarded it as a piece of 'Belgian stupidity',
since 'the working class is not yet sufficiently organised to exert
a decisive influence on the course of events'.[2]

STRIKES AND MACHINERY

The next debate on the strike weapon was remarkable for
the unanimity with which it was approved. Even the Parisians,

— see Marx to Engels, September 25, 1868. For Blanqui's views on the
International and his criticism of the Proudhonists, see his posthumously
published *Critique sociale*, Paris, 1885, vol. II, pp. 163-5 and 171-4.
   [1] The phrase 'for benefit of Russia' was omitted from Eccarius's report
— see Marx to Engels, September 16, 1868.
   [2] Marx to Engels, September 16, 1868. See also Marx to Eccarius and
Lessner, September 10, 1868, giving them their instructions for the Congress.

Tolain and Tartaret, now supported strikes 'as a means of transition from our present state of affairs to one of association'. Shaw, as a British trade unionist, defended strikes as a means of improving conditions under the existing system and showed the normal working-class suspicion of 'would-be economists' who tried to prove that they only brought ruin. The suggestion by Brismée, for the Belgians, that the International should organise a central strike fund was opposed by Lucraft who feared that it would reinforce the impression that the Association encouraged strikes. But Cohn, of the Cigar Makers, was keen on the suggestion. While the International should not 'promote strikes . . . it was bound to assist men who were on strike, provided their cause was just'. Further, unless the International supported strikes it would become a mere political institution, with little appeal to trade unions. But for Cohn, as for everyone else at the Congress, trade unions and strikes were only 'means to a higher idea — that of co-operation'.[1] Brismée's suggestion was formally adopted[2] though never put into practice.

The next debate on the effects of machinery opened with a statement by Lessner along the lines of Marx's earlier speech to the General Council and including a long quotation from *Capital*. Both on the General Council and at the Brussels Congress the economic debates displayed a high level of understanding and responsibility. Issues which were to become perennial in the labour movement were now raised publicly for the first time; some of the suggestions made — especially by de Paepe — are still topical nearly a century later.

The Parisian mutualists had moved a long way on the question of strikes since 1866. On public ownership, too, their position had changed. At Lausanne in 1867 they had supported the nationalisation of mines, canals and railways. But these, it could be claimed, were natural monopolies and the mutualists at Brussels remained implacably opposed to State interference in agriculture, industry or commerce. On the question of machinery, therefore, as previously over the eight-hour day, they were opposed to any suggestion of State control.

Like the Parisians, the Belgian socialists considered themselves mutualists. At Lausanne de Paepe had tried to support the case for land nationalisation on mutualist grounds. In

---

[1] *Beehive*, September 19, 1868.   [2] *Compte Rendu . . .*, p. 18.

relation to industry, the Belgian leader was described in the *Beehive* [1] as 'one of the ablest, as he is one of the most energetic of the managers of the Congress', was beginning to see the answer in terms of workers' rather than State control. He told the Congress that while machinery had adverse effects on the worker, it need not do so 'if introduced under proper conditions destined to serve him as well as other classes'. The workers, therefore, should approve and supervise the installation of new machinery. They should be fully consulted before it was introduced, and compensated for adverse effects, including unemployment.

The General Council's resolutions on the immediately damaging, but ultimately revolutionary, effects of mechanisation as drafted by Marx were carried unanimously. De Paepe's resolution on compensation for redundancy was opposed by all the English delegates who clearly regarded it as unpractical and by one or two others. But it was carried with the support of the overwhelming Belgian delegation, together with an addendum stating that machinery would not be of real service to the workers until they operated their own system of co-operative production.

PROUDHON AND MARX

In the debate on education, the French again opposed the intervention of the State, quoting extensively from Proudhon's *Idée générale de la révolution du XIXe siècle*. The German delegation countered by recommending the workers of all countries to study *Capital* and calling for its widespread translation. The Congress became openly a clash between the ideas of Proudhon and Marx when the Parisians introduced a debate on mutual credit. Their resolution called for the establishment of Banks of Exchange, granting loans at nominal interest, 'according to a model prepared by Proudhon'. The English described the proposal with the characteristic adjectives 'unsound', 'visionary' and 'illusory'.[2] Moses Hess, an old colleague of Marx and Engels from the 1840s, described it as the proposal of 'a small sect whose doctrines had been refuted by Marx in the *Poverty of Philosophy*'. Marx's book had appeared in 1847. His ideas were only now, twenty-one years later, becoming international currency.

[1] September 19, 1868.   [2] *Beehive*, September 19, 1868.

Eccarius had his instructions and acted accordingly. Marx had written that 'if the question of mutual credit comes up Eccarius will simply have to explain that the workers of England, Germany and the United States have nothing to do with the Proudhonist dogmas and that they consider the credit question of secondary importance'.[1] Eccarius's speech followed the line laid down. In opposition to the Proudhonists he was convinced that 'the working men of other countries were going to work out their emancipation through the State'.[2] He was strongly supported by Cohn, the cigar maker, who while advocating the State ownership of railways, gas and water works and the development of producers' co-operation, was convinced that for the rest the commercial system and its attendant apparatus of credit would last his lifetime. After some further discussion the resolution on mutual credit was on de Paepe's own suggestion referred back to the sections for further study.

This was in marked contrast to Lausanne where the Proudhonist resolutions on mutual credit had been carried without difficulty, but there was more to come. The resolution demanding the collective ownership of 'land, railways, mines and forests' was supported by the English delegations. The French and some of the Belgians — excluding de Paepe — wanted to postpone a decision until the next Congress. After the arguments used at Lausanne had been repeated on both sides, the resolution was carried by the surprisingly small vote of nine to four with fifteen abstentions. Doubts were expressed as to how far the International could be committed on such an important issue by so small a vote, but when Tolain tried to annul the decision at the following session he was defeated by a very large majority. In his closing address to the Congress, Dupont referred to this vote and to the attempts which would be made by the opponents of the International to incite the 'cultivators of the soil' against it. The Association must make it clear, he insisted, 'that the enfranchisement of agricultural labourers was as much their object as was that of the workmen in towns. They laboured for all humanity.' The Congress closed on a note of enthusiasm.

Brussels marked the end of a phase in the International's history. For the first time it was committed, unambiguously, to socialist aims. The banner of 'anti-statism', which the

<hr>

[1] Marx to Eccarius and Lessner, September 10, 1868.

[2] *Reynolds's*, September 20, 1868.

Proudhonists had carried up to then was soon to be taken over and defended, more vigorously, by the Bakuninists. Indeed, Michael Bakunin himself had made his unobtrusive *début* in the International with a policy statement which he sent to Congress and which contained many of the aims for which his Alliance was subsequently to struggle.[1] Meanwhile the influence of Marx, as shown by many of the resolutions and by much of the tone of the Congress debates, was becoming dominant and through the alliance of the English and German delegations with de Paepe's Belgian followers, he had fulfilled his declared aim of inflicting a decisive defeat on Proudhonism. The alliance with de Paepe was to prove temporary, and when a few years later, the Belgians moved away from Marx and towards Bakunin, it was Marx himself who faced defeat and who resorted to desperate measures to avert it.

The history of the International can be divided into two periods — the first, stretching from the foundation meeting to the Brussels Congress, the second, from Brussels to the Hague. 'During the first period the Collectivist struggle against the Proudhonists who are defeated at the Brussels Congress' — so runs the terse but accurate verdict of the historian.[2] Marx and Engels could congratulate themselves that they had laid the ghost of Proudhon [3] because they had no inkling of what was in store for them at the hands of Bakunin.

[1] *Compte Rendu* . . ., p. 41.
[2] Compère-Morel, in the *Encyclopédie Socialiste*, Paris, 1912, pp. 497-8.
[3] Marx to H. Jung, September 14; to Siegfried Meyer, September 14; to Engels, September 12, 19; Engels to Marx, September 16, 1868.

CHAPTER IX

From Brussels to Basle

THE Brussels Congress aroused more interest in England than any of its predecessors. *The Times*, which had asked Eccarius to act as its correspondent, devoted four editorials in ten days to comments on the proceedings. These were, as could have been expected, largely unfavourable, but *The Times* took pleasure in the support given by the Congress to producers' co-operation. Here, at least, the workers' representatives were putting forward an alternative to capitalism so that 'the point . . . at which the working men diverge from the existing system is rendered perfectly definite, and becomes open to intelligent discussion'.[1]

The Tory *Standard*, in contrast, was prepared to agree with many of the social criticisms made at the Congress, whose proceedings were described in an editorial as 'practical and dispassionate'.[2] Strikes were often justified in view of the inequality in bargaining power between capital and labour and there was also much truth in what Eccarius and Lessner had said about the adverse effects of machinery. However, Tolain had gone too far in attacking profits, while de Paepe's proposals on compensation for redundancy would only delay or prevent technical progress.

The Liberal Press was mostly friendly in its comments. The *Daily News* of September 11 was pleased with the resolute opposition to war which had been expressed. The *Morning Star* of September 15 was more enthusiastic about the discussions on social and economic questions which it described as 'of greatest practical interest'. In a perceptive comment the *Star* remarked that it was, of course, easy 'to criticise the Utopian tone of the resolutions arrived at ; but it would not

---

[1] *The Times*, September 19 ; see also *ibid.*, September 9, 12, 15, 1868.

[2] September 16, 1868. The writer may well have been Maltman Barry, a 'Tory socialist' and correspondent of the *Standard*. His later dealings with the International and with the labour movement during the 1880s and 1890s were to give rise to speculation and controversy.

be at all easy to prove that the practice of European statesmen is wiser than the preaching of European artisans'. There were similarly favourable comments in the *Morning Advertiser* of September 16.

The close attention which papers of various trends were beginning to pay to Congresses of the International must have owed much to the Reform Act of 1867. For the first time the working class constituted a majority of the electorate and all parties were anxious to secure, so far as they could, support from this new source of political strength. Moreover, unlike the proceedings at succeeding Congresses, the tone of Brussels was not overtly revolutionary, and superficial observers of the labour scene could feel justified in a certain complacency in their assessments.

THE PROGRAMME OF THE INTERNATIONAL

While the Brussels resolutions had been framed so as not to run ahead of the opinions of British workers they had in Marx's view the additional advantage of being free from concessions to Proudhonism. The General Council therefore decided to publish as the programme of the International a pamphlet containing the Brussels resolutions together with some of those passed at Geneva. The Lausanne resolutions and those passed at Geneva of which the General Council disapproved — those 'incorrigible stupidities', as Marx described them [1] — were simply omitted. The *Beehive*, reporting the decision in its issue of November 21, 1868 also reprinted Marx's *Instructions to Delegates* at the earlier Geneva Congress. On December 12 it also published the Brussels resolutions with a highly commendatory editorial. The International in England, it advised, should 'make a special effort to circulate the said resolutions, and report to all unions and unionists'. Early in the following year the pamphlet duly appeared. No one seems to have complained about the cavalier treatment of the Proudhonist resolutions adopted at Geneva and Lausanne and Engels's shrewd remark that the Lausanne resolutions would have 'no value as long as the General Council remains in London' [2] was vindicated.

The pamphlet was well received. The radical *Lloyd's*

[1] Marx to Engels, February 24, 1869.
[2] Engels to Marx, September 11, 1867.

Weekly Newspaper was particularly impressed by its moderation and good sense. It saw nothing revolutionary about the
proposals which it interpreted as an attempt by the workers to
secure 'a fairer adjustment of the proportions of the profits
realised jointly by capital and labour'. The International, it
pointed out, aimed 'to combine and generalise the spontaneous
movement of the working classes, but not to dictate or impose
any doctrinary system whatever'. The resolutions deserved
the widest study among all classes.[1]

At least one trade union — the West-End of London Boot-
closers' Society — recorded its 'warmest approval' of the
Geneva and Brussels resolutions and decided, on the strength
of the publication, to join the International.   The most
prominent member of the union, Charles Murray, follower and
close personal friend of the late Bronterre O'Brien, was in the
chair at the meeting which decided to affiliate. Up to the end
of the effective existence of the International in England both
Murray and his union were to play an important part in its
affairs.   Two delegates were at once elected to the General
Council.[2]

SOURCES OF FRICTION

Murray's union, however, was small, and there was no
sign of the International conquering any substantial new
territory in the British trade-union movement. Meanwhile the
time of the General Council was taken up with squabbles
which looked petty enough at the time but which were later
to play their part in speeding the disintegration of the International. The London French branch had submitted a formal
protest to the Brussels Congress against the failure of the
International to undertake republican propaganda. This was
due, they were convinced, to the baneful influence of the French
Proudhonists and they complained of 'the conduct of certain
members of the International who profess absolute indifference
in political affairs; who declare loftily that the International
Working Men's Association must not be republican. . .'.[3]

---

[1] March 21, 1869.   [2] *Beehive*, March 20, 1869.
[3] *L'Association International des Travailleurs*, 1870, p. 6. This pamphlet
is described in the London University Goldsmiths' Library catalogue as
apparently a police report to Napoleon III on the activities of the International. It is, in fact, the official indictment against the members of the
International in Paris at their trial in May 1870.

Dupont had referred obliquely to this attack in his closing address to the Brussels Congress when he said that 'the revolution has now become more of a social than a political question. . . . They had no special antipathy to any particular government. . . .'

Relations had deteriorated further since Brussels. Unsavoury personal allegations were made against members of the London French branch to which they — Vésinier in particular — were quick to reply with counter-charges. A little wearily the General Council set up a sub-committee to investigate. Marx, originally favourably disposed towards the French republicans, was now thoroughly disillusioned. He told Engels on October 24 that 'the London French branch have organised a meeting with Pyat and proclaimed the Commune but the Press ignored them. Tonight there is the meeting of the sub-committee to consider the evidence of the witnesses who have testified that amongst this bunch . . . there was a procurer, another a gambler, a third — a spy of the employers during the tailors' strike, and so on and so on. . . .' The report of the sub-committee was highly unfavourable to the London French branch which accordingly repudiated the General Council.[1] It continued, however, to describe itself as a section of the International and as such held a public meeting in February 1869 to celebrate the twenty-first anniversary of 1848 at which Charles Bradlaugh spoke alongside Pyat and the German Lassallean, Weber.[2]

Another source of friction, later to become much more serious, was the growing strain in the relations between Eccarius and Marx. There is reason to believe that Eccarius, while regarding Marx as his intellectual leader, was jealous of him. Eccarius in his reports to *The Times* had attributed Marx's resolution on machinery to himself, for which he was roundly attacked by Lafargue. After that, he aroused further criticism by omitting to report Marx's authorship of the address on the Belgian massacres, for which he was taken to task by Lessner. His explanations in each case were lame.[3]   Marx, in contrast

---

[1] G.C. *Minutes*, October 20 and November 3, 1868.

[2] *Reynolds's*, February 21, 28, 1869. See also G.C. *Minutes*, April 13, 27, 1869, for further acrimonious correspondence between the General Council and the London French. See also Marx's unflattering reference to Weber in his letter to Kugelmann, December 5, 1868. Weber later translated Vésinier's book on the Paris Commune into English.

[3] G.C. *Minutes*, October 6, 1868 and May 11, 1869.

to some of his followers, continued to hold Eccarius in some esteem, attributing his undoubted 'stupidities' to a narrow egoism 'which can, possibly, be explained by the circumstances of his life'. Marx generally defended Eccarius against the English, though 'occasionally my patience broke down, then I gave him a bashing'.[1]

Had the state of the International in England been healthy, the quarrel with the London French and the tension between Eccarius and his colleagues need have done no great damage. But in an organisation which had stagnated since 1867 the quarrels were to fester, grow and finally erupt in the last fatal illness of the Association in 1872.

THE BASLE AGENDA

By July the General Council was ready to begin discussing the agenda for the Basle Congress. The first item on the 'question of landed property' was soon disposed of. The Council was unanimous in supporting the nationalisation of land.[2]

There was a more substantial discussion on the second item — 'the right to inheritance' — on July 20. This had been inserted at the request of the Geneva branch and was in fact the unobtrusive opening of the titanic struggle between Marx and Bakunin.[3] Marx, who opened the debate, argued that the abolition of inheritance would be either impossible or unnecessary since 'a parliament that might have the will and power to abolish the laws of inheritance would equally have the power of expropriation. A law that all the tenant farmers should pay the rent into the public treasury instead of paying it to the landlords would act at once and provide the government with funds', while a law to abolish inheritance would have

---

[1] Marx to Siegfried Meyer and August Vogt in New York, October 28, 1868. Regarding Eccarius's egoism, see Lessner's report to Marx from the Basle Congress, September 6, 1869, 'Friend Eccarius is exceptionally busy with himself. He asks each foreigner whether he has heard of Eccarius. And sometimes he asks : has anything been heard in your place of Eccarius ?' *Baselski Kongress Pervovo Internationala, 1869*, Moscow, 1934, p. 147.

[2] G.C. *Minutes*, July 6, 13, 1869. See *Beehive*, June 26, 1869, for the first announcement of the Basle agenda.

[3] The controversy which opened publicly at Basle had started a year earlier at Brussels — see Chapter VIII. 'The programme of the Russian Socialist Democracy published by Bakunin in Geneva' had, as its main items, the abolition of the right to inherit property, of sex inequality and of marriage.

L

little immediate effect. Marx's views were generally endorsed.

In the debate which followed on education, there was general condemnation of the Proudhonists' hostility to State education. Marx urged that education should be compulsory, secular and adequately inspected. He was full of praise for the American system of federal finance combined with decentralised control which he contrasted favourably with 'the Prussian system of national education . . . only calculated to make good soldiers, not citizens'. In the resumed debate on the following Tuesday, Jung insisted that controversial subjects were unsuitable for children. Harris, the O'Brienite,[1] objected that compulsory primary education without the right political instruction had produced soldiers in Prussia, mercenaries in Switzerland and grasping characters in the U.S.A. Harriet Law wanted a scientific, humanist education, financed by the proceeds of Church disestablishment.

Summing up the debate, Marx expressed decidedly liberal views. Political economy, religion and other controversial questions 'could not be admitted into the primary, nor even the higher schools', but should be confined to adults. 'Nothing but the physical sciences, truths that were independent of all party prejudices, and admitted but of one interpretation, were fit subjects for schools.' The Council then resolved unanimously that 'education must be compulsory and gratuitous, and that the Church funds ought to be devoted to the education of the people'.

The last debate was concerned with Socialism and by this time nearly all the vocal elements on the Council — except for Odger, who attended but did not participate in the discussion — favoured Socialism in one form or another. The question for debate was 'To what extent can credit be immediately utilised by the working class?' The ensuing discussion provided a remarkable recapitulation in miniature of the development of socialist thought from Owen, through O'Brien to Marx.

First, Milner, of the National Reform League, urged the trade unions to sponsor co-operative production for the employment of their members when out of work which would initiate a process by which the workers could be emancipated 'from the wages system'. This at once raised the question of finance and markets. Cohn declared that his own Society had

[1] Probably the Harris who wrote for Ernest Jones's paper, *Notes to the People*, as early as 1851.

wanted to use its surplus to finance co-operative production, but its members made a luxury product which might well be unsuitable for experiments of this kind. Why could not the Cigar Makers use their surplus to finance co-operative production elsewhere? Should there not be a 'central bank, in which all societies could deposit their money, to be lent to such as carried on production?'

At this point, Martin Boon, also of the National Reform League, pointed out that a central bank would not solve the problem of markets and for this he favoured Owen's solution. 'If they had some central store where all could deposit their goods and receive notes to the value of it, they might exchange them for something else that was in the store.' Equal labour would then be equally rewarded.[1] Harriet Law, no doubt bearing in mind the fate of Owen's labour exchanges, urged the need for a central plan. 'If a man has a right to get the value of his labour at the store it would have to be regulated how much of each was to be made. If a man was allowed to make tables and chairs without limit when nobody wanted any, he might choke the store with them.' Central planning in fact was the only alternative to a market economy. When production was no longer regulated by supply and demand there would be need for 'a directing power that could determine how much was to be produced of each particular kind of goods'.

Other members of the Council were apparently not prepared to commit themselves to State Socialism and Hales proposed, with Cohn seconding, a resolution recommending 'the establishment of Labour Banks in conjunction with Labour Exchanges' so that the workers could make use of the capital already in their possession. At this point Odger intervened to move the adjournment so that no vote was taken.

THE BASLE CONGRESS: PRELIMINARIES

A few weeks later on September 5 the fourth Congress of the International opened in Basle. There were seventy-eight accredited delegates of whom six — Applegarth, Lucraft, Lessner, Eccarius, Cowell Stepney and Jung — were members

---

[1] Boon was the most prolific of the O'Brienite propagandists, producing a large number of pamphlets on land and railway nationalisation, credit and emigration.

of the General Council.[1]   Once again the General Council's
report to Congress had been drafted by Marx,[2] though it was
signed by Applegarth, Stepney and Eccarius — respectively
the Chairman, Treasurer and Secretary to the Council.   In
contrast to previous reports this dealt almost exclusively with
developments on the Continent, especially 'the guerilla fights
between capital and labour — we mean the strikes which during
the last year have perturbed the continent of Europe, and
were said to have sprung neither from the misery of the labourer
nor from the despotism of the capitalist, but from the secret
intrigues of our Association'.

The Report went on to deal with the strikes in Basle and
Geneva and with the Belgian massacres, for all of which the
International had been held responsible.   In France the past
year had seen repressive measures against the International
and widespread strikes resulting from economic distress.[3]   With
the granting of limited rights of association in Austria following
the war of 1866, the Austrian workers, 'especially those of
Vienna', had 'at once occupied a vantage ground'.[4]   They had
sent delegates to the recent Congress of German workers at
Eisenach at which a Social Democratic Party had been established.   The German workers, though forbidden by law to
affiliate, had declared their adhesion to the principles of the
International.   New branches of the Association had also been
reported from Naples, Barcelona and Amsterdam, where a
Dutch organ of the International was being launched.

In contrast to these encouraging developments, there was
noticeably little to say about England.   Though the Report
could draw attention with pride to the unanimous resolution of
the Birmingham T.U.C., it is significant that the only working-
class action referred to was a riot of striking miners in Denbigh-
shire, in which five had been killed by soldiers, but in which the
International had played no part.[5]

---

[1] The other delegations numbered twenty-six from France, twenty-five
from Switzerland, ten from Germany, five from Belgium, five from Italy,
two from Spain and one from the U.S.A.

[2] G.C. *Minutes*, August 31, 1869.

[3] For French Government measures against the International, see
Marx to Kugelmann, March 3, 1869, and the indictment at the third Paris trial
of members of the International, *L'Association Internationale des Travailleurs,
1870*, p. 13.   Also O. Testut, *L'Internationale*, Paris, 1871, pp. 61-75.

[4] For the discussion of the Austro-Prussian War of 1866 on the General
Council, see *Commonwealth*, July 14, 21, 1866.

[5] *Report of the Fourth Annual Congress of the I.W.M.A.*, p. 13.

The General Council's delegation at Basle was small. Nevertheless it exerted considerable influence. Eccarius urged the formation of independent workers' parties to fight for political power and 'the overthrow of the rule of capital'. Land nationalisation and the eight-hour day would provide a suitable short-term programme.[1] More significant was the speech by Applegarth in a preliminary address to the Congress. If the International had done no other good, he proclaimed, it had stopped the English employers from freely importing European workers to break strikes. 'But it had done more. It had enlarged the views of English trades' unionists, and showed them that trade unions could be used for higher purposes than simple wage-quarrels, and that an international union was necessary to attack the evil that oppressed them at the root.' Both English and European workers could learn from each other; the Europeans might possess more 'spirit', but the English 'always stood their ground . . . every inch they gained they held for good'.

After reports had been given by several delegates on the position in their respective countries, Applegarth spoke again providing a summary of the situation in England. He referred to the rise of his own union from a membership of five hundred in 1860 to nine thousand five hundred members and £17,000 in the bank by 1869.[2] Characteristically, he pointed with pride to the £30,000 paid out in friendly benefits since the formation of the Society. He described the campaigns of the British unions to extend the franchise, to improve the legal status of trade unions and to secure labour representation in Parliament. He drew attention to the unanimous resolution of the Birmingham T.U.C. in support of the International. Applegarth clearly saw the International not as an instrument of revolution but as the logical sequel to the successes already achieved by labour in his own country. 'Much that I have heard here', he

---

[1] *Report of the Fourth Annual Congress* . . ., pp. 4-5. Eccarius became, with Martin Boon, Joint Secretary of the Land and Labour League founded in the following month in London. For the programme of the League see Dr. Royden Harrison, *The Land and Labour League, Bulletin of the International Institute of Social History*, Amsterdam, 1953, p. 170.

[2] Oscar Testut apparently mistook Applegarth's report on the A.S.C.J. for a report on the International in England. He then transferred a zero from the cash to the membership figure, making Applegarth claim a membership of ninety-five thousand, with funds of £1,700 for the English section. *L'Internationale*, p. 214. The error was copied by G. Stekloff, *History of the International*, 1928, p. 135.

told Congress, 'were settled questions with us twenty years ago. We have now got into thorough working order, and we want to extend our alliances all over the world. . . . We are in want of education, and the State must give it free from religion. You want some of your obnoxious laws repealed, and we may help you there.'

PUBLIC OWNERSHIP OF LAND

The first debate was on land nationalisation. In the year since Brussels there had been a remarkable change in international opinion. At Brussels, with an inflated delegation from the General Council and an overwhelming preponderance of Belgians, land nationalisation had been carried on a vote so small as to cast doubts on its validity. At Basle there could be no doubt about the feeling of Congress. Only the Parisian old guard was left to defend peasant proprietorship and to argue, with Chemalé, that 'if private property in land was abolished individual liberty would be abolished too, it would lead to communism'.

The first major speech in defence of nationalisation came from an Englishman, Benjamin Lucraft. Poverty, he contended, was largely due to the concentration of land ownership in a few hands. But it would not help matters to break up the large estates. On his way through France he had seen some of the effects of peasant proprietorship and they seemed to involve the perpetuation of poverty. Land 'should be cultivated on a large scale, by machinery and the application of science for the benefit of the whole community'.

At Lausanne, Longuet had argued that a strong and independent peasantry was a necessary safeguard of personal freedom against the overweening power of the State. At Basle, the point was made more brutally by the Parisian, Langlois. He thought that if the Brussels decision were endorsed, 'the country people whom you have not consulted, and who are not represented here, will turn against you as in June 1848. I have seen the days of June and I do wish that they may never occur again.' [1] He warned Congress that 'despite their intention, those who only claim to preach a liberal communism may be impelled by logic and the very force of circumstances to-

[1] *Standard*, September 17, 1869.

wards authoritarian communism . . . that is the system of Citizen Lucraft'.[1]

Bakunin, making his first major speech at a Congress of the International, and Lessner, for the London Germans, both argued that personal freedom and the right to work required the common ownership of land. Lessner recognised the danger of alienating the peasantry but insisted that the peasant could be shown through effective propaganda 'that the transformation would be for their benefit'.[2]

The result of the debate was a foregone conclusion, in view of the size of the German delegation and the fact that the Belgians had now broken with the mutualists of Paris. For this Marx was very largely responsible.[3] Hins said candidly that 'last year he had been an individualist, but since then he had become convinced of his error; he was now for the proposition'. Hins was still sufficient of a mutualist, however, to oppose Lucraft's views on State cultivation. Like de Paepe he wanted State-owned land to be cultivated by producers' co-operatives. When put to the vote, the necessity for land nationalisation was carried by fifty-three to eight, with ten abstaining and four absent. The extent to which collectivism had triumphed was indicated by the fact that six of the eight who voted against the resolution were Parisians, while the delegates from Rouen, Lyons and Marseilles voted with the majority.[4]

The next issue — the abolition of the right of inheritance, called for by Bakunin's Geneva section — split the collectivist majority. Marx had drafted the statement of the General Council,[5] which argued that inheritance was the effect of private property, not its cause. The abolition of inheritance might be justified in a modified form through transitional measures such as an extension of death duties and some

---

[1] *Compte Rendu* . . ., p. 79.

[2] *Reynolds's*, September 19, 1869 and *Report of the Fourth Annual Congress* . . ., p. 23.

[3] For the part played by Marx in the Belgian conversion, see de Paepe to Marx, June 9, 1869. De Paepe asked Marx to prepare a draft for the resolution on land ownership, since 'the followers of Proudhon' were preparing to reverse their defeat at Brussels and would produce a carefully reasoned case. *Baselski Kongress Pervovo Internationala*, p. 145. For Marx's view 'that the Proudhonists are representatives of the small peasantry', see G.C. *Minutes*, July 6, 1869.

[4] *Compte Rendu* . . ., p. 90.

[5] G.C. *Minutes*, August 3, 1869.

limitation on the right to bequeath property. But such policies must be auxiliary to, not a substitute for, the nationalisation of land.

De Paepe gave his powerful support to the General Council's position. Not only land, but 'machinery and the other instruments of production should become the property of the associated producers'. Supporters of the resolution were looking for a means of compromise with the bourgeoisie. But the bourgeoisie did not want to compromise. There were countries where the demands of the workers were met with 'powder and lead'. 'In the great French revolution, the *bourgeoisie* had wound up the feudal State by confiscating the estates of the Church and the nobility.' The workers could learn from this example.

Bakunin argued for his proposal as a means of conciliating, not the bourgeoisie, but the peasantry. He thought that if the peasants were allowed *de facto* possession of their land while they lived, they would not mind it passing to public ownership after death. Despite this rather unconvincing argument, the resolution secured thirty-two votes, with twenty-three against. But with thirteen abstentions it lacked an absolute majority and was declared lost.

On the next item, trade unionism, there was no resolution from the General Council. A committee of the Congress produced a very general statement calling for 'an international organisation of trades' unions'. Liebknecht told the Congress that 'In Germany they had made a beginning to organise on the English and American pattern'. Chemalé gave lukewarm support to the resolution as an interim measure, while convinced that trade unions 'would disappear in the social democratic state'. Then Hins of Brussels outlined the first syndicalist programme to be presented to an International Congress.

It is significant of Bakunin's poverty as an original thinker that the first and by far the clearest statement of what came to be called Anarcho-Syndicalism was presented to the International not by himself but by a Belgian colleague of de Paepe. Hins said that 'trades' unions would some day overthrow the present state of political organisation altogether; they represented the social and political organisation of the future. The whole labouring population would range itself, according to occupation, into different groups, and this would lead to a new political organisation of society. He wanted no intermeddling

of the State, they had enough of that in Belgium already. . . .
By trying to reform the State, or to take part in its councils,
they would virtually acknowledge its right of existence. Whatever the English, the Swiss, the Germans, and the Americans
might hope to accomplish by means of the present political
state the Belgians repudiated theirs.'

Applegarth had of course nothing to say about the ideological arguments from France and Belgium. He 'desired to
give a practical turn to the discussion' by proposing an international federation of trade unions; a monthly exchange of
information on trade conditions, with the technical assistance
of the local sections and the General Council of the International; support for the principle of 'arbitration for the
settlement of trade disputes' and 'the utilisation of the funds of
trades unions' for the fostering of co-operative production;
and trade-union support for 'a national compulsory and un-
sectarian system of education', which was essential if social
and political reforms were to have any permanent effect.

After a fraternal address from A. C. Cameron of Chicago,
editor of the *Working Man's Advocate* and delegate of the
National Labor Union of the U.S.A., Jung, from the chair,
made his concluding remarks. 'Three years ago,' he said, 'at
our first Congress at Geneva, we were looked upon as rather a
queer lot. The Press slighted or ridiculed us. . . . Today our
principles are discussed without hesitation, they are proclaimed
everywhere, the Press of Europe notices our doings, sometimes
not in the most amiable way, but it is manifest we have become
a power.' Another verdict on Basle, however, was that of
Fribourg, lamenting the final defeat of mutualism. 'The international of the French founders was dead, quite dead; now
the only possible question for the Parisians was how to save
mutualist socialism from this general shipwreck'.[1] Fribourg
was right, but the split in the collectivist majority, of which only
the first signs had appeared at Basle and which was to dominate
the closing years of the International, still lay ahead.

[1] *Op. cit.*, p. 140.

PART FOUR

THE WAR AND THE PARIS COMMUNE

CHAPTER X

From Basle to the French Republic

THERE was a curious lull in the activities of the International in the year following Basle. In England there were no new trade union affiliations though the General Council was instrumental in developing liaison between English and continental trade unions in textiles, painting and, most significantly, in engineering. While in the last quarter of 1869 there was a vigorous campaign in support of the Fenian prisoners in which the International participated fully, the movement died away from the beginning of 1870. The only lasting effect of the brief revival of the Irish question was to bring to a head the already developing split between the International and the *Beehive*.

In the absence of important industrial movements in England, the attention of the unions was increasingly taken up with two related issues — the improvement in their legal position and the winning of labour representation in the House of Commons. For those workers whose interests were more widely political, the Land and Labour League, set up a few weeks after Basle and the new Republican movement led by Bradlaugh, tended to divert energy away from the General Council.

The outbreak of the Franco-Prussian War in July, and the establishment of the French Republic in September 1870, brought the lull abruptly to an end. Once again, as Marx quickly perceived, the situation held revolutionary possibilities and there might be work of major importance for the International.

REACTIONS TO BASLE

After Basle the English Press was for the first time openly hostile to the International. Even the *Beehive*, which wanted to be friendly, was shocked by *Égalité*, the Geneva organ of the International now under Bakuninist control. That journal had printed a form of enrolment committing members of the Geneva section to a 'war between the workmen and masters' which could 'only end in the destruction of the latter'. Blinding itself to the speeches and resolutions at the Congress, the *Beehive* urged that the International was not really advocating 'socialism and communism' but only 'what is good in those ideas'. The trouble really came, it felt, from the attitude of the 'unyielding capitalists'.[1]

Other papers were even more confused by the proceedings at Basle. *The Times*, understandably horrified by the tone of the speeches, drew comfort from the belief that the six votes against the public ownership of land were those of 'our fellow countrymen', which caused Applegarth and his friends some amusement on the General Council.[2] *The Times* was unable to understand what benefit 'Mr. Applegarth and his English fellow-delegates' could hope to derive from associating with 'men who aspire to domination through revolution and whose first act aims at the abolition of property'. Similarly, the *Daily Telegraph*[3] drew attention to the foreign names of Jung and Eccarius while taking it for granted that the English delegates had voted against the socialist resolutions. More crudely, the *Builders' Trade Circular*, organ of the building employers, wrote that 'three of the number were named respectively Eccarius, Jung and Lessner, being probably Germans or Polish Jews'. The real Englishmen, it was sure, were only enjoying a cheap holiday.

Even earlier, on September 13, *The Times*, in warning Bright against his allies among the trade union leaders, had decided that the Bakuninist enrolment form printed in *Egalité* was an 'oath of engagement' taken by all the delegates at Basle. After Odger had sent in a refutation[4] *The Times* returned to the attack, claiming that trade unionism was inherently protectionist and to be deplored by all liberal-minded men. Had not Applegarth at Basle pointed to the success of the International in preventing the importation of foreign workers during strikes? What was this, asked *The Times*, but an illegitimate interference with free trade?[5]

---

[1] September 18, 1869.   [2] G.C. *Minutes*, September 14, 1869.
[3] September 17, 1869.
[4] *The Times*, September 21; see also *The Times*, October 1, 1869 for a further letter from Odger.
[5] *The Times* was not liberal enough to print Applegarth's reply which appeared in the *Morning Star* on October 11. Applegarth could see no

Besides the reports and comments in *The Times*, the Press in general gave more attention to Basle than to any other Congress of the International. A most interesting and extremely hostile account appeared in the Tory *Standard* on September 17. Its correspondent, paraphrasing the attitude of the International to the League for Peace and Freedom due to hold its second Congress in a few days' time at Lausanne,[1] wrote that according to the International the League 'maintains the economic inequality; all it wants to destroy is the military dictatorship; but that dictatorship is the only force that can postpone for a little while longer the social reckoning. The middle classes know that perfectly well, and it explains why they content themselves to bark at that dictatorship.' Of Bakunin's appearance, the writer said : 'I have rarely seen such a colossal man; his features are deeply accentuated, and seem antediluvian, so to say; his aspect is half-savage and half-illuminated'. It seems likely from the style that the *Standard*'s Basle correspondent was French or French-Swiss. In 1871 after the Paris Commune further articles were to appear in the same paper on the history of the International, scurrilous, anonymous and also in Gallic English. Shortly after that a book based on the *Standard* articles of 1871 was to appear and win some notoriety as *The Secret History of the International* by 'Onslow Yorke'. There seems a strong possibility that 'Onslow Yorke', about whose identity there has been a good deal of dispute, was the *Standard*'s Basle correspondent of 1869.[2]

The first hostility of the *Standard* and *The Times* was

---

connection between keeping out foreign labour during strikes and import or export duties. For the controversy between Applegarth and *The Times*, see A. W. Humphrey, *op. cit.*, pp. 102-7. For further discussion of trade unionism and protection in connection with Basle, see *Eastern Morning News*, Hull, September 25 and *Pall Mall Gazette*, October 2, 1869.

[1] This Congress received little attention in the English Press — but see *Morning Advertiser*, September 16, 1869 for a comparison of the rival Congresses at Basle and Lausanne.

[2] The British Museum catalogue describes 'Onslow Yorke' as the pseudonym of the Rev. Hepworth Dixon. Dixon wrote travel books on Russia and on visits to American communist-religious colonies. His style is in impeccable English and unless he was more subtle than appears, he can hardly have written the *Secret History*. Besides being written in Gallic English, the book has a foreword written from Geneva. The British Museum's identification of 'Onslow Yorke' with the Rev. Hepworth Dixon is probably based on a statement by 'M. B.' — also anonymous! — in *Zur Geschichte der Internationale*, Leipzig, 1872, p. 143. It is highly improbable as is the identification of 'Onslow Yorke' with Maltman Barry by S. Maccoby, *op. cit.*, p. 420.

general throughout the Press with one conspicuous exception. The *Pall Mall Gazette* was intelligently critical.   It admitted that the Congress genuinely represented the labour movements of France and Germany and that its influence was spreading in Europe.   An editorial on September 20, however, speculated about the proposal made at Basle to hold the next Congress of the International in Paris.   This would bring the Socialism of the International on to the very doorsteps of the French peasants.   'It is possible that the result of this may be to throw the whole weight of the small proprietors on the Continent on the side of the bourgeoisie, a consideration of some moment if a conflict of classes is spreading.'   The French Revolutionary land settlement, wrote the *Gazette*, had made the peasantry an anti-socialist force and there might be lessons in this for Britain.   In a perceptive anticipation of Gladstonian policy, the article noted that the Irish were potentially revolutionary, but that 'supposing some settlement of the land question can be arrived at . . . there will be a counteracting influence at work which may convert Ireland into the firmest bulwark conceivable against the spread of a revolutionary propaganda'.[1]

THE LAND AND LABOUR LEAGUE

Soon after the Congress, Hales revived on the General Council his earlier demand for the establishment of an English section of the International.[2]   The discussion was adjourned, however, after Weston had announced a forthcoming conference at the Bell Inn, Old Bailey, to start a public campaign on the land question.   At the General Council meeting on October 19 Eccarius successfully urged the postponement of further discussion, since the forthcoming meeting might give rise to a new society which would be, in effect, the British Section of the International.

On October 27 the proposed conference was held and the

[1] For a contemporary day-by-day account of Basle see also Applegarth's articles in the *Sheffield and Rotherham Independent* beginning with the issue of September 9, 1869.   Applegarth kept a scrapbook with thirty-six pages of Press cuttings on Basle, now in the British Library of Political and Economic Science, London.   For another contemporary account of Basle in English, see reports of A. C. Cameron in *Workingman's Advocate and Anti-Monopolist*, Chicago, November–December 1869, reprinted in *Documentary History of American Industrial Society*, vol. IX ,Cleveland, by J. R. Commons and J. B. Andrews, 1910, pp. 341-50.
[2] G.C. *Minutes*, October 5, 1869.

Land and Labour League formally established. The new society soon adopted a programme based on land nationalisation which had been part of the International's programme since 1868. Many members of its executive were, or had been, members of the General Council and with Weston as Treasurer and Boon and Eccarius as Joint Secretaries, the Land and Labour League could well be regarded as an offshoot of the International. The executive included Hales, Murray, Eccarius, Mottershead, Milner and Odger among present members of the General Council as well as such past members like Osborne, Le Lubez and Cremer.

The formation of the League gave rise to a lively controversy. Some labour leaders, like Dunning, made it clear that their belief in private property and free trade led them to support John Stuart Mill's Land Tenure Reform Association, formed three months earlier to advocate the abolition of primogeniture and entailment.[1] One ex-member of the General Council and a delegate to its Lausanne Congress — the old O'Brienite, A. A. Walton — also declared his support for Mill's Association, explaining that while he still supported nationalisation, 'free trade in land' was a necessary first step.

Though Marx had some hopes that the Land and Labour League could serve as a political instrument of the International, it succumbed, like other political and trade union movements of the early seventies, to the Great Depression. Its agitation no doubt helped to prepare the way for the land movement of the 1880s which was on a much more formidable scale.[2] Its immediate effect on the International was to cause Hales to drop for the time being his proposal to establish an English section. In reply to a question from Marx, he explained that with the formation of the Land and Labour League and in view of the fact that 'many Council members were on the executive of that League it was not necessary to go any further at present'.[3]

IRELAND AND THE FENIANS

Leaving the movement on land nationalisation to the Land and Labour League, the General Council began to concern

[1] Cf. T. J. Dunning's letter in *Beehive*, October 23, 1869.
[2] See Dr. Royden Harrison, 'The Land and Labour League', in the *Bulletin of the International Institute of Social History*, 1953, No. 3.
[3] G.C. *Minutes*, November 2, 1869.

M

itself once again with Ireland.   With Gladstone's refusal, in a
carefully worded statement, to agree to an amnesty for the
remaining Fenian prisoners, a mass campaign was started to
secure their release.   A number of well-attended meetings
had been held in Ireland and an 'English Amnesty Committee'
led by J. P. McDonnell, a Fenian since the 1850s, began
work from offices in Holborn.[1]

A great demonstration was called in Hyde Park for Sunday
October 24, and some tens of thousands responded.[2]   The
Beehive's report — almost identical with that of *The Times* —
estimated the attendance at 'from forty to fifty thousand' and
commented editorially on 'the perfect wisdom and right feeling'
of Gladstone's reply to the amnesty request.[3]   By contrast,
Reynolds's[4] thought that 'there must have been at least 120,000
present'.   It devoted a lot of space to reporting amnesty
demonstrations in the provinces and said in an editorial that
Gladstone's letter of refusal 'contains much that is illiberal
and illogical'.

On November 9 the question came up for discussion on the
General Council.   Marx opened with a carefully prepared
statement in which he tried to use the Irish issue to drive a
wedge between Gladstone and the labour movement.   Gladstone's conduct, he claimed, in refusing an amnesty to the
remaining prisoners, compared unfavourably with that of other
governments, including the American, Austrian and French.
Gladstone had made great show of opposing the treatment of
political prisoners in Naples in 1851.   Now it was being argued
that there was no analogy because 'the Fenians were tried
according to lawful custom and found guilty by a jury of their
own countrymen'.[5]   But the Irish judges and juries were at
least as venal as the Neapolitan.   'In England the judges can
be independent, in Ireland they cannot.   Their promotion
depends on how they served the government.'   Finally, Marx
contrasted Gladstone's support for the slaveowners' rebellion in

---

[1] McDonnell was later to act as Secretary for Ireland on the General
Council, and the collection of his papers in the University Library of
Wisconsin contains valuable information on the activities of the Irish
section of the International.

[2] An interesting eye-witness account was that of Jenny Longuet, Marx's
eldest daughter, in a letter to Kugelmann on October 30, 1869. She thought
that the general Press estimate of seventy thousand attending was too low.

[3] October 30, 1869.   [4] October 31, 1869.

[5] For this argument, see *Beehive*, October 30, 1869.

the American Civil War with his preaching of 'passive obedi-
ence' to the Irish.   The policy of repression was as futile as it
was stupid.   It would not crush Fenianism in Ireland and
most certainly not in the United States.[1]   Marx's very full
statement seems to have made a considerable impression on
the Council.   The veteran G. E. Harris,[2] who reported the
meeting in Bradlaugh's *National Reformer* on November 28,
wrote that: 'Dr. Marx's address on this occasion is only
equalled by the *exposé* he gave of Palmerston, some years ago,
in the *People's Paper*, a treatise which ought to be in the home
of every Englishman'.[3]

Odger spoke first against the resolution.   He had, at the
time of his prospective candidature in Chelsea, called for a
public demonstration in support of Gladstone's Irish Church
policy and had been under attack from the right for hankering
after yet 'another of those physical force demonstrations . . .'[4]
and from the left, by Lucraft, on the General Council, for
supporting Gladstone.[5]   Now he urged that it was 'impolitic
to make demands on the Liberal Government' and 'prejudiced
the case of the prisoners.   The Church Bill was a matter of
history now, and he hoped Mr. Gladstone's Land Bill would
be as good.'[6]

Jung in reply retorted that 'in this country, nothing was
carried except under pressure from without', while Applegarth
'thought it was no use to apply soft language, the time had
come to demand'.

Only one speaker on the Council supported Odger. Mottershead[7] accused Marx of having 'greatly exaggerated if not
wholly falsified the position of affairs'.[8]   If England walked out
of Ireland, France would walk in.   'Ireland could not be

---

[1] G.C. *Minutes*, November 9, 16 and *Reynolds's*, November 21, 1869.
Also Marx to Engels, October 30; Engels to Marx, November 29, 1869.

[2] For Harris's earlier activities in the 1850s see Chapters I and II.

[3] Cf. Marx to Kugelmann, November 29, 1869.

[4] *Chelsea News*, October 3, 1868.

[5] G.C. *Minutes*, October 13, 1868.

[6] *Reynolds's*, November 28, 1869.

[7] He had, nearly two years earlier, opposed Home Rule for Ireland on
the Council of the Reform League — see *Reform League Minutes*, January
8, 1868.   George Julian Harney, Mottershead's old friend from Chartist
times, shared his views on Ireland.   In a letter to the General Council from
America, Harney 'declared a disgust of Fenianism and contended that
Ireland was an integral part of the British Empire'.   Nevertheless he sent £1
as a donation to the General Council, G.C. *Minutes*, May 24, 1870.

[8] *National Reformer*, December 5, 1869.

independent.' Suspicion of Louis Napoleon, combined with anti-clericalism, could easily lead a sincere democrat like Mottershead to oppose the Irish national movement and he had already on the Council of the Reform League urged the intolerance practised by the Catholic religion as an argument against Irish Home Rule. 'I never', he now told the General Council, 'found the Irish in the field with the English in any movement, but they have often been against us. I remind you of the Garibaldi riots.' Like Odger, Mottershead had a high regard for Gladstone, but was more explicit. He approved of Gladstone's free-trade treaty with France in 1860 and of his Italian policy. Gladstone had also 'advanced German unity' by keeping Britain out of the war over Schleswig-Holstein. He had been right on every issue except the American Civil War, and even there he had relented. Mottershead 'wished the prisoners and all the Irish free', but could not vote for a resolution attacking Gladstone.[1]

After Odger had again expressed sympathy with the Fenians while deploring the 'wholesale denunciation of Gladstone's policy', Eccarius castigated the narrow nationalism prevalent in England. While 'in the eyes of the English public Garibaldi was a great patriot, the Fenians were traitors. They never dreamt that England was to Ireland what Rome, Naples and Austria had been to Italy.' Jung developed the point by saying that the Clerkenwell explosion was 'certainly a shocking affair but Garibaldi had caused much bloodshed . . . the police were as much to blame in the Clerkenwell affair as anyone'.

In his reply to the debate, Marx was diplomatic. Though on the General Council only Odger and Mottershead had resented his criticisms of Gladstone, they clearly spoke for a considerable body of labour opinion. Marx made clear that his attack on Gladstone had not been personal. 'Castlereagh was as good a man as Gladstone & I found today in the Political Register that he used the same words against the Irish as Gladstone, and Cobbett made the same reply as I have done.'[2] 'His resolution was not intended to release the prisoners. The Irish themselves had given that up. It was to express sympathy

---

[1] G.C. *Minutes*, November 26 — this is a mistake. The weekly meeting was held as usual on Tuesday, which was November 23. See Marx to Engels, November 26, 1869 in which he gives a full report of the debate.

[2] *Reynolds's*, November 28, 1869.

with the Irish, and review the conduct of the Government.'
Gladstone was under heavy pressure from such organs as *The
Times* and *Saturday Review*,[1] but 'the people could strengthen
Mr. Gladstone in his power to overcome difficulties, or they
could aid him in the perpetuation of political crime'.[2]

Marx's views were endorsed by the General Council. But
of the three most representative trade unionists present, Odger
and Mottershead had strongly objected, while Applegarth had
spoken in support of Marx with manifest reluctance.[3] The
Beehive was omitting all reference to the Irish debate from its
reports and on November 30 when the vote was taken Marx
gave notice that he was going to raise the question of the
paper's conduct and its future relations with the General
Council.

Marx knew that in denouncing Gladstone he risked alienating the most active elements in the British labour movement.
He explained his reasons in a letter to Kugelmann on November
29. He had 'of course other objects besides that of speaking
out loudly and decidedly for the oppressed Irish against their
oppressors'. Marx had become 'more and more convinced —
and the only question is to bring this conviction home to the
English working class — that it can never do anything decisive
here in England until it separates its policy with regard to
Ireland in the most definite way from the policy of the ruling
classes, until it not only makes common cause with the Irish,
but actually takes the initiative in dissolving the Union established in 1801 and replacing it by a free federal relationship'.
Independence for Ireland would mean the overthrow of Irish
landlordism which was in fact absentee English landlordism.
Contrary to his earlier views, Marx now saw this as an essential
prerequisite for social revolution in England.[4]

---

[1] *National Reformer*, December 5, 1869.
[2] *Reynolds's*, November 28, 1869.
[3] Marx to Engels, November 26, 1869. In his next letter to Engels, on
December 4, Marx complained of inaccuracies in the reports of the G.C.
debates appearing in the *National Reformer* and *Reynolds's*. From the
other side, the *Irishman*, edited by Richard Pigott, omitted to publish the
G.C. resolution — see Eccarius's letter of complaint to Isaac Butt, the
Fenians's chief defence counsel, December 20, 1869, McDonnell Papers.
Marx attributed this to narrow Irish nationalism in his letters to Engels of
December 4.
[4] Marx to Engels, December 10, 1869. Cf. the Confidential Circular
written by Marx for the General Council published on January 1, 1870: 'If
England is the bulwark of European landlordism and capitalism, the only
point at which the great blow against official England can be struck is

The Irish resolution was circulated by the General Council to all the trade unions with which it was in contact. It was apparently received with approval — or at least without complaint — by all except the Curriers who, after hearing a deputation from the General Council, withdrew from the International, 'not having any faith in Workingmen's Societies that meddled with politics'.[1]

In the meantime Odger was standing for Parliament in a by-election at Southwark where there was a substantial Irish population. Marx thought it was for that reason that he had finally voted for the General Council's Irish resolution, 'despite all his diplomatic observations'.[2] Odger's association with the International was something of an asset to him in his campaign. The Carpenters and Joiners of Barnet pledged support for his candidature. They objected in general to 'mere class candidates' but saw in Odger's 'connection with the International Working Men's Association . . . that cosmopolitan spirit so much needed in the national Legislature. . . '. Through the medium of the International a collection was opened as far afield as Marseilles in support of Odger's campaign — the Marseilles section remembering him as 'formerly president of our association'.[3] In the event Odger proved unsuccessful.[4] Marx was not altogether sorry and attributed his defeat to the fact that a portion of the Irish workers had abstained 'because he kept on trimming as in the discussions of the General Council, about which they learned from *Reynolds's*'.[5]

SOCIALISM AND FREE TRADE

Marx had intended a further discussion of Ireland on the General Council in the New Year, but the debate was never resumed. Instead there was a discussion on free trade in which

Ireland. . . . The average English worker hates the Irish working man as a competitor who lowers his wages and his standard of life. . . . The position of the International Association with regard to the Irish question is thus quite clear. Its first concern is to forward the social revolution in England. To do this, the decisive blow must be struck in Ireland.' See Marx to Kugelmann, March 28, 1870. Cf. Marx's letter to Meyer and Vogt, April 9, 1870.

[1] Marx to Engels, December 10, 1869 and G.C. *Minutes*, May 31, 1870.
[2] Marx to Engels, December 12, 1869.   [3] *Beehive*, January 8, 1870.
[4] The Tory candidate, Colonel Beresford, having polled 4,686 votes and Odger receiving 4,382.
[5] Marx to Engels, February 19, 1870.

the members tried to clarify their attitude to the Manchester School which was dominant in radical circles and to agree on an alternative economic philosophy.

The Owenite, Weston, opened the debate on January 18. Since free trade meant buying in the cheapest market it could only depress the standards of the workers. It was essentially a gospel for the non-producers. He was followed by Milner, the O'Brienite, whose remarks followed the general line of Tolain's speech at the foundation meeting of the International in 1864. Genuine free trade, he argued, must mean 'complete freedom of exchange'. But in 'the sense of the Manchester School' it meant the ruin of the small producer, the destruction of entire national industries and lower wages for the working class.

Harris supported Milner, saying that what they wanted was neither orthodox free trade nor protection but 'reciprocity to exchange equal values of labour'. He did not use the Proudhonist phrase 'free exchange', but he meant exactly that. Marx was apparently not present to criticise the 'Petty Bourgeois Socialism' of Milner and Harris, nor would he necessarily have wished to do so. His hostility to the Proudhonists had been based on their attitude to the eight-hour day, to Poland and more especially to land nationalisation. However eccentric, from Marx's viewpoint, might be the O'Brienite policies on currency and credit, and however much they might recall the phrases and attitudes of Proudhon, on the key issue of land nationalisation they were his valued allies.

TRADE UNION ACTIVITIES.   THE PARIS IRONMOULDERS' STRIKE

In the months that followed Basle, the General Council's relations with the unions remained good. The Cigar Makers were seriously worried by the number of Belgians arriving in the East End, lodging with compatriots and willing to work for 'anything that was offered them'. Through the medium of the General Council an address drawn up by the unions was translated and contact established with the Cigar Makers of Brussels and Antwerp.[1]

At about the same time the Council was instrumental in making contact between the velvet weavers of Lyons and

[1] G.C. *Minutes*, November 9, 1869 ; January 11, February 8, 1870.

London; between the lithographic printers of Paris and the London compositors and between the painters of London and Paris.[1]

More remarkable were the new relations between the Council and the proud, aloof Amalgamated Society of Engineers which had rebuffed all previous overtures from the International. The Society was gradually becoming aware that engineering was no longer a British monopoly. On April 12 Jung reported that the Council of the A.S.E. had declared its readiness to 'enter into communications with the Engineers of Germany and France and desired particulars as to the state and administration of the Engineers' societies in the respective countries'. They were particularly concerned to know about conditions among the German metalworkers — hours, wages, union contributions, friendly benefits and degree of union organisation. Though the A.S.E. never got to the point of affiliating to the International, Danter, their President, asked for details of affiliation fees on May 10, 1870.[2]

The results of this contact soon became apparent when the Paris ironmoulders went on strike for wage increases, the abolition of overtime, piece-work and Sunday work and for the payment of wages fortnightly instead of monthly. The International referred the Paris appeal to a number of British unions and for the first time the A.S.E. replied favourably. Allan in his monthly report to the Society for June 1870 felt the need to tread his way warily. He was fully aware, he said, of the 'delicacy' of the question, owing to the 'long and severe strain which the depression of trade has made upon the resources of our members'. Nevertheless, he favoured a loan of £264 to the Parisians which was endorsed in a ballot vote of the membership by the huge majority of 7,045 to 557. The Ironfounders, who had earlier regretted their inability to help because of the financial position, were stimulated by this example to contribute a loan of £25, with apologies for the smallness of the sum.[3]

---

[1] G.C. *Minutes*, March 8, 22, April 26, 1870. On April 26 a deputation consisting of Applegarth, Hales and Jung was appointed to present the address of the Paris painters to their London colleagues.

[2] G.C. *Minutes*, April 26, 1870. See also letter from Marx, as Corresponding Secretary for Germany, in the Zürich *Tagwacht*, June 4, 1870. This letter is not in the *Sochinenia*.

[3] G.C. *Minutes*, June 7, *Beehive*, August 6 and *Fortnightly Review*, November 1870.

RELATIONS WITH APPLEGARTH

In the year preceding the Paris Commune, the International retained considerable prestige among the British trade unions which had come to accept it as a useful and even necessary adjunct to their work. Marx still wielded, whenever he chose to exert it, the dominant influence on the General Council and he no doubt hoped through this position to win in time a measure of understanding and support for his ideas in England. Among trade union members of the Council, Applegarth was probably closest to Marx, and when Lord Lichfield, concerned at the report that Applegarth had voted for land nationalisation at Basle, asked him for a memorandum on his views, Applegarth, as a matter of course, asked Marx for help. Marx duly sent him a four-page draft. Land, he pointed out, had originally been expropriated by the few through right of conquest. By organisation the majority could win back their rights. Adequate production could only be obtained through cultivation in large-scale units and public ownership was the only just way of securing this.[1] Marx was overjoyed and wrote to Engels that Applegarth, accepted by both houses of Parliament as the leading representative of trade unionism, had asked his advice. Engels was suitably impressed. 'The request of Applegarth', he replied, 'is remarkable . . . these damned lords and members of Parliament think that the whole labour movement is in their pocket, because Odger and Potter play with them and the *Beehive* sold out. These gentry will be surprised.'[2]

But Marx and Engels were too sanguine. Applegarth's support for the International was sincere and deep enough to survive the Paris Commune, but his approach to politics remained eclectic. He not only served on the committees of the Labour Representation and National Education Leagues, whose objects were at least compatible with those of the International, but also gave public support to the launching of the Emigration League, a much more dubious proposition from Marx's point of view. The League's objects were 'to remove by emigration the superfluous hands from the labour market in England, and by that means to mitigate distress at home, and to strengthen the British empire through the extension of prosperous colonies

[1] *Chronik*, p. 287. Reprinted in *Marx-Engels-Lenin-Stalin Facsimiles.* Moscow, 1939 — no pagination — and in *Labour Monthly*, September 1952,
[2] Marx to Engels, December 4; Engels to Marx, December 9, 1869.

abroad'. On the platform at the inaugural meeting were Beales, Potter, Guile, Druitt and Applegarth — the last two of whom had close associations with the International. Druitt justified his support by referring to the high level of unemployment in the tailoring trade. Applegarth was more apologetic in tone. No doubt there would one day be better means of dealing with unemployment in the building trade, 'but at present the evils existed' and no alternative policy was to hand.[1]

THE GENERAL COUNCIL'S FINANCES

Marx did not then, despite his personal prestige, succeed in influencing to any considerable extent the political thought of the trade union leaders with whom he worked harmoniously on the General Council. Nor did anyone ever succeed in converting trade union good-will into cash to salvage the shaky finances of the Council. The annual report of the finance committee presented on May 10, 1870 disclosed an expenditure of £47 : 7 : 5 against an income of £36 : 1 : 6. The income included a donation of £10 from Cowell Stepney who had just resigned as Treasurer on the grounds that the position should be held by a worker. A balance of £4 remained. Things would have been much more serious but for the fact that for a whole year — from June 1867 to June 1868, when the Council had moved to Truelove's premises at 256 High Holborn — Maurice had not charged rent for the use of a room at his coffee house in 16 Castle Street. Despite this, there were arrears of rent amounting to £4 : 4 : 0 and Eccarius reminded the members that £19 was still outstanding from the Geneva Congress in 1866. There seemed also to be some slackness in collecting subscriptions from affiliated organisations.[2]

THE *BEEHIVE*

In addition to a chronically unstable financial position, the General Council was suffering even more than usual from the

[1] *Beehive*, January 8, 1870. For further discussion, see *An Appeal to Edmond Beales, Esq., M.A., to Publicly Renounce or Justify his Connection with Sir George Grey and Co.'s Emigration League . . . with Mr. Beales's Reply* by J. Weston, Treasurer of the Land and Labour League. For the strong opposition in the American labour movement to attempts to stimulate European emigration see S. Bernstein, *The International in America*, New York, 1962.

[2] G.C. *Minutes*, May 3, 10, 1870.

lack of an effective Press organ. Relations with the *Beehive*, never very good, had now reached breaking point. Hodgson Pratt, friend of the Liberal magnate, Samuel Morley, had saved the paper financially and secured the appointment, as controlling editor, of the Rev. Henry Solly, a Unitarian clergyman. Since then the paper had tended to give less space to reporting working-class activities. 'Last Sunday', Engels told Marx on November 17, 1869, 'the *Beehive* had nothing about the International but of course an account of the wedding of the Duke of Abercorn's daughter instead.'

Despite an occasional complaint in the *Beehive*'s correspondence column, the situation persisted. On April 26, 1870 Marx proposed that the General Council should sever all relations with the paper. 'He said it had suppressed our resolutions and mutilated our reports and delaying them so that the dates had been falsified. Even the mention that the Irish prisoners were being discussed had been suppressed. Next to this the tone of the Bee-Hive was contrary to the rules and platform of the Association. It preached harmony with the capitalists and the Association had declared war with capitalist rule.'

On the General Council the condemnation of the *Beehive* was unanimous. Even Mottershead, who had less reason than most to complain of its Irish policy, insisted that the break be made as publicly as possible. It was no longer a working-class paper, he added — 'It used to be milk and water. The milk has evaporated.' Some embarrassment was caused by the fact that Applegarth was a member of the *Beehive*'s Consulting Committee. He had once, he explained, had hopes of the paper becoming useful. But as things stood, he valued his connection with the International too much not to resign from the *Beehive* if he were forced to a choice. Three weeks later the General Council unanimously and publicly severed all relations with the paper which, except for an interval of two years, had served as its organ since 1864.[1] By the end of the year it was arranged to publish reports from the General Council in the *Eastern Post*, a radical weekly appearing in the East End of London.

As over Ireland, Applegarth had voted for the decision on

---

[1] G.C. *Minutes*, April 26 and May 17, 1870. The names of Applegarth and Odger continued to appear on the list of members of the Consulting Committee which was published from time to time in the *Beehive* until the end of 1870. But there is no evidence that this body was ever consulted by the Rev. Solly during his editorship.

the *Beehive* with mixed feelings.[1] His uneasiness may well have been due to a recognition that however much agreement there might be on current issues, his own outlook differed fundamentally from that of Marx and many of his other colleagues on the Council. Marx might condemn the *Beehive* for preaching 'harmony with the capitalists', but Applegarth's outlook was closer to that of the *Beehive*, however he might criticise its treatment of the news. In his own trade he deemed it a matter for congratulation that employers and workers 'not only meet on a footing of equality, and adjust any casual differences by arbitration; but, by their combined efforts, technical schools for the building trades have been established' — for example, in Bradford.[2]

If Applegarth's support for the International was none the less wholehearted it was because his vision, however empirical, was not restricted to the narrow confines of his trade. Speaking a month later at the annual dinner of the Islington branch of his Society he 'defended the policy of taking up all questions affecting the welfare of the members of the society, and working men generally, whether political or social. He complimented the society upon . . . their aid to the Reform League, the International Society, the National Education League, and similar movements, with all of which he had earnestly and consistently worked. (Cheers !).' [3]

THE PARIS 'PLOT'

The public breach with the *Beehive* merely formalised a situation which had existed for many months. While the statement was being prepared, events in France compelled the General Council to make public another and more longstanding breach — that with its erstwhile London French section, which had for some time been operating as a separate society while continuing to describe itself as a branch of the International.

These events were precipitated by the action of the French police in arresting in preparation for the Emperor's forthcoming plebiscite a number of known opponents of the régime, including some members of the International. At the same

[1] Marx to Engels, April 28, 1870.
[2] Tenth annual report to the A.S.C.J., *Beehive*, May 7, 1870.
[3] *Beehive*, June 11, 1870.

time the police announced the discovery of a plot to assassinate the Emperor and denounced Gustave Flourens, at that time in London, as the principal plotter. Flourens was associated publicly with the so-called London French branch of the International. The General Council was therefore obliged to repudiate the French society, though not in such a way as to give credence to the fabrications of the French police.

On May 3, with Applegarth in the chair, Marx read to the Council a statement on the affair which was unanimously adopted. In a letter to Marx on November 29, 1869 Engels had derided the Fenian propensity for 'empty conspiracy and the fabrication of small coups', while applauding their decision to contest an election at Tipperary — 'a path of action which, even if legal in appearance, is still far more revolutionary than what they have been doing since the failure of their insurrection'. In his statement on the French 'Plot', Marx took the same line. Branches of the International must act as centres of working-class organisation, while helping on 'all political movements tending to . . . the economical emancipation of the working class'. The very nature of an association which identified itself with the workers 'would exclude from it every form of a secret society'. If the working classes, who formed the great bulk of society and who produced all wealth, could be said to conspire, 'they conspire publicly, as the sun conspired against darkness, in the full consciousness that without their pale there exists no legitimate power. . . . The noisy and violent measures against our French sections are exclusively intended to serve one single purpose — the manipulation of the plebiscite.' [1]

At a time when the International was 'undergoing severe persecutions on the part of the Austrian and French Governments, who eagerly catch at the most flimsy pretexts', the General Council was not prepared to be saddled with responsibility for statements and, perhaps, actions which might emanate from the associates of Félix Pyat. On May 10, therefore, a resolution drafted by Marx was adopted by the Council, declaring that 'the so-called Federal French Branch ceased two years ago to form part of the "International", and to

[1] *Beehive*, May 7, 1870. See also *The Times*, May 4, *Reynolds's*, May 8 and G.C. *Minutes*, May 3, 1870. See also the long report in *The Times*, May 5, 1870, on the functioning of the General Council and its relations with trade union and political movements on the Continent.

have any connection whatever with the General Council in London, or any of the branches of that association on the Continent'.[1]

In opposition to the Proudhonists, Marx had successfully upheld the necessity of political action by the working class. He maintained this point of view consistently against other groups which advanced terrorism as an adjunct to political action — the Fenians and the London French. The issue was soon to recur in a new form when the Bakuninists and the Blanquists — from opposite poles — were to form secret societies for conspiratorial purposes. Of these the Bakuninists, who advocated conspiracy and spontaneous insurrection as an alternative to political action, were by far the more dangerous. The conflict was due to break out into the open at the Congress of the International to be held at Mainz in September, 1870. Owing to the outbreak of war the Congress was not held, and the acute phase of the conflict was postponed for a year.

THE FRANCO-PRUSSIAN WAR

The situation in France made it clearly inadvisable to persist in the original decision to hold the fifth annual Congress in Paris. On May 17 Marx told the General Council that the German Social Democrats had invited them to hold their Congress in Mainz and by June 28 an invitation had duly arrived from the Burgomaster. The Franco-Prussian War which broke out on July 19 made this impossible and at once pushed all other issues into the background.

Marx wrote a short address on the war, dated July 23, which the General Council approved and ordered to be printed. It predicted with devastating accuracy that 'whatever may be the incidents of Louis Bonaparte's war with Prussia, the death knell of the Second Empire has already sounded at Paris. It will end as it began, by a parody.' While condemning the foreign policy of Prussia, Marx still considered that 'on the German side the war is a war of defence . . .', adding the warning that 'if the German working class allow the present war to lose its strictly defensive character and to degenerate into a war against the French people, victory or defeat will prove alike disastrous'. But Marx felt confident enough to say that the principles of the International had spread too widely

---

[1] *Beehive*, May 14; *The Times*, May 12; *Reynolds's*, May 15, 1870.

and sunk too deep for this to happen and he quoted from statements and public meetings in both the warring countries. He expressed the hope, which his followers were to maintain with even more disappointing results, that the workers of all countries would join hands to put an end to war. The address was issued in the form of leaflets in English, German and French.[1]

The address was well received. A thousand copies were originally printed and on August 2 the General Council decided on a further thousand. A message was read to the Council from John Stuart Mill who declared himself 'highly pleased with the address. There was not one word in it that ought not to be there; it could not have been done with fewer words.' *Reynolds's* praised it in a glowing editorial on August 7, while John Morley, in the September issue of the *Fortnightly Review*, expressed his approval.

The policy of the General Council, as displayed in its first address on the war, was distinctive in stressing the danger that 'the dark figure of Russia looming in the background' might gain in power as a result of 'this suicidal strife'. Otherwise it was not as yet very different from that of other radical and labour organisations. The *Beehive*, in an editorial on July 23, insisted that while Germany was fighting a defensive war, the struggle ought not to end in a purely military triumph of Germany over France. The *Republican*, a journal close to the Land and Labour League, placed the main blame for the war on Louis Napoleon in its first issue in September 1870. Edmund Beales's Workmen's Peace Committee, on the other hand, was more pacifist in tone, calling for the war to be ended by arbitration. The manifesto of the Labour Representation League, though less pacifist, maintained a similar neutrality and denounced the war as being 'purely dynastic in character' on both sides and also appealed for it to be submitted to arbitration. England should not participate in the war unless the 'honour or legitimate interests of the nation' were found to be at stake.[2]

Such differences in analysis and approach did not interfere

---

[1] The distribution list — G.C. *Minutes*, undated but end-July 1870 — included twenty-five trade unions, four trades councils, two weekly papers — the *Examiner* and the *National Reformer* — and the Land and Labour League, as well as a number of prominent radicals.

[2] *Beehive*, July 30, 1870. The signatories included William Allan, of the A.S.E., as Treasurer and Lloyd Jones as Secretary.

with the unity of the various societies and individuals who stood for one or another brand of liberal or working-class internationalism — a unity that was to last until the proclamation of the Paris Commune in March 1871. On July 31, 1870 a manifesto appeared drawn up by Eugene Oswald and Charles Cassal, a radical German and Frenchman respectively, domiciled in England. The large number of signatures from Germany and France included those of Élie and Élisée Réclus, the future anarchist leaders, Louis Blanc, August Bebel and Wilhelm Liebknecht.[1] The terms of the manifesto resembled those of the General Council. The peoples on both sides were urged to end the war which was described as having been forced on both countries by their respective rulers. As in the International's Address, emphasis was laid on the existence in Europe of 'a dark power which has an interest in the weakening of civilised nations! How that power must rejoice in this way! . . . How worthy is this war of applause of Russian autocracy.' A number of signatories — Marx, Engels, H. J. Rothschild, Alfred Talandier, Liebknecht, Bebel and P. Robin — appended a footnote stating that: 'We agree with the above address, so far as its general sentiments coincide with the manifesto on the war issued by the General Council of the International Working Men's Association'.[2]

And, indeed, there was one significant difference between the two manifestoes. In the Oswald-Cassal document there was no special emphasis on the defensive character of the war for Germany, stressed in the first manifesto of the International. For more than twenty years radicals and socialists, with considerable justification, had denounced Louis Napoleon as the enemy of democracy beyond as well as within the borders of France. The national unification of Germany and Italy was in the view of Marx and Engels a progressive development, facilitating the development of capitalism and hence of socialism. Finally, the day after the declaration of war, Marx explained to Engels: 'The French need a thrashing. If the Prussians win, the centralisation of the state power will be useful for the centralisation of the German working class', a class which since 1866 had begun to show itself 'superior to the

[1] Bebel and Liebknecht had recently been elected members of the North German Parliament. For their declaration on the war, speaking as members of the International, see G.C. *Minutes*, July 26, 1870.

[2] *Reminiscences of a Busy Life*, by Eugene Oswald, pp. 411-17, London, 1911.

French both theoretically and organisationally. This predominance over the French on the world stage would also mean the predominance of our theory over Proudhon's, etc.' [1]

THE FRENCH REPUBLIC

Such differentiation between France and Germany was, however, unusual and the more straightforward 'plague on both your houses' Internationalism of the Peace Society was by far the most common attitude in labour circles. But with the spectacular German victories and the likelihood that they would be followed by territorial annexation, opinion began to change. In his pamphlet, *A Word for France*,[2] written just before the abdication of the French Emperor, Professor Beesly explained how he had supported Germany at the beginning of the war because of his hostility to French militarism. But once the Germans became the aggressors and threatened to annexe Alsace-Lorraine, they must be opposed. As the pamphlet was in the press, news came through of the proclamation of the French Republic on September 6 and Beesly added a postscript: 'Since this pamphlet went to the printer the Republic has been proclaimed. Now I know what London workmen will do. The grand cause is once more before them. The Republic against monarchy and nobles, national independence against foreign domination — it is a simple issue.'

The Labour Representation League rallied at once to the French cause, warning against the dangers of aggressive German expansion and also of a possible holy alliance against the new Republic. 'Holy alliances', it warned, 'acting openly or covertly in favour of kings and aristocracies, will never again receive countenance from the people of England.' [3]

The General Council was meeting on the day the Republic was proclaimed. Among some of its members there was a carry-over of the earlier hostility to France. Weston suggested that the second address from the Council should be principally directed against France, since the Republic was continuing the Emperor's war. Serraillier resisted this, pointing out that the new Government had offered terms for peace.

---

[1] Marx to Engels, July 20, 1870.
[2] Published by E. Truelove, from 256 High Holborn, now also the meeting place of the General Council.
[3] *Beehive*, September 10, 1870.

N

Harris appealed to the stronger side to show magnanimity, but Boon was quite happy to let the Germans have Alsace-Lorraine, providing 'the people themselves had a voice in the annexation'. As so often before, Marx clinched the discussion. His reaction to the birth of the Republic was instantaneous. His earlier pro-German attitude vanished completely, as he predicted that 'the French would revive under the revolution & the Germans would become what the French had been'. So far from being a peaceful race, as some of the English papers were arguing, the Germans had dismembered Poland and oppressed both Hungary and Italy. The Council agreed that Marx, together with Jung, Milner and Serraillier, should form a committee to draw up the new address.[1]

Meetings were held in many parts of the country to support the French Republic. Joseph Cowen was again active in Newcastle. A public meeting was held in Bradford. At a London meeting of the Workmen's Peace Committee addressed by its Secretary, Cremer, and by Odger, Beales moved a resolution from the chair welcoming the French Republic 'as calculated to lead to a speedy end of the war'. At another meeting in Hyde Park, members of the General Council — Odger, Weston, Applegarth and Mottershead — spoke alongside such ex-members as Cremer, Le Lubez and Howell.[2] At a meeting of twenty thousand 'Republicans' in Trafalgar Square, with the Land and Labour League represented on the platform, Mottershead moved a resolution calling for a British initiative to promote an armistice followed by arbitration.

The traditional working-class and radical policy of support for republics and opposition to 'Holy Alliances' was once again in evidence. At the other extreme, the *Standard*, in a highly critical article, blamed Positivism and its Francophile traditions for the propaganda of such labour spokesmen as Odger and Holyoake.

The International found itself completely in harmony with these currents of radical opinion. The second address of the General Council, written like the first by Marx, is also too well known to need detailed examination. The most important statement by Marx on foreign affairs during the whole period of the International, it was almost uncanny in its grasp of the

---

[1] G.C. *Minutes*, September 6, 1870.
[2] Another speaker was Shipton, of the House Painters, subsequently Secretary of the London Trades Council.

world situation and the accuracy of its long-range forecasts. It could justly claim that the predictions in the first address about the fall of Bonapartism, together with its warnings of the danger that the war would lose its strictly defensive character for Germany 'and degenerate into a war against the French people' had been quickly confirmed.   A further warning was now given, also to be vindicated by history — in this case over the next fifty years.   If, said Marx, 'the arrogance of success and dynastic intrigue lead Germany to a dismemberment of France', France would become either 'the *avowed* tool of Russian aggrandisement' or prepare for a war of revenge which would become 'a war with the combined Sclavonian and Roman races' against the Teutons.   'Do the Teuton patriots', Marx asked pertinently, 'really believe that liberty and peace will be guaranteed to Germany by forcing France into the arms of Russia ?' [1]

The first address had predicted that the German workers would prevent their Government from turning the war into one of aggression.   In the second, Marx abandoned his wishful thinking.   'If the French workmen amidst peace failed to stop the aggressor, are the German workmen more likely to stop the victor amidst the clangour of arms ?'

Turning to the position in France, Marx, while welcoming the Republic, pointed out that 'the Orleanists have seized the strongholds of the army and the police, while to the professed Republicans have fallen the talking departments'.   The new French Republic 'inherited from the Empire, not only ruins, but also its dread of the working class'.[2]   At the same time Marx issued a clear warning against a premature insurrection by the workers of Paris.   They were admittedly faced with 'circumstances of extreme difficulty'.   But 'any attempt at upsetting the new Government in the present crisis, when the enemy is almost knocking at the doors of Paris, would be a desperate folly'.   For the time being, the task of the French workers was less spectacular.   'Let them calmly and resolutely improve the opportunities of Republican liberty,

[1] 'And a war No. 2 of this kind will act as the midwife to the inevitable social revolution in Russia', wrote Marx to Sorge, on September 1, 1870, with even more uncanny precision.

[2] In its first issue, September 1870, the *Republican* had foreseen some such development.   'I presume', it wrote of Louis Napoleon, 'that his reign and dynasty are at an end . . . All the *respectable* rascals will soon be clamouring for the Orleans dynasty.'

for the work of their own class organisation.' [1]

Finally, the address praised the stand already taken up by the British labour leaders in bringing pressure on their own Government to recognise the French Republic, and to oppose 'the dismemberment of France which part of the English press is so shameless enough to howl for . . . the same press that for twenty years deified Louis Bonaparte . . . that frantically cheered on the slave-holders' rebellion. . . '. In this address there was no facile prediction of an inevitable victory for the workers, but instead the stark warning that if they failed to respond correctly to the situation 'the present tremendous war will be but the harbinger of still deadlier international feuds, and lead in every nation to a renewed triumph over the workman of the lords of the sword, of the soil, of capital'.

One of the first to recognise the outstanding merits of the two addresses was Edward Beesly, with whom Marx's relations were now very close. After thoroughly reading both documents, he wrote to Marx on September 14th: 'I think their importance can hardly be overrated. They are admirably reasoned, & the spirit is excellent. I now recognise as I never did before the importance of the International and I repent that I have not co-operated with its meetings in the past, though I have always sympathised.' [2] Beesly's support was firm and like that of other leading Positivists in England, was to survive the period of storm that opened six months later with the proclamation of the Commune in Paris.

[1] Cf. Marx to Engels, September 12, 1870. 'If anything at all could be done in Paris, a rising of the workers before peace is concluded should be prevented.'

[2] The letter is in the Institute of Marxism-Leninism, Moscow.

CHAPTER XI

From the Fall of France to the Paris Commune

WITH the proclamation of the French Republic, English radical opinion swung round from a position of neutrality tilted against France to one of support for the Republic and hostility to German aggression and annexation. Marx's second address on the war was entirely in line with this mood and, though there had been prior discussion, there was no disagreement on the General Council when the address was presented.

The only notable exception to this trend seems to have been Engels, who had as early as August 15 in a letter to Marx criticised his friend's view that the war was losing its defensive character for Germany. On September 4 he wrote again to Marx saying, in a spirit of apparent levity, that the defence of Paris might prove 'an entertaining episode' and sneering at the 'perpetual little panics of the French'.

Marx reacted more quickly to the change and he revealed to Engels his fear of precipitate action on the part of the Paris workers. There were already, he told him on September 6, enough adventurers like Félix Pyat in Paris to make it likely that 'stupidities' would be committed 'in the name of the International'. Luckily, he added, the General Council had sent Serraillier to Paris to discuss the position with the French Council on the spot.

Apart from Serraillier, Marx was encouraged by the attitude of Eugène Dupont who was also opposed to the adventurism of the London French and who, like Marx, wanted the workers to take advantage of the political freedom to build up their organisations, but otherwise to pursue a cautious policy until the peace treaty was signed.[1]

THE CAMPAIGN FOR RECOGNITION

Besides giving cautionary advice to the Parisians, Marx saw the task of the General Council as being to campaign, together

[1] Marx to Engels, September 7, 1870.

with other sections of the labour movement as well as many leading Positivists, for the recognition of the French Republic. On his initiative, a deputation to Gladstone was arranged.[1]   It included Applegarth, Coulson, Dunning, Howell, Potter, Osborne, Hartwell, Weston, Hales and Cohn among others and represented every section of the London labour movement. Potter, the chief spokesman, said that any annexation of territory would provoke the speedy resumption of hostilities and would be opposed by democratic opinion in Germany. Howell contrasted Britain's delay in recognising the Republic with the speedy recognition granted by the U.S.A. and Switzerland.   Applegarth made similar points.[2]

The movement in support of France was meanwhile gathering momentum.   Odger drafted an address to Jules Favre, the new French foreign minister, which was adopted at a Hyde Park meeting on September 8.   The meeting asked the British Government to recognise the Republic and use its influence to secure an armistice and arbitration.   Odger left for Paris to deliver the address to Favre in person.   Beesly and other leading Positivists wrote a number of articles in support of the Republic, while the Conservative Press, which on the whole deprecated the campaign, treated the Positivists and the labour movement as a united force.

Marx was anxious to involve Beesly more directly in the International's activities.   He wrote to him on September 12 to stress the importance of recognition and to tell him of the work of the Association.   Beesly replied in friendly terms two days later, enclosing £1 towards the support of Serraillier in Paris.   On September 16 Marx wrote suggesting that Beesly should write an article on the International in the *Fortnightly Review*.   The article appeared in the November issue and Beesly drafted it in close consultation with Marx.[3]   It provided by far the fullest account of the International's history and organisation to appear in the Press up to that time.   It also defended the International against the more sensational attacks. From time to time there appeared 'paragraphs, with the well

---

[1] Marx to Engels, September 10, 1870 and *Karl Marx, Chronik seines Lebens*, p. 297.

[2] *Beehive*, October 1, 1870.   For Gladstone's cautious, non-committal reply, see *Standard*, September 26, 1870.

[3] Letters from Marx to Beesly in the *Social Democrat*, London, vol. VII, 1903, pp. 231-2, and Beesly to Marx, September 18, 20, October 18, 24, 1870, in Institute of Marxism-Leninism, Moscow.

known smack of the police office or the counting house . . .
containing alarming statements as to the aims of the association, its mysterious activity, and still more mysterious resources'.   Beesly was especially concerned to defend 'the
foreign members, in whose hands the continental correspondence necessarily lies' as 'men of great ability and information'.
His praise of Marx was wholehearted.   To no one, he insisted,
was the success of the International due so much 'as to Dr. Karl
Marx, who, in his acquaintance with the history and statistics
of the industrial movement in all parts of Europe is, I should
imagine, without a rival'.   Beesly concluded with a statement
of the International's attitude to the Franco-Prussian War and
he stressed in particular the value of the Association in spreading internationalist and anti-militarist teachings among the
workers.[1]

The campaign for the Republic touched off a strong
revival of interest in international questions throughout the
labour movement.   In November the Manchester and Salford
Trades Council affiliated to the International following a visit
from Eugène Dupont.   Shortly afterwards the Birmingham
Trades Council followed suit.[2]   These were the only trades
councils ever to affiliate and in the case of Birmingham at least
the grounds for joining were explicitly internationalist.[3]

For the first few months from September 1870 the campaign
united all sections of the labour movement.   The International
took part in an enthusiastic and packed meeting of workers in
London to demand recognition.   Odger, Lloyd Jones, Howell,
Bradlaugh and Lucraft spoke — the latter on behalf of the
General Council.   Beesly's close collaborator, Frederic Harrison, sent a message of support stating that no class had a more
direct interest in democracy and self-determination than the
workers.[4]   Marx carried the campaign into the Press in a letter
to the *Daily News* attacking the arrest of Social Democrats in
Brunswick and the banning of socialist papers in Germany as a

[1] See also Marx to Beesly, October 19, 1870 for Marx's views on the fiasco
of the Lyons Commune, following the disastrous intervention of Bakunin
and Cluseret.

[2] G.C. *Minutes*, November 8, 29, 1870; January 17, 1871. *Beehive*,
December 10, 1870; *Eastern Post*, January 21, 1871; Birmingham Trades
Council *Minutes*, August 4 and September 2, 1870.

[3] Wm. Gilliver, a cordwainer, was Chairman of the Birmingham Trades
Council.   For his correspondence with the General Council in 1867 on
the Irish question, see Chapter VIII.

[4] *Beehive*, January 7, 14, 1871.

whole. Bismarck, he said, was using diplomatic pressure to stop criticism of Prussia in foreign papers. He concluded optimistically: 'France — and her cause is fortunately far from desperate — fights at this moment not only for her own national independence, but for the liberty of Germany and Europe'.[1]

DIVERGING VIEWS

Though all sections of labour were agreed on recognition, divisions soon appeared on other issues. The first cause of dissension was Odger's desire to link the campaign for the French Republic with support for the Orleanist Government of Jules Favre. Marx was strongly opposed and after accusing Odger of 'speaking against the truth' gave the General Council a detailed and highly derogatory account of Favre's career which he was later to elaborate in his address on the Paris Commune.[2] He laid an accurate finger on the dilemma of Favre's Government when he wrote to Siegfried Meyer in America that it 'thinks it can wage a revolutionary war without a revolution'.[3]

Another cause of disagreement arose over the policy to be pursued by Britain in relation to the war. On one side, there was the pacifism of Cremer, Beales and their Workmen's Peace Association who confined themselves to demanding recognition of the Republic, followed by a British initiative to secure a settlement through arbitration. Mottershead, though a member of the General Council, supported this approach.[4] At the other extreme, a meeting called by the Labour Representation League condemned Germany's war as an attack by despotism on democracy and called for British intervention on the side of France.[5]

The position of the Labour Representation League found some supporters on the General Council. Eccarius, Boon and Weston all demanded active British intervention against

---

[1] Letter of January 16, published in *Daily News*, January 19, 1871. Reprinted in *Marx-Engels Selected Correspondence*, 1956, pp. 308-10.
[2] G.C. *Minutes*, January 17, 1871. See also Marx to Jung, January 18, 1871, in *Soc.* XXVI, pp. 85-6 and *Chronik*, p. 300.
[3] Letter of January 21, 1871 in Marx and Engels, *Letters to Americans, 1848–1895*, New York, 1953, p. 81.
[4] *Beehive*, February 25 and *Eastern Post*, February 26, 1871.
[5] *Beehive*, December 31, 1870.

Germany.[1] Engels, who had joined the General Council,[2] supported the more moderate line arguing that the International should support the broader movement for recognition. As ever, he, like Marx, judged the question principally in terms of its effect on the power of Russia. Following the French defeat, he pointed out, Russia had repudiated those clauses of the Treaty of Paris imposed on her after the Crimean War which prohibited her from keeping warships in the Black Sea. Britain's naval position in the Eastern Mediterranean was threatened and at that point she could, with advantage, have declared war on Russia. That would have saved not only France, but also Poland. Unfortunately, the moment had been allowed to pass and now the most that could be secured was recognition of the Republic. If the popular movement was not strong enough to secure that, it was hardly likely to push Britain into a war.

Marx took the same line and also urged the Council to demand no more than recognition — 'if that failed all the rest must fail'. In both France and England the bourgeoisie was basically anti-Republican, since both feared that a republic must eventually develop along socialist lines and that it was 'the political form of government under which the changes required by the working class can best be effected'. For this reason and because of the family link between the English and Prussian courts, England 'followed in the footsteps of the Holy Alliance'.[3] Bitterly, Marx concluded that 'the only place where the English Government can employ physical force is Ireland'.

Towards the end of February Serraillier's first report arrived from Paris. It made gloomy reading. The French section of the International had been confused by the defection of its foundation member, Tolain, now a member of Parliament. Varlin, whose loyalty was never in doubt, was still, under Proudhonist influence, opposing political action by the workers. Serraillier had helped to reorganise the French

[1] Weston, probably under the influence of Odger and Le Lubez, had reversed his earlier anti-French stand — G.C. *Minutes*, September 6, 1870, — see above.

[2] After many years of patient waiting, Engels had at last sold out his share of the family business and moved to London. He became a member of the General Council and Corresponding Secretary for Italy — G.C. *Minutes*, September 20, 1870 and *Chronik*, p. 298.

[3] *Eastern Post*, February 19, 26, 1871. See also *Pervy International v dni Parishkoi Kommuny*, p. 9, n. 1.

Federal Council, but his task had not been made easier by
Odger's public support for Favre. Parisians were assuming
that Odger spoke for the General Council and Serraillier suggested that he be publicly repudiated.

Only one member of the Council spoke up for Odger.
Citizen Weston, the old Owenite, was moving politically to the
right. On February 21 he had tried to get the Council to consider joint action with John Stuart Mill's Land Tenure Reform
Association.[1] A week later he repeated the suggestion and also
defended not only Odger but Le Lubez, who as leader of the
French republicans in London was campaigning in support of
Favre. Marx pressed the charge against Odger. While no one
in Paris took notice of Le Lubez, Odger was widely identified
with the International and assumed to speak for its General
Council.[2] Within a matter of weeks the heroic and tragic
episode of the Paris Commune was to take place and the breach
with Odger became final.

At its last meeting before the Commune, the General
Council received a message from the Birmingham Trades
Council, writing as 'a branch of the International'. On the
initiative of Gilliver and Loughton — characteristically enough,
a cordwainer and a carpenter — the Trades Council proposed
that an address be circulated in France and Germany in favour
of peace and the strengthening of the International — 'the only
association that appears likely at present to produce that
fraternal feeling by which the curse of war and its primary
causes may be swept from the earth'.[3]

Before the meeting broke up, Hales raised for the third
time the question of establishing an English Federal Council.
He gave notice that he would put it on the agenda for the next
meeting, but by March 21 there were more urgent matters to
consider. Hales had asked for an autonomous English section,
separate from the General Council, for the first time in 1866
when it had simply been brushed aside. On the second
occasion, after Basle, the Land and Labour League was about
to be started and it seemed as though this might provide what

---

[1] Mill's demands included taxation based on land betterment and the
repeal of the laws of primogeniture and entail. Characteristically, these
proposals were aimed at improving the distribution of wealth while preserving private property intact.

[2] G.C. *Minutes*, February 28, 1871.

[3] Birmingham Trades Council *Minutes*, March 4 and G.C. *Minutes*,
March 14, 1871.

Hales was looking for. Now, nearly eighteen months later, it was clear that it would not. Moreover, although two trades councils had affiliated to the International and the T.U.C. had once again recommended trade unions to support it,[1] attendance at meetings of the General Council was poor and the finances as chaotic as ever. There had been no strike of importance since that of the Paris ironmoulders in the middle of 1870 and while trade unionists had plenty of good will for the international, their effective participation in its affairs was pitifully small. Beesly in his *Fortnightly* article had deliberately avoided this rather embarrassing subject, 'because to have done so without making some precise and incontrovertible statement as to the number of English members would have had, in my judgement, a bad effect. . . '.[2] Marx himself made the same point to the General Council a few weeks later, when he told them that: 'Respecting the list of members it would not be well to publish what the real strength was as the outside public always thought the active members much more numerous than they really were'.[3] Still, Marx was not too disturbed about the state of the General Council. What mattered to him was its potential, the possibility that in a crisis it might be able to convert its trade union good will into positive action. It must be kept in being, 'this powerful engine', to be used in the service of the revolution whenever it came.

THE COMMUNE

Suddenly, it came. On March 18 an insurrection in Paris transferred political power to the National Guard. Three days later the General Council had its first detailed report from Serraillier. Then Engels gave an account from his own sources of how the National Guard had refused to hand over its arms to the Government and of how Thiers and his followers had withdrawn to Versailles, leaving Paris in the hands of a people's army.[4]

In England opinion was at first stunned then divided. Beesly came at once to the defence of the Commune. In a

[1] The resolution was moved by Eccarius in a speech on the eight-hour day in which he also advocated international working-class unity as an antidote to wars. Supported by Beesly and Odger, it was passed unanimously.

[2] Beesly to Marx, October 24, 1870.

[3] G.C. *Minutes*, December 20, 1870.

[4] G.C. *Minutes.*

courageous article in the *Beehive* [1] he referred to the attacks on the Commune which had already appeared as being 'coloured by bitter antipathy to the workmen of Paris'. Although, he said, in the course of ordinary party warfare debate was reasonably free and the public able to read both sides, 'when it is a question between poor and rich, between genuine Republicanism and the manifold forms of privilege, then the writers in the press merely sing the same song, which they fancy will please the upper and middle classes'. It was a great misfortune that the workers of London had no independent source of information. Beesly dealt in detail with the misrepresentations which had already appeared and described the circumstances under which the French generals, Lecomte and Thomas, had been shot by soldiers under their command. He was as forthright and unapologetic in his defence of the Commune against charges of atrocities as he had been four years earlier in defending trade unions against attacks arising from the 'Sheffield Outrages'. Republicans, he insisted, were usually 'merciful in their hour of triumph. They leave slaughter in cold blood to the Bonapartists and Governor Eyre.' [2] As in the case of the 'Sheffield Outrages', Beesly did not justify the killings, but he insisted that 'with the exception of this solitary act of savagery, the revolution has been conducted with remarkable forbearance'. With a shrewd idea of what was to follow Beesly concluded that: 'If the reactionists should win, in the end, the upper hand, we shall see executions enough'.

On March 28 Hales moved a resolution of sympathy with the workers of Paris which the General Council unanimously approved. It was not yet clear to everyone that support for the Commune would involve a feud with Odger and a bitter public controversy with Bradlaugh, though both men and the republican movement they sponsored identified their cause

---

[1] March 25, 1871.

[2] Cf. the report of Beesly's speech at the meeting on the 'Sheffield Outrages' called by the London Trades Council on July 2, 1867, reprinted in *Labour's Formative Years, 1849–1879*, ed. James B. Jefferys, 1948, pp. 101-4. In this speech Beesly also contrasted prevailing attitudes to deaths brought about by working-class action with those resulting from the protection of property by 'such means . . . as Governor Eyre has adopted' — *ibid.*, p. 102. Eyre was Governor of Jamaica from 1862 to 1866. His suppression of a Negro riot with revolting brutality and the loss of 586 lives had provoked an outcry in England. Eyre, however, found many supporters among men of rank and property who were vociferous in denouncing trade union 'violence' and 'intimidation'.

with the Government of Thiers and Favre. But it may well
have been clear to Marx, who had already attacked Odger for
his statements on France and who now, in an obvious reference
to the republican campaign in England, told the Council that
'no republican movement can become a serious force unless it
is turned into a social movement. The wire-pullers of the
present movement, of course, have no such intention.'

At the end of the meeting Marx proposed that the Council
should issue a call to the people of Paris. This was unanimously
approved, as was Cohn's suggestion that Marx should write it.
But at the next meeting on April 4 Engels asked for a postponement in view of the confused situation prevailing in Paris. The
manifesto was not destined to be written during the lifetime of
the Commune, though requests came in from many parts of the
world for a statement on the events and on the position of the
International.[1]

Meanwhile, information was reaching Marx from a number
of correspondents, including Serraillier who was sending
reports via his wife. He described the economic position as
reasonably good and reported his own election to the Commune.[2] Leo Frankel, the Hungarian socialist and founder of
the Lyons branch of the International, had been elected to the
Commission of Labour — the first foreigner to serve in the
Commune. He told Marx that he regarded his election 'not as
a personal honour, but as a compliment to the International'
and asked for his advice on social legislation.[3]

The first pessimistic note in the correspondence from Paris
was struck by Lafargue on April 8. He said that the people
were enthusiastic but seriously short of leaders. He wondered
whether Engels could come over to Paris and help.[4]

On the basis of such correspondence, Marx and Engels
formed their impressions of the position in Paris and the Commune's chances of survival. Marx was clear, at least by April 6,

[1] Cf. the letter from H. Scheu to Marx, from Vienna, March 27, 1871,
in *Pervy International v dni Parishkoi Kommuny*, Moscow, 1941, pp. 169-70.
[2] *Ibid.*, pp. 173-4.   [3] *Ibid.*, p. 175.
[4] *Ibid.*, p. 180. Lafargue no doubt had in mind the plan of military
operations worked out by Engels for the defence of Paris against the Germans. After Engels's death, his literary executors, August Bebel and
Eduard Bernstein, destroyed the plan because they wanted to remove
evidence of Engels's 'treason' to the 'fatherland'. Cf. Gustav Meyers,
Friedrich Engels, vol. II, p. 197 and pp. 544-5 ; also B. Nicolaevsky, 'Towards a History of the Communist League, 1847–1852', in *International
Review of Social History*, 1956, p. 239, n. 1.

that the position was practically hopeless. 'It seems the Parisians are succumbing', he wrote to Liebknecht, adding that this was 'due to their too great decency.' The central committee of the National Guard, into whose hands effective power had passed when the Government withdrew from the city, should have marched at once on Versailles. Instead it had tried to avoid giving the impression that it was starting a civil war — 'as if Thiers had not already started it by his attempt at the forcible disarming of Paris' — and had then tried to regularise the constitutional position by holding elections to the Commune to which power was then transferred. All this cost time which could not be spared. Thiers and the Versaillese had been able to consolidate their position and the results would probably be fatal for the Commune.

This letter from Marx goes far to explain an apparent mystery. The Commune of Paris arose out of the only proletarian revolution to occur during the lifetime of the International. Yet during the brief two months' life of the Commune, the International remained completely silent without issuing an appeal for solidarity or even an expression of sympathy and support. Marx's brilliant and moving obituary — *The Civil War in France* — was written after its overthrow. The passivity of the International throughout the whole of that critical and tragic episode surprised many of its members. Yet in the light of Marx's known views, reflected in his letter to Liebknecht on April 6 and Lafargue's letter of April 8, the explanation seems only too obvious. From its very inception Marx knew that the Commune was doomed. With the victorious German army surrounding Paris and with the Commune effectively isolated from the rest of France, the workers could not hold on to the power they had precipitately seized. Yet something of value might have been achieved. If the Bank of France had been seized and Versailles occupied, the Commune could have exercised considerable leverage in its subsequent bargaining with the Government of Thiers. Control, however temporary, over France's reserves and access to State documents — no doubt with their share of compromising material — would have provided the Communards with the means to bargain. 'With a small amount of sound common sense', Marx wrote to the Dutch socialist, Domela Nieuwenhius, on February 22, 1881, 'they could have reached a compromise with Versailles useful to the whole mass of the people — the only thing that could be reached at the time.' But by early April Marx knew that the opportunity had been let slip. Nothing could now prevent complete disaster. But he could not say this while the Communards fought on. Nor did he feel justified in raising false hopes. Hence his silence.

When the General Council met on April 11 Marx was absent through illness, but Engels gave a grimly realistic account of the position. The Parisians had wasted too much time in talk. The favourable moment for action had been allowed to pass and now Versailles was gaining the upper hand. The Communards, under siege, were 'losing ground, wasting aimlessly their arms supply and eating up their provisions'. Though the workers had done incomparably better than in June 1848, the position was difficult and in the past two weeks had started to deteriorate.

MARX'S SILENCE

Whatever Marx might have been thinking, demands were soon raised on the General Council for some sort of action in support of the Commune. Mottershead attacked Engels's report as unduly pessimistic. Milner wanted the Council to issue a public statement on the events in Paris. The dissident London French branch had set up a body known as the International Democratic Association whose moving spirits were Le Lubez and the German Lassallean, Weber. Against opposition from Engels, the General Council agreed to co-operate with the I.D.A. in a public meeting. The meeting took place in Hyde Park on April 16 and Weston and Murray from the General Council spoke alongside Le Lubez.[1]

Meanwhile Marx was actually at work on a statement which was not issued and of which the drafts were to remain unpublished until 1934.[2] In a letter to Kugelmann on April 12, however, Marx included extracts from his first draft praising the Communards in glowing terms and comparing 'these Parisians, storming heaven, with the slaves to heaven of the

---

[1] The meeting was described as 'the war of the penny against the pound. . . . It is ignorance defying knowledge to try a fall.' *Graphic*, April 29, 1871. Quoted from *Contemporary British Opinion during the Franco-Prussian War*, by Dora Neill Raymond, Ph.D., in *Studies in History, Economics and Public Law*, vol. 100, p. 392, Columbia University, New York, 1921. The meeting received some publicity on the Continent, but little in England; see Engels to Liebknecht, April 20, 1871. *Soc.* XXVI, pp. 110-11.

[2] See *Archiv Marksa i Engelsa*, vol. III (viii), Moscow, 1934, pp. 318, 234, 348, 428.

German-Prussian Holy Roman Empire, with its posthumous masquerades reeking of the barracks, the Church, Cabbage-Junkerdom and above all, of the philistine'. The Paris Commune was demonstrating in practice what Marx had argued theoretically in his *Eighteenth Brumaire* in 1851 when he predicted that 'the next attempt of the French Revolution will be no longer, as before, to transfer the bureaucratic military machine from one hand to another, but to *smash* it, and that is essential for every real people's revolution on the Continent'. It was true that Marx had warned the Parisian workers against the 'desperate folly' of attempting an insurrection and had pleaded with them to stick to constitutional methods, at least until after the peace settlement. The presence of the Prussian troops made a workers' victory impossible. But of this, 'the bourgeois *canaille* of Versailles were also well aware. Precisely for that reason they presented the Parisians with the alternative of taking up the fight or succumbing without a struggle. In the latter case, the demoralisation of the working class would have been a far greater misfortune than the fall of any number of "leaders".'

When the General Council met on April 18 Marx faced further demands for a public statement and temporised as best he could. It was not only on the General Council that voices were raised expressing a sense of urgency and alarm. Perret wrote to Jung from Geneva to say 'what a disaster it will be for us if Paris is defeated'.[1] From Paris itself there came an appeal from the Russian woman, Eugenia Toumanovskaya, who played a distinguished part in the Commune. She wrote to Jung asking that the General Council should conduct a public campaign for aid to the Commune.[2] De Paepe wrote from Brussels to express his fears that a defeat for the Commune might lead to a renewed triumph of reaction as after the June days in 1848. The Belgian section of the International, he told Marx, had opened a campaign in support of the Commune and he suggested that the General Council do the same and also issue an address.[3]

When the General Council next met on April 25 there was still no report from Marx. He told the Council, however, of a letter from Lafargue which described both the isolation of Paris and the support of its citizens for the Commune. The rich had fled and the social legislation of the Commune, par-

[1] Letter of April 23, 1871, in *Pervy International . . .*, p. 191.
[2] *Ibid.*, pp. 192-4.   [3] *Ibid.*, pp. 194-5.

ticularly on rents and debts, had rallied the lower middle classes
to the support of a workers' government. The guillotine had
been publicly burned, and 'the highest officials receive six
thousand francs a year and the rest the same wages as a worker'.
Marx also told the Council of the attacks being made on the
International in Paris by Pyat and his followers and was asked
by the Council to draw up a statement which would make clear
once again that Pyat had no connection with the International.
Finally, a resolution was passed expelling the foundation
member, Tolain, from the Association for having 'betrayed in
the most dastardly fashion the working class' by taking up his
seat in the Assembly at Versailles.

When the General Council next met on May 2 Marx was
again absent through illness and Engels apologised for the fact
that the address was still not ready. At the same meeting two
members of the General Council who had not attended for some
time — Applegarth and Odger — were reported to be expressing concern at the possibility of their names being appended
to an address in support of the Commune. Applegarth had
recently resigned his post as Secretary of the Carpenters and
Joiners following a serious dispute with his Executive [1] and,
not being fit enough to return to the bench, was worried about
his future. He had spoken to Jung about the forthcoming
address while Odger had apparently — the *Minutes* are not
entirely clear on this — raised the same point with Eccarius.
Eccarius in fact urged that while it was admittedly the practice
to sign official statements with the names of all members of
the General Council, the practice should be suspended in
the present case. To this there was strong opposition on the
Council and it was finally agreed to ask Jung and Eccarius to
discuss the matter again with Applegarth and Odger.

When the General Council met on May 23 it had to face
the certainty of impending defeat. Marx again apologised for
not having finished the address, pleading illness, and promised
to complete it within a week. He was frank about the position
in Paris. 'The end was near but . . . the principles of the
Commune were eternal and could not be crushed. They would
assert themselves again and again until the working classes
were emancipated.' [2] The Prussians were helping Thiers and

---

[1] See A. W. Humphrey, *op. cit.*, Chapter XI.
[2] The identical phrase occurs in *The Civil War in France* which must
by this time have been practically complete.

O

Favre to crush the Commune, but this was 'only the old story. The upper classes always united to keep down the working class. In the eleventh century there was a war between some French and Norman knights and the peasants rose in insurrection ; the knights immediately forgot their differences and coalesced to crush the movement of the peasants.' Similarly, the Prussians had arrested five hundred people in Rouen on the pretext that they belonged to the International. 'The International was feared' and demands for its suppression were beginning to be raised in France.

Boon seems to have been the first to mention the need to help the refugees who might be expected to arrive soon from Paris. He was supported by Harris, whose memories of 'what was done previously in 1851' were still very much alive. Boon anticipated that those failing to escape would fall victims to the 'beastly reprisals' of Versailles and Marx suggested a public meeting, with a deputation to the British Government, to protest against atrocities which all knew to be imminent. Lucraft, who spoke almost for the last time on the Council, made remarks completely at variance with his subsequent performance. In an attack on the republican campaign of Odger and Bradlaugh he said that 'to awaken sympathy for the Commune amongst real workers will give better results, but the movement which is led by other leaders, who interfere in everything, will only be harmful'. He apologised for his frequent absences, pleading ill-health, 'but all the time he was on the side of the Commune and the Council. If the English trade unionists will not undertake this then you cannot rely on them.' Boon was pessimistic about the response from the trade unions on any political issue and Hales agreed that it would be unwise to count on them for support, 'as so many distorted views are spread about the Paris Commune'. It would be better to appeal to democratic opinion in general. On a motion of Boon, seconded by Lucraft, a propaganda sub-committee was elected to expose the cruelties of Versailles.[1] The General Council was about to be subjected to the severest test of its existence up to that time. It is doubtful whether many of its members realised the weight or intensity of the propaganda barrage they would have to withstand.

---

[1] G.C. *Minutes*, May 23, and very abridged version in *Eastern Post*, May 27, 1871.

CHAPTER XII

From the Paris Commune to the London Conference, 1871

DURING the period of the Commune there were favourable accounts and comments in the *Eastern Post*, *Reynolds's* and the *Beehive*. Public men, except for the small group of English Positivists, united to condemn it. Beesly wrote an outspoken series of articles in the *Beehive* expressing deep sympathy with the workers of Paris.[1] More guarded and more representative was the reaction of Lloyd Jones in the same paper.[2] If 'these revolted men', he wrote, 'should indulge in a reckless destruction of life or a wanton attack on the rights of property', nobody would condemn them more heartily than the workers. If, on the other hand, they laboured 'to found a permanent and popular government in the interest of the nation, to the perpetual exclusion of princely pretenders of all sorts, then the honest men of England will hail with high approval their great and good work'. This was straightforward radical republicanism with little grasp of the social issues involved in the destiny of the Commune.

Beesly was attacked in the *Beehive* by the bookbinders' leader, Dunning, a consistent opponent of 'Red Republicanism' throughout his career, who criticised Beesly's 'too innocent judgement'. Because the Commune stood for the abolition of private property it constituted a threat to 'civilised existence'.[3] By contrast, the *Beehive* published an editorial a week later which asserted that the Commune had 'proclaimed the programme of the future' not only for France, but also for Germany where 'thousands of workmen were watching with painful anxiety this contest of Paris, on which the interests of labour are staked for a generation'.[4]

In a further article Beesly [5] stressed the significance of the

---

[1] See especially *Beehive*, April 1, 1871.   [2] *Ibid.*
[3] *Ibid.*, April 8, 1871.   [4] *Ibid.*, April 15, 1871.
[5] *Ibid.*, April 22, 1871.

fact that many foreigners including Germans held leading positions in the Commune, a good omen for the future of international co-operation for which the International deserved its share of the credit. Beesley was also responsible for publishing a pamphlet by 'A French Positivist' — possibly the well-known scholar, Robinet — which gave the first detailed and friendly account of the events in Paris from March 18 to April 22.[1]

The fact that Beesly and his fellow Positivists were critical of the social aims of the Commune did not in the least diminish their admiration for the 'simple working men, who have only just learnt to handle their weapon' and who, said Beesly, 'have bid adieu to wives and little children and gone to face death for the cause of the working class as calmly as an English workman faces a strike or lock-out'. If Beesly opposed the collectivism of the Communards, this did 'not alter the fact that they are defending the cause of labour' and in defending their own aims were 'also fighting the battle of labour all the world over. . . '.[2]

Such views were not uncommon among the working class who, according to Thomas Wright, 'did sympathise with the Commune, though not upon strictly Communistic grounds . . . while the working classes generally had no particular sympathy with the Paris Commune, simply as such, they entertained a warm and very decided sympathy with the Communists on the broader ground that they believed them to be thorough patriots and true republicans. . . . Knowing that . . . a fusion of interests among the working classes throughout the world, was the chief object of the Commune ; that some of the leaders of the Commune were also leading men in the Workmen's International Association ; knowing this, they sympathised very heartily with them on that point, and wished for their success as a means to that end.'[3]

While the Press was for the most part jubilant at the fall of the Commune, a more cautious note was struck by *The Observer*. In an editorial comment on May 24 it described the leaders of

[1] *Political Notes on the Present Situation in France and Paris.* Robinet, a doctor of medicine and leading French Positivist, was probably Beesly's main correspondent in Paris during the Commune — see Beesly to Marx, June 13(?), 1871. Institute of Marxism-Leninism. Marx quoted from this pamphlet in his *Civil War in France* without mentioning its title or author.

[2] *Beehive*, May 20, 1871.

[3] *Our New Masters*, 1873, pp. 194-9. This essay first appeared as an article in *Fraser's Magazine*, July 1871, under the pseudonym 'Journeyman Engineer'.

the Commune as men who 'governed well, very patiently —
quite as well as an English vestry would have done'.[1] It dwelt
on the moderation of the Commune's social policy — the
cautious measures of rent control, prohibition of night-work
for journeymen bakers and the transfer to co-operative control
of 'a few shops whose proprietors had run away'. Nor was
The Observer in much doubt about the nature of the new rulers
of Paris, the 'Cosmopolitan Party of Order', whom 'the
removal of fears of reprisals from below would render dangerously headstrong, if not revengeful and cruel'.

A very similar estimate of the character of the Versaillese
had been made seven weeks earlier by a British eye-witness,
William Gibson, whose letters from Paris were published in
Paris During the Commune, 1871, which appeared in London in
the following year. Gibson concluded, 'from what has trans-
pired in the Assembly at Versailles, that there are many of the
deputies who would be glad to see Paris bombarded and the
city burned to the ground. They seem to forget that burning
Paris would not destroy the weeds they are striving to uproot,
which would crop up elsewhere if turned out of their favourite
soil in Paris. The cause of the tumult lies deep . . . this
"proletariat" controversy, which is at the bottom of all, is the
greatest question for the next generation to settle.'[2]

THE CIVIL WAR IN FRANCE

'The Commune has fallen ! Long live the Commune !' —
this phrase summed up the content and conveyed the spirit of
the pamphlet in which Marx expounded the lessons of a
decisive episode in working-class history. He produced his
remarkable obituary analysis in a matter of five days. Whatever doubts and hesitations he had experienced during the two
desperate months vanished at once. Under the stimulus of

---

[1] Cf. article by 'A Vicar of the Church of England', signed H.S.F., in
Fraser's Magazine, August 1871 : 'The Commune was a mistake ; but it
did keep Paris clean and morally wholesome ; it did manage its police, its
schools, its hospitals strangely well'.

[2] William Gibson, *Paris During the Commune*, 1871, p. 75. See also
J. A. Froude, editor, in *Fraser's Magazine*, August 1871 : 'If, as I believe
also, the insurrection arose from causes inherent in the modern industrial
system — causes which are at work in England as powerfully as in France —
it behoves us all to attend to what is said about it by its friends as well as by
its enemies'. For other favourable Press comments — exceedingly rare —
see *The Irishman*, April 1 and the *Daily News*, March 31, April 1, 1871.

overwhelming defeat, Marx rose to the height of his political and literary powers in a document only surpassed by the *Communist Manifesto* of 1848. *The Civil War in France* achieved its immediate object enshrining the memory of the Commune in unforgettable phrases and identifying the Commune with the International indelibly in the public mind. In the long term, the pamphlet was even more important for its effects on the thinking of Marx's followers, most notably in the case of Lenin and the Bolsheviks.

From one point of view *The Civil War in France* was an intellectually brilliant and emotionally moving defence of the Commune. From another, it represented a new departure in Marx's thinking — the idea that the workers of Paris had spontaneously, by their own efforts, discovered the political form in which the international working class would one day establish its supremacy. Seven years earlier when the International had just been founded Marx had written into the *Rules* the idea 'that the emancipation of the working classes must be conquered by the working classes themselves'. The truth of this idea had in Marx's view just been exemplified briefly but decisively by the workers of Paris. There were lessons to be drawn from this experience about the nature of the State, the way in which a bourgeois would be replaced by a workers' State and the possibility that the capital of a country, providing it were a centre of working-class life and activity, could lead an entire country towards revolution.

On May 30, 1871 Marx read his belated *Address* on the Commune to the General Council of the International. The members, overwhelmed by the document's sweep and power, adopted it unanimously and without discussion. Marx was returning to the old 'boldness of speech' which he had abandoned for tactical reasons in October of 1864. As the members of the General Council listened to Marx reading his *Address* they can hardly have anticipated the storm which its forthcoming publication would unleash. In its earliest years the International had often complained about lack of publicity; from now on there was to be no more cause for complaint.

The last phase in the history of the International — a phase centring on the appearance of *The Civil War in France* — had opened with the French defeat at Sedan and the proclamation of the Republic in September 1870. Marx was now preoccupied with two major issues, the campaign to defend the

Republic for which it was essential to win the recognition of the British Government and the attempt to warn the workers of Paris against precipitate action. In the campaign for recognition, he had the support of most members of the General Council and of the radical Positivists, Professor Beesly, Frederic Harrison and Dr. Harry Bridges. Marx, like Engels, opposed the extreme demand by some members for British military intervention. The campaign for recognition would have wider support, mobilise more working-class opinion against Gladstone and be more likely to succeed. At one point Marx became absurdly over-optimistic, as when he told Siegfried Meyer: 'We have worked up a powerful movement among the working class over here against Gladstone . . . which will probably bring about his downfall'.[1] In pursuing this policy, Marx came into conflict with Odger and Bradlaugh who identified the republican cause with the Orleanist Government of Thiers and Favre. Moreover, the very breadth of the support he was receiving at one time worried Marx. He was concerned, as he told the General Council, that the workers should not allow themselves to be confused by those middle-class liberals who 'enter the movement only to undermine it'.[2]

Marx's other main object had been to warn the Parisian workers against a premature rising when, in the words of the *Second Address on the War*, written only five days after the establishment of the Republic, 'the enemy is almost knocking at the doors of Paris'. On his advice Serraillier had been sent over by the General Council to warn the workers against committing 'stupidities there in the name of the International'. Marx expressed the same fear in letters to his friends such as Ludwig Kugelmann. From the opposite side of politics the same danger was seen by *The Times* when it warned Bismarck that too harsh a policy towards the vanquished might undermine the authority of the Thiers Government. In that case, 'the Reds will have the upper hand in many places, and a state of fearful anarchy will arise which will be utterly beyond the treatment it can supply'.[3]

The first move from the workers came not from Paris but from Lyons where a radical government was established with

---

[1] January 21, 1871, in Marx and Engels, *Letters to Americans, 1848–1895*, p. 81.
[2] G.C. *Minutes*, February 28, 1871.
[3] *The Times* editorial, September 6, 1870.

the participation of working-class members of the International. There were similar developments in Marseilles, Toulouse and Rouen. The Lyons story ended in a comic-opera *putsch*. Bakunin, with the help of the ex-officer and republican conspirator, Gustave Paul Cluseret, seized the town hall and had just time to abolish the State before being dispersed by a handful of gendarmes.[1] Apart from this setback, however, developments in many ways seemed favourable for the workers. 'The middle class has discovered', wrote a *Beehive* correspondent,[2] 'that the safety of France depended upon the revolutionary working class, who had at last been armed.' The report ended on a note of excessive optimism that Wilhelm I of Prussia and Bismarck between them had willy nilly 'laid the foundation for a universal social republic'. Nevertheless, with the collapse of the Empire and the demoralisation of the middle class, the tactical position of the workers was very strong. The war, Marx wrote to Kugelmann on December 13, had 'given the French proletariat practice in arms, and that is the best guarantee of the future'. But he repeated his earlier warnings about the dangers of a premature rising in which the workers 'would be needlessly crushed by the German armies and thrown back another twenty years'.

When the rising nevertheless occurred Marx saw no alternative to giving it his enthusiastic support. The heroic workers of Paris were 'storming heaven' and setting an example to the international working class which, whatever its immediate outcome, would bear a rich harvest in the future. *The Civil War in France* contained a record of the Commune's origin and activities in which Marx stressed those elements which he considered to be important for the future rather than the errors which he hoped would be buried in its fall.

The address opened with an account of the Empire's collapse on September 4 when the abdication of Napoleon thrust power into the hands of the people, and particularly the workers of Paris. Thiers and Trochu had lost no time in occupying the vacated seats of authority. 'At that time', wrote Marx, 'they were imbued with so fanatical a faith in the mission of Paris to represent France in all epochs of historical crisis, that to legitimatise their usurped titles as governors of France, they thought it quite sufficient to produce their lapsed mandates as representatives of Paris.' Meanwhile, with the leaders of the

[1] Marx to Beesly, October 19, 1870.   [2] December 10, 1870.

workers remaining in prison, the people of Paris accepted the new régime with reluctance and on the sole condition that it pursued 'the single purpose of national defence'. With the destruction of the French forces this could only mean arming the workers for the defence of the capital. 'But Paris armed was the Revolution armed.' In that event the victory of France over the Prussians 'would have been a victory of the French workman over the French capitalist and his State parasites'. Inevitably Thiers had shrunk from the consequences. While preaching defence he had prepared for capitulation and on January 28, 1871 had emerged with his colleagues in the shameful rôle of 'the Government of France by Bismarck's permission' which even Louis Bonaparte had declined at Sedan.

In a style reminiscent of Swift, Marx then sketched a series of scathing, bitter portraits of Thiers, Jules Favre, Trochu, Jules Ferry and Ernest Picard. With a few strokes of the pen he presented a remarkable rogues' gallery worthy of Daumier. 'Thiers, that monstrous gnome, has charmed the French bourgeoisie for almost half a century, because he is the most consummate intellectual expression of their own class corruption. . . . The chronicle of his public life is the record of the misfortunes of France.' 'Jules Ferry, a penniless barrister before the 4th of September, contrived, as Mayor of Paris during the siege, to job a fortune out of famine. The day on which he would have to give an account of his maladministration would be the day of his conviction.' 'Jules Favre, living in concubinage with the wife of a drunkard resident at Algiers, had, by a most daring concoction of forgeries, spread over many years, contrived to grasp in the name of the children of his adultery, a large succession, which made him a rich man.' These savagely accurate attacks on the political leaders of France were toned down versions of what the author had written in his two earlier drafts.

Marx moved on to an analysis of events. In the confusion which followed capitulation it had not been possible to arrange elections, since communication with the Provinces was still uncertain. The National Guard, which had proclaimed the Republic on September 4, had at least as much claim to be the legitimate Government as Thiers and his Ministers. Moreover, Thiers desired the destruction of the Republic, because then 'the appropriators of wealth could hope to shift on to the shoulders of its producers the cost of a war which they, the appropriators, had themselves originated'. This could only come about if Paris were disarmed. Thiers duly ordered the National Guard to surrender its cannon and was met with a blank refusal. The National Guard elected a central committee which assumed supreme control. In doing so it became 'the champion of France, whose salvation from ruin and whose regeneration were impossible without the revolutionary overthrow of the political and social conditions that had engendered the Second Empire'.

Repudiating the authority of the Thiers Government at Versailles, Paris was determined to resist the Prussians. It had no intention of engaging in civil war against Versailles, unless this was forced on it. Thiers attacked Paris, civil war had begun and the Central Committee of the National Guard became the provisional Government of the Commune.

Marx defended the Commune against charges of atrocities. The shooting of the Generals, Lecomte and Thomas by their own troops became inevitable when the soldiers were ordered to fire on innocent people. The execution of Darboy, Archbishop of Paris, had been decided on by Thiers when he refused the Commune's offer to exchange the Archbishop for the imprisoned revolutionary, Auguste Blanqui. 'The real murderer of Archbishop Darboy is Thiers', wrote Marx. 'He knew that with Blanqui he would give to the Commune a head; while the Archbishop would serve his purpose best in the shape of a corpse.' In dealing with the charge of incendiarism levied against the Commune, Marx was at his most trenchant. Exposing the middle-class preoccupation with property as against human lives, he explained that 'The working men's Paris, in the act of its heroic self-holocaust, involved in its flames buildings and monuments. While tearing to pieces the living body of the proletariate, its rulers must no longer expect to return triumphantly into the intact architecture of their abodes. . . . The bourgeoisie of the whole world, which looks complacently upon the wholesale massacre after the battle, is convulsed by horror at the desecration of brick and mortar!'

Marx did not limit himself to defending the Commune against its enemies. He treated it as a prototype of working-class government. Crime almost vanished during its reign despite the hardships of battle and the resulting food shortages. Its government had been democratic, its social legislation benevolent. The Commune had shown that when the working class seized power it could not simply utilise the existing machinery of State. The State had to be smashed and replaced by a new apparatus controlled by the working class. The standing army must be replaced by a people's army. Members of the Commune had been 'chosen by universal suffrage . . . responsible and revocable at short terms'. The Commune had consisted, in the main, of working men and had combined both executive and legislative functions. All of its members and public service employees had been paid workmen's wages. Vested interests had disappeared 'along with the high dignitaries themselves'. The Church had been separated from the State. 'The priests were sent back to the recesses of private life, there to feed upon the alms of the faithful in imitation of their predecessors, the Apostles.' Education had been made free of charge and free from Church control. Judges and magistrates had been elected by the people.

Had the Commune been given a respite from civil war and from the silent, ominous and incessant threat of intervention from the Prussian troops which ringed the city, it would have confronted the whole of France with an alternative to capitalist rule. In Marx's view, the Paris Commune was 'to serve as a model to all the great industrial centres of France'. And the industrial centres would of course lead the countryside since this was the rôle which they assumed with the development of capitalism.[1]

In his first draft of *The Civil War in France* Marx wrote explicitly that 'Paris, true to its historical antecedents, seeks the regeneration of old society, making the social regeneration of mankind the national business of France'.[2] In the published version of the pamphlet Marx went on to add a sentence which has later been taken as a concession to Proudhon and the anarchists.[3] 'The communal *régime* once established in Paris and the secondary centres, the old centralised Government would in the provinces, too, have to give way to the self-government of the producers.' In the context, however, it is

[1] 'The bourgeoisie has subjected the country to the rule of the towns. It has created enormous cities, has greatly increased the urban population as compared with the rural, and has thus rescued a considerable part of the population from the idiocy of rural life.' *The Communist Manifesto.*

[2] *Arkhiv Marxa i Engelsa*, vol. III (viii), Moscow, 1934, p. 282.

[3] Cf. E. Bernstein, *Evolutionary Socialism : A Criticism and Affirmation*, 1909, p. 156. See also Martin Buber, *Paths in Utopia*, 1949, pp. 84-9.

clear that Marx was telescoping a long period of hypothetical development which would have followed the stabilisation of the Commune in Paris. Then, on the model of the capital, working-class power would have spread to other parts of the country. The oppressive features of the State would have been abolished at once with the right of the people to recall its public functionaries and with the employment of everyone on useful labour. But Marx made clear his difference with the anarchists in saying that, had the new social order been given time to develop, 'the few but important functions which still would remain for a central government were not to be suppressed, as has been intentionally mis-stated, but were to be discharged by Communal and therefore strictly responsible agents'. In contrast to the Proudhonists, who tended to idealise the mediaeval Communes, Marx pointed out that 'the new Commune, which breaks the modern State power, has been mistaken for a reproduction of the mediaeval Communes, which first preceded, and afterwards became the substratum of, that very State power. . . . The antagonism of the Commune against the State power has been mistaken for an exaggerated form of the ancient struggle against over-centralisation.' But this Marx thought was a superficial view. What was decisive and essentially new about the Commune of Paris was the fact that 'it was essentially a working class government, the product of the struggle of the producing against the appropriating class, the political form at last discovered under which to work out the economical emancipation of labour'.

All the social implications of the Commune would have taken time to become manifest, but time was not granted to the workers of Paris. Even in its short life, however, the Commune had introduced advanced social legislation, such as 'the abolition of the nightwork of journeymen bakers; the prohibition, under penalty, of the employers' practice to reduce wages by levying upon their workpeople fines under manifold pretexts'. Expressing its spirit of working-class internationalism, the Commune had appointed 'a German workingman its Minister of Labour' — Leo Frankel, member of the International and one of the founders of Hungarian Social Democracy. It also paid homage to 'the heroic sons of Poland by placing them at the head of the defenders of Paris' — most notably, General Dombrowsky.

The Commune had made its share of serious blunders, such

as failing to confiscate the Bank of France, march on Versailles and keep up at all costs the military initiative. Moreover, the Commune had not been homogeneous. In every revolution there were to be found, besides genuine revolutionaries in tune with the needs of the time, 'men of a different stamp ; some of them survivors of and devotees to past revolutions' — Marx no doubt meant Delescluze who had taken over unaltered the outlook and politics of the Jacobins. Yet again, there were 'mere brawlers, who repeated year after year the same set of stereotyped declamations against the Government of the day' — Vésinier and Pyat, veteran antagonists of the General Council, were no doubt included in this category. Such men were 'an unavoidable evil ; with time they are shaken off ; but time was not allowed to the Commune'.[1]

Marx ended by exposing the atrocities and cruelties of the Versaillese with the help of Bismarck and the Prussian Government against helpless prisoners and fleeing Communards. Mindless and degrading orgies of brutality had always characterised the ruling class on the morrow of an unsuccessful revolution and the government of Thiers lived fully up to this tradition. 'After Whit-Sunday, 1871', wrote Marx towards the end of his pamphlet, 'there can be neither peace nor truce possible between the working men of France and the appropriators of their produce. The iron hand of a mercenary soldiery may keep for a time both classes tied down in common oppression. But the battle must break out again and again in ever-growing dimensions, and there can be no doubt as to who will be the victor in the end, — the appropriating few, or the immense working majority. And the French working class is only the advanced guard of the modern proletariate.' And in his final paragraph Marx proclaimed that 'Working men's Paris, with its Commune, will be for ever celebrated as the glorious harbinger of a new society. Its martyrs are enshrined in the great heart of the working class. Its exterminators history has already nailed to that eternal pillory from which all the prayers of their priests will not avail to redeem them.'

[1] An Englishman, John Leighton, was told by an *habitué* of French revolutionary circles of the three groups comprising the Commune — members of the International, who had to be taken seriously, Jacobins and 'thirdly, and by far the largest proportion, unsuccessful plotters in former revolutions, journalists, orators, and conspirators — noisy, active, and effervescent. . . '. *Paris Under the Commune ; or, The Seventy-Three Days of the Second Siege*, 1871, pp. 75-7.

In *The Civil War in France* Marx returned to the tone and language of the *Communist Manifesto*. For nearly seven years, in the period of the International, Marx had expressed himself publicly in language of studious moderation. Now, in the shadow of a resounding defeat, he ran up once again the red flag of proletarian revolution. Even so, the published version was in some respects more reticent than the two preliminary drafts. In these he had drawn attention to the part played by members of the International in running the Commune. In the published pamphlet this was considerably toned down. Thiers and Favre were circularising governments to demand the suppression of the International and Marx had no wish to provide them with ammunition. Similarly, he modified and in some cases removed attacks on the Positivists. Whatever his criticisms of French members of that school, English Positivists such as Beesly and Harrison had rallied publicly, and with considerable courage, to the defence of the Commune.

The Civil War in France was a moving and powerful obituary on an unsuccessful proletarian revolution and an inspiring vision of the future which would follow from the first real victory of the working class. Its publication marked the climax of Marx's constructive work in the International and his achievement as a creative thinker. The struggle with the Bakuninists which loomed ahead was to tear the Association apart. Marx gave his declining energies to thwarting the anarchist attempt to take over the International. And after that, the creative period in his life was at an end.

Press Reactions

As was to be expected, a storm of criticism blew up in the English Press on the publication of the address. One of the first attacks appeared in the *Spectator* which in an editorial on June 17 said that the fact that English workers had signed such an address was 'perhaps the most significant and ominous of the political signs of the times'. By instinct or otherwise, it attacked Odger and Lucraft by name and wondered how Englishmen could bring themselves to sign, not 'an apology' for the Commune, which could have been understood, but 'a thorough-going panegyric'. 'The writing, as vigorous as Cobbett's, reminds us of earlier documents of the same Association, which have been attributed to . . . Karl Marx.'[1] The *Standard* was even more forthright and in an editorial on June 19 it also singled out 'the familiar names of Lucraft and Odger'.

The Times, as at the time of Basle, did not quite know what to make of the International, but was happy to publish whatever came to hand. On June 5 it had summarised in all seriousness the nonsense of a sensational French book, *Les Mystères de l'Internationale*, according to which the International had been founded by a mysterious Irishman called Patrick Howell. This was only one item in a long list of forgeries, distortions and atrocity propaganda with which the French Press was filled in the months following the overthrow of the Commune.

On June 6 Jules Favre released a circular letter to all the European governments calling on them to suppress the International. The circular was full of inaccuracies, including the description of a statement from the Bakuninist 'Alliance', demanding the abolition of religion and marriage, as an official pronouncement of the International. On June 13 *The Times* published a letter from John Hales, who had replaced Eccarius as Secretary of the General Council,[2] pointing out that the statement in question had been issued by the Geneva 'Alliance de la Démocratie Socialiste' and repudiated by the General Council.[3]

On June 19 *The Times* returned to the attack and condemned the International for having 'accepted the responsibility of the Communist revolution'. But it went on to distinguish between the Continental members who preached revolution and the English who 'did generally confine themselves to such questions as occupy the attention of ordinary trade unions'. The French Government, at least, was justified in suppressing the International. On June 21 it once again published as the programme of the International the rubbish which Hales had repudiated in its own correspondence columns eight days earlier. Later in the year, however, *The Times* published a serious historical survey of the Association, probably written by

[1] A writer in the *National Reformer*, July 9, 1871, also remarked on the similarity between the styles of Marx and Cobbett.

[2] Eccarius had resigned on May 9, pleading pressure of work, but saying, at the same time, that he was not prepared to discuss the matter further — G.C. *Minutes*. His successor, Hales, was close to Marx politically, and Marx drafted most of his public statements, including the letter to *The Times* which appeared on June 13.

[3] The letter to *The Times* was included, as an appendix, in the second and third editions of *The Civil War in France*.

Eccarius, who had previously supplied it with reports of every Congress since Lausanne.[1]

While the attacks on Marx, the Commune and the International varied in intensity, there was general agreement that *The Civil War in France* expressed an attitude of iconoclastic extremism which could not be treated as a subject for rational discussion. This was the line taken by a review of the pamphlet in the radical *Eastern Post* on June 17, though an editorial in the same issue described it as 'invaluable as giving in compendious form what can be said in explanation of the acts and aims of the Communists — to put an end to the despotism of capital over labour'.

On the same date the *Beehive* contented itself with giving a summary of the pamphlet without comment. That journal had already together with Beesly, the trade union movement and the International, been attacked by the *Builders' Trade Circular* — organ of the master builders — for having, directly or otherwise, 'had some hand in the horrible scenes lately enacted in the French capital'. In its reply the *Beehive* pointedly refrained from identifying itself with either view. It had merely, it insisted, kept a fair balance in presenting the arguments on both sides. It went on to identify the author of the anonymous attack in the *Builders' Trade Circular* as Mault, Secretary of the Master Builders' Association and added that the sole object of the attack was to discredit the *Beehive* in the building trade. The employers' journal did not take up the argument again.

ODGER AND LUCRAFT

The Press barrage no doubt had some influence on the attitude of Odger, who had expressed his concern to the General Council even before Marx's address had been written and Lucraft, who had fervently declared his support for the Commune as recently as May 23. Both resigned from the General Council at its meeting on June 20.[2] George Jacob Holyoake, co-operator and popular writer on secularism, wrote to the *Daily News* attacking the address which, he said, being 'full of French ideas and English expressions, cannot be an

---

[1] *The Times*, October 27, 1871. Authorship of the article was attributed to Eccarius by Ryazanoff, in 'Zur Geschichte der Ersten Internationale', *Marx-Engels Archiv*, vol. 1, 1927, p. 168.

[2] Odger declared that 'he wouldn't be dictated to, if the satellites of Dr. Marx liked they could, but he wouldn't'. G.C. *Minutes*.

English production, though manifestly revised by some Saxon or Celtic pen'. The 'best known among the British signatories', he added, had told him that his name had been appended without his having been consulted or even shown a copy of the address. Hales replied that Marx had indeed written the address, but that it had then been unanimously adopted by the General Council. It was the custom of the Council, he explained, to append the signatures of all its members to public statements and he added, knowing nothing of the impending resignations, that 'it will be time enough for Mr. Holyoake to interfere when the members themselves complain'.[1]

On the day Hales's letter appeared in the *Eastern Post* other papers carried the news of Odger's and Lucraft's resignation. This was the first notable secession of English working-class representatives from the International and was greeted with joy by the *Spectator*. No doubt Lucraft, it remarked, had just been elected a member of the London School Board under the 1870 Education Act, owed his constituents a 'very full explanation' about his attitude to 'principles which touch the very basis of moral and practical education'. The editorial ended by asking rhetorically whether the leaders of the working class, on which the future of England depended, were 'going to sink their individuality in a council chiefly guided by foreigners'?[2]

Lucraft did his best with a rather embarrassing situation. He replied to Hales that he had been absent from the Council meeting at which the address was endorsed but that after its appearance he 'felt so much disgusted with some of its sentiments' that he attended the next meeting, 'denounced its authors, and withdrew altogether from the Council'.

The reply of the General Council was contained in a letter signed by Hales and written by Marx which appeared in the *Eastern Post*. Lucraft, it was pointed out, had been present on May 23 at which it was announced that the draft of *The Civil War in France* would be discussed at the next weekly meeting. He had declared 'his entire sympathy with the Commune of Paris' on May 23, but had been absent the following week, when the address was adopted. In accordance with the custom, of which Lucraft himself had been 'one of the most strenuous supporters', the names of all members of the Council had been appended. Nothing more was heard from him until the Council

---

[1] *Daily News*, June 20, and *Eastern Post*, June 24, 1871.
[2] June 24, 1871.

meeting on June 20 when he was forced to admit that he had not yet read the address, but that his impressions were gathered entirely from Press comment. With regard to Odger, Hales insisted that he had been 'waited upon personally and informed that the Council was about to issue an address and was asked if he objected to his name appearing in connection with it and he said "No" '.

Neither Odger nor Lucraft replied to the letter and Lucraft, who comes rather badly out of the whole episode, had no further dealings with the International. This was not the case with Odger, who was conducting under Bradlaugh's leadership a vigorous and nation-wide republican campaign. He emphatically refused to repudiate his past associates, whatever his differences might be on current policies. Being asked at a meeting of the Newcastle and Gateshead Republican Club in June to explain his connection with the Association, he referred proudly to his part in founding it and quoted at length from his address to the French workers in November 1863. The International, he insisted, had been formed to promote the thoroughly worthy objects of peace and the raising of continental wages to British levels.[1]

There was, nevertheless, considerable hostility in radical circles to Marx's attack on Favre and Thiers. This resentment was shared by the *Beehive* which wrote approvingly on July 1 of the resignations of Odger and Lucraft, adding that 'these two English working men, at any rate, leave to Dr. Marx the responsibility which he assumes for his personal accusations against Messrs. Thiers, Favre and their colleagues'. To the defence of Marx came the well-known London Positivist, Dr. Harry Bridges.[2] He told the editor of the *Beehive* that Thiers, not the Commune, was responsible for the killing of the hostages. In a second letter to the paper on July 22 he suggested that the mistakes of the Commune lay in undue caution and legalism rather than in destructiveness and bellicosity — a view identical with that of *The Civil War in France*.

The Press attacks on the International soon became more general. English papers began to copy the French in describing the Association as a vast cosmopolitan conspiracy which em-

---

[1] *The Times*, June 29, 1871.
[2] During the first siege of Paris, he had written a leaflet, *Why We Should Stand by France*, in which he expressed a view almost identical with that of Marx in the second address of the General Council on the war.

broiled innocent native workers in the snares of international revolutionaries. The *Pall-Mall Gazette*, to which Engels had a short time before contributed a series of articles on the Franco-Prussian War and which had published a balanced account of the International after the Basle Congress,[1] now wrote on July 20 that 'Marx an Israelite by birth . . . caused utopia to merge into reality by placing himself at the head of a vast conspiracy having for its object to create political communism'. The *Saturday Review*, which had been the first English journal to draw attention to the appearance of *Das Kapital*, in a favourable review [2] now wrote on July 8 that 'The German prophets of revolution probably despise the English artisans who, only half understanding their doctrines, allow them to speak in their name'.

Many of the International's critics took at its face value the quotation from the programme of Bakunin's *Alliance* which Jules Favre's circular of June 6 [3] described as the programme of the International. Favre had quoted from the Geneva document the telling sentence : 'The Alliance declares itself Atheist ; it desires the abolition of religion, the substitution of science for faith, of human justice for divine justice and the abolition of marriage. . . '. This was enough to make the *Spectator* declare in horror on June 24 that 'principles of this kind go to the very root of national society' and warn trade unionists, fortified by the examples of Odger and Lucraft, against 'permitting themselves to be made the catspaw of foreigners who use them for far sighted purposes in which they themselves apparently are hardly permitted to participate'.

Much of the sensationally inaccurate material in the English Press was taken straight from French papers such as *Paris-Journal* and *Le Gaulois*.[4] Marx spent a good deal of time denouncing these productions as forgeries.[5] But he and

---

[1] See Chapter X.   [2] January 18, 1868.

[3] The full text of the circular was reprinted in George Bourgin's article 'La Lutte du Gouvernement français contre la Première Internationale', in the *International Review of Social History*, vol. IV, p. 54, 1939.

[4] Cf. the editorial on Marx, 'Le Grand Chef de l'Internationale' in *Paris-Journal*, March 17, 1871.

[5] Cf. *Morning Advertiser*, July 11, and Marx's reply, July 13 ; *Standard*, July 12, and Marx's reply, July 17 ; *Public Opinion*, August 26 ; Marx's letter to *Spectator* and *Examiner*, June 24 ; Marx's letter to *l'Internationale*, August 8 ; Marx's letter to *Pall-Mall Gazette*, June 9 ; the forged interview with Marx in the *New York Herald*, August 3 and Marx's letter, August 17 ; Marx to *Le Gaulois*, August 24 and to *La Vérité*, September 9, 1871.

Engels were not altogether displeased at the attention which the pamphlet was receiving. Marx wrote to Kugelmann on June 18:[1] 'It is making the devil of a noise and I have the honour to be at this moment the best calumniated and most menaced man in London. That really does one good after a tedious twenty years' idyll in my den.'

Though the English Press was on the whole milder than its French counterpart, condemnation was almost, though not quite, universal.[2] Even the *Eastern Post*, which was publishing regular accounts of the General Council's meetings, was mildly censorious, and the *Beehive* was non-committal, though it gave publicity to the views of Beesly and Bridges. On the other hand, the English Positivists had all been 'ardent supporters' of the Commune from the start, as Beesly was able to assure Marx in his letter of June 13 (?), 1871.[3] While recognising that Marx was radically opposed to Positivism for its defence of private property, Beesly was at pains to stress that 'The one point we and you have in common is our indignation against the individualist theories of the propertied classes and their anti-social conduct. We both believe that the working class suffers terrible wrongs at the hands of the middle class and that the social question is more important than the political.' The Commune, as a movement of the workers against the 'terrible wrongs', and as an attempt, however misguided, to solve 'the social question' must clearly be supported.

Apart from a defence of the Commune by Frederic Harrison in the *Fortnightly Review* for August 1871, Press unanimity was apparently broken by only two papers. *Reynolds's* on June 18 declared that the flag raised by the Commune would rally not only the people of France, 'but the masses of the whole of Europe' and quoted extensively and approvingly from Marx's address. The *Examiner*, edited by the radical Fox-Bourne, a frequent visitor to Marx's house during the period of the Commune,[4] said that the International had been right to defend the Commune. The Association promised to be 'a powerful

---

[1] See also Engels to Liebknecht, June 22, 1871, in *Briefe an Bebel, Liebknecht und andere*, p. 27.

[2] For an attack from an extreme Tory standpoint, in which the Commune and the International are seen as indirect consequences of parliamentary reform and religious equality, see *Quarterly Review*, No. 262, 1871.

[3] I.M.L. The date of the letter is not very legible.

[4] See E. Belfort Bax, *Reminiscences and Reflections of a Mid and Late Victorian*, 1918, pp. 31-2.

machinery for the thoroughly healthy improvement of the conditions of the working class in this and other countries', and deplored the attacks being made on it as 'altogether ungenerous and dishonest'.[1]

Despite or perhaps because of these Press attacks, *The Civil War in France*, unlike any previous publication of the International, was issued in three editions in England in a period of two months. Besides this, Engels reported to the General Council that it had been 'translated and published in Dutch, German and French, in which language it had been published, both in Belgium and Switzerland. Translations were also in progress in the Italian, Spanish and Russian languages, and would soon be ready.'[2]

THE REFUGEES

After the fall of the Commune, the General Council began to organise help for the refugees who were soon expected to arrive in large numbers. Though a small number of papers were demanding that they should be prohibited entry into Britain,[3] the more general view was that 'no Communist refugees can be surrendered for any acts whatever done during the Civil War'.[4]

A public meeting was held in support of the refugees, to which John Stuart Mill sent a message deploring 'the horrors now being perpetrated at Paris'.[5] The meeting resolved to send a deputation to the Government to demand that there should be no extradition of escaped Communards. Branches of the International passed resolutions of sympathy with the victims of the terror, and pledged assistance.[6]

---

[1] June 24, 1871. For a working-class view, see also *Minutes* of the Birmingham Trades Council, Fifth Annual Report, for year ending June 1871. The Trades Council still firmly supported the International, whose opinions were 'making headway amongst the thoughtful portion of the working population in this country in spite of all the slanders and misrepresentations to which the Association may for the time being be subjected'.

[2] *Eastern Post*, July 22, 1871. The address was also published in full in two American papers, the *Woodhull and Clafflin's Weekly* and the Chicago *Workingman's Advocate* and in long extracts in the *World* and the *Irish People*. See letter from Sorge to General Council, August 6, 1871, in *Pervy International* . . ., p. 227; also pp. 220-1.

[3] *E.g.* the *Express*, May 30 and June 1 and 10 and the *Saturday Review*, June 10, 1871.

[4] Beesly to Marx, June 10, 1871, summarising the views of *The Times* and *Pall-Mall Gazette*.

[5] *Daily News*, June 2, 1871.   [6] *Eastern Post*, June 10, 1871.

When the General Council met on June 20 Marx reported on meetings held in Geneva, Brussels, Munich, Vienna and Berlin 'denouncing the Thiers-Favre massacres'. It was decided to open a Refugee Fund [1] and the number of applications for relief was soon so great that the Council set up on June 27 a special committee to deal with them. The 'work of the International', Marx wrote to Kugelmann on July 27, 'is immense, and in addition London is overrun with refugees, whom we have to look after'.

Meanwhile, there was some concern as to how the British Government would react to the Favre circular of June 6 calling for a European-wide ban on the International. There was little public support for the demand in England, though a meeting called by the Universal Republican League [2] in Clerkenwell Green to demand political asylum for the refugees, was broken up by Irish Catholics, and a riot nearly ensued.[3] On July 5 A. O. Rutson, private secretary to Bruce, the Home Secretary, sent a messenger to Beesly to ask for a 'list of the documents' published by the International and an indication of where they could be obtained. Beesly referred him to Marx, as Truelove, the printer, had no copies left except for the recent address on the Commune.[4] Marx sent Rutson a copy of every official statement which he had written for the General Council, presumably to enable the Home Office to distinguish between the genuine pronouncements of the International and those being ascribed to it in various forgeries.[5] In the event, the British Government saw no reason to suppress the International and had not the legal power, even if it had the wish, to prevent the entry of Communard refugees or to molest them once they had arrived.[6]

THE INTERNATIONAL AND THE UNIONS

In the midst of its other and often tragic preoccupations, the International still found time to take part in a collection of funds for the cigar workers of Antwerp who were locked out

---

[1] G.C. *Minutes*, June 24, July 1, 1871.
[2] A small body, founded in April. See G.C. *Minutes*, April 25, 1871.
[3] *The Times*, June 19, 1871.
[4] Beesly to Marx, July 5, 1871. I.M.L.
[5] Marx to A. O. Rutson, July 12, 1871, in *Soc.* XXVI, pp. 130-1. Also *Chronik*, p. 309.
[6] See also Chapter XIV.

for sixteen weeks. On July 18 Cohn reported to the General Council that more than £600 had been raised in England. While much of the money had been contributed by the London and Liverpool cigar makers there had been a response from an impressively wide range of trade unions.[1]

More spectacular was the appeal addressed to the General Council by the Amalgamated Society of Engineers which had persistently ignored invitations to affiliate. Now the Newcastle engineers were on strike for the nine-hour day and the employers were threatening to bring in foreign workers particularly from Belgium and Denmark.[2] A deputation which included John Burnett, leader of the Nine Hours' League, and Whetstone, President of the A.S.E., attended a meeting of the General Council on August 8. Marx did not fail to point out that trade unions had a habit of coming to the International when they were in trouble while otherwise ignoring its existence. Whetstone replied, rather awkwardly, that his Society's Council 'had the subject of affiliation under discussion'[3] and that they could see the advantages of belonging to 'such a powerful and homogeneous association'. The General Council appointed Cohn and Eccarius to go to Belgium as delegates.

Apparently Cohn went on his own and it was not long before the Belgian Government deported him.[4] But before he left Belgium, Cohn managed to make contacts through the Antwerp Cigar Workers' Mutual Association. As a result of his efforts, many Belgians were dissuaded from leaving for England.[5] After his deportation, Cohn was sent to Newcastle where the Belgians were already expressing their discontent with working conditions. Many of them left as a result of 'the persuasive tongue of Mr. Cohn who sent off a batch with nearly every boat that left for the Continent'. Burnett paid a

---

[1] Societies reported as contributing were the compositors, gilders, basket makers, tinplate workers, coopers, hatters, bookbinders, plumbers, brass finishers, elastic web weavers, bricklayers, paperhangers, plasterers, blind makers, tailors and furriers. G.C. *Minutes* and *Eastern Post*, June 17, July 22 and 29, 1871.

[2] Cf. letter from Applegarth to General Council, read on June 13, 1871. Jung wrote to Brismée, in Belgium, to ask for help. G.C. *Minutes*.

[3] There is no evidence of this. In 1867, however, during the Paris ironmoulders' strike, the A.S.E. had considered sending one or two delegates to the Lausanne Congress of the International, but that was as far as it went. A.S.E. *Monthly Report*, June, and *Minutes*, June 29, 1867.

[4] See Cohn's report to the G.C., *Eastern Post*, September 9, 1871.

[5] For an account of Cohn's activities in Antwerp and Brussels, and of his deportation, see *Morning Advertiser*, September 7, 1871.

generous tribute to Cohn, saying that 'by the manner in which he induced foreigners to leave Newcastle he was of great service to the cause'.[1]   Despite this, relations between the A.S.E. and the International became no closer, and Whetstone's half-promise of affiliation was never fulfilled.   A year later by the time of the Hague Congress in September 1872 the A.S.E. had decided to forget the services requested, and received from the International a resolution denouncing it as having become 'the mouthpiece of the disaffected from all parts of Europe'.[2]

TAKING STOCK

The International was now at the height of its fame, and the most extravagant views prevailed about its objectives and the part it had played in the Commune.   An American journal sent a representative to interview Marx, who denied categorically that the International had organised the Commune.   The International, he insisted, 'does not write down the form the political movement is to take;   it only demands that these movements be directed to a given aim'.   In different countries the approach would be different.   In England, with its political freedom, 'the working class has the possibility of showing its political strength.   An insurrection there would be idiocy when a peaceful agitation can lead to the achievement of the aim more quickly.'   In France, the degree of repression and the intensity of class antagonism made a forcible clash inevitable. Even in England, where the bourgeoisie had acquired the habit of accepting majority decisions so long as it retained overall control, Marx was sure that 'the moment it becomes a minority on those questions which it considers most vital, we shall have a new war of the slaveholders against the slaves'.   The essential thing was that 'the working class of each country must choose its own path.   The International cannot dictate this.'   The Association aimed rather to serve than to dictate and Marx referred proudly to the International's achievements during strikes.[3]

[1] John Burnett, *A History of the Engineers' Strike in Newcastle and Gateshead.   The Nine Hours' Movement,* 1872, pp. 42–5.   See also, for another contemporary tribute, Thomas Wright, *op. cit.,* p. 271.

[2] Abstract Report of the Council's Proceedings, 1870–2.   A.S.E., London, 1873.   Quoted in James B. Jefferys, *Labour's Formative Years,* 1948, p. 190.

[3] Interview with the New York *World,* August 3, 1871, reprinted in *Woodhull and Clafflin's Weekly,* August 12.   Retranslated from the Russian

Meanwhile, two years had passed without a Congress of the International. The world-wide attacks to which it was being subjected and the widespread confusion between its programme and that of the Bakuninist 'Alliance' suggested that it was now time for another international gathering. On July 25, 1871 Engels proposed at the General Council that a 'private conference' be called in London on the third Sunday in September. A public conference, he explained, would be impossible, since the International was banned in France, 'subject to prosecution' in Germany, Spain and Belgium and split by the Bakuninist controversy in Switzerland. England remained the only practical centre, but not for a Congress, since 'scarcely any of the sections could send delegates'. The General Council agreed accordingly on a conference which, unlike a full Congress, would concern itself with organisational and not theoretical questions. The agenda therefore consisted of items such as membership fees, organisation under conditions of illegality and the rules of the Association. The indefatigable Hales added the question of forming an English Federal Council.[1] It was also suggested that there should be neither advance publicity nor open sessions at the conference, in view of the danger of spies and the likelihood of the continental delegates being prevented from leaving or prosecuted on their return.

Six weeks before the opening of the London Conference, an incident took place which clarified the position of Applegarth in relation to the International and its controversial pamphlet on the Commune. Before the appearance of *The Civil War in France*, Applegarth, like Odger, seems to have had misgivings about the publication of his signature on the statement.[2] Throughout the storm which followed the publication, Applegarth, having his own preoccupations over his resignation as Secretary of the Carpenters and Joiners, remained silent. In deference to his wishes, his name had been left out of the first three editions of *The Civil War in France*. However, the

---

in *Pervy International* . . ., pp. 261-6. Cf. Marx's rather different emphasis in his speech at Amsterdam in September 1872. Rudolf Meyer, *Der Emancipationskampf des Vierten Standes*, Berlin, 1882, vol. I, pp. 159-62.

[1] G.C. *Minutes*, July 25; cf. *Minutes* of August 15, September 9, 11, 12 and 16, 1871. Also letter from Marx to Utin, July 27, 1871, in *Soc.* XXVI, pp. 134-5 and *Chronik*, pp. 313-16.

[2] See Chapter XI.

meeting of the General Council which received the Engineers' deputation also heard a letter from Applegarth, apologising for his absence and saying that he still regarded himself as a member. 'With regard to the use of his name', he added, in an oblique reference to Odger and Lucraft, 'he considered it the property of the Council so long as he remained a member, and it had a right to use it when the interests of the Council required it'.[1]

It is very generally believed that the trade unions deserted the International after the Commune, but the evidence suggests that their attitude was in fact completely unaffected and that the resignations of Odger and Lucraft were in no way representative. No trade union withdrew its membership after the International's defence of the Commune and the Engineers, who were not members, made use of its services without the least inhibition. What Engels complained of to his colleagues on the General Council was not the hostility of the British workers but their apathy. This only provoked from Hales the inevitable reply that such apathy was the fault of the General Council itself 'for not taking the initiative in establishing an English section'.[2]

After the London Conference, Hales was at last to realise his ambition with the formation at last of a British Federal Council. Even two months before the conference of September 1871, two English branches had already been set up in East London.[3]

The International, despite the terrible defeat suffered by its French section, was very much alive. In August and September there were encouraging reports of progress in America and of a slow recovery in Germany. Headway was also being made in Belgium and Spain. More surprising was an application from a branch in Calcutta which hoped to destroy privileges based on colour and caste. The Indian workers would be helped to win their rights, political and social. 'Capital, the real juggernaut which crushes down labour, would no longer be allowed to use up human energy like so much fuel, but would be

[1] Applegarth's name duly appeared in the *Rules* and *Resolutions* of the London Conference, September 1871 and in the French edition of *The Civil War in France*, issued in Brussels, 1872.

[2] G.C. *Minutes*, August 8, 1871.

[3] In Bethnal Green and City Road, London. G.C. *Minutes*, July 11, 1871.

brought under the control of the workers themselves.' [1]

Towards the end of September the London Conference assembled to inaugurate what was to be the last year of effective existence for the International.

[1] *Eastern Post*, September 2, and a briefer report, *ibid.*, August 19, 1871. This is probably the first statement from India to deal with the labour movement. Hales wrote to Calcutta to advise the presumably all-white branch of 'the necessity of enrolling natives in the Association'. G.C. *Minutes*, August 15, 1871.

PART FIVE

THE LAST PHASE

CHAPTER XIII

The London Conference of 1871.
Bakunin in the International

THE Commune sealed the fate of the International, not directly but through a complex chain-reaction. Before this can be discussed, however, it is necessary to describe briefly the rôle of Bakunin and the rise of his movement in opposition to Marx which reached its climax in the year which followed the Commune. There is no need to consider this story in detail since Bakunin's political theories made no impact whatever on the British labour movement. While in the earlier struggle against the ideas of Proudhon, the English members had given valuable support to Marx, in the fight with Bakunin they played little active part. The entire controversy was quite outside their grasp and it is significant that while the statements of the General Council on other questions were in every case written in English, the statements against Bakunin all appeared in French.

Bakunin paid a brief visit to London soon after the International was founded. He did not join and had no part in its establishment. His relations with Marx at the time were amicable, and when Bakunin left for Italy at the end of 1864 it seemed to both Marx and Engels that he might be a useful ally against Mazzini. Nearly two and a half years later Bakunin appeared at the Geneva Congress of the League of Peace and Freedom. Within the League he organised a group of supporters around himself, trying both to capture the League and to bring it as an affiliated body into the International.

After failing in both attempts, Bakunin founded the International Alliance of Socialist Democracy, at first limited to Geneva, though soon acquiring an international membership. Joining the International in 1868, Bakunin developed his Alliance as a centre of influence independent of the General Council. To Marx and Engels this was intolerable. In a confidential circular sent out by the General Council on December

22, 1868 it was argued that if the Alliance were allowed to remain a 'State within a State' there would be nothing to stop other bodies from doing the same and the International would degenerate into a conglomeration of warring sects. Only national bodies and local sections, it was pointed out, were eligible for membership. The Alliance as an organisation with an international membership was ineligible.

On March 4, 1869 the General Council received the reply from Geneva. The Alliance accepted the ruling and declared itself dissolved. Its former members and sections would apply for membership in the usual way. Though none too happy about receiving Bakunin's followers in Geneva, France, Spain and Italy into the International, Marx felt that he had no option but to accept the apparent capitulation.

Bakunin attended the Basle Congress of the International — the only one he did attend — with a substantial following. Though differing from the General Council on the question of inherited property [1] the Bakuninists gave it full support against the Proudhonist rearguard action on the public ownership of land and industry. Unlike Proudhon, Bakunin was a collectivist. He agreed entirely with the Frenchman, however, in opposing the political authority of the State. He described his agreement with Proudhon in a letter to the Parisian *La Démocratie* which was reprinted in the English *Social Economist* [2] in August 1868. 'The great and true master of us all, PRUDHON' (*sic*), read the letter, 'has said . . . that the most disastrous combination that could be formed would be that which united socialism with absolutism — the tendencies of the people towards economic emancipation and material well-being with the dictatorship and the concentration of all the political and social powers of the State.' In a speech to the League of Peace and Freedom shortly before his resignation, Bakunin explained that he stood for the abolition of the State and its replacement by a 'free association' in which there would be no exercise of authority 'from above downwards'.[3]

[1] See Chapter IX.

[2] This short-lived paper published in its issues of August and September 1869 long excerpts from the *Communist Manifesto*, translated by Cowell Stepney. The author's name was not given, though he was referred to editorially as 'an eminent expositor of social ideas . . . if we quoted in full we would scare our readers, whom we are told we have already terrified'. There is no evidence that Marx or Engels ever knew of this pirated translation. The *Social Economist* ceased to appear immediately afterwards.

[3] Guillaume, *L'Internationale*, Paris, 1905, vol. I, pp. 74-9.

Once his supporters were inside the International, Bakunin's ideas made rapid headway, though chiefly in countries with large populations of peasants and handicraftsmen. England, with a developed industrial working class and Germany, where the ideas of Lassalle had struck root and those of Marx were gaining ground, remained impervious to Bakunin's influence. In less developed countries his revolutionary *élan* and headlong assault on Church and State were more immediately attractive than the less spectacular approach of Marx with its emphasis on tactics and organisation and its insistence on the need to build up the political, as well as the industrial power of organised labour. By the end of 1869 there were journals in Geneva, Le Locle, Barcelona and Naples, all disseminating Bakunin's ideas and Marx began to express alarm.[1] It was probably for this reason that Marx decided to hold the fifth Congress of the International in Mainz, where the Germans would have given him decisive support, as the Belgians had done at the crucial Brussels Congress in 1868. Shortly before the Mainz Congress was due to assemble, Marx suggested to the General Council on June 28, 1870 that it propose to Congress the removal of the General Council from London to Brussels. The proposal was not meant to be taken seriously. 'The Congress', Marx explained after making his suggestion, 'may not accept the proposition, then we can put conditions.'

Already in fact by the middle of 1870 Marx was sufficiently alarmed by the growth of anarchism in the International to resort to a dangerous expedient. If the General Council had accepted his proposition, Marx must have been counting on the Mainz Congress to reject it. He would then have been able to impose conditions in return for London remaining the seat of the General Council. These conditions would have been such as to strengthen the Council against national sections in which Bakuninism was strong or dominant. Marx was to achieve this at the London Conference of September 1871, but he was already manœuvring for the same result fifteen months earlier. It was a desperate manœuvre. Congress might, indeed, have declined the offer, but there seems no evidence that he could count on this as a certainty. The centre of power would have passed to Brussels and to a national section by no means completely under his control. Because of the Franco-Prussian War the Mainz Congress was never held and nothing more was

[1] Marx to Engels, December 17, 1869.

Q

heard of Marx's proposal. Two years were to pass before the fifth Congress could meet at the Hague and by that time the International was split beyond repair.

THE SECOND LONDON CONFERENCE, SEPTEMBER 1871

After the fall of the Commune it was decided to hold a Conference in London in September 1871. The Conference had no power to determine policy, but could take decisions on organisational matters. Delegates arrived from Brussels, Liège, the valley of the Vesdres, Verviers, Antwerp, Geneva and Spain. The General Council elected a contingent of six, of which Mottershead was the only Englishman. In contrast to all the Congresses and to the first London Conference of 1865, the English took next to no part in the proceedings. Besides Mottershead, Hales the General Secretary, and J. P. McDonnell from Ireland put in an occasional appearance, but they showed little interest in the organisational debates which they regarded, rightly, as being concerned with continental matters.

Marx's position was strong. The Bakuninists were underrepresented and he could count on the support of the French followers of Blanqui who had joined the General Council in some numbers after the fall of the Commune. On the two main issues under dispute, political action and the powers of the General Council, they agreed with Marx against Bakunin. In fact, they went beyond Marx in demanding a disciplined, centralised international party with a reorganised General Council at its head.[1] De Paepe and the Belgians also supported Marx, though with qualifications.

Marx was successful in extending the powers of the General Council which, Conference agreed, must include the right to correspond with foreign sections direct and not necessarily through the appropriate Federal Council. A proposal of Vaillant which committed the International explicitly to political action was passed against strong Bakuninist opposition. But Marx did not succeed in getting a vote of censure passed against Bakunin's 'Alliance of Socialist Democracy'. A com-

---

[1] See *Internationale et révolution à propos du Congrès de la Haye par des réfugiés de la Commune, ex-membres du Conseil Général de L'Internationale*, by Édouard Vaillant and others, 1872. In this pamphlet the Blanquists declared that the time had come for the General Council to constitute itself the 'vanguard' of an 'international revolutionary workers' party', but that the General Council had refused to face up to its task. *Ibid.*, p. 10.

mission which had been investigating the position in Geneva reported that the Alliance, while masquerading as a local section, was in fact an international organisation.   But de Paepe insisted that whatever the errors of the 'Alliance', it contained many sincere people and should not be treated as a hostile body.   His conciliatory policy carried the day.

The Conference then turned to the Netchaev affair which had achieved considerable and highly unwelcome publicity for the International.   Claiming to be a member of the Association, Netchaev had set up a terrorist organisation in Russia, the terrorism being directed mainly against his own supporters. Following the murder of a student, Netchaev was awaiting trial at the time of the London Conference.   It became very necessary that the International should place on record its attitude to secret societies.   Marx accordingly denounced them in the most emphatic terms.   While they might have been 'suitable for the Carbonari' they did 'not correspond to the needs of the working-class movement.   It is necessary to educate the workers, and to educate them in a spirit of freedom and independence.'   There was no opposition to this view at the Conference, but Marx also wished to implicate Bakunin, who had been closely associated with Netchaev, in the condemnation.   Once again de Paepe came to Bakunin's assistance pointing out that there was no evidence which implicated him in Netchaev's crimes.   Marx had to accept a resolution condemning Netchaev alone.

At long last Hales's project of an English Federal Council was to be realised.   At a meeting of the General Council on September 11, six days before the Conference opened, Marx had agreed to support the proposal.   He personally moved it towards the end of the Conference and went through the motions of explaining his own past hostility to the idea.   Previously, he claimed, it had been necessary to permeate the English workers with the spirit of internationalism.   This could only be done through the General Council but it had now been accomplished.   Marx knew better than to believe this.   If now, after almost six years, he was prepared to abandon his opposition, there could be only one explanation and it was hardly one which he could have given to the Conference.   The rising of the Paris workers had not touched off as in 1848 an international revolution.   The French working class lay prostrate and neither the German nor any other working class was in a position to take its place. For the foreseeable future there would be no European revolution and no need therefore to keep the 'great lever' under his personal control.

In the new situation, English affairs need no longer be afforded the old priority. There was a much more urgent task to hand. The Commune had created a legend and in the minds of workers all over the world the International, with which the Commune was indelibly associated, had become the symbol of revolutionary labour. The symbol must now be preserved for future use but there was a serious danger of it being appropriated by Bakunin. This must be prevented at any cost, and this in Marx's view was the function of the second London Conference.

This task the Conference achieved only in part. It strengthened the powers of the General Council in any future dealings with refractory sections and individuals. It firmly committed the International to political as well as industrial action. For Marx these were important tactical gains. But they were not enough. Through the ambivalence of de Paepe and his Belgians it had been impossible to clinch matters and to register an explicit repudiation of Bakunin. The anarchists, however, were now in a position when they must either abdicate or launch an all-out offensive in defiance of both the General Council and the decisions of the London Conference.

AFTER THE CONFERENCE

How far Marx's assessment of the position had changed may be judged from his speech at a semi-public meeting which followed the end of the Conference. The International, he maintained, was not the creation of politicians. It was the product of a historical situation. It was no part of its purpose to formulate a particular creed. 'Its task was to organise the forces of labour and link the various workingmen's movements and combine them.' Governments might persecute the International but they could no more destroy it than the Roman Empire could destroy the early Christians. Unlike the revolutions of 1848, the Commune had shown how capitalism could be destroyed by transferring to the workers the ownership of the means of production. But for this to be possible, the workers would have 'to emancipate themselves on the battle field' by creating a 'proletarian army' and setting up a 'proletarian dictature' (*sic*). 'The task of the International was to organise and combine the forces of labour for the coming struggle.'[1] This was the language of the *Communist Manifesto*, not the *Inaugural Address*. In one respect it went even further than the *Manifesto* which had said nothing about a proletarian dictatorship. But if Marx reverted to his earlier outspokenness it was not as in 1848 in anticipation of an early revolution. Now it was the impossibility of speedy developments which led him to abandon the cautious, diplomatic language of the *Address*. In *The Civil War in France* Marx had thrown caution to the winds. That this was no momentary aberration under emotional stress was shown by his speech following the London Conference.

Hardly had the Conference Resolutions been published[2] when news reached London that the Bakuninist offensive against the General Council was being organised in a number of countries. The London Conference decisions became the target for a general attack. In London itself the Section Française de 1871 consisting of a number of Communard refugees was working in collaboration with Bakunin's followers in Switzerland. In the United States, Bakunin was receiving support from the followers of Victoria Woodhull.[3]

From Italy came the news that the Naples and Turin sections were refusing to accept Conference resolutions. Similar news arrived from Spain and it was soon clear to Marx, Engels and the General Council that drastic action was required. The Belgian section, which had carefully kept to a middle position at the London Conference, was clearly going to give trouble. On the other hand, the Conference decisions were supported by the Germans, the English Federal Council, the Dutch, the German Swiss and by some of the Belgians, French and Americans. Even in Spain, a minority still adhered to the General Council.

The breach became public when the Jurassian section in Switzerland, overwhelmingly Bakuninist, issued a circular declaring that the London Conference was invalid because of its unrepresentative character, repudiating its decisions and demanding an immediate Congress to consider the differences

[1] New York *World*, November 15, 1871.
[2] They first appeared, unofficially, in the daily newspaper published for a short time in London by Vermersch and a group of Communard refugees, the *Qui Vive*, November 7, 8, 1871. I.I.S.G.
[3] S. Bernstein, *The First International in America*, 1962, Chapter VII.

within the International. On March 5, 1872 the General Council issued Marx's pamphlet — *Les Prétendues Scissions dans l'International, circulaire privée du Conseil Général de Londres*. The anarchists answered with the *Réponse de quelques Internationaux* from Neufchâtel. Without attempting a detailed reply it denounced the Council for operating a dictatorship within the Association and for exercising a usurped authority by prolonging its existence beyond the expiry of its mandate in September 1870. The attacks on Bakunin, it insisted, were largely the work of Jews.

From this time onwards it was open war. *Les Prétendues Scissions* had been signed by all members of the General Council, English included, and though the English were not directly involved, they were prepared to support Marx and the Council against what had every appearance of being a disruptive attack on the unity of the International. Engels felt confident that whatever progress the anarchists were making in Europe, 'here in England, of course, none of these intrigues finds any support'.[1] This position was to change decisively during the year when the defection of Hales, with a strong following on the English Federal Council, was to bring the controversy to England, though in an altered form.

[1] Engels to Cuno, January 24, 1872. For the progress of the conflict, see Marx to Sorge, November 9 and Engels to Liebknecht, November 4, December 15, 1871; Engels to Carmelo Palladino, November 23 and to *Proletario Italiano*, November 29, 1871. Engels to Liebknecht, January 2, 1872. Engels to J. P. Becker, February 16 and to Pio, March 7, 1872. This correspondence is reprinted in *Soc.*, vol. XXVI and in *Londonskaya Konferentsia*. *Les Prétendues Scissions* — there is no English translation — is reproduced in *Soc.*, vol. XIII/2, pp. 391-433. For Bakunin's case, see Bakunin, *Werke*, vol. 3, pp. 217-50 and Guillaume, *Bakunin*, vol. 3, pp. 153-231 and vol. 4, pp. 232-56.

CHAPTER XIV

From the London Conference to the Hague

FROM the moment when in connection with the Commune, the International had sprung into public attention, estimates of its size and influence ranged from one extreme to the other. The Catholic *Tablet* on July 15, 1871 described thus, in somewhat heightened language, Truelove's modest bookshop at 256 High Holborn which specialised in editions of Voltaire and Paine and allowed the notorious Association to meet on its premises : 'There is a booksellers' shop in High Holborn. It is in every sense an unpretending establishment. . . . An inscription above it calls it "The Reformers' Library". . . . There are sights more hunted after by mere sight-seers. There are edifices linked with many a historic narrative or fable. Yet we would venture to set that undistinguished shop above more than one palace and monument. For there are the head-quarters of a society whose behests are obeyed by countless thousands from Moscow to Madrid, and in the New World as well as in the Old, whose disciples have already waged desperate war against one Government, and whose proclamations pledge it to wage that war against every government — the ominous, the ubiquitous International Association of Workmen.' At the other extreme, the tight-lipped *Scotsman* thought that 'there is generally among us a wholesome distrust of theorists and a desire rather to be guided by the teaching of facts. Hence it is that, in respect to the Paris Commune, apologists have not had much success here.' Like the *Tablet*, the *Scotsman* had no hesitation as to the responsibility for the Commune and its excesses. 'Paris', it concluded, 'has been made a sort of vicarious sacrifice, that the rest of Europe might be saved from the misdoings of the Internationale.' [1]

On September 15 the *Express*, concerned about the danger to civilisation which it perceived, drew attention to the fact that the Chancellors of Germany and Austria — 'the two

[1] July 4, 1871.

master minds of Continental Europe' — were meeting to discuss ways of checking the progress of the International. England
should co-operate, but the paper doubted whether Gladstone
would risk antagonising 'the chiefs of the democracy which
he is constantly lauding'.

Gladstone's views on the International were duly expressed
later in the same month when he received an address from the
Aberdeen Trades Council.   In a country whose institutions
were not 'in the main honestly addressed to the welfare of the
community at large' there was always the danger of violent
upheavals when the workers discovered their power.   Further-
more, 'with respect to that very remarkable combination that
has lately been formed under the name of the International
Society, no person can question, I think, that that may grow
into an institution productive of important and in some cases
of critical results'.   With regard to Britain, however, 'I take a
sanguine view of the whole question between capital and
labour', though there was admittedly 'a great deal to adjust, a
great deal to rectify and improve'.[1]

OPPOSITION TO THE GENERAL COUNCIL. THE CONTROVERSY
WITH BRADLAUGH

While outright attacks on the International had been characteristic of the Conservative Press, the controversy over the
Commune gave rise to an attack from a new source — Bradlaugh's *National Reformer*.   In the issue of September 17, 1871
Bradlaugh described the International as having 'but few
members and but little influence in England' and added that
its Secretary had 'justified the burning of *public* buildings in
Paris as a piece of military strategy'.   Hales replied in a letter
to the *Eastern Post* on September 23 attacking Bradlaugh for
his Malthusian economic views, justifying the burning of
buildings as a military necessity and adding that Bradlaugh's
friends Thiers and Favre must bear the main blame for the
destruction of property.

The two replies which appeared in the following issue of
the *Eastern Post* attacked, not Hales who had signed the letter,
but Marx who was becoming increasingly recognised as the
effective leader of the International.   'Thou shalt have no
other prophet but Marx' had become the watchword, wrote

[1] *Manchester Guardian*, September 27, 1871.

Charles Wade, so that the Association had been diverted from its original worthy aims. 'Mr. or rather Herr Karl Marx', wrote the foundation member, Le Lubez, had 'changed the "Central Council" into an arena where he may insult with impunity the honest and disinterested men who would like to restore it to its primitive mission.'

When the French section originally split, Marx had, how-ever reluctantly, sided with the workers Tolain and Fribourg against the 'bourgeois republican' Lefort. Le Lubez had not forgiven Marx and his followers. Now the London French branch was being reinforced by refugees from the Commune whose political allegiances, ranging from Pyat to Bakunin, brought them into conflict with Marx and the General Council. Towards the end of 1871 a body calling itself the 'Section Française Fédéraliste' of the International issued a leaflet printed in London — in French — attacking the decisions of the London Conference and calling for a grouping of all like-minded national sections which stood for 'the federative idea' and against the 'radically authoritarian' outlook of the General Council.[1]

As yet the French federalists, like their Bakuninist allies of the Jura Federation, had no support in England. Hales, who later joined them, was still Marx's staunchest English ally on the General Council. At the first meeting of the Council following the London Conference it was Marx himself who re-nominated Hales as General Secretary and there was now no controversy over the resolution which announced the forma-tion of 'a Federal Committee for England, so that the influence of the Association might be brought to bear more directly upon English politics, than it had hitherto done'.[2]

With branches already existing in Bethnal Green and Middlesbrough [3] the English Federal Council was formally set up in October at a well-attended meeting of the London members. The enigmatic figure of Maltman Barry made his first appearance in the International taking the chair and being elected provisional Chairman — with Hales as provisional Secretary — at the conclusion of the meeting.

A news item appearing in *The Times* [4] alleged that English

[1] Leaflet in I.I.S.G.
[2] G.C. *Minutes*, September 26 and *Eastern Post*, September 30, 1871.
[3] G.C. *Minutes*, October 17 and *Eastern Post*, October 21, 1871.
[4] October 23, 1871.

trade unionists, disgusted by the Commune and refusing any longer 'to find the sinews of war for foreign agitations', had withdrawn their support from the International and that the English Federal Council had been formed as a result by 'members of this secret society'. In his reply [1] Hales denied that the International was in any sense a secret society. All its meetings he claimed were open and of the 'many thousands of members we have in England only two have withdrawn their names or entered a protest'.[2]

The charge that the International conducted its affairs in secrecy was taken up by Charles Bradlaugh in a lecture on 'pauperism' at the Hall of Science on November 26. While the 'duty of every country was to help the people of other lands', different policies were appropriate in different countries. In England the great question was land monopoly; in France, the struggle between the bourgeoisie and the working class. The tasks of an International Association therefore were complex and regarding the International, he was in favour of 'the rules of the society as printed, but not as carried out, for in a semi-secret society of which they did not understand the objects, they might be committed to things of which they could not approve'.[3]

Bradlaugh returned to the attack at a meeting in support of Communard refugees. Distorting the analysis of the Second Empire in *The Civil War in France* he attributed to Marx the view that 'the Empire was the only Government possible, while the middle class could not be entrusted with the Government, and the working class had not become fitted to rule. Bradlaugh contended, however, that government should not have a class character at all, but should belong 'to all classes equally'. On these grounds he denounced the Commune as a minority dictatorship, but he also condemned the behaviour of the Versailles Government.[4]

---

[1] *Eastern Post*, October 28, 1871.

[2] Hales's statement was borne out by *The Times* itself, which printed a very well informed history of the International, presumably by Eccarius, which ran to four and a half columns on October 27. It pointed out that there had been few new trade union affiliations after 1867 and that of all the unions which joined, only three had seceded, none of them as a result of the Commune. (The three to leave, on the Fenian issue, were the Amalgamated Cordwainers, the Birmingham House Painters and the Curriers.) In the *Eastern Post* on October 7 Hales gave the current English membership as eight thousand.

[3] *Eastern Post*, December 2, 1871.

[4] *Eastern Post*, December 16, 1871.

In a letter to the same issue of the *Eastern Post* Bradlaugh attacked Marx personally, accusing him, in rather vague terms, of having denounced people to the Prussian police. Marx replied in the following issue that ever since the publication of *The Civil War in France* Bradlaugh had joined in the 'world-wide chorus of slander against the International and myself'. Marx had 'treated him, like the other revilers, with contemptuous silence. This was more than the grotesque vanity of that huge self-idolator could stand.' If Bradlaugh would make his charges more specific, Marx would consider legal action. Hales wrote in the same issue defending Marx and accusing Bradlaugh of hob-nobbing with Bonapartists in Paris.[1]

INTRIGUES OF MALTMAN BARRY

Much more dangerous than the antagonism of Bradlaugh were the machinations within the International itself of Maltman Barry, a correspondent of the *Standard* and a Conservative Party agent.[2] Marx's friendship with Barry, who acted as his agent at the Hague in 1872, is incongruous and reminiscent in some ways of his earlier collaboration with the High Tory, David Urquhart.[3]

Barry first appeared on the General Council on November 7, 1871 when with Charles Kerr he was accepted as the representative of the English Federal Council. In less than a month he seems to have begun actively intriguing to set Marx against Hales. On December 2 he reported to Marx and Engels at

[1] For a reference to this controversy, see Bradlaugh's daughter, Hypatia Bradlaugh Bonner, in *Charles Bradlaugh*, 1894, vol. I, p. 331.

[2] For Barry's subsequent activities as a Conservative agent, see *Will Lloyd George Supplant Ramsay MacDonald?* By Joseph Burgess, n.d., pp. 59-100, and *The Apostle of Free Labour*, the autobiography of William Collison, 1913, pp. 235-42. Burgess was the editor of the *Workman's Times* and one of the founders of the Independent Labour Party. His strangely titled book, though written much later — *c.* 1930 — is well documented.

[3] According to Adolphe Smith, Jung later produced evidence that Barry acted as a spy on the Communard refugees — Burgess, *op. cit.*, p. 66. Max Nettlau compared Marx's weakness for Barry with Engels's for Aveling and commented that both aberrations cost them influence amongst British workers. 'Ein verschollener Nachklang der Internationale : The I.L.U. *Minutes*, London, 1877–78' in Grünberg's *Archiv*, vol. IX, 1921, p. 140, n. 2. See also the similar comment of H. M. Hyndman, *op. cit.*, p. 285. Marx provided Barry with material for articles in the *Examiner*, *Standard* and *Hour* in 1874 and 1875. See *Chronik*, pp. 346 and 351. Barry also acted as Marx's agent at the Ghent Congress in 1877 — Marx to Sorge, September 27, 1877. Marx later became more critical of Barry, see letter to Engels, September 18, 1878.

length on the activities of the Federal Council and, in particular, on Hales, who was aiming, he said, to strengthen the Federal at the expense of the General Council.[1] This produced its effect and three days later at a meeting of the General Council Marx, on Barry's suggestion, moved successfully that Hales should not be Secretary of both Councils and should withdraw from Secretaryship of the Federal Council.[2] He was replaced by C. Keen.

Barry next opened an attack on Hales for allegedly reporting a private meeting of the Federal Council in a news item appearing in the *Standard* on December 5. From internal evidence, the article may well have been written by Barry himself. None the less, it served to increase the tension between Hales and Marx who was persuaded to move formally that Hales relinquish his post on the Federal Council. A few weeks later Barry must have written to Marx warning him of a party led by Hales on the General Council since Marx replied on January 7, 1872 denying that there was any such thing. 'If we ever came out against Hales', he wrote, 'when we considered him wrong, then we carried out our duties as members of the Council. The same would apply to any other member. Why then a party? There are no parties in the Council. Amongst Hales's friends there are many who have worked for long for our aims.'

Barry had not yet succeeded in opening a rift between the two. In a letter to the *Eastern Post* on February 3 replying to another attack by Bradlaugh, Hales was emphatic that 'there are no official subordinates to Dr. Marx on our Council. He is secretary for Germany, and would as little dream of interfering in English affairs as I should in German.' Marx, Hales added, would be 'the first man to resent an assumption that he held a superior position'.

At some time in January Hales and his supporters had Barry expelled from the British Federal Council. This does not seem to have affected Barry's relations with Marx whom he no doubt continued to feed with more or less tainted information about Hales. Some resentment was expressed in the St. Luke's Branch, and no doubt elsewhere at the fact that Barry, even after his expulsion from the Federal Council, was still treated by the General Council as a bona fide member. But the anomalous situation persisted.

[1] *Chronik*, p. 320.   [2] G.C. *Minutes*, December 5, 1871.

GROWTH OF BRANCHES. THE *INTERNATIONAL HERALD*

At the beginning of 1872, however, the friction did not yet appear serious. The Federal Council, with Keen as Secretary, had been fairly successful in recruiting. Keen presented a report on January 9 showing provincial branches in Manchester, Middlesbrough, Liverpool, Loughborough and Nottingham. Trade unions written to were listed as Boot Closers, Cigar Makers, Tailors, Bricklayers, Portmanteau Makers, Day-working Book Binders and Alliance Cabinet Makers.[1] With the withdrawal of the Carpenters and Joiners which took place with Applegarth's resignation as General Secretary, this probably represents the extent of trade union affiliation in England and is compatible with Hales's estimate of the nominal membership as eight thousand. J. P. McDonnell, who had been active in the Fenian movement, had started to form Irish branches in London, the Provinces and Ireland itself.[2] He was only accepted as Irish Secretary on the General Council after an acrimonious dispute. The *Irishman*, the leading nationalist journal, denounced him as a middle-class adventurer,[3] but Marx, after what he described to Sorge as 'a most searching enquiry', gave McDonnell his full backing.[4] McDonnell's efforts bore their first fruit with the formation of a Soho Irish branch on February 4, 1872. Though the branch in a preliminary declaration considered its first duty was to help emancipate Ireland 'from foreign domination and class rule', it also recognised the obligation to co-operate, 'through the International with the working classes of all other nations'.[5]

The Manchester branch, which was destined to be the most successful of all, was addressed by Harriet Law on behalf of the French refugees at one of its earliest meetings.[6] Eugène Dupont who was working in Manchester kept Engels informed

[1] MSS. report in I.I.S.G. This list, with the addition of the Boot Closers and Portmanteau Makers, of which the West End of London branches had affiliated and with the omission of the Carpenters and Joiners, corresponds to Eccarius's list of unions making financial contributions, G.C. *Minutes*, October 31, 1871.

[2] *Eastern Post*, January 6, 1872.

[3] See undated draft of a letter from Murphy, who managed the *Irishman* for Piggott and letter from McDonnell to Engels, September 30, 1871. I.I.S.G.

[4] Marx to Sorge, November 29, 1871.

[5] *Eastern Post*, February 10, 1872. The manifesto also appears as a printed leaflet in the McDonnell papers, Wisconsin.

[6] *Ibid.*, January 13, 1872.

about developments and constantly sought his advice on policy.
Manchester's delegate to the General Council was Dr. Sexton,
a prolific writer of rationalist tracts who had, somewhat to
Dupont's surprise, declared himself a communist.[1]   Dupont
was pleased with developments in Manchester, but very
worried, and with reason, about the developing Bakuninist
offensive.   A circular issued by the Jura section had just
reached England.   It attacked the General Council for exercising a usurped authority, since no Congress had met for over
two years and for arrogating to itself despotic power over
affiliated sections.   'I read the circular of the Jura sections',
wrote Dupont to Engels, adding in some alarm, 'have the other
sections not protested?   They tell me that the Italians have
also pronounced against the General Council.   Is it true?'[2]

In England, at least, there seemed little cause for alarm.
New branches were still being formed and whatever personal
friction existed between the Federal and General Councils,
there was as yet no conflict of political views.   On the contrary,
the Federal Council passed unanimously in February a resolution supporting the decisions of the London Conference 'in
their integrity'.   'Every member', the resolution emphasised,
'was in favour of combining political and social action, and
thoroughly endorsed the policy of the General Council.'[3]
Besides preserving a broad agreement of outlook, in a period
when the International was deeply split, the Association in
England seemed about to acquire an organ of its own for the
first time since 1867.

On March 2, 1872 the first number of the *International
Herald* appeared published by W. Harrison Riley.[4]   In a letter
to Marx on February 9, 1872 Riley asked him to write for the
journal[5] and on February 10 he wrote to Engels also asking
for help and promising to print full reports of the Inter-

---

[1] Later, in 1872, Dr. Sexton announced his conversion to spiritualism,
which disconcerted some of his new friends in Manchester.   Nevertheless,
he attended the Hague Congress in September as a staunch supporter of
Marx.
[2] Dupont to Engels, January 11; see also letter of January 8, 1872.
I.I.S.G.
[3] *Eastern Post*, February 17, 1872.
[4] Riley was born in Manchester and worked for some time in the clothing
trade.   After spending a few years in America he came to London in 1871
where he came under the influence of Marx and Engels.   For a further
account of Riley see p. 270, n. 3.
[5] *Chronik*, p. 324.

national's activities. Appearing fortnightly at first, the paper
became a weekly from May 11. Its statement of objects
covered all the demands of contemporary working-class
radicalism, ranging from shorter working hours and universal
suffrage to 'the nationalization of land and currency' and the
liquidation of the National Debt. Though not specifically an
organ of the International, the *Herald* aspired to be 'the special
organ of such societies as are not already specially represented
by *The Beehive* or the *National Reformer*'.

The second issue of the *Herald* published in full the first
'Address of the British Federal Council to the British working
class'. In seven years, it pointed out, the International had
'acquired a position such as no other Labour organisation ever
attained in the history of the world'. Extending into nearly
every civilised country 'its adherents may be counted by
hundreds of thousands, if not by millions. It has become a
power dreaded by most of the European Governments.' It
was 'neither a rival of, nor in conflict with, any Labour or
Democratic organisation . . .' but on the contrary sought to
promote the maximum common action.[1]

The reference to the dread of the International felt by
European governments was timely. Early in March the Spanish
Government sent round a circular to all countries with which
it had diplomatic relations calling for the suppression of the
International. At about the same time, the French Government introduced a Bill for the same purpose. In England the
more Liberal papers opposed any repressive action. 'The
English Government', wrote the *Saturday Review* on March
16, 'wisely declined to recommend to Parliament any change
in the law, and not a single demand for extradition of a Communist has been made by the French Government'. The
International was, in its view, basically an association of trade-
union movements in various countries. Since trade unions
had a right to organise, it was hard to see why they should be
denied the right of international association. This remained
true, it thought, despite such occasional aberrations as the
'Sheffield Outrages' and *The Civil War in France*. The *Daily
News* feared that the only effect of the French legislation would

---

[1] The address was published as a pamphlet of six pages, printed by the
Eastern Post, together with the rules of the Federal Council and the subscription rate, which was 3d. per annum for each affiliated member, of
which 1d. went to the General Council. I.I.S.G.

be to increase 'the fund of that class hatred which is the fatal legacy of civil war' and so make moderate reform more difficult. By contrast, the *Standard* of March 18 complained that 'our shores are already regarded as the refuge of conspiracies that fail and the starting point of conspiracies that are to succeed'. It thought that the British Government could with advantage emulate the legislation of the new French Republic.

All that the British Government did, however, was to introduce a Bill curtailing the right of meeting in public parks. There were suggestions of outside pressure when the proprietors of St. George's Hall in Langham Place cancelled at the last minute the booking for the International's Commune anniversary meeting.[1] A meeting was held by the French republicans at which Landeck, Weber and Vésinier spoke, in the Hall of Science, St. Luke's. The occasion was used to make a public attack on the General Council. The tenor of the meeting was described by the *Eastern Post* on March 23. 'The fact that the International has a council which is not subject to more frequent overhaulings by a congress seemed to be the chief ostensible grievance; but there were mysterious whispers which would lead a stranger to imagine that a horror of "Dictatorship" and the iron system of Germanic organisation attributed to Dr. Karl Marx, was at the bottom of the schismatic feeling. Indeed, we heard fond regrets uttered in low tones that it had not pleased Allah (or Somebody Else) to take the doctor to the other world instead of Mazzini', although Mazzini had denounced the Commune, while Marx had defended it, 'with perhaps more valour than discretion'. Weston, a foundation member of the International, spoke at the meeting. He was moving closer to the London French, although he refrained on this occasion from joining overtly in the attack.

REPRESSION IN IRELAND. BAILLIE-COCHRANE IN THE HOUSE OF COMMONS

If it was sometimes possible to defend the Commune at public meetings in England, there could be no question of doing so for long in Catholic Ireland. John De Morgan

---

[1] See Engels to Sorge, March 17; also *Express*, March 20, 1872. A poster announcing the meeting, with a list of intended speakers, is in the McDonnell papers.

addressed a meeting in Cork which culminated in a riot. He
was a teacher of elocution, a colourful, voluble and unstable
character. For the meeting, his 'ordinary slender attire, half
theatrical, half clerical in appearance — tight-fitting frock coat,
white neck tie and round peakless cap — was exchanged for a
comfortable brown overcoat, bright green tie and billy cock
hat'. The meeting had been well leafleted in advance by the
Catholic opposition. One of the leaflets, addressed to the
'Working Men of Cork', began : 'The apologist of the Communists of Paris is amongst you' and ended 'God save Ireland !'
Canon Maguire had called for the International to be driven
forcibly from Cork and he was taken at his word. Though
De Morgan denied that he supported the Commune, he was
thrown out of the hall at an overwhelmingly working-class meeting. Many of his most strenuous assailants had served prison
sentences in the Fenian cause.[1] The Dublin branch ran into
equally heavy weather and it was in vain that a Danish speaker,
at its inaugural meeting, declared that they 'had no alliance
or sympathy with the Commune, except in so far as the rights
of labour were concerned'.[2] *The Times* was not exaggerating
when it wrote : 'Their connection with the atrocities of the
Communists of Paris has made a union with the working
classes here impossible'.

For a short while, however, the Carpenters' and Coach
Makers' Societies in Cork affiliated to the local branch. The
Coach Makers were locked out for demanding a fifty-four hour
week and the General Council issued a printed leaflet appealing
for aid and addressed to 'the Irish Sections of the International
and the *Working Classes in General*'.[3]

Official pressure, including the stationing of policemen at
meetings taking the names of those participating and passing
them on to their employers, caused the Coach Makers to withdraw their affiliation, while De Morgan, unable to earn a living
in Cork, had to leave for England.[4] All members of the
General Council signed a statement drafted by Marx, Milner
and McDonnell issued as a leaflet entitled 'Police Terrorism in
Ireland'. The national antagonism between English and
Irish workers, it said, had been 'one of the mainstays of class
dominion in England as well as in Ireland. The spread of the

[1] *Express*, March 25 ; cf. *Freeman*, March 25, 26, 1872.
[2] *Express*, March 30 and *The Times*, April 1, 1872.
[3] McDonnell papers.	[4] *Eastern Post*, April 14, 1872.

R

International in Ireland and the formation of Irish branches in England, threatened to put an end to this state of things.' Hence the violence of the repression, more possible in Ireland than in England because of the 'truly Prussian way' which 'the exceptional legislation and the practically permanent state of siege' made possible. It is hard to say what effect, if any, this vigorous and well written leaflet which had on it the unmistakable stamp of Marx produced. But repression which had the support of the masses was bound to succeed and McDonnell tacitly admitted that the two branches in Ireland were dead at the General Council meeting of May 7.[1]

Things were very different in England. When on April 12 Alexander Baillie-Cochrane introduced a motion in the Commons calling for the suppression of the International, his speech fell flat. His argument was based on an uncritical assimilation of current French propaganda and followed substantially the lines of a letter he had written to *The Times*, appearing on October 31, 1871. Bakunin's programme, he believed, had been adopted by the General Council in July 1869. The International stood for atheism, the abolition of all forms of worship and marriage. It had seven million members, including one hundred and eighty-six thousand in England. Henry Fawcett, a prominent Liberal and future Postmaster-General, opposed the motion, but not out of sympathy with the International. Its views could produce 'incalculable mischief', but repression would only give them 'a factitious importance'. The Government itself was not free from blame because its last Budget had been based on 'the first principles of the International', teaching the people that it was legitimate to pay for reforms by taxing property. Fawcett went on to develop his attack on land nationalisation, free education, progressive taxation and other modifications of *laissez-faire* which seemed to him instalments of the International's programme of which he went on to give a largely fanciful account.

Replying to the discussion the Home Secretary, Bruce, explained that 'from enquiries he had instituted' more than six hundred thousand trade unionists had joined the International [2] 'for the immediate purposes of trade, and without entertaining any of those terrible opinions to which his hon. friends had adverted'. Its paid-up membership in England was only

[1] *Eastern Post*, May 11, 1872.
[1] This was, presumably, its world membership.

eight thousand. While he did not want to underrate 'the dangers of this society', they should be dealt with by 'education with some religious teaching'. With little Parliamentary support, Baillie-Cochrane's proposal was quietly dropped.[1] Commenting on the debate, *The Times* was apprehensive that trade unionists who adhered to 'the old English claim of a fair day's wage for a fair day's work' might be contaminated by the 'strange theories . . . respecting the constitution of society in general' which Parisian workers had imported into the International. Nevertheless, it thought that the Home Secretary had been right in refusing to 'take arbitrary measures for the suppression of a Society which, so far as we know, is within the pale of our law'.[2]

This remained the Government's view. Replying to the Spanish circular, Lord Granville reiterated the view that the 'revolutionary designs' which were attributed to the International were restricted to its 'foreign members'. Its British section was mainly concerned with trade unions and strikes and had 'but very little money at its disposal for their support'. He ended by pointing out that the British Government had no legal right to expel refugees who obeyed the law and had not committed crimes covered by the treaty of extradition.[3]

MANCHESTER, NOTTINGHAM, THE IRISH SECTION

Secure from legal interference, the International went its way with an increasing number of branches of which those in Manchester and Nottingham were beginning to show stability and vigour. Both branches were meeting regularly to discuss their political programmes. Manchester was divided on land policy between advocates of nationalisation and supporters of redistribution to peasant proprietors. Dupont, who kept Engels well briefed about the affairs of the Manchester branch, favoured nationalisation as decided at Basle on the grounds

---

[1] Baillie-Cochrane asked, in one form or another, for the suppression of the International five times in the Commons. See *Hansard*, 3rd series, CCIX, 1025-6, CCX, 244-5; 401; 1183-210, 1268. February 26, March 19, March 21, April 12 and April 15, 1872.

[2] April 15, 1872.

[3] *The Times*, April 16, 1872. The Spanish Press deplored the British reaction as a sign of lamentable weakness, 'which that country may one day regret'. *The Times*, April 19. The exchange of notes was published in Britain as *Correspondence between the British and Spanish Governments respecting the International Society*, 4, 1872.

that 'Sharing, fragmentation would run contrary to modern ideas and means of production, which require large-scale exploitation'. These differences did not impede the activities or recruiting of the branch which held a successful public meeting in April — 'Nous marchons très bien' was Dupont's optimistic conclusion.[1]

The Nottingham branch, which met weekly at Lester's Coffee House in Houndsgate, issued its own programme calling for 'political and social revolution'. Its five points, differing in emphasis from the International's official policy authorised by its successive Congresses, called for freedom of expression and education, the abolition of privileges based on class and sex, 'emancipation of the land', including the 'right and duty of men to enjoy the fruit of their own labour' and 'capital the servant of labour, and not labour the servant of capital' — a vague provision, as compatible with the views of Mill as with those of Marx — universal suffrage, national and racial equality and, unique among the British branches, 'the protection of the rights of minorities by the principle of federalism and by decentralisation of power — so as to take away the temptation of the central government to trample on the rights of its opponents'.[2] The statement was signed by Thomas Smith, the Branch Secretary and the most original political thinker among the English members of the International.[3]

A conference of the Irish sections in London was held on April 21 under McDonnell's chairmanship to discuss the building of the organisation in the various districts of London and the inauguration of a 'propaganda fund' to carry on the work in Ireland.[4] This innocent-looking proposal was to add its contribution to the split already developing within the British section.

THE UNIVERSAL FEDERALIST COUNCIL AND THE REVOLT AGAINST MARX

The first signs of revolt against Marx came from outside the General Council. A large gathering in the Black Swan, Leicester Square, with Englishmen speaking alongside French-

---

[1] Dupont to Engels, March 8, April 28, 1872. I.I.S.G.
[2] *International Herald*, April 13, 1872.
[3] See Chapter XV.
[4] *Eastern Post*, April 27, 1872. The delegates were strongly advised to find alternative accommodation to public houses.

men and Germans, inaugurated the Universal Federalist Council in April. The Secretary at the meeting was Richard Dennis Butler, a compositor and delegate to the London Trades Council. A foundation member of the International, he had formally proposed Professor Beesly as Chairman at the inaugural meeting in 1864. He now claimed that the members of the Universal Federalist Council still regarded themselves as belonging to the International, but that they had united to oppose the General Council which had 'constituted itself into a centralizing and despotic power' expelling individuals and sections without appeal and generally tyrannising over the membership.

The Englishmen participating in the secession were few in number and would probably have had no effect on the General Council had there not been on that body members already in revolt against Marx for a variety of other reasons. There was firstly the controversy over the dissident, anarchist section 12 of New York which, led by two enterprising sisters, Victoria Woodhull and Tennie Claflin, was campaigning for free love, spiritualism, currency reform and other causes which appealed to its exclusively middle-class and decidedly cranky membership.[1] The General Council sided with the more working-class and largely foreign-born American section led by Friedrich Sorge and Frederick Bolte. Using the decisions of the London Conference it ordered section 12 to dissolve. But Marx had been aware for some months of the existence on the General Council of sympathisers with section 12. As early as November 23, 1871 he had written to Bolte that G. Harris and Martin Boon were known to be corresponding with the New York dissidents. Both the Englishmen, he explained, 'belong to the sect of the late Bronterre O'Brien, and are full of follies and crotchets, such as currency quackery, false emancipation of women, and the like. They are thus by nature allies of section 12 in New York and its kindred souls.' As yet, Marx was not too concerned nor inclined to take a strong line against the O'Brienites. He explained to Bolte that 'in spite of their follies' they constituted 'an often necessary counterweight to trade unionists in the Council. They are more revolutionary, firmer on the land question, less nationalistic, and not susceptible to bourgeois bribery in one form or

[1] Samuel Bernstein, *The First International in America*, New York, 1962, pp. 109-27.

another. Otherwise they would have been kicked out long ago.' [1]

Much more disturbing for Marx was the behaviour of Eccarius. After his resignation as General Secretary, Eccarius had been appointed Corresponding Secretary for America. Personally disgruntled and increasingly tending to favour an alliance between the workers and the liberal middle class, he had in his correspondence with America encouraged section 12 and incited it, so far as any incitement was needed, against Sorge. On April 12 Marx charged Eccarius on the General Council with abusing his position as Corresponding Secretary.[2] There followed a bitter exchange of letters between Eccarius and Marx. Eccarius was convinced that both Marx and Engels were intriguing against him. On May 3 Marx reminded Eccarius of the number of times he had protected him over the years against English attacks — first, from Odger, Cremer, Howell and others over the *Commonwealth*, later, against Fox and finally, against Hales when Eccarius was General Secretary. 'The day after tomorrow is my birthday,' wrote Marx, 'and I should not like to start it conscious that I was deprived of one of my oldest friends and adherents.' Eccarius probably did not reply and so ended a friendship going back at least twenty-five years.

On May 28 Marx took further measures to curb Eccarius's activities by proposing that the General Council should support only the New York section led by Sorge. 'Eccarius was thunderstruck', as Marx told Sorge next day, but Marx himself was probably disturbed by the fact that Hales who had replaced Eccarius as General Secretary was now voting with him in support of the autonomy of sections against the claims of the General Council. Ostensibly, opposition to Marx in England was coming from minute bodies with impressive titles incorporating the old London French branch under Vésinier, the handful of German Lassalleans such as Weber and a scattering of Englishmen such as Butler whose connection with the International had been minimal and who had probably been added at the last minute to give an impression of English respectability to an assemblage of unrepresentative and disintegrating

---

[1] For an O'Brienite view of their good relations with Marx on the General Council, see W. Townshend to Marx Beer, 1895, in the latter's *Fifty Years of International Socialism*, 1937, pp. 133-4.

[2] G.C. *Minutes*.

refugee bodies.[1] Hales's antagonism to Marx almost certainly dated from the time when he was made to resign on Marx's motion but at Maltman Barry's instigation from his position as Secretary of the English Federal Council. From April Hales was at loggerheads with McDonnell over the formation of the Irish branches which Hales insisted must come under the control of the English Council. On May 14 he had reached the stage of demanding the dissolution of the Irish branches as being contrary to the objects of the International which were, he now claimed, to obliterate national barriers. Engels was scathing. The Irish were as much a 'distinct nationality' as the Poles under Russian rule. 'In a case like that of the Irish', he added, 'true Internationalism must necessarily be based on a distinct national organisation', the first task of which must be the fight for national independence. Hales was defeated by a vote of twenty-two to one, which did nothing to improve his relations with Engels or Marx.

THE BRITISH FEDERAL COUNCIL ON THE EVE OF NOTTINGHAM

By June two approaching Congresses overshadowed all other business — the Nottingham Congress of the Federal Council arranged for July and the fifth Congress of the International at the Hague for September. For Nottingham it was arranged that each branch send one delegate for every fifty members, and the *International Herald*, which announced itself from May 11 as 'The Official Organ of the British Section of the International Working Men's Association', announced the existence of twenty-one branches on May 25.

Of all the branches, that in Manchester was by far the most vigorous. It held regular open-air meetings on Sundays to audiences estimated at four to five hundred and on one occasion seven hundred. The West End of London branch, to which Charles Murray's Society of Boot-Closers was affiliated, had twenty-nine members. The Nottingham branch was strengthened considerably by the affiliation of the

---

[1] See the sixteen-page pamphlet of the *Universal Federalist Council of the International Working Men's Association and of Republican and Socialist Societies Adhering*, 1872. See also a handbill, dated in ink, April 21, 1872, announcing the formation of the Universal Republican League, which developed out of the International Democratic Association and adhered to the Universal Federalist Council.

International Labour Protection League of Nottingham which had developed out of the local Nine Hours League. Its object was to co-ordinate strike action between the various trades so that only one trade struck at a time receiving assistance from all the others. It also aimed at securing joint action with European workers. On June 22 one hundred and two plaster workers and farm labourers joined the League, no doubt stimulated by the aid which the General Council was planning for Joseph Arch's campaign to organise farm workers in Warwickshire.[1]

Unlike the General Council, the local branches of the International inevitably became socialist propaganda bodies and equally inevitably the ideas propagated were those of Bronterre O'Brien, whose followers formed the only coherent body of socialists in England at the time. Charles Murray was a leading member of this school. When he took the chair at a meeting of the 'Mutual Land Emigration and Colonization Company' — a body which aimed at establishing an O'Brienite colony in America — he referred to those 'just laws on land, credit, currency and exchange' as being 'identical with those upon which the International is based'. Hales later addressed the same 'crowded audience' on land nationalisation.[2] The West End branch of the International, in which Murray and Milner were leading members, was addressed by Martin J. Boon of the National Reform League on the theme 'That the land and currency laws are of vital importance to the people'.[3] And in Manchester one of the earliest meetings, addressed by Walker, had as its subject 'Land, Currency and Credit'.[4]

In addition to the National Reform League and the Colonisation Company, the *International Herald* itself preached the O'Brienite gospel. The 'Notes and Comments' feature on May 18, 1872 attacked the recent increase in the bank rate as a plot by the big banks. 'What matters it to them', it asked rhetorically, 'if a thousand working tradesmen are ruined and a hundred thousand more are distressed ? They are the dis-

[1] *International Herald*, June 29, 1872. Cf. Eccarius's article, *ibid.*, June 8, and three-page prospectus of the International Labour Protection League, I.I.S.G. The *Herald* also published weekly a full list of the International's British branches which were: Manchester, Liverpool, Nottingham, Sunderland, Dundee, Birkenhead, Newcastle-on-Tyne, Hinckley, Loughborough, Middlesbrough, Buckfastleigh, Blackpool, Leeds, Glasgow, Woolwich, Grimsby, Ryde, London West-End, Bethnal Green, Stratford, St. Luke's, Aberdeen, Hull and Birmingham.
[2] *International Herald*, June 1, 1872.
[3] *Ibid.*, May 25, 1872.   [4] *Ibid.*, May 11, 1872.

pensers of the only money of the nation and they obtain their wealth by keeping the supply insufficient to meet the natural demand. We must have national bank notes and not leave our only mediums of exchange to the control of Jews.' [1]

INTRIGUES OF HALES

In the intrigues which preceded the Nottingham Congress of the British Federal Council, the Manchester branch played an important part. After the departure of Dupont from Manchester Edward Jones took over the leadership of the branch and kept up a regular correspondence with Engels.[2]   Hales probably knew that Manchester was under Engels's influence. Both he and the Federal Council were accused by Engels at the General Council meeting of June 18, 1872 of neglecting their administrative duties towards the branch.   Besides his antagonism to Manchester, Hales was also known, together with Eccarius, to be in correspondence with the anarchists in New York. Marx did not at first take this as a sign of treachery, but was inclined to attribute it to Hales's self-importance. He warned Sorge on May 27 not to send any material to Hales, 'because he wants to play an important rôle, regularly commits stupidities. Regarding him and Eccarius there is an investigation in connection with the American history.'

For his part, Hales was already playing a double game. On the eve of Nottingham he wrote Sorge a soothing letter extolling the virtues of unity and saying that he would make 'almost any concessions upon questions of policy rather than see the Association dissolved'.[3]   While advising Sorge at all costs to 'bear and forbear and do nothing to widen the breach' he was inciting the dissident American sections against the General Council.[4] Publicly, he was still presenting himself as a mediator between rival groups and a man who placed the unity of the International above every other consideration. Speaking to the

---

[1] For an anti-semitic attack on Disraeli, see *International Herald*, April 13, 1872. The idea that finance was the common enemy of capital and labour and the identification of finance with the Jews forms a strand which runs, perhaps without interruption, through currency reformers from Cobbett to the Social Credit movement in the twentieth century.

[2] See especially Jones to Engels, June 23, 1872, with the suggestion that the Federal Council might be transferred to Manchester, which would have brought it under Engels's control.

[3] Letter of July 2, 1872. I.I.S.G.

[4] For evidence of Hales's duplicity, see S. Bernstein, *op. cit.*, pp. 125, 137.

British Federal Council on June 20 he referred scathingly to 'those who, with democracy on their lips and jesuitry in their hearts, tried to sow discord in the ranks of the International'. He concluded that the present attempts to disrupt the International with pleas for greater democracy would fail as they had failed in the past.[1]

Ostensibly, Hales was referring to the public campaign of the small Universal Federalist Council against the 'dictatorship' of the General Council. In fact, his position was coming closer than ever to that of the open dissidents. While still unready to attack the powers of the General Council in public, his attacks on that body in private correspondence with Americans were by now well known.[2] When the General Council met on June 25, Engels, with the support of Dupont and Marx, demanded that the General Council should have the right of suspending any Federal Council at will. Eccarius and Hales unsuccessfully opposed. After the vote, Roach, a strong supporter of Hales, again expressed the resentment of the British Federal Council that the Irish branches in England were not subject to its control.

For most of the period in which he had been Secretary to the General Council Hales had been completely loyal to Marx. Except on two subjects, he was prepared, almost without question, to follow Marx's advice. The two exceptions, significantly, were Ireland and Britain. As early as March 14, 1871 Hales had declared on the General Council that he did 'not believe in the separation of Ireland from England' for which he was sternly rebuked by Marx. Almost from the moment he had joined the General Council in 1866, and long before 'autonomy' had become an issue in the International, Hales had persistently demanded the establishment of a separate Federal Council for Britain. From the moment he got his way, friction developed rapidly. Hales had neither the wish nor, probably, the confidence to operate as Secretary to the General Council without leaning heavily on Marx. For a short time Hales had been Secretary to both the General and the British Federal Councils. When, as a direct result of the intrigues of Maltman Barry, he had been forced to give up his

[1] *Eastern Post*, June 22, 1872.

[2] G.C. *Minutes*, June 25, 1872. The *Minutes* are not very explicit on this point. They were, of course, written by Hales, who was still General Secretary. He was accused of falsifying them at the General Council meeting of June 18 and offered his resignation.

post on the Federal Council, he continued in effect as leader of the British section. Roach, who replaced him as Secretary to the Federal Council, remained Hales's obedient follower. From that point onwards Hales used his remaining post on the General Council to further the autonomy of the British section. This inevitably brought him into alliance with the anarchists, with whom he had ideologically nothing in common, but with whom he was prepared to fight jointly for the rights of the national sections against the General Council.

On July 23 Marx secured the suspension of Hales as Secretary to the General Council pending an enquiry into his conduct. He had evidence, he said, 'that the secretary works against the Council while he is paid by the Council'. During Hales's suspension the General Council elected a provisional Secretary at each meeting. Since relations with the British Federal Council were clearly becoming crucial, the General Council established the new post of Corresponding Secretary for England. Significantly, an Irishman, Milner, who was Secretary of the National Reform League, was elected to the post, against Eccarius, who was described by Jung accurately enough, as being 'placed in the same position as Hales'.[1]

THE NOTTINGHAM CONGRESS

The Nottingham Congress opened on July 20 with all branches represented except for Newcastle, Blackpool and Ryde which three may never have had more than a paper existence. Besides regional branches, there were representatives from the German Arbeiterbildungsverein (Friedrich Lessner), the Nottingham French, the Nottingham Labour Protection League and the Operative Bricklayers of Manchester, who had apparently affiliated to the local branch. W. E. Harcourt was present as a fraternal delegate from the Democratic Association of Victoria, Australia which had affiliated to the International on June 18. Five delegates — John Roach, John Hales, H. Mayo, G. B. Clark and G. Bennett — represented the British Federal Council.[2] Engels's friend, Jones from Manchester, was elected Congress Secretary, Thomas Smith of Nottingham, Chairman, and Alex Clark of Liverpool, Vice-Chairman.

[1] G.C. *Minutes*, July 23, 1872.
[2] The Congress *Minutes*, as an unsigned manuscript, are in the I.I.S.G. See also, *Eastern Post*, June 22, 1872.

After a report on the Federal Council from Roach, who spoke of a small financial surplus and nineteen branches, including one being formed in Aberdeen, there followed some acrimonious discussion on the powers of the new Federal Council in relation to its affiliated branches. Then Hales issued his first open challenge to Marx and the General Council with a motion to permit the British Federal Council to communicate freely with federal councils abroad. The procedure, he argued, was particularly necessary during strikes. Dr. G. B. Clark [1] supported him, 'quoting the case of the agricultural strike in Warwickshire where an attempt was made to bring labour from Ireland. The correspondence in this case had been conducted through the General Council, and it might happen that the General Council might be in America. To conduct a correspondence relating to a matter on the other side of the Channel via America was absurd.' The reference to the General Council's removal to America was strange, since this was precisely what occurred at the Hague Congress less than two months after Nottingham. But Marx's plan, even if it had been formulated as early as this, was a well-kept secret and took the majority of delegates at the Hague by complete surprise. It is inconceivable that Dr. Clark was privy to Marx's scheme and the episode must be regarded as a remarkable coincidence.

Clark was opposed by Dupont who, after his move to London, had played an active part on the General Council. Dupont was supported by the Conference Chairman, Thomas Smith, who despite his strongly federalist views on politics, was a centralist on matters of organisation and insisted that 'the other plan would be tantamount to doing away with the General Council altogether'. The resolution was, however, carried. Dupont was furious. 'I have no need', he wrote to Engels from the Congress,[2] 'to draw your attention to this resolution which coming from Hales is neither more nor less than treason.'

The next debate on political action was more subtle. Edward Jones moved that the time had arrived 'for the formation of a third political party in this country, based upon the claims of the labourer. . . . The rule that they must keep in view was that laid down by the International Association, that

---

[1] Later prominent in the crofters' agitation during the 1880s. Radical M.P. for Caithness and a friend of Keir Hardie.

[2] Letter of July 21, 1872. I.I.S.G.

the freedom of the working classes must be worked out by the working classes themselves.'   After the motion had been seconded by Heys, another Manchester delegate, Hales moved a remarkably far-sighted amendment. He proposed that 'while we recognise the fact that the social emancipation of the working classes is the greatest end to which our efforts should be directed, we also recognise the fact that it is necessary to take political action to work out that social emancipation, and we hereby pledge ourselves to establish a distinct Labour Party, based upon the principles of the International'.

Taken literally, Hales's amendment was compatible with the motion, but the emphasis was very different and the words 'while' and 'we also' suggested the difference.   Jones had asked for the International to set up a third party 'based upon the claims of the labourer' and in the spirit of the Inaugural Address, though organisationally distinct from the Association. The International, however, would continue to work for its long-term social revolutionary aims.   Hales wanted a labour party 'based upon the principles of the International' and working for political reforms, with the long-term social aims, while not formally abandoned, very much in the background.

After an interesting speech by Alex Clark of Liverpool in which he proposed a limitation of the profits of non-working capitalists to five percent of their investments, while working for the gradual extinction of capitalists through progressive taxation — close in substance and in spirit to some of the later proposals of the Fabians — Jones withdrew his motion in favour of the amendment.   Whether he did this for tactical reasons or because he did not realise the implications of the amendment, Dupont had no illusions.   Hales's amendment, he told Engels, which had been modified by its author before being put to the vote, demanded 'that a workers' party be formed and that it should be recognised that only *through political action*, etc. (that is the spirit, if not the letter of his proposal)'.   Dupont complained that only the inexperience of most of the delegates had permitted the amendment to be carried.   Had it been possible to operate Hales's proposal, the International would have sponsored a political party which with its trade union affiliations would have been politically and structurally an anticipation of the Labour Representation Committee as it appeared in 1900.

There emerged from the Congress resolutions a political

platform consisting of ten points accurately reflecting the preoccupations of contemporary British radicalism. The demands
were for: (i) Political equality, based on adult suffrage and
proportional representation; (ii) Eligibility of all citizens for
all offices; (iii) Nationalisation of the land; (iv) Abolition of
all hereditary titles and privileges; (v) Abolition of unpaid
Justices of the Peace; (vi) Religious equality — disestablishment and disendowment of the Church of England; (vii)
Education to be free, compulsory and secular; (viii) Abolition
of all private banks of issue — establishment of a National Bank
of issue; (ix) An executive committee, to implement this programme, to be set up in Manchester; (x) This committee to be
elected by the Manchester Federation.[1]

The decision to entrust the Manchester Federation with the
task of organising the political campaign was, like so many of
the Nottingham decisions, the result of a compromise. An
earlier resolution to transfer the Federal Council to Manchester
had been defeated, though it was agreed to hold the next Congress in that City.[2]

A report of the Congress appeared in *The Times* of July 22.
The *Saturday Review* of July 27 which doubted whether the
'meeting of a score or so of obscure agitators at Nottingham
. . . deserved the compliment of a report in *The Times*' correctly appraised the resolution empowering Federal Councils to
communicate directly with each other as an expression of revolt
against the General Council.

After Nottingham the fight between Hales and the General
Council was unrestrained. Hales attended the meeting of July
30 to hear his conduct described as 'treason against the General
Council'. After attacking both Marx and Engels Hales refused
to hand over the books and papers of the Association 'until he
had a satisfactory reason given him'. On August 6 Engels presented his report on Bakunin's Alliance which after a good deal
of argument was endorsed against strong opposition from
Hales by only twelve votes to eight. Finally, and with a very
bad grace, Hales returned the documents of the Association.[3]

---

[1] I.I.S.G. For the branches composing the Manchester Federation,
see Chapter XV.

[2] *Eastern Post*, July 27, 1872. Hales had been warned in advance that
the resolution was coming up — Dupont to Engels, *ibid.*, and no doubt
prepared just such a compromise to forestall it.

[3] G.C. *Minutes*, July 30, August 6 and August 27, 1872. For a more
detailed indictment against Hales and his collaboration with G. B. Clark to

With a state of incipient revolt inside the British section, Marx was also worried about the outcome of the approaching Congress at the Hague. Both he and Engels arranged, where they could, that national delegations favourable to their side should be as heavily represented as possible. On July 29 Marx wrote to Kugelmann : 'It will be a matter of life and death for the International ; and, before I retire, I want at least to protect it from disintegrating elements'. The German section should send 'as many representatives as possible' and credentials could no doubt be procured for Kugelmann himself if he cared to attend. Engels was also alarmed at the strength the anarchists could muster. He told J. P. Becker on August 5 that the delegations from the Jura, Italy and Spain would be dangerously strong and he was afraid that some of the Belgians would support them.

THE HAGUE. OPENING STAGES

The fifth Congress of the International opened, inappropriately at the Concordia Hall, the Hague, on September 2. Barry's reports from Congress began to appear in the *Standard* on September 6. About a year later they appeared as a booklet together with the text of the resolutions and the division lists, omitted from the original articles.[1]

The English delegation was evenly divided ; Barry and Dr. Sexton — an unrepresentative pair — voted consistently with Marx, while Roach and Mottershead of the British Federal Council were in the other camp. Hales who attended the Congress at the beginning soon left, and the *Manchester Guardian* of September 7 made it clear that 'Citizen Hales, of London, came to the Congress at his own expense simply to see the leaders of the anti-Marx party, and to exchange addresses, so as to be able to co-operate with them in the schism which

discredit the General Council, see the testimony of Frederick Lessner in his letter of August 14, 1872 — I.I.S.G.

[1] *Report of the Fifth Annual General Congress of the International Working Men's Association held at the Hague, Holland, Sept. 2-9, 1872.* By *Maltman Barry Ex-Member of General Council & Member of British Federal Council*, London, 1873. In his preface to the booklet, Barry contrasted the treatment given to the Congress by the Tory *Standard* with the 'caricature presented by the "Liberal" Press, the servile flunkeys of the base *bourgeoisie*'. Barry's articles are reprinted, without the preface, in *The First International Minutes of the Hague Congress of 1872 with Related Documents*, ed. Hans Gerth, Madison, 1958.

was to follow the triumph of Marx'. McDonnell, representing
the Irish section, was on Marx's side. Of the two Germans on
the General Council delegation, Lessner remained faithful to
Marx while Eccarius was no longer on speaking terms. The
Frenchmen on the General Council — Johannard, Dupont,
Lafargue and Serraillier — were in Marx's camp, as was the
Communard, Leo Franckel, who voted with him on every issue
except the move to New York. The Bakuninist, Guillaume
from Switzerland, abstained on every issue on principle, while
the seven Belgians, led by Brismée, justified Engels's fears and
for the most part supported Bakunin.[1]

There was, inevitably, a good deal of wrangling over
credentials. Mottershead wanted to know how Maltman Barry
came to represent the Chicago Germans, but Marx was able to
satisfy the Congress that the mandate was valid. In reply to
Mottershead's scarcely disputable statement that Barry was
'not a recognised leader of English working men', Marx said
he thought 'that was an honour, for almost every recognised
leader of English working men was sold to Gladstone, Morley,
Dilke and others'. If this remark seemed harsh to members of
the British labour movement who were to show their resentment after the Congress, it seemed to the *Saturday Review* of
September 14 that 'Perhaps, after all, it is true that Odger and
Bradlaugh are sold to Gladstone and Morley'.[2]

Marx was equally adamant in urging the rejection of
William West's mandate, as representative of the middle-class
anarchists of New York's section 12. That section, said Marx,
was 'well known in America as an organisation got up primarily
to forward the chances of Mrs. Victoria Woodhull for the
Presidency of the United States of America'. With its concentration on free love and spiritualism, Marx did not think it
qualified to be a section of the International quite apart from
the fact that it had not paid its subscriptions. West, who
impressed Barry as having the manner of 'a veritable Stiggins

[1] 'Personally (and along with most of the Belgians) we are not at all
with the Jura but fully with the General Council', wrote de Paepe to an
unknown correspondent in London on August 22, 1872. But something
seems to have happened at the Hague to make the Belgians change their
minds. Letter in I.I.S.G

[2] For evidence of the financial links between the Liberal Party and
Howell, Cremer, Potter, Odger, Hales, Mottershead and others in the
General Election campaign of 1868, see Royden Harrison. 'The British
Working Class and the General Election of 1868' in the *International
Review of Social History*, Part 3, 1960, Part 1, 1961.

in the pulpit of an indubitable Bethel', did not improve his case by arguing that 'the best leaders are not the working men themselves, but those who mixing more in intellectual society, see with a clearer eye'. His mandate was duly rejected.

The skirmishing over credentials went on for three days, and behind closed doors. All that *The Times* correspondent could hear, listening from outside, was 'the tinkling of the President's bell, rising now and again above a storm of angry voices'.[1]

When this was settled and Congress moved into public session, the proceedings were opened by the General Council's report which was read in four languages and excited no controversy. Since the last Congress, it began, two great wars had changed the face of Europe, the Franco-Prussian War and the Commune. Now a third war was in progress, the war against the International which the Emperors of Germany and Austria together with the Pope were concerned to denounce and repress. The International had been made illegal in France, Spain and Italy, while in Germany its representatives, Bebel and Liebknecht, had been sentenced to two years in a fortress for attempted high treason.

Although in Britain the Gladstone Government had been 'unable to act', it had more than made up for this by the grossest display of 'police terrorism' in Ireland. More pervasive than repression had been 'the war of calumny undertaken by the lying power of the civilised world. Apocryphal histories and mysteries of the International, shameless forgeries of public documents and private letters, sensational telegrams. . . .'[2] The Chicago fire had been blamed on the International — why not the West Indian hurricane:

Since Basle, the Association 'has been extended to the Irish in England and to Ireland itself, to Scotland, Holland, Denmark and Portugal; it has been firmly organised in the United States, and has established ramifications in Buenos Aires, Australia and New Zealand'. The experience of the Commune had shown the difference between 'a working class without an International and a working class with an

[1] September 7, 1872.
[2] The forgeries continued almost right up to the time of Congress. On August 15 *The Times* published a circular convening the Congress which purported to be signed by Karl Marx as General Secretary. In the following issue a letter from Marx exposed the fabrication.

S

International'. 'Years were required for the working class itself
to recognise the insurrection of June 1848, as the work of its
own vanguard. The Paris Commune was at once acclaimed by
the universal Proletariat.'[1]

POWERS OF THE GENERAL COUNCIL

The first major debate was on a resolution giving the
General Council the responsibility for carrying out Congress
resolutions and for ensuring in each section the strict observ-
ance of the 'principles, statutes and general rules'. Brismée
for the majority of the Belgian delegation opposed. Some of his
delegation, he pointed out, wanted to abolish the General
Council, others to limit its powers and none of them wished
to see its powers actually increased. Longuet and Serraillier
spoke in support of the motion. Guillaume, who opposed, said
bluntly that 'they all understood each other; discussion was
useless. The majority were there with matured plans and it
was idle to oppose them.' He was as good as his word and
abstained on every issue. The resolution was carried by forty
to four with eleven abstentions.[2] On this issue, and by way
of exception, Hales's friend Roach voted with the General
Council.

Marx took up Brismée's point, in moving the next resolution which gave the General Council greater powers to suspend
sections, federal councils and federations, subject to confirma-
tion by Congress. Those critics, said Marx, who favoured
abolishing the General Council were more logical than those
who wanted to reduce it to being 'merely a centre of communication'. What was the point of turning the General
Council into a 'letter-box'? It would be more simple and
natural 'for the sections and federations to correspond with
each other direct; why pass the letters through the mechanical
letter-box?' The sections had their journals, so there need
not even be any letters and power would pass from the 'responsible General Council' into 'the hands of the irresponsible
journalists'. Equally absurd was the demand that the Council's
suspensory powers should be limited to 'foreseen and specified
cases', since it was 'just for the unforeseen that we most

---

[1] Barry, *op. cit.*, pp. 17-21.
[2] *Résolutions du Congrès Général*, a leaflet published by the Comité
Fédéral Romand, now in I.I.S.G.

require provision'. Those who were inclined to 'chafe under the authority of the general council' should remember that its power was 'not one of arms, of soldiers, nor the law. It is a moral power' which only existed to the extent that the Council retained the confidence of the members.

Guillaume's opposing speech is of some interest, since it showed with complete clarity the link between the organisational views of the anarchists and their crudely mechanical version of the materialist philosophy.[1] The idea of an international of labour was not 'the conception of a brain' but 'was the outgrowth of the economical conditions that surrounded us. Without these conditions no Council in the world whatever its attributes could produce the idea and fructify it.' Since the conditions did exist, 'the tie of union and combination existed, and it required no central head to organise it and guard it against heresy'.[2]

The voting on this resolution fully brought out the split among the English delegates. Thirty-two votes were cast in favour with six against and sixteen abstentions.[3] Guillaume's abstentionists were joined by the two representatives of the British Federal Council, Mottershead and Roach. Barry, Sexton and McDonnell voted with the majority.

THE CLIMAX

The Congress was approaching its climax. 'After the adoption of the two articles in their revised form', wrote Barry, 'there was a slight pause. It was the lull before the storm. Knowing what was coming, and whom it would most affect, I stood up and watched the operation. Up got Engels, Marx's right hand, and said he would make a communication to the Congress. It was a recommendation from a number of members of the general council respecting the seat of the council for the next year.' London had been an appropriate centre in the past because of its safety and its cosmopolitan

---

[1] This speech, like Sorge's which followed, was not reported by Maltman Barry, but appeared in *The Times*, September 10, 1872. It was also included in the *Minutes* which Sorge took and which are published in *The First International. Minutes of the Hague Congress of 1872 with related documents*, p. 207. Sorge's account is in substantial agreement with Barry's, which is reprinted, *ibid.*, pp. 259-94.

[2] *The Times*, September 10, 1872.

[3] These figures are from Maltman Barry's account. There are slightly different figures in *Résolutions du Congrès Général* and in Sorge's *Minutes*.

The Last Phase

population which had 'resulted in a truly international com-
position of the general council'. Now, however, this very fact
was frustrating the work of the Council, since 'almost all
shades of socialist opinion' were represented on it and its
'debates had, at times, been quite as excited as those of the
present Congress'. The numbers and disunity had both
increased with the arrival of the French refugees after the fall
of the Commune. It was proposed, therefore, to limit the
numbers on the Council in future to fifteen and, since Europe
was out of the question as a seat for the Council, it should be
moved, for a year at least, to New York.

'Consternation and discomfiture', wrote Barry, 'stood
plainly written on the faces of the party of dissension as he
uttered the last words.' New York, said Engels, had like
London the advantages of safety and cosmopolitanism. The
Council there would be in the hands of men who, though new
to the movement, had already 'demonstrated their capacity and
zeal'. The recommendation was signed by nine members of
the Council — Marx, Engels, McDonnell, Sexton, Barry,
Longuet, Le Moussu, Serraillier and Lessner.

'It was some time', remarked Barry, 'before any one rose
to speak. It was a *coup d'état*, and each one looked to his
neighbour to break the spell'. Vaillant, the 'extreme Blanquist',
was first on his feet to oppose the move. The Blanquists,
apostles of centralised, disciplined, conspiratorial revolutionary
leadership, supported Marx in all his other fights with the
anarchists, but on this issue Vaillant was sure that the place for
the leadership of a workers' international was 'close to the field
of battle — France and Germany'.

When the decisive vote was taken there was a narrow
majority of twenty-six to twenty-three in favour with nine
abstentions. The minority included some of Marx's strongest
supporters who felt like Frankel that 'his personal supervision
and direction is absolutely essential'. For the same reason the
majority included some of Marx's opponents, such as Brismée,
David and Roach.

However carefully Engels's arguments are weighted, they
add up to a remarkably weak case for so drastic a move and it is
doubtful whether without a good deal of mandate-fixing before
the Congress it could have been carried at all. Engels could
clearly not say outright that with developments in Switzerland,
Belgium, Spain, Italy and France, the Bakuninists and their

allies might well secure a majority at the next Congress and so put their — to Marx and Engels — fatal stamp on the international labour movement at a formative stage in its development. And neither Marx nor Engels was prepared any longer to expend the enormous amount of energy that would have been needed to keep control under those conditions. Both were preparing, as after 1848, to retire from active politics at least for a time. But the decisive consideration was probably the fact that, with the divisions among the French and the impending split in the English section, the General Council itself could no longer be counted on to support Marx as it had done on every major issue since 1864.

That this last consideration was decisive is confirmed by Barry who, after referring to the effect on Marx's health of his prodigious work on the General Council, in addition to his editing of the several translations of *Capital*, went on to explain how 'during the last year or so, since the accession to the Council of a number of "representative" Englishmen, it had taxed all his efforts (and these have sometimes failed) to keep the council to its legitimate work. If he retired from the Council, and it still remained in London, it would be in great danger of falling into the hands of men who would make it either a pothouse forum or an electioneering machine' — the last in obvious reference to Hales's plan for converting the British section into a reformist labour party.

At a meeting in Amsterdam following the end of the Congress Marx made his last speech as a member of the International. His main stress, in sharp and pointed contrast to the anarchists, was on the need for the workers to conquer political power as the only way in which they could 'establish the new organization of labour'. If they failed to overthrow the old political system they would suffer the fate of the early Christians 'who neglected to overthrow the old system, and who for that reason, never had a kingdom in this world'. But the means for doing this would not be the same in every country. 'We know', Marx stressed, 'that special regard must be paid to the institutions, customs, and traditions of various lands.' In England, the U.S.A. and perhaps Holland the workers could 'hope to secure their ends by peaceful means'. But in most continental countries 'force will have to be the lever of the revolution'. Marx ended with an excessively optimistic estimate of the prospects of the International in the United

States — now 'pre-eminently becoming the land of the workers'. Half a million of them were going there yearly, and 'the International must perforce strike deep roots in this soil upon which the workers are supreme'.[1]

In England it was widely recognised that the decision to move the General Council to New York meant the end of the International as an effective organisation. The *Daily News* on September 10 thought that whatever Baillie-Cochrane might say about the 'formidable character of this Society', he would not be believed after the Hague. *The Times* on the same day recognised the end of the International in its existing shape though it counted on 'its stubborn vitality, on its manifold resources, on its versatile instincts for indefinite reproduction' to ensure its reappearance in one form or another.

The *Eastern Post* on September 7 drew attention to the apparent incongruity between the meeting of the three Emperors — of Germany, Austria and Russia — discussing how to fight the menace of the International and 'the deliberations of a score of mechanics in a Dutch town'. However, it was not really so incongruous. Perhaps the Emperors knew that 'but for the workmen they could not exist for a week'. Possibly they also realised that 'principles might do for the proletariat what heat does for the harmless water and give it an expansive power which would shiver in a moment the most perfect embodiment of material force'.

With another kind of prescience, the *Spectator* on September 14 predicted that 'the star of the Commune has already passed its not very elevated meridian altitude, and, — unless it be in Russia, we shall hardly ever see it so high again as it was in the year of the great war between the two great military governments'.

[1] Rudolf Meyer, *op. cit.*

CHAPTER XV

After the Hague

THE fight against Marx united men of widely differing beliefs. His first opponents had been the French republicans whose London branch had been disaffiliated in 1868. Then, the Proudhonists had challenged State Socialism, but were defeated at Brussels in 1868 and decisively at Basle in the following year. By 1869, however, Bakunin had taken over the banner of anti-statism and his teachings, more collectivist and more aggressively revolutionary than those of Proudhon, had made rapid headway in the year and a half between Basle and the Paris Commune. With the fall of the Commune a number of French refugees arrived in London. Some, like Vaillant, were Blanquists. Agreeing with Marx in political action and in the State as an indispensable instrument for establishing Socialism, the Blanquists differed from him in their conception of revolution as the work of a conspiratorial *élite*. Up to the Hague, Marx could count on their support against the anarchists though they broke with the International after the decision to transfer the General Council to New York. Others among the refugees, like Landeck, were republicans of the Lefort school, long-standing antagonists of Marx, and they soon joined with Vésinier and his German ally, Weber, in bitter attacks on the General Council.

The London Conference of September 1871 had dissolved Bakunin's 'Alliance' and as was perhaps inevitable, the anarchists and the dissident French made common cause against the 'centralizing and despotic power' of the General Council. The French republicans set up the Section Française Fédéraliste and henceforth their slogan was 'Federal Autonomy' which they could claim had been the principle for which the Communards had fought and died. Adolphe Smith [1] returning from Paris after the Commune and Richard Butler who had represented the London Trades Council at the International's

---

[1] He later served as translator at Congresses of the Second International.

foundation meeting, agreed with the French critics of the General Council. Their Universal Republican League joined with the followers of Vésinier and Landeck to form the Universal Federalist Council. This remained a tiny and ephemeral body and would have had no significance but for the fact that in the course of 1872 John Hales, with his own axe to grind against the 'centralizing and despotic power' of the General Council, adopted identical arguments and slogans.[1]

It is not certain that Hales had any direct contact with the U.F.C., though he complained bitterly when, on Marx's insistence, two of its members were expelled from the British Federal Council.[2] It is quite clear, however, that during a brief visit to the Hague at the beginning of September 1872 he reached an understanding with the anarchists of the Jura Federation. On returning to England he began at once to work for a split.

THE BRANCHES

To all appearances the English branches of the International continued with their normal activity when the delegates returned from the Hague. Manchester, which was now a Federation with a foreign section and a branch in Hulme besides the original Central branch, held a public meeting addressed by Odger on 'Capital and Labour'. The meeting was a great success and Odger paid glowing tribute to the services which the International had performed for trade unionism in Britain and Europe while condemning its support for the Commune as 'a great mistake'.[3]

Hales was quick to attack Marx's influence where it was strongest. He wrote to the Manchester Federation denouncing the Hague decisions. 'I do not say that Marx is absolutely dishonest', he explained, 'but I do say that his life of exile and proscription has led him into tortuous paths of intrigue that would damn the association.' Jones of course reported the letter to Engels; the Manchester District Council and some of

[1] For the Conference of the Universal Federalist Council immediately after the Hague and the speeches of Landeck and Vésinier, see *Daily News*, September 19, and *The Times*, September 20, 1872.

[2] See unpublished letter to Hins's Brussels paper, *La Liberté*, of which there are two drafts in I.I.S.G.

[3] Jones to Engels, September 25, 1872, I.I.S.G. *International Herald*, October 5, 1872.

the London branches protested strongly against Hales's behaviour.[1]

Nottingham, like Manchester, was a Federation having besides its Central branch the Labour Protection League and a French branch eighty strong based on the local silk workers.[2] Thomas Smith, Secretary of the Central branch, had written at the time of the Commune a series of letters to the *Nottingham Daily Express*. The letters, with dates ranging from March 25 to July 13, 1871, were collected and published as a pamphlet.[3] In what was probably the only attempt made by an English member of the International to expound a philosophy of history, Smith wrote that 'all phenomena are the results of laws eternal in their operation. . . '. Each period of history — ancient, mediaeval and modern — had its own distinctive tendencies and laws of development. The modern period — 'the era of the revolution' — had started with the Reformation. Its inherent principles included universal suffrage and political decentralisation. The Commune was an expression of this tendency and social upheavals, accompanied by bloodshed, would continue until those principles were recognised and applied.[4]

The pamphlet was sent to a number of prominent people and elicited a friendly reply from John Stuart Mill, who expressed his warm approval of the general approach, dissenting only from the use of 'revolution' as an abstract concept in the French fashion instead of dealing with specific historical revolutions in the scientific way developed by English empiricism.[5]

Other branches of the International were developing regular public activity. The Birkenhead branch was selling the *International Herald* in the docks,[6] while Liverpool was publicising the appeal of the local dockers against the attempt to impose non-unionism by importing Belgians.[7] It was some

[1] Jones to Engels, October 3 ; also Jones to Jung, who was beginning to side with Hales, October 8, 20, 1872. I.I.S.G. Also Engels to Sorge, October 5, 1872.

[2] Charles Hazard was Secretary. Dupont to Engels, July 21, 1872.

[3] *Letters on the Commune. The Law of Revolution ; or the Logical Development of Human Society*, March 1872, price 2d., published by the Nottingham Branch of the International Working Men's Association.

[4] Cf. the programme of the Nottingham branch, summarised in Chapter XIV.

[5] *International Herald*, October 26, 1872. See editorials, praising Mill's reply, in *Daily News* and *Daily Telegraph*, October 28, 1872. See also *Letters of J. S. Mill*, ed. H. Elliott, 1910, vol. II, pp. 346-8.

[6] Letter from W. Dodd to Vickery, September 29, 1872, I.I.S.G.

[7] *International Herald*, October 26, 1872.

weeks before the effects of the split began to be felt in the branches. When they were, the result was devastating.

HALES SECEDES

On November 6, 1872 Hales wrote a long statement to the Jura Federation declaring that despite differences regarding the need for political action and although the British Federal Council was 'in favour of a *waiting* policy', he was at one with the anarchists on 'the principle of Federalism'. His letter was published in the Federation's *Bulletin*, together with a cordial reply from Adhemar Schwitzguebel saying that political differences need be no bar to co-operation.[1]

Next day Hales, who had replaced Roach as Corresponding Secretary to the Federal Council, was elected to the post of General Secretary, responsible in addition for correspondence and finance.[2] Engels wrote to Sorge on November 16 in some alarm. Hales and Mottershead, he believed, had captured the Federal Council with the votes of 'delegates from non-existent sections'. Engels asked Sorge for authority to act in England on behalf of the General Council. The *International Herald* would be important in the struggle despite its limitations and the shortcomings of its editor, W. H. Riley, 'an honest man . . . but he is weak and depends to a certain extent on the Federal Council in connection with his paper'.[3]

Riley's political views, like those of almost all his socialist contemporaries, were O'Brienite with the characteristic blend of physical-force Chartism, producers' co-operation and land and currency reform. The enemy of the worker was the monopolist of land and money, not the employer. In his pamphlet, *Strikes, Their Cause and Remedy*, he wrote: 'The

---

[1] Guillaume, *L'Internationale, documents et souvenirs, 1864-1878*. Paris, vol. III, pp. 24-7.

[2] *International Herald*, November 16, 1872.

[3] A more favourable account of Riley was given by Edward Carpenter in *Sketches from Life in Town and Country*, 1908, where he is portrayed as a dynamic character, 'restless, inquisitive, sensitive; of rather searching mind, stimulating and paradoxical in his talk and writing . . .'. There is not much sign of any of these qualities in Riley's writing, but Carpenter may well have sentimentalised the memory of one of the small band 'whose names are now unknown or forgotten' but who 'did a great work in their time, bridging over the interval between the old Chartism of '48 and the Socialism of the early eighties. . . .' *Ibid.*, pp. 205-7; p. 109. For an account of Riley's later activities, with a less favourable picture, see Professor W. H. G. Armytage, *Notes and Queries*, May 1956.

active employer who organises and superintends labour, and buys, and sells, is really a working man, and, as such, his interests are identical with those of his employees.[1] By contrast, 'No man has any more right to make a profit upon the mere use of money than he has by letting land'.[2]

Immediately after the Hague, Riley was hostile to the General Council. When he came to appreciate the dangers of a split and the effect which this would have on the sales of his paper, he worked for a compromise between the two sections.[3] By December when it was clear that Hales would force a split at any cost, the *Herald* swung round to support the 'official' section, the section which accepted the decisions of the Hague.

On November 21 the British Federal Council received a communication from the General Council in New York. S. Vickery, a stalwart supporter of the official group, proposed a friendly reply. He was seconded by Adam Weiler, a German cabinet-maker, member of the Arbeiterbildungsverein and later active on the British T.U.C. Jung still favoured compromise, but Hales poured scorn on the Hague resolutions which committed sections to 'Political action . . . under the control and direction, not of the country itself, but of a General Council sitting three thousand miles away'. Vickery, who was blunt to the point of crudeness, based his case on the need for international unity. 'Federalism meant having a number of petty dictators, while Centralisation meant having one dictator ; he was in favour of the one.' Jung's amendment, proposing a non-committal reply, was carried with Riley's support.

At its last meeting in November the Federal Council was joined not accidentally by three partisans of the General Council ; Charles Murray, representing Normanby, George Milner, from the National Reform League, and Eugène Dupont, with a mandate from Manchester. Weiler gave notice that at the next meeting he would propose Hales's removal from the post of General Secretary. A week later the British Federal Council split into two bodies each claiming the title and the leadership of the International in England.[4]

Within a fortnight each side had prepared a statement of its

[1] P. 6. The pamphlet is undated, but published in Leeds, *c.* 1873.
[2] *Ibid.*, p. 5. See also Riley's pamphlet, *c.* 1873, *British Slavery. A tract dedicated to all Working Men.* Leeds.
[3] Riley to Jung, October 14, 1872. I.I.S.G.
[4] *International Herald*, November 30, 1872 and Hales's account at the London Congress of his party in *Eastern Post*, February 1, 1873.

case for the branches.[1] Hales's circular appearing on December
17 claimed to speak for the majority of the old Federal Council
which took its stand on the decisions of the Nottingham
Congress and repudiated the Hague. Hales's dilemma was
that he believed in reformist politics while most of his allies
abroad called for revolutionary abstention from politics. His
statement, therefore, referred to the 'many phases' through
which the working-class struggle must pass in different
countries and welcomed as allies all opponents of the Hague
decisions. Hales's circular ended by repudiating the New
York General Council and calling for a Congress of the British
Federal Council on the first Sunday in January. There was
an impressive number of signatures to the statement, including
Hales, Mottershead, Jung and G. B. Clark together with the
representatives of sixteen branches.[2]

In reply, two statements — both written by Engels [3]— were
issued. The first on December 21 was signed by the leading
members of the Manchester foreign section. The second on
December 23 was issued by the official British Federal Council
and signed by Lessner, Riley, Murray, Milner, Weiler, Vickery,
Dupont and Mitchell. The two circulars, though differing in
detail, covered much the same ground. Both insisted on the
representative character of the Hague and the soundness of its
decisions.

The Manchester document made a good debating point by
drawing attention to the peculiarity of a majority secession.
'Hitherto', it claimed, 'minorities have seceded often enough.
This is the first instance of a *majority* seceding.' The reason
for this anomaly, wrote Engels, was that an understanding had
been reached between the minority at the Hague and its supporters in the national sections 'to call all sorts of congresses
in all countries about Christmas and get them to confirm their
secessionist action'. Belgium and Spain, for instance, were to
have Congresses on December 25 and the 'English sections
are now to be bamboozled into assisting the plot without
knowing what is going on'. This was true and it accounted
for the precipitancy of Hales's action which ruined whatever

[1] *International Herald*, December 7, 1872, and Engels to Sorge, same
date. See also Hales's second circular, December 1872, reproduced in
Guillaume, *op. cit.*, p. 28.
[2] Hales's circular was reproduced in full in the *Minutes* of the official
British Federal Council, December 19, 1872.
[3] Engels to Sorge, January 4, 1873.

chance he might have had of establishing an effective English section of an anarchist led International.

On December 21 the *International Herald* carried a letter from Marx and Engels containing a detailed indictment of Hales's intrigues. In a letter appearing a fortnight later, Hales did not attempt a detailed reply, but blamed Engels's influence for his own breach with Marx. Referring to the letter of December 21, Hales did 'not for one moment believe that Citizen Marx had anything to do with such a miserable production except to father it, the same as he has done other effusions from the same pen'.[1] Hales was convinced that he was really being attacked because of his successful resolution at Nottingham which tried to uphold the rights of national sections against the overweening powers of the General Council. In a passage which is striking in the light of later developments in international Socialism, Hales accused Engels of trying 'to turn the Association into a secret one, with an infallible pontiff at the head of it, who shall thunder excommunication against all who shall dare to enquire or doubt. I decline', he concluded, 'to be a party to such a degradation of the Labour struggle.'

Hales's over-hasty withdrawal from the Federal Council, though no doubt determined by his international commitments, proved a fatal mistake. It enabled the minority to appeal successfully to the loyalty of the branches by appearing as the official council confronted by a breakaway. Before the end of January a large proportion of the branches, including the West-End of London, Nottingham, Leeds, Leicester, South Lambeth, Birkenhead and possibly Middlesbrough had repudiated Hales and the secessionist majority of the old Federal Council. The *International Herald* was now firmly in Marx's camp and outside London only the Hulme and Liverpool branches, where the influence of Thomas Mottershead was strong, adhered to Hales.[2]

[1] The view of Engels as Marx's evil genius was also expressed by Jung at the London Congress of the breakaway British Federal Council which met on January 26, 1873 and later by Hyndman and, to some extent, Belfort Bax. See *Eastern Post*, February 8, 1873, Hyndman, *op. cit.*, p. 279 and Bax, *op. cit.*, pp. 52-5. Townshend, an O'Brienite member of the General Council, later told Max Beer that throughout their political differences on the Council, Marx always behaved as a 'gentleman', Engels as a 'domineering German'. Beer, *op. cit.*, p. 134.

[2] Engels to Sorge, January 4; *International Herald*, January 4, 11, 18; letters from W. Dodd to Vickery, January 20 and from De Morgan to Engels, January 8, 1873 — in I.I.S.G.

THE LONDON CONGRESS

The weakness of the secessionists became apparent at their London Congress which took place on Sunday January 26, 1873 in City Road, London. The eleven delegates included three old-established members of the General Council — Eccarius, who was now convinced of the need to collaborate with middle-class Liberals, Weston, long in close contact with the London French, and Jung, who had supported Marx almost to the end but who was finally alienated by tactics of the majority at the Hague.

The first of the main speeches was given by Hales, who reiterated his case against the General and the official Federal Council. He again put the main blame on Engels whom he accused of offering money from an unnamed source to finance the General Council's delegation to the Hague.[1] Jung also held Engels chiefly responsible for the split. He said that since Engels's arrival in London Marx had ceased to consult his former friends before deciding on policy. After the Hague Jung had learned from members of the Manchester foreign section that Engels had been 'writing letters everywhere, giving people advice who to elect as delegates and who not'. Jung did not agree with the Bakuninists, but was sure that they 'should have been opposed with political arguments, not with intrigue. . . . We killed the opposition on the land question with arguments, we should have succeeded in this.'

Eccarius, who made the last formal speech to Congress, believed in political action, but it should not, he was careful to add, be applied in all countries, irrespective of local conditions. In three countries — England, U.S.A. and Switzerland — 'the next step in the labour movement must be to get working men into the legislature, and this, in the first instance, requires combinations and alliances with the advanced men of the middle classes'.[2]

[1] *Eastern Post*, February 1, 1873. Some of the money may have come from Cowell Stepney. There is a letter from him in the I.I.S.G., offering to provide £7 for a delegate. His death on November 7, 1872 deprived the International in England of a loyal and generous friend. See obituary in *International Herald*, November 23, 1872.

[2] *Eastern Post*, February 8, 1872. In 1872 Eccarius had given a lecture to the Labour Representation League, under the chairmanship of Thomas Brassey, a Liberal M.P. The lecture appeared as a pamphlet, *The Hours of Labour*, published by Mottershead as Secretary of the Labour Representation League. It was reviewed in the *International Herald*, on November 16,

The Congress resolutions inevitably denounced the Hague and called for a new international Congress in which the British would participate alongside the anarchists of Europe. An executive of nine was elected, including Weston and Mottershead, with Hales as Secretary.[1] Engels felt justified in describing the Congress as a miserable fiasco supported only by Hales's personal following in the East End.[2]

RAPID DECLINE

The 'official' British Federal Council held its Congress on June 1 of the same year. The story of the International in Britain between the two rival Congresses is one of almost uninterrupted decline. For one thing the branches, deprived of effective leadership, simply did not know what to do and either became, or remained, discussion groups. The Nottingham branch was exceptional in having a clear-cut outlook and programme which it owed to Thomas Smith. More characteristic was Hull which had a programme of demands headed by free education, government control of gin palaces and pawnshops, extension of the franchise, the nationalisation of 'all great commercial undertakings' and the punishment of drunkenness other than by fines.[3] While the General Council remained in London, the International always had an obvious value to British trade unions. But, apart from the Liverpool dockers already referred to, there is no record of British workers approaching the International for help after the Hague, though appeals from foreign workers occasionally reached one or other of the Federal Councils.[4] Hales wanted to turn the Association

1872. The statistics and general argument of the pamphlet followed very closely the treatment by Marx in *Capital*, vol. I. Eccarius had, however, like George Julian Harney and later, Ernest Jones, both also former friends of Marx, become convinced of the need for an alliance with middle-class radicals. Eccarius's chairman, Brassey, one of the 'advanced men of the middle classes', wrote scathingly of the 'vague theory of the International Society, founded on atheism, and in a narrow and contemptible spirit, acknowledging the existence of only one section of society. . . '. *On Work and Wages*, by Thomas Brassey, M.P., 1873, p. 283.

[1] *Eastern Post*, February 8, 1873. The resolutions of the London Congress were also issued as a four-page leaflet, I.I.S.G.

[2] Engels to the General Council in New York, February 8, 1873.

[3] *International Herald*, January 11, 1873.

[4] Cf. the appeal of the Lisbon shipwrights and caulkers to the Federal Council before the split — *International Herald*, October 5, 19; Engels to Lessner, October 16; Hales to Engels, October 28, 1872 — I.I.S.G. Also the Amsterdam cigar makers appealed to Hales's Federal Council for help

into a political party with trade union affiliations, but the unions were not nearly ready for such a commitment. The International might have survived in England as a small political party conducting propaganda for Socialism of the O'Brienite school. But even for this modest aim the Association would have needed a clear and energetic political leadership which the mutually warring Federal Councils were incapable of providing.

One by one the branches withered and died. Aberdeen which, after a period of uncertainty adhered to the 'official' Federal Council, was virtually dead by the middle of 1873. Nottingham, despite its promising start, failed to win the support of the local trade unions for its Labour Protection League, while part of its French branch broke away in April to join up with Hales. The split at the centre was also tearing the other branches apart. In Leicester, the Internationalists were about to begin a joint propaganda campaign with the strong local Republican Club when a visit from Mottershead to the Republicans persuaded them to break off all relations.

Manchester also suffered in the same way, though its foreign section was able to keep going in a modest way until after the Manchester Congress in June, for the organisation of which it was largely responsible. It met fortnightly with an attendance of twelve to fifteen, but suffered from the big turnover in Manchester's foreign population. Like the French section in Nottingham, the Manchester foreign section had been active in collecting aid for the Geneva goldsmiths. The position was even worse in the Manchester Central branch. Edward Jones wrote to Engels complaining of apathy. 'The unfortunate quarrel that you had in London', he explained, 'had a very detrimental effect on our work in Manchester.' In Hulme, J. S. Murchie, who claimed to have proof of Engels's intrigues against Hales, attempted to form a branch of the breakaway Federal Council but apparently met with no success. As in other centres, workers of radical views were more likely to be attracted by Republicanism than by a squabbling and leaderless International and it is not surprising to read Murchie's complaint in the *Eastern Post* that one of the former Manchester

in a lock-out, in which the employers were demanding that they sever connection with the International. The English cigar makers contributed over £145 which their President, Cohn and the Secretary of the union, took over to Holland.

branches 'had been turned into a Republican club'. With variations in detail the story was repeated in Liverpool, Halifax, Stratford in East London and the West-End branch.

A momentary exception to the general tendency towards disintegration and collapse was provided by the Woolwich branch which flickered briefly into activity when the workers at the Siemens plant in Charlton went on strike for the payment of special night rates. H. G. Maddox, Secretary of the branch, wrote to the official Federal Council on February 6, 1873 to outline the men's grievances. He reported that eight to ten Germans had been introduced into the works with more expected. The Woolwich branch was successful in establishing friendly relations with the Germans, who agreed to go home. At a joint party arranged by the branch the Germans had sung the Watch on the Rhine while the English responded with Rule Britannia. But a month later Maddox had to report that while the strike had been completely successful, the branch had almost collapsed as 'in this town of Government hacks anything in advance of what is termed Liberalism has no favour with the men'. On April 3 he told the Federal Council that it had been impossible to find any support among the workers at the Arsenal for fear of Government victimisation.[1]

While the official Federal Council had inherited a network of branches which fell rapidly into decay after the split, the breakaway Council had difficulty in maintaining any kind of branch organisation. It managed to establish for a short time a number of branches in East London — City Road, Hackney, Bethnal Green, Limehouse and the vacillating Stratford branch — while in the provinces they had Liverpool, Greenock, Hulme and, just possibly, Leicester.[2]

THE MANCHESTER CONGRESS

Though Hales could not establish his own movement, his propaganda was effective in reducing the morale of his rivals. 'Our weakness', wrote Vickery to Engels on May 7, 1873, 'lies

---

[1] James T. Brownlie, however, the first President of the A.E.U., once told Professor G. D. H. Cole that the Woolwich branch of the Social Democratic Federation claimed direct descent from the local branch of the International.

[2] For a fuller account of the history of the branches after the split, together with the sources, see Henry Collins, 'The English Branches of the First International' in *Essays in Labour History*, ed. Asa Briggs and John Saville, 1960.

T

in our want of all propagandist matter and our want of rules to distribute to the sections.' The British Federal Council could not even afford the £2 needed to print its Rules. Vickery went on to complain that Hales's knowledge, experience and prestige were of inestimable value to the secessionists. The official General Council had nothing to set against this except the *International Herald* whose editor, Riley, 'we have done our best to alienate'. Finally, Bradlaugh's Republican campaign was attracting much needed support away from the International.[1]

For reasons which are not quite clear, relations between the Federal Council and the *International Herald* grew rapidly worse. It could not call on much journalistic talent and Riley was bitter with Marx and Engels for refusing to help.[2] Engels told Sorge on April 15 that the paper was on its last legs, adding that it was 'not worth much except as an organ of publicity for the B.F.C. but as such, for the moment, it is almost indispensable'. The *Herald*, however, published only the briefest account of the Manchester Congress which took place on June 1 and 2, 1873 and Riley said that even this had only reached the paper through the courtesy of a volunteer.[3]

An official report of the Congress was published as a pamphlet by the B.F.C.[4] Apart from the Rules of the International as originally formulated in 1864 and amended at Basle and the Hague, there was not much of interest in the account. The Federal Council's Report to Congress contained little except the customary abuse of the secessionists and a good deal of revolutionary rhetoric.

In the debate on land nationalisation an amendment moved by De Morgan on behalf of the National Reform League, which called for 'equitable' compensation for the dispossessed, was defeated by eight votes to seven. De Morgan was, however, successful in securing the adoption of the National Reform League's resolution on 'the right of the working class to the use of the national credit for the purposes of co-operative industry'.

The remaining resolutions for the most part repeated the

---

[1] Letter in I.I.S.G. See also B.F.C. *Minutes*, March 27, April 3, 1873.
[2] Vickery to Engels, March 13, 1873, I.I.S.G.
[3] The fullest Press account appeared in the *Manchester Guardian*, June 3, 1873.
[4] *General and British Federative Rules of the International Working Men's Association together with a Report of the Second Annual Congress of the British Federation held at Manchester, June 1st and 2nd, 1873.*

demands of previous Congresses on the eight-hour day, educational reform and public ownership. Two new resolutions called respectively for aid to the farm workers who were attempting under the leadership of Joseph Arch to build a trade union and for the recognition of the Spanish Republic set up in March 1873. The resolution congratulated 'the working class of Spain on the election to the Cortes of members of the International'.

The *Eastern Post* on June 7 deplored the 'very alarming resolutions' of the Congress and particularly its 'extreme views' on expropriation of property. After Manchester, reports of the International in the *Post* ceased almost entirely. Vickery declared himself satisfied with the results of the Congress[1] and Engels expressed similar sentiments in a letter to Sorge on June 14. Yet Engels, at least, knew better and in writing to Bebel on June 20 he said, almost apologetically, that while 'every party leadership wants to see successes', there were times when '*momentary* success' must be sacrificed to longer-term considerations. The 'sectarians' had come flooding into the International after the fall of the Commune, and to have postponed the split would merely have given the 'sectarians, especially the Bakuninists . . . another year in which to perpetrate, in the name of the International, even much greater stupidities and infamies'.

THE END OF THE INTERNATIONAL

Before the end of the year the *International Herald* had ceased to appear.[2] The Federal Council still existed well into 1874, though Marx described the English section as being 'as good as dead. The Federal Council exists as such only in name, although some of its members are active individually.'[3]

Theoretically, a sixth Congress of the International was held in Geneva from September 8, 1873, but although it had been called by the General Council in New York, no member of the Council attended. Most of the delegates were Swiss from Geneva whipped up locally. In a letter to Sorge, who was leading the General Council in New York, Marx wrote on

[1] Letter to Engels, June 16, 1873, I.I.S.G.
[2] The last number appeared on October 18, 1873. No copies of its announced successor, the *Republican Herald*, have been found.
[3] Marx to Sorge, August 4, 1874.

September 27 that the Congress had been a fiasco. 'As I view European conditions', he explained, 'it is quite useful to let the formal organisation of the International recede into the background for the time being but, if possible, not to relinquish control of the central point in New York so that no idiots like Perret or adventurers like Cluseret may seize the leadership and discredit the whole business'. He had every confidence that 'events and the inevitable development and complication of things will of themselves see to it that the International shall rise again improved in form'.

A week before the official Congress, the secessionists had met also in Geneva and also describing themselves as the Sixth Congress of the International. Eccarius and Hales attended as delegates of the dissident B.F.C. Hales admitted to the Congress that his movement was in a parlous state, but attributed this to 'the intrigues and calumnies of the Marxist coterie' which had induced apathy among former Internationalists. He looked to the Geneva Congress to revive interest in England.[1]

The whole Congress agreed without question that there should be no attempt to erect a new General Council exercising powers over affiliated national sections. But, committed as they were to national autonomy as an article of faith, they could not agree on the machinery for securing international co-operation without a General Council. Hales suggested a central commission whose powers would be limited to exchanging information. But he could not agree with his hosts on anarchism as the basis, either for future society or for the labour movement in the present. 'Anarchy means individualism', he explained, 'and individualism is the basis of the existing state of society which we want to overthrow. Anarchy is compatible with collectivism. Take, for instance, a strike. Could one hope for its success with an anarchical organisation?' Hales was also for changing the name of the Association to the International Federation of Labour which should be exclusively working class in membership, since he blamed the admission of intellectuals for the subsequent divisions in the Association.

In 1874 the anarchists held what they described as the

---

[1] *Compte-Rendu Officiel du Sixième Congrès Général de l'Association Internationale des Travailleurs*, Geneva, 1873, 1-6 septembre. *Au siège du Comité Fédéral Jurassien*, 1874.

Seventh Congress of the International. Eccarius was now the only delegate from England.[1] He could neither report progress at home nor reach agreement with his hosts in Brussels. No more was heard of the dissident Federal Council in England.

Meanwhile, the official General Council in New York had languished. Isolated from the fragmentary remains of the movement in Europe, it had nothing of substance in America on which to build.[2] Sorge's resignation in September 1874 brought its effective existence to an end. Its formal abolition at the Philadelphia Convention in 1876 was no more than a belated death certificate. If it is impossible to identify the precise moment of death, it is certain that the fatal blow was struck at the Hague Congress in 1872.

The blow had been delivered, after careful preparation, by Marx and Engels. Engels wrote the obituary in a letter to Sorge following his resignation in September 1874. The International, wrote Engels, belonged to the period of the Second Empire, 'when the oppression throughout Europe prescribed unity and abstention from all internal controversy for the labour movement, then just reawakening. It was the moment when the common, cosmopolitan interests of the proletariat could come to the fore . . . German communism did not yet exist as a workers' party, Proudhonism was too weak to be able to insist on its particular fads, Bakunin's new trash did not yet exist in his own head, and even the leaders of the English trade unions thought they could enter the movement on the basis of the programme laid down in the Preamble to the Statutes.' The Commune, however, and its aftermath, had brought all these latent differences fully into the light. 'The Hague Congress was actually the end — and for both parties. The only country where something could still be accomplished in the name of the International was America, and by a happy instinct the executive was transferred there. Now its prestige is exhausted there too, and any further effort to galvanise it into new life would be folly and a waste of energy. The International dominated ten years of one side of European history — the side on which the future lies — and can look back on its work with pride. But in its old form it has outlived itself.' Only the revival of a common oppression could

[1] *Compte Rendu . . . du VIIe Congrès . . . Bruxelles. Septembre 7-13, 1874*, Verviers, 1875.

[2] S. Bernstein, *The First International in America*, New York, 1962.

CONCLUSIONS

Failure and Success of the International

THE International arose out of the labour revival of the 1860s. It could not have existed earlier. Its predecessors, the Fraternal Democrats and the International Association, were cosmopolitan rather than international. The former, though it had contact with the Democratic Association in Brussels, had no sections outside Britain and in all probability no branches outside London. The latter society was even more limited in size and caused scarcely a ripple in the wider labour movement.

Yet the English workers were far from being indifferent to foreign affairs. What they lacked were stable organisations on which to build. The Fraternal Democrats appeared in 1846, when Chartism was already past its peak and when the trade societies which existed were small, scattered and weak. The International Association was founded at an even less auspicious time when the poor remnants of Chartism were about to be disbanded and when the unions, though growing in numbers and cohesion, were utterly disinclined to embark on independent political activity.

Change came quickly in the early 1860s. The New Model unions from the beginning were interested in the Nine-Hour Day. From the time of the London building strikes of 1859–60 this ceased to be of purely industrial significance. The episodes at Chelsea Barracks and at Chatham Docks during the course of the dispute seemed to show the need for trade unions to acquire political influence if their industrial struggles were to be successful. Old Chartists, such as Benjamin Lucraft, were at hand to point the moral. The London Trades Council, the Amalgamated Society of Carpenters and Joiners and the *Beehive* were all products of the builders' movement and each in its own way contributed to the political awakening.

Nor was the change confined to England. Industrial development in France, Germany and some parts of Northern

Italy was stimulating a labour revival. By the early 1860s the workers had begun to recover from the disasters of 1848. The appearance of French workers' candidates in the elections of 1863, the movements founded by Lassalle in Germany and by Mazzini in Italy were all pointing in the same direction.

By 1864 there existed at least in rudimentary form an international labour movement. More than that, from the Italian Risorgimento onwards, there appeared a series of international causes, each arousing a different degree of response in Britain. By a coincidence they occurred precisely in the order best calculated to give rise to a workers' international. Italy's cause had supporters in every section of English society. The American Civil War divided opinion horizontally with radical and labour opinion supporting the North from the beginning of 1863 and the Whig and Tory establishment upholding the South. The Polish insurrection, coming at the very moment when Lincoln's emancipation proclamation was winning him new support from British labour, divided the unions from their allies among the Bright radicals and strengthened the tendencies making for an independent labour intervention in politics.

Contacts between workers' societies in England and France had been developing since the French visit in 1862. Poland provided a rallying point. Odger's address on Poland was widely circulated in England and France and was in a very real sense the foundation document of the International. The Anglo-French meeting in support of Poland in September 1864, at which German and Italian workers' societies were represented and at which Odger's address was read, brought the International into being.

By 1864 the idea of an International was in the air and some attempt at a permanent association of British and European labour was inevitable. Before the beginning of the year the Marquis of Townshend had established his Universal League for the Elevation of the Working Classes with substantial trade union support. Its object included not only shorter hours but also 'a fraternal communication with the industrial populations of all other countries' for joint action in the interests of labour. Members of the Universal League were elected to the first General Council of the International and an attempt was soon made to merge the two organisations. Whatever their disagreements with Bright on economic and industrial matters, British labour leaders were very ready to collaborate with philanthropic and liberal-minded men from other classes and there seemed every chance that the International would soon lose its independent working-class character. That this did not happen and that the International retained its independence and developed along the lines it did, was largely due to another accident — the presence in London of Karl Marx and his decision to accept the invitation to attend the foundation meeting.

At first sight it seems surprising that Marx was invited at all. For nearly two years he had been isolated from public life. He was unknown to most, if not all, of the British trade union leaders who were arranging the foundation meeting. He in turn knew little about them and it was through the Jersey Frenchman, Le Lubez, that the organisers of the meeting made their first contact with Marx.

This is perhaps not surprising, since Marx spent his politically formative years in Paris where he had met and argued with Proudhon. Arriving in Paris in 1843 Marx was a journalist and a left-Hegelian philosopher, ignorant as he well knew, of both political economy and the working class. When he left, in 1845, he was a communist steeped in the literature of revolutionary France and already decided about his rôle in life. The French visitors whom Le Lubez took to Marx's house, in the late September of 1864, may well have known him by repute. In any event it was the French who in their list of 'distinguished exiles and friends of the people' to be invited to the meeting, included the name of Marx.

Despite his lack of previous contact with the British and French leaders, Marx saw at once that 'this time real "powers" were involved both on the London and Paris sides'. For that reason alone he was ready to waive his 'usual standing rule to decline any such invitations'.

Once installed on the provisional General Council, Marx had little difficulty in establishing his intellectual ascendancy. His next problem was harder. The English workers with whom he would mainly be dealing were not revolutionary and would not quickly or easily become so. On international affairs their outlook was closer to Mazzini than to Marx. During his years in London Mazzini had got to know many of the leading trade unionists, including Cremer and Howell. Odger's address on Poland had unmistakably Mazzinian undertones. For Mazzini what was in question was not only Italy's right to independence. At least three other propositions were equally involved. United Italy must be a republic responsive to the needs and ideas of the labour classes; her cause was therefore uniquely the concern of labour. Morality must be the basis of both social and international relations, morality being founded on a recognition of the reciprocal character of duties and rights. Finally, and as a corollary, diplomacy must have as its object the liberation of subject peoples. But this would not be achieved by conventional alliances between monarchs. The situation called for an alliance of the subject peoples themselves — Italians, Hungarians and Poles in particular.

This was precisely the kind of approach which appealed to the mid-Victorian Nonconformism of the British labour leaders. To Marx, however, it was unrealistic and sentimental. For him the crucial task was to establish the political supremacy of the working class which would then carry through the social revolution. All international questions must be subordinated to this central aim. The struggles of subject peoples were to be encouraged in so far as they strengthened labour by weakening its main opponents. This was clearly the case in Poland and Ireland. It was clearly not the case in the Slav provinces of the Austrian Empire whose national movements were exploited by the Czar in the interests of Russian imperialism. Even the Italian Risorgimento was viewed with mixed feelings, since it accepted aid from Napoleon III and since the weakening of Austria might rebound to the benefit of Russia.

On domestic policy too, there seemed little in common between Marx and the English trade unions. Though they might strike out on their own in campaigns to improve their legal status, the unions normally and almost as a matter of course adopted the politics of advanced liberalism. They tended to look for political leadership to such men as Bright, Mundella and Gladstone and they showed no inclination to emerge as an independent political force, as distinct from a mere pressure group.

The *Inaugural Address* was designed to bridge the gap between Marx and the unions. It fulfilled its purpose admirably. Industrial development, he could claim, while it increased the wealth of society, brought little tangible benefit to the working class as a whole. Some sections, well organised and favourably placed, might temporarily improve their conditions but for the majority, capitalism could offer nothing but increasing misery and a subsistence standard of life. No social, economic or political reforms within the framework of capitalism could change this state of affairs. But it did not follow from this that the struggle for such reforms was futile. On the contrary, struggle could bring temporary alleviation and, more important, could lead to a permanent growth in unity and understanding. The workers must, therefore, be convinced that their partial struggles would culminate in the winning of political power and that this power would in itself be the instrument for transforming society from its basis of private ownership to one of common property in the instruments of production.

Though Marx was convinced and had made clear in the *Communist Manifesto* that such change could only occur through revolution, he made no mention of this in the *Inaugural Address*. Later, he explained to Engels, after a period of political education, a reawakened movement would allow 'the old boldness of speech'. Meanwhile the watchword would be '*fortiter in re, suaviter in modo*'. Since 1846 there had been two encouraging developments in Britain, neither of them revolutionary. The Ten Hours' Act, won largely through working-class pressure, had established the fact that the workers could on occasion compel the capitalist State to intervene on their behalf. The co-operative movement in its modest way had shown that large-scale enterprises could be carried on 'without the existence of a class of masters employing a class of hands'. With all its moderation of phrase, the *Address* embodied some of the principles laid down in the *Communist Manifesto* of 1848. There it was stated that the Communists did not 'set up any sectarian principles of their own, by which to shape and mould the proletarian movement'. Marx, therefore, based his tactics on what the labour movement had done and was doing, hoping in this way to awaken it to an understanding of its historical destiny.

For the immediate future Marx aimed at a political labour movement which, if not revolutionary, would at least be independent of the liberal middle class. For that reason the whole emphasis of the *Address* was on the position of the workers in capitalist society. Less than a tenth of the document dealt with foreign affairs and the omission of all reference to the Risorgimento must have been deliberate. Though, for tactical reasons,[1] he wrote in Mazzinian terms of 'the simple laws of morals and justice . . . as the rules paramount of the intercourse of nations', it was the complex laws of class power-politics which dictated the tone and context of the *Address*.

THE APPEAL OF THE INTERNATIONAL

The appeal of the International to the British worker was, therefore, simple and straightforward. It made no attempt to preach unfamiliar doctrines. It offered to augment their existing struggles, political and industrial, with the power of international combination. British trade unionists had often been ready to support democratic movements abroad both on general humanitarian, democratic grounds and because they agreed with Harney that 'a blow struck at Liberty on the Tagus is an injury to the friends of Freedom on the Thames'. Now the International could offer them for the first time aid from the Continent in their own trade union struggles. By means of the electric telegraph a council sitting in London could quickly establish contact with trade unions abroad and discourage or prevent the arrival of strike-breakers. Again and again this aspect of the International's achievements was stressed by British trade unionists in their appeals for support. The success of the General Council during the London tailors' strike in 1866 established the International as a force in the labour movement. There seemed no reason why the Association should not go on to secure the affiliation of a large part, if not an actual majority, of the organised working class.

In 1867 there were, according to George Potter, eight hundred thousand trade unionists in Britain.[2] Yet the unions affiliated to the International at its height numbered some fifty thousand members. By 1867 it had almost reached the limits of its expansion and it never achieved the dimensions that had at one time seemed likely.

THE LIMITS OF ADVANCE

The reasons for the failure were complex. At its inception the main strength of the International was in the building

[1] Marx to Engels, November 4, 1864.
[2] Conference of the London Working Men's Association, March 5-8, 1867.

trade. Of the twenty-seven Englishmen elected to the first General Council, eleven were building workers; a fact which reflected the tremendous impetus which the strikes of 1859–60 had given to the labour movement. Besides the bricklayers and carpenters it was the shoe-makers, tailors, cabinet makers, bookbinders, ribbon weavers, saddlers, web weavers, cigar makers and the like who constituted the overwhelming majority of the International's trade union membership. Unskilled workers were unrepresented except for the united excavators. The heavy industrial trades were absent with the sole exception of the malleable ironworkers. The International was never able to transcend these limitations, for reasons which may be briefly considered.

From start to finish the International was London based. This, while an asset politically, was from the industrial point of view a devastating liability. The few provincial Societies to affiliate were mostly, like the shoemakers or tailors, following the example already set for them in London. Apart from the malleable ironworkers, the only other exceptions were the ribbon weavers of Coventry whose trade was rapidly dying. London was the centre of the country's political life and of its commerce, but it was remote from the main centres of industry. Nor did the General Council try to offset these disadvantages by initiating political campaigns which could have had repercussions in the provinces. These were left to such bodies as the Reform League and the Land and Labour League, many of whose leaders served on the General Council. But the General Council was principally an international co-ordinating body, linking and seeking to guide the development of affiliated national sections. Hales was right when he said that it could not at the same time serve effectively as the leadership of the English section.

Besides this, there were powerful economic forces which helped to determine the limits of the International's expansion. The 1860s and early 1870s saw the maintenance by the British engineering industry of its technical lead over other countries. World trade was growing rapidly and a large part of the increased demand for engineering products inevitably came to Britain. The period of Britain's industrial monopoly was necessarily one in which powerfully based craft unions could bargain successfully with the employers. In contrast, the building industry could derive no direct benefit from expanding exports and while its firms were growing in size, there was no rise in the productivity of labour remotely comparable to that occurring in engineering. In even sharper contrast to engineering, the traditional craftsman in tailoring and shoemaking was finding his position undermined by the growth of machine production. It is not therefore surprising that of the five men comprising the Junta, Odger the shoemaker, Coulson the bricklayer and Applegarth the carpenter were members of the International, while Allan the engineer and Guile the iron-founder were not.

If the expansion of the International was limited in area it was also restricted in time and 1867 was the last year to see any appreciable increase in trade union affiliations. The reason for this was twofold. Trade unions were by that time firmly established and within their accepted limitations powerful. For them there remained two outstanding political tasks — to secure their legal position and to win an extension of the franchise. The Reform Act of 1867 gave the workers an important share in political power, while in the same year a Royal Commission was set up which was to report favourably on the objects and activities of the unions. From then onwards there could be no serious challenge to their right of existence. If there was still much to be fought for — the total repeal of the Master and Servant Act, protection for trade union funds and the right to picket peacefully during strikes, it was reasonable to hope that the normal processes of political pressure would secure what was wanted. By 1867, in fact, the fourth estate and its institutions had become accepted as part of society. This was true of no other country in Europe.

In Switzerland strikes were treated as abnormalities, in Belgium as acts of war. In France where strikes had been legal since 1864, trade unions continued to operate under severe legal restrictions. Combinations of unions into local *chambres syndicales* developed strongly in the 1860s, but effective nation-wide organisation was unknown.[1] In Germany trade unionism was even weaker and collective bargaining almost non-existent outside the printing trade.[2] In no other country could the leaders of national unions meet regularly in the capital city and as a matter of course combine to bring political pressure

[1] Paul Louis, *Histoire du mouvement syndical en France*, Paris, 1920, pp. 115-31.
[2] J. H. Clapham, *Economic Development of France and Germany, 1815–1921*, Cambridge, 1921, pp. 330-1.

on the government. In England the labour movement in all its aspects was legal. On the Continent it was, at best, tolerated. If the International stopped expanding in England by 1867 because there were other, more immediately profitable, outlets for working class energies, it continued to advance in Europe for another three years. The difference in climate struck Applegarth forcibly as he listened to the speeches at Basle in 1869. 'Fortunately, in England,' he reminded his fellow delegates, 'we have no need of creeping into holes and corners lest a policeman should see us.' Many of the rights for which his continental colleagues were striving were, he told them, 'settled questions with us twenty years ago'.

English Influence on the International

If the differences between England and the rest of Europe were well known at the time, their consequences for the fate of the International were not foreseen. Marx, who knew well enough that the British workers were not revolutionary, hoped that they could be drawn into an international revolution starting on the Continent. And on one level at least, his expectations did not seem unrealistic. When issues of policy were debated at Congresses of the International, the English delegates sided almost invariably with Marx. On Poland, on the legal Eight Hour Day and even on land nationalisation they supported him against the followers of Proudhon. In doing so they helped to ensure that when anarchists fought their first battle with Marxists for the future of the world socialist movement, it was the Marxists who came out victorious. At the Basle Congress in 1869 international Socialism was firmly committed to the 'centralist' and against the 'libertarian' trend. It seemed incredible to *The Times* that such Englishmen as Applegarth and Lucraft had helped to bring about the decision, but it was so.

At the same Basle Congress Bakunin presented his first challenge to Marx, though on the peripheral issue of inheritance rights. During the next two years Bakunin's following increased rapidly. Marx's doctrines were the product of a highly sophisticated political tradition. Bakunin's destructive frenzy, with its contempt for politics and its violent repudiation of authority and the State had more appeal in those parts of Europe where the proletariat was a recent creation and where the traditions of a pre-industrial society of peasants and handicraftsmen lingered strongly. In Switzerland, Spain, Italy and parts of France the anarchists gained ground so quickly that by 1870 they were in a position to challenge Marx for control of the International.

Meanwhile, Marx had taken a strange decision. In January 1870, in the body of a private circular against the Bakuninists, he had listed a number of valid reasons for opposing the creation of an English Federal Council. The anarchists in Switzerland had just taken up the four-year-old demand of Hales for the creation of such a body. Why, they were asking, did the General Council assume the double burden of leading both the International and the English section? Why, alone of all the countries represented in the International, had England no separate Federal Council of its own. In his confidential reply Marx pointed to the decisive rôle, for good or ill, which England must play in a future European revolution. Located in London the General Council had a controlling influence over the strongest working class in the world. But while they were strongest numerically and organisationally, the English workers were certainly not the most politically advanced. This being so, 'it would be sheer folly, we would almost say it would be an outright crime, to allow that hold to fall into purely English hands!' 'The English', Marx claimed, 'have all the material requisites necessary for the revolution. What they lack is the spirit of generalisation and revolutionary ardour.' All of which was equally true five months later when Marx suddenly proposed moving the seat of the General Council to Brussels.

In the *Minutes* of the General Council for June 28, 1870 Marx was reported as asking 'that the General Council be transferred from London to Brussels. We must not let it crop up as a privilege that the Council sits in London.' On the face of it, this looked like capitulation to one of the main tactical demands of the Bakuninists. In Brussels the General Council would have lost all direct contact with the English workers' organisations which Marx had argued was so crucially important. The separate British Federal Council which he had been resisting for four years would have been formed a year earlier than in fact it was. Marx would have lost control of the General Council and of the International two years before the Hague.

It is hard to believe that the proposal was seriously meant.

Had the General Council endorsed it, it would have gone to the Congress due to be held at Mainz in September for a final decision. 'The Congress', Marx explained after making his suggestion, 'may not accept the proposition, then we can put conditions.' Already in fact by the middle of 1870 he was sufficiently alarmed by the growth of anarchism to resort to a dangerous expedient. If the General Council accepted the proposition, Marx must have been counting on the Mainz Congress to reject it. He would then have been able to impose conditions in return for London remaining the seat of the General Council. These conditions would have been such as to strengthen the Council against national sections in which Bakuninism was strong or dominant. What Marx achieved at the London Conference in September 1871, he was already manœuvring to secure fifteen months earlier. It was a desperate manœuvre; Congress might, indeed, have declined the offer, but there seems no evidence that he could count on this as a certainty.

Whatever the explanation, the proposal was no momentary aberration, since Marx returned to it on July 12. The question was only laid aside because of the pressure of business concerning the agenda for the projected Congress at Mainz — the first Congress planned to take place in Germany. But a week later the Franco-Prussian War broke out and the matter was never raised again.

It was fortunate for Marx that his proposal failed. In the middle of 1870 he could rely on de Paepe and the Belgians to support him against Bakunin. But Hins had outlined a complete syndicalist programme at the Basle Congress and there was always the possibility that Bakunin's anarchism and Belgian syndicalism might come together. This actually happened over a period of two years and by the time of the Hague in September 1872 Bakunin and de Paepe were united against Marx. Had the General Council moved to Brussels in 1870 it is exceedingly likely that it would not have moved to New York in 1872. It would have stayed in Europe controlled by anarcho-syndicalists with unforeseeable consequences for the future development of Socialism.

THE FRANCO-PRUSSIAN WAR AND THE PARIS COMMUNE

None of this was apparent, however, when the war broke out and Marx's suggestion was shelved. War inevitably revived

U

interest in international issues and there was considerable agreement with Marx's first Address which, laying the main blame for hostilities on Louis Napoleon, predicted his early downfall. There were differences in emphasis between the various peace organisations, but Marx's views did not differ significantly from those expressed by the majority. In his second *Address* issued immediately after the fall of France, Marx laid particular stress on the need to secure British recognition of the new Republic. While the war had become a defensive one for France, the French workers were warned against the 'desperate folly' of attempting to seize power. They must, instead, take full advantage of republican freedom to develop their organisations. Here again, Marx and the General Council found themselves in harmony with the main currents of labour opinion. The Labour Representation League, founded in 1869 to win working-class representation in Parliament, always displayed the liveliest interest in foreign affairs. Its statement after the fall of France, like that of the General Council, demanded international support for the new Republic.

Marx and the General Council had reacted quickly to the outbreak of war and to the fall of France. There was no such speed in their reaction to the establishment of the Commune in March 1871. At first sight Marx's silence and comparative inactivity during the one socialist revolution of the nineteenth century is astonishing. This strange passivity can be explained only in the light of events which took place before and after the Commune. For one thing, Marx must by that time have given up hope of the British labour movement for the foreseeable future. True, he had written in his Confidential Circular on Bakunin that it was vital for the General Council to secure control over the British trade union movement. Yet by 1870, in his more realistic moments, Marx must have wondered whether this was being achieved. The stagnation of the International in England from 1867 has already been discussed. By 1870 Applegarth, the one outstanding trade union leader over whom Marx had some influence, had ceased to attend meetings of the General Council because of the upheaval in his own Society. With Odger, who still attended from time to time, Marx had long been disillusioned and Lucraft was not of major importance in the trade union world. Marx knew that the English workers for all their organisational achievements lacked 'the spirit of generalisation and revolutionary ardour'. It was 'only the General Council', he wrote in the Confidential Circular, which would 'supply this deficiency, which can thus accelerate the truly revolutionary movement in this country and consequently everywhere', but he must have doubted at least by the middle of 1870 whether it really could.

When the clash came in Paris between Thiers and the National Guard, Marx gave up hope in France too. The workers disregarded his advice and rose in patriotic revolt against what they regarded as a government of national betrayal. But the Paris workers could hardly hope to defeat both the French bourgeoisie and the besieging German forces. The affair would have been more hopeful had Paris been backed by risings in the countryside, but of this there was no sign. The reactionary stolidity of the rural population which had sealed the fate of Paris in June 1848, was still unbroken.

The main hope, as Marx saw it, was that the workers would play a vigorous opposition rôle in republican France forcing the Government to the left and paving the way for a socialist revolution. This had been the tactic of the *Communist Manifesto* and it was essentially the same advice which he gave to the French in his second *Address* on the war. So far as the British workers were concerned, they must bring pressure on their Government to recognise the Republic and so help stabilise its international position. This was as far as they should go. While the Labour Representation League pressed for armed intervention in support of France, Engels argued on the General Council for the more moderate line. With the Commune, all this was pushed into the background. For a time Marx hoped that the Communards, through the seizure of strategic points and compromising documents, could negotiate a settlement with Versailles which would have left some elbow room for the labour movement in the new Republican *régime*. Marx had no illusion that the Commune could win and his diplomatic and tactical approach to the whole question, once the Parisians had disregarded his advice and taken up arms, no doubt explains his unwillingness to issue, or allow the General Council to issue, any statement or call for solidarity while the Commune lasted.

As Marx feared, the outcome of the rising was the triumph of reaction and a devastating defeat for the French workers.

For two years following the disaster of June 1848 Marx had hoped for an early revival of the revolutionary movement. In 1871 he knew better. The defeat would be lasting in its effects and international in its repercussions. No one could foresee when revival would come. Meanwhile, in the ebb which must follow, the Commune would be an inspiration and a legend. At last, in a major capital city in Europe, the workers had taken power and held it for two months. Encouragement could be drawn from the experience and there were lessons to be learned in the technique of revolution. Marx, therefore, wrote a moving obituary to the Commune after its fall. He had had no hope of its victory while it was alive.

MARX: THE LAST TWELVE YEARS

The Commune and his brilliant, moving if not very analytical defence of it marked a climax in Marx's life of which the last twelve years were strangely barren both in political activity and in theoretical work. It is well known that the second and third volumes of *Capital* were published posthumously and unfinished by Engels. Less well known and so far unexplained, is the fact that Marx did extraordinarily little work on those volumes in a period when for the first time in his adult life he was free from political and financial distractions. The material used in volumes II and III comes overwhelmingly from the 1850s and 1860s. Sources from the 1870s are exceedingly sparse and of little consequence.[1] Nor do his other writings after the end of the International occupy many pages. An article on 'Political Indifferentism' for the *Almanacco Repubblicano* in 1873 and an epilogue to the *Revelations on the Cologne Trials* in the same year; the *Critique of the Gotha Programme*, not meant for publication in 1875 and his reply to Howell's *Nineteenth Century* article, distorting the history of the International in 1878 which Marx published in Harriet Law's *Secular Chronicle* after the *Nineteenth Century* had refused to publish it;[2] prefaces written, jointly with Engels, to the German and Russian editions of the *Communist Manifesto* in 1872 and 1882 — they do not add up to a very considerable total.

[1] Cf. *Capital*, vol. II, pp. 18, 86, 383; vol. III, p. 287, Calcutta, 1945–6.
[2] James Knowles to Marx, July 21, 1878 (wrongly dated as 1871) — I.I.S.G.

'I am terribly overworked,' Marx wrote to Danielson on May 29, 1872, 'and meet so many obstacles in my theoretical studies that after September I am determined to leave the General Council, all the work of which lies on my shoulders.' Marx left the Council as planned and resumed his theoretical studies. Between 1872 and 1875 he revised the French edition of *Capital* which was published in instalments. He studied Russian and Turkish and maintained an active interest in the development of Socialism in a number of countries. But his work for the most part remained unpublished. His style of life had changed. The Liberal politician, Sir Mountstuart Grant Duff, lunching with him at the Devonshire Club, met a scholarly, urbane man, with a dry wit and an interest in philology. 'It was all very *positif*, slightly cynical, as I thought, showing very correct ideas, when he was conversing of the past or the present, but vague and unsatisfactory when he turned to the future.' Marx told him that he expected the revolution to begin in Russia and then spread to Germany as a revolt against militarism. The immediate result would be republican democracy, not Socialism. 'It would merely be a step to better things,' he concluded, 'as your revolution of 1688 was only a step on the road.' [1]

This casual comment is not by itself of great significance, but it harmonises perfectly with what is known of Marx's last twelve years. He had lost none of his intellectual and political acumen, but something had gone. He no longer had the capacity for sustained creative work. He was only fifty-three when the Commune fell, but this was the turning point in his life. He had been thirty when the June uprising was crushed in Paris and he was quite ready in the 1850s and early 1860s to retire to the study in preparation for the time when the movement would revive. Revival had come. With it had come the International and the hope that when the next revolution occurred, 'this powerful engine' would be at hand to co-ordinate activities in a number of countries and ensure victory. The revolution had come and the International proved powerless. Engels on the General Council expressed his bitterness at the passivity of the English workers and there can be little doubt that he also spoke for Marx. Marx could not face the prospect of a long period of painfully slow

[1] Sir Mountstuart E. Grant Duff, *Notes from a Diary*, 1898, vol. II, pp. 105-6.

development as he had faced it in his thirties. He does not seem to have expressed, and may not have realised, the depth of his disappointment. But on March 8, 1881 he wrote to Vera Zasulich : 'A nervous disorder which has troubled me for the last ten years, has prevented me from replying before. . . .' [1] One may guess at the origin, if not the nature, of his nervous disorder.

MARX'S TACTICS

If this hypothesis is accepted, the rest becomes clear. The Commune had become a legend. Marx's brilliant pamphlet linked it indelibly with the International in the public mind. Then the International became a legend, a symbol of the world labour movement. Whoever controlled it spoke with the authority of that movement. If Bakunin controlled it he would place his stamp on future developments. This could not be allowed.

At the London Conference of September 1871, Marx strengthened the General Council so as to use it more effectively against local Bakuninist sections. He could still count on the support of the English who, so far as they understood what was going on, were opposed to the disruptive manœuvres of the Bakuninists. The fall of the Commune had actually strengthened Marx's position on the Council since with the arrival of the Blanquists he had a new source of support against the political abstentionism of the anarchists. Towards the end of the Conference Marx, having secured his main points, readily agreed to the formation of an English Federal Council. Since there was to be no revolution in the foreseeable future the backwardness of the English was no longer an argument for continuing to resist Hales's five-year-old proposal. So the English Federal Council came into existence with profound effects on the future of the International.

The Commune itself had had little direct effect on the General Council and none at all on its relations with the unions. In a sense the formation of the English Federal Council was an indirect result, because of the effect of the Commune on Marx's political calculations. At first the two Councils now existing in London were on the friendliest of terms and it was

[1] Ryazanoff, *Marx-Engels Archiv*, I, p. 341.

Marx himself who renominated Hales as General Secretary immediately after the London Conference. At the same time Hales remained Secretary of the English — later British — Federal Council and there seemed no reason why the two bodies should not continue to work in harmony.

The first breech resulted from the intrigues of Maltman Barry who joined the English Federal Council soon after it was formed. 1871 was the year of the 'Scott-Russell' plot in which a number of leading Conservatives made a concerted attempt to win over the leading trade unionists.[1] Barry was a correspondent of the Tory *Standard* and then, and for many years to come, an agent of the Conservative Party. It would be surprising if his adhesion to the Federal Council had no connection with the 'plot'. He soon set to work to discredit Hales whose past associations had been with the Liberals and who was, of all the members of the Council, most closely identified with the moves to establish an autonomous British workers' party. In correspondence with Marx, Barry charged Hales with using his position as Secretary of both Councils to develop the Federal Council along autonomous lines. Hales was forced to give up his position on the Federal Council, but he left it in safe hands and soon after was able to resume complete control. What brought Hales and his followers to side with the Bakuninists and with the veteran French republican antagonists of the General Council was not a concordance of political outlook but a common adherence to the principle of national autonomy. By the time of the Nottingham Conference of the English Council in July 1872 it was clear to Marx and to Engels who was increasingly acting as his political adjutant, that without an enormous expenditure of time and energy, which they were not now prepared to consider, the English section could not be kept in line. The Hague Congress in September was most carefully packed by Engels, but at any future Congress it seemed only too likely that the Bakuninists would win control.

It is not certain exactly when Marx took the desperate decision to move the General Council to New York where, under the care of his friend Sorge, it could be kept out of harm's way. But the defection of Hales and his followers was

[1] See *The Times*, October 25, 26, 1871. For a contemporary socialist account, see George Jacob Holyoake, *Sixty Years of an Agitator's Life*, vol. II, pp. 194-8.

a material fact in driving Marx to his decision. This is confirmed by Barry himself who in his report on the Hague wrote of the 'accession to the Council of a number of "representative" Englishmen' who sought to make of it 'either a pothouse forum or an electioneering machine'. Determined to retire from the General Council, Marx, with the defection of a majority of the English section, no longer dared leave the centre of the International in London. For want of a better alternative, he despatched it to New York, where it died.

FATE OF THE ENGLISH SECTION

Even a united English section would have been hard put to survive in the conditions of the 1870s. Hales was a generation too soon in his hopes of a Labour Party based on trade union affiliation. The quarter century of mid-Victorian prosperity had affected the outlook of the unions and the rags and hunger of the 1840s seemed remote, at least to the skilled craftsmen who constituted the bulk of the movement's leadership. Had they been met with a blank wall of opposition from the propertied classes, it might have been a different story. But the partial enfranchisement of 1867 and the report of the Royal Commission on trade unions appearing in 1869 convinced them that the path to reform was not blocked. Moreover, they were right. Functioning as a pressure group the trade unions were remarkably successful in winning the industrial and social legislation they required. In contrast to France and Germany where trade unionism did not develop strongly in the basic industries until some time after the appearance of socialist parties, liberal-labourism was to dominate working-class politics in England for the rest of the century. The unique strength of craft unionism in England which Marx had failed to notice in his *Inaugural Address*, proved decisive for the future.

Formed at an inauspicious moment in a basically unfavourable situation, the English section of the International split and foundered. Marx and Engels took practically no interest in its activities except to prevent Hales and his followers from taking over the 'official' Federal Council. In this they were helped by Hales's decision to secede while his followers constituted an actual majority of the Federal Council. In the best conditions it seems impossible that the autonomous English section could have lasted long. As things stood, it was certainly too weak to survive a split and little was left of it by the middle of 1873. The remnants of O'Brienism had adhered to the International and they provided the English section with its ideology. But, as G. D. H. Cole pointed out, 'in the Great Britain of the eighteen-fifties agrarian democracy was out of date, and it was still too soon to rouse the people against monopoly capitalism'.[1] This was also true of the 1870s.

In England the I.W.M.A. had established itself as the unofficial international department of the trade union movement. As such it achieved some quite remarkable successes and in that capacity it could have continued on a course of modest usefulness. But after the Paris Commune Marx was not much interested in Britain and the consequences for the British section of his decision to move the General Council to New York did not concern him.

The lasting effects of the International in England are hard to assess, but they undoubtedly existed. The Labour Representation League was largely founded in 1869 by men who had served or were still serving on the General Council. Though started primarily to secure labour representation in Parliament, it maintained throughout its existence the liveliest interest in international affairs. Eccarius, Hales, Mottershead, Walton and Cohn were active on its executive almost to the end of the 1870s. One of the League's last acts was to campaign together with the Eastern Question Association against war with Russia in 1877-8. Mottershead and Hales were at the head of the movement. It was not a cause which commended itself to Marx, but it brought William Morris into political activity. When Morris and his friends formed the Socialist League in 1885 its Rules were, except for a few words, identical with those drawn up by Marx for the General Council in November 1864.[2]

The International, in fact, succeeded in keeping alive the idea of international Socialism in England between the decline of Chartism and the revival of the 1880s. It was identified in the public mind with Socialism which, but for its existence, would probably have been forgotten. When Mrs. E. Lynn Linton published her political novel, *The True History of Joshua Davidson* in 1872, she made her socialist hero as a

---

[1] *Chartist Portraits*, 1941, p. 242.
[2] *Commonweal*, No. 1, February 1885. Friedrich Lessner was one of the signatories and the same issue of *Commonweal* announced a lecture by Belfort Bax on the history of the International.

matter of course a member of the International.[1] Contemporaries had no doubts about the effectiveness of the International in providing English Socialism with the continuity it would otherwise have lacked. Henry Fawcett, the Liberal M.P. and Postmaster-General, saw in it an important link between the Socialism of the latter-day Chartists and the agrarian policies of Alfred Wallace and Henry George in the 1880s.[2] And, indeed, both Charles Murray and Benjamin Lucraft served on the Executive of the Land Nationalisation Society founded in 1881 under the Presidency of Alfred Wallace, twelve years after the Basle Congress had first made its cause an international issue.[3]

It was not only land nationalisation which came to be identified, in contemporary minds, with the notorious International Society. The International had in 1869 advocated the cause of compulsory State education.[4] A delegate from the London Trades Council, giving evidence before a Royal Commission as late as 1887, argued for the same ideas. But was not this, asked the Rev. Dr. Rigg, a 'plank of the international?' The witness agreed that it was, and that it could be described as 'communism'. He supported it none the less.

More important was the demand for the legal Eight-Hour Day which the International had first raised at its Geneva Congress in 1866. With the rise of the 'New Unionism' at the end of the 1880s the demand was revived, and became a central issue at the T.U.C. The part played by the International in popularising the idea was not forgotten. On August 12, 1890 the veteran Tory agent, Maltman Barry, told the Aberdeen Trades Council: 'The prominence which the Eight Hours Question now enjoys is due, in large measure, to the teachings of Karl Marx and to the active practical exertions of his disciples. . . . Marx founded the "International". . . .'[5]

---

[1] Pp. 145-58.

[2] Henry Fawcett, M.P., *State Socialism and the Nationalisation of the Land*, 1883, p. 3.

[3] Dr. G. B. Clark was another former member of the International to work actively in the Land Nationalisation Society, writing for it a forty-page pamphlet, *A Plea for the Nationalisation of the Land*, n.d.

[4] See Chapter IX.

[5] Maltman Barry, *The Labour Day*, Aberdeen, 1890, p. 7. From the time of Marx's death, Barry had tried persistently to ingratiate himself with Engels, to whom he sent a copy of *The Labour Day*. By 1890, however, Engels had grown tired of him, see Barry to Engels, September 27, October 13, 1890; January 10, 1891. I.I.S.G.

There is abundant evidence to show that the ideas of the International lived on in the labour movement through the activities of its former members. Such men as Adam Weiler, of the Alliance Cabinet Makers, Thomas Mottershead, of the Preston Trades Council and A. A. Walton, of the Operative Masons, were prominent in the Trades Union Congress throughout the 1870s. The socialist revival of the 1880s was stronger because the International had existed in England and because many of those participating in the revival knew that they were continuing in its tradition. Belfort Bax, a leading publicist for the Social Democratic Federation, included Hermann Jung among his early political teachers. James Macdonald, for seventeen years the Secretary of the London Trades Council and one of the founders of the Labour Party, was introduced to Socialism, in the form of Engels's articles in the *Labour Standard* in 1881, by Adam Weiler, the German cabinet-maker who had served on both the General and the British Federal Councils [1] and had remained loyal to Marx throughout. Marx's youngest daughter, Eleanor, worked closely with Tom Mann and Ben Tillett in the 'New Unionist' agitation at the end of the 1880s.

The most convincing evidence for the lasting influence of the International came, however, from George Lansbury. 'My adviser and friend', he wrote in his autobiography, 'was John Hales who, during the days of the Commune, was secretary of the First International established by Marx and his friends in 1864. . . . Hales told me about the International and taught me the need of working-class solidarity . . . the fact is that although men like Hales and early working-class Radicals like Howell, Lucraft, Applegarth and Odger failed to follow Marx and establish a Socialist organization, they did see farther than most of those with whom they came in contact. It is true most of these men lived the latter part of their lives in the odour of sanctity of the Liberalism of Mr. Gladstone and died therein; nevertheless, they deserve honour because they helped establish the First International, and by so doing made the present International possible.' [2]

[1] *How I became a Socialist : A Series of Biographical Sketches*, 1896, pp. 56-66.

[2] George Lansbury, *My Life*, 1928, pp. 31-2.

The Problem of Eccarius

THE real character of the talented, clumsy and over-sensitive German tailor who played a leading part in the First International has long been a subject for speculation. In 1909 Howard Evans, in his biography of Cremer, wrote of Eccarius that he 'was afterwards falsely accused of selling the secrets of the International, but those who knew him best protested that a more honest fellow never lived'.[1] Much more serious was the accusation by Brügel, which followed the opening of the Austrian Archives in 1918, that Eccarius was a spy who provided the Austrian Government with confidential information about the International.[2] Edward Fuchs, who edited the English edition of Mehring's *Karl Marx*, repeated the charge without apparently having checked the evidence [3] and, more recently, Giuseppe Del Bo has repeated it again.[4]

It is certain that throughout his entire career in the International Eccarius was a controversial figure, disliked by the English members of the General Council — against whom Marx had frequently to defend him — and finally quarrelling irreparably with Marx and Engels themselves. Up to the death of Eccarius in 1889, Engels felt bitterly about him and refused to write for the *Labour Standard* if contributions were accepted from 'the traitor to our cause'.[5]

Yet Eccarius had been a member of the League of the Just and, later, of the Communist League which commissioned Marx and Engels to write the *Communist Manifesto*. He had taken part in the famous Chartist demonstration on Kennington Common on April 10, 1848 [6] and had contributed an article on

[1] *Op. cit.*, p. 36.
[2] *Der Kampf*, vol. XVIII, Vienna, 1921.
[3] *Op. cit.*, p. 553.
[4] *Movimento Operaio*, Milan, 1955, p. 263, n. 5.
[5] Engels to Shipton, August 15, 1881; see also Engels to Schlueter, December 7, 1885; to Bebel, August 18, 1886 and to Sorge, June 8, 1889.
[6] F. Lessner, *op. cit.*, p. 16.

the London tailoring trade to the last issue of Marx's *Neue Rheinische Zeitung — Politisch-Oekonomische Revue*.[1] In 1864 Marx recommended him to speak as a representative of the German workers at the foundation meeting of the International and he was elected to its first General Council. After Marx he was the most important German member of the Council; he was its General Secretary from 1867 to 1871 and was the only member to attend every Conference and Congress. All the reports of the General Council to Congress were written by Marx except that for Lausanne which was the work of Eccarius. At first sight it might seem strange that with such a record of service he should have been an object of distrust and suspicion.

The Englishman, Fox, disliked Eccarius as an embodiment of German influence on the Council, more vulnerable than Marx because he was Marx's mouthpiece. A little later there was acute rivalry between Eccarius, Howell, Cremer and Odger for the editorship of the *Workman's Advocate* and considerable annoyance when Eccarius was appointed. After the English had been further annoyed by the majority of the Council's hostility to Mazzini, Marx dropped Eccarius in favour of Odger, no doubt to conciliate them. A man gifted with subtlety and finesse might have negotiated such difficulties; Eccarius who was humourless and gauche in the extreme probably exacerbated them.

In his article on the London tailoring trade Eccarius had written about the struggle between large and small capital which he knew about from personal experience. By the 1860s life had become still harder for the small tailor and there is reason to believe that Eccarius was often in dire financial straits. The work he did as Secretary of the General Council was not well paid and the reason he gave for resigning — that he needed to give more time to tailoring — may well have been true, though it was probably not the only reason.

The reports which Eccarius wrote of the Lausanne and subsequent Congresses for *The Times* among other papers were criticised by his colleagues on various grounds. But there seems to have been no question raised about his right to be paid for such reports until Hales argued that the money was rightly the property of the General Council. After his resignation as General Secretary, Eccarius attended the London Con-

---

[1] No. 5-6, pp. 293-303, reprinted, Berlin, 1955.

ference of 1871 and soon after reports appeared in the *Scotsman* which all concerned knew had emanated from Eccarius. This may have been the occasion on which he was accused of 'selling the secrets of the International' and technically, since the Conference was private, the charge was true. It is also noticeable, however, that in his four reports which appeared in the *Scotsman* [1] Eccarius wrote nothing to the discredit of the International and revealed the names of no delegates except for that of Marx which was sufficiently well known. On the contrary, Eccarius made it clear that the Conference 'had not been a secret one in the sense in which the word secrecy had been generally understood', but that it had been necessary to protect the French and German delegates from persecution on their return.[2] In his last report [3] Eccarius reported some of the Conference resolutions, including the one which barred secret societies from membership of the International. There were in fact private resolutions passed by the Conference which were not recorded in the *Minutes* and they did not appear in the reports of Eccarius.

This episode shows Eccarius as guilty of nothing worse than indiscretion. Another more mysterious episode occurred seven years later which may or may not have involved Eccarius, but which deserves to be recorded. It seems likely that in 1878 the secrets of the International were sold to the German consulate in London, not by Eccarius, but by George Howell.

On January 22, 1878 Howell wrote to James Knowles, editor of the *Nineteenth Century*, to tell him that efforts were being made to reorganise the International and that an article on the Association's history might be timely. On February 7 he wrote again to Knowles to say that 'I have gone over the entire article and copy with the secretary of the International'. The Secretary concerned may have been Eccarius, but was more probably Hales, since Howell wrote to him on April 4, 1878, 'I want to ask your opinion and advice about a little matter or two'. Since the article was almost certainly completed before April 4 [4] the 'little matter or two' may well have concerned another project in which Howell was interested. On May 4, 1878 he wrote to the German Consul promising to call the next day with a report and he felt able to say that 'Much of

---

[1] September 25-7 and October 2, 1871.
[2] *Op. cit.*, September 27, 1871.   [3] *Op. cit.*, October 2, 1871.
[4] See Howell to Knowles, April 6, 1878.

the information given is not to be found elsewhere in any form whatever'.[1]   When Howell, much later, was preparing notes for his autobiography, he referred to a report which he had written for the German Consulate and which he said was concerned with British labour legislation.   His notes give the date as 1876 which may have been a deliberate error to distract attention from the real content of the report.   In 1878 the German Government, concerned with the attempt on the Emperor's life, passed legislation making socialist organisations illegal.   It is more than likely that it sought information about the International which was regarded as a secret society.[2] Howell, who had served on the General Council, but whom no one considered a revolutionary, would be an obvious source of information.   His unusually intense interest in money was remarked on by Soutter and is confirmed by his correspondence, diary and notes.[3]

It is just possible that Eccarius helped Howell with his article and report, either directly or in collaboration with Hales with whom he was associated in the International Labour Union, an unsuccessful attempt to revive the International in 1877.   Howell's article on the history of the International appeared in the *Nineteenth Century* in July 1878.   Soon afterwards the International Labour Union condemned Howell's article as inaccurate, which indeed it was.   There is no record that Hales, who had checked the article with Howell, dissented from the resolution.[4]   Though Eccarius may have been concerned with Hales in the affair, there is no evidence that he was and this does not seem to have been the origin of the discreditable rumours about him.

It is much more likely that Eccarius, who wrote for a number of foreign journals, corresponded with Heinrich Oberwinder, editor of the Viennese labour paper the *Volkswille* to

---

[1] See also Howell to German Consul, September 26, 1878.

[2] For the attempt by Lothar Bucher, Secretary of the Berlin Congress, who had previously had dealings with Marx, to implicate the Socialists in the attempt on the Emperor's life, see letter of Marx in *Daily News*, June 12, 1878.

[3] 'Mr. George Howell has never worked for or been connected with any reform movement where money was scarce and hard work the only reward.'   F. S. Soutter, *Recollections of a Labour Pioneer*, 1923, p. 120.   The remark was first made by Soutter in a leaflet published in 1881.

[4] See I.L.U. *Minutes* published by Max Nettlau in 'Ein verschollener Nachklang der Internationale: The International Labour Union, London 1877–8' in Grünberg's *Archiv*, vol. 9, pp. 134–45, Leipzig, 1919.

which Eccarius contributed about the British labour movement. In 1888 Oberwinder was exposed internationally as a spy.[1] Without an examination of the Austrian police archives the whole question must remain partly speculative, but it seems at least possible that reports which Eccarius sent to Oberwinder in good faith found their way to the Austrian police and seemed later to incriminate Eccarius. On the basis of available evidence, the case against Eccarius is not proved and seems incompatible with what is known of his character.

[1] See the list of police spies in *Commonweal*, January 7, 1888.

Two Contemporary Sources on the History of the First International

NEARLY all historians who have dealt with the International have leaned heavily on the contemporary accounts of the Frenchmen, Fribourg and Testut. Though both versions contain material of value, both were written with specific political objectives and neither is reliable.

Fribourg, writing soon after the fall of the Commune, set out to prove that the International had followed the wrong path through ignoring the advice given by himself and Tolain. The Proudhonists intended the International to be an association of study circles investigating such questions as mutual credit banks, co-operation and the place of women in society. Had the International followed the advice of Fribourg and his colleagues it would not have meddled in politics or strikes.[1]

The English members of the International, on the other hand, believed strongly in both political and industrial action while tending to ignore or disparage the social theories of Proudhon. Fribourg, accordingly, gives scant attention to the English influence in the International. Odger's address of 1863 signed by a group of English trade unionists which led directly to the Foundation Meeting in the following year is not mentioned.

Other omissions in Fribourg's history stem directly from the 'ouvrierisme' of the Proudhonists, their antagonism to intellectuals and their wish to exclude them from working-class societies. There is therefore no mention of the fact that Beesly took the chair at the Foundation Meeting or that Marx wrote the Inaugural Address and Rules.[2] Fribourg seems, in fact, to have been totally ignorant of Marx's work and ideas. He did not read Marx's statement of his case against Proudhon, apparently believing that Marx wrote a chapter in his book

---

[1] Fribourg, *op. cit.*, pp. 141-2 and 146-7.
[2] *Ibid.*, p. 12.

Capital against Proudhon called *Misère de la philosophie.*[1]

In accordance with his political position, Fribourg presented a distorted account of every Congress of the International. At the Geneva Congress the Proudhonists tried to prohibit non-manual workers from holding official positions in the Association. This would of course have excluded Marx who was vigorously defended by Cremer and Carter. The attempt failed, but the Proudhonists were more successful in their attack on Lefort since the principle had been accepted that each national section would determine its own representation. In his account of Geneva, Fribourg makes no mention of the first controversy, while giving a detailed treatment of the second. Similarly, of the Brussels Congress, at which his party was decisively defeated, Fribourg says little about the proceedings except that Tolain protested against 'the communists'.[2] In his account of Basle, Fribourg reprints statements by Tolain, Langlois and Bakunin and nothing whatever from the General Council or its delegation.[3]

The General Council in fact fared badly at Fribourg's hands. Not a single document from the Council was published, except the Rules, and those appeared in the distorted French version which was subsequently repudiated.

Finally, in the course of a discussion on the relation of the International to the Paris Commune, Fribourg summarised the attacks by Lucraft and Odger on the General Council while quoting nothing from *The Civil War in France*, the document around which the controversy was raging.[4]

Fribourg's work is not a history of the International, but a mutualist tract against 'Russo-German collectivism'.[5] As such, it provides a useful source for the statements and opinions of the original Paris section. For an understanding of the work of the General Council, of Marx or of the English members, however, it is useless.

In contrast to Fribourg, Testut is full and well-documented. The Lyonnese lawyer published in 1870 and 1871 three books and one pamphlet on the International, which have been widely accepted as authoritative. He also gave evidence before the

---

[1] *Ibid.*, p. 46.   [2] *Ibid.*, pp. 123-6.   [3] *Ibid.*, pp. 136-40.
[4] *Ibid.*, pp. 198-200. For the view that in his repudiation of the Paris Commune, Fribourg went to even greater lengths than Tolain, see the Anarchist historian, Max Nettlau, *Der Anarchismus von Proudhon zu Kropotkin*, Berlin, 1927, p. 135.
[5] *Ibid.*, p. 140.

French Government's Commission of enquiry on the Commune.[1] It was not realised until 1952 that Testut was himself a police spy and it is still not known who were his agents on, or with access to, the General Council.[2]

What Del Bo discovered in the archives of the French police could have been guessed at by a close student of Testut's writings. In May 1870 his most important book, *L'Internationale*, appeared in Lyons. In the same month the indictment of the Paris section of the International was published under the title of *L'Association Internationale des Travailleurs*.[3] The indictment was presented by the prosecution to the court on June 22, 1870.[4] It consisted largely of the correspondence of the General Council and French members which had been seized by the police. A good deal of this material had already appeared in Testut's book though there was no mention of the indictment or trial.[5] Only one prominent member of the Paris section of the International, Fribourg, was not mentioned in Testut or in the proceedings at any of the three trials of the Paris section.[6]

Because of his relations with the police, Testut was well supplied with material not available elsewhere and his writings are useful as a source of information. However, he had the bad habit of omitting sentences from the material quoted without indicating that he had done so.[7] More serious was his

[1] *Enquête parlementaire sur l'insurrection du 18 mars, 1871*, Versailles, 1872, vol. 2, pp. 599 *et seq.*

[2] Giuseppe Del Bo, 'Lo spinaggio intorno alla Internazionale. Oscar Testut, agente segreto "Numero 47"' in *Movimento Operaio*, November-December 1952.

[3] Paris, 1870. No printer's name is mentioned. A copy of this publication is in the Goldsmith's Library, London, the catalogue wrongly describing it as 'apparently an official report to the Emperor, setting forth the grounds for the suppression of the Internationale'.

[4] *Troisième Procès de l'Association Internationale des Travailleurs à Paris*, Paris, July 1870, pp. 6-65 ; but see also pp. 4-5.

[5] See *L'Internationale*, 3rd edition, pp. 52, 221-3, 226-7, 236, 244. See also *L'Internationale et le jacobinisme au ban de l'Europe*, vol. I, pp. 41, 56-7, 59, 63-4, 65-6, 71, 419-20.

[6] Suspicion is inevitably thrown on Fribourg, at least until some other explanation for these omissions has been found. Testut's activities as a police agent were not suspected at the time ; Marx and Engels referred to him merely as 'the former Bonapartist prosecutor (procureur) Oscar Testut'. Statement of the General Council, signed by Hales but written by Marx and Engels. *Eastern Post*, November 11, 1871, and *Soc.* vol. 13/2, p. 372.

[7] Among many examples, cf. letters from Dupont to Chemalé, April 17, May 12 and November 1, 1867, as reproduced in *L'Internationale et le jacobinisme* . . ., vol. I, pp. 8, 9, 14 and in the *Troisième Procès* . . ., pp. 42, 43 respectively.

practice of quoting statements from Bakunin and his followers as though they expressed the official policy of the International. This was deliberately deceptive since Testut and the French police knew that the General Council had repudiated Bakunin. The Confidential Communication from the General Council of January 1870 was quoted by Testut, but he printed only the statement on the possibility of social revolution in Ireland, not the attack on Bakunin.[1] Similarly, Testut quoted statements from Felix Pyat and the dissident French Branch in London without mentioning that both had been denounced by the General Council.[2]

Testut attributed a fantastic membership to the International and credited it with branches so far afield as Sweden and China.[3] Inevitably, he blamed the International for the Paris insurrection and for the burning of public buildings. In the spate of writings on the International which appeared after the fall of the Commune, Testut was widely quoted as an authority. Though historians of the International have relied on his works for source material, and though Postgate has described them as 'of the greatest value',[4] they should be treated with considerable caution.

---

[1] Cf. *L'Internationale, ibid.*, pp. 237-8. For the full text of the Confidential Communication, see *Letters to Dr. Kugelmann*, pp. 102-9.

[2] *L'Internationale*, pp. 211-13 and *L'Internationale et le jacobinisme . . .*, vol. I, pp. 19, 30-4.

[3] *L'Internationale*, pp. 159-214 and 215.   [4] *Op. cit.*, p. 120.

BIBLIOGRAPHY

PRIMARY SOURCES

PRIMARY sources consist of all statements issued by the General Council of the International, together with manuscripts, newspaper articles, pamphlets and books written by participants in or opponents of the International during the period 1860–74. Other material is classified in a separate section devoted to secondary sources. Newspapers, periodicals and pamphlets are from London unless otherwise stated. The year denotes the first reference to a newspaper or periodical to appear in the book. Location of material is given for manuscripts and leaflets.

This section is subdivided as follows:

    (a) MSS.
    (b) Statements of the General Council; Congress Reports and Resolutions
    (c) Newspapers and Periodicals
    (d) Marx-Engels
    (e) Contemporary Pamphlets, Articles and Books

(a) *MSS.*

(1) Minutes of the Amalgamated Society of Engineers — Amalgamated Engineering Union, London

(2) Minutes of the Birmingham Trades Council, 1870–2 — Birmingham City Library

(3) Minutes of the British Federal Council of the I.W.M.A. 1872–1873 — Biblioteca Feltrinelli, Milan (F)

(4) British Federal Council Draft Programme. Nottingham, July 1872 — International Institute of Social History, Amsterdam (I.I.S.G.)

(5) British Federal Council Report by C. Keen. 9.1.1872 — I.I.S.G.

(6) Minutes of the General Council of the I.W.M.A.
    1864–6
    1866–9 — Bishopsgate Institute, London (Bis.)
    1869–72 — I.I.S.G.

The Minutes for 1864–8 have now been published in Russian Translation: Generalny Soviet Pervovo Internationala 1864–1868. Protokoly Londonskaya Konferentsia 1865 goda, Moscow, 1961–3. English edition in preparation.

(7) George Howell's Summary of the Minutes of the G.C. of the I.W.M.A. 1866–9 — Bis.

(8) The copybook of the International American Section, and of General Council after its transfer to New York. — Wisconsin State Library. Microfilm, Chimen Abramsky. (CA.)

(Partly published by S. Bernstein.) — Annali; Istituto G. Feltrinelli

(9) Minutes of the Labour Representation League. 1873–8 — London School of Economics and Political Science

(10) Minutes of the London Trades Council, 1860–76 — Microfilm, CA.

(11) National Reform League 1865–9. Secretary's letter books, 4 vols. Executive Council Minutes, 5 vols. Account, Ledgers, Cashbooks, etc., 6 vols. Miscellaneous papers, 3 vols. — Bis.

(12) Beesly's letters to Marx. 1867–1877 — Institute of Marxism-Leninism, Moscow. (I.M.L.) Microfilm, Dr. Royden Harrison

(13) Letters to British Federal Council — I.I.S.G.

(14) Letter from George Eccarius to Isaac Butt, 6.1.1870, written on behalf of the G.C. — Dublin National Library

(15) Letters to Engels on International in Engels Nachlass — I.I.S.C.

(16) John Hales. Two drafts of letter to *La Liberté*, April 1873. One also signed by Jung and de Paepe — I.I.S.G.

(17) G. J. Holyoake's Diary — Bis.

(18) George Howell's Diaries from 1864 to 1870 — Bis.

(19) George Howell's Notes for an Autobiography — Bis.

(20) Letters to Jung on International — I.I.S.G.

(21) R. S. Kirk. The Second Annual Congress of Trades Unions (August 23–28, 1869) — Birmingham City Library

(22) MSS. of Marx's address to the   I.I.S.G.
G.C. on Poland, 1865, 57 pp.

(23) MSS. Marx's letter to an anonym-   Auctioned at Sotheby's in
ous correspondent, 14.7.1875   London, February 6,
                                            1952

(24) Letters to Marx on International   I.I.S.G.
in Marx Nachlass

(25) H. H. Sparling. Collections for   British Museum Add.
History of 'First International'.   MSS. 41,089
(A bibliography of published
material by son-in-law of William Morris, 1893)

(26) Correspondence of Waring Bros.   H.O. 450.5.7853, August
and Home Office on Belgian   1866. Public Records
riots   Office

(b) *ADDRESSES AND STATEMENTS OF THE G.C.,
CONGRESS REPORTS AND RESOLUTIONS*
(Chronologically arranged. The name of the writer is in brackets)

BRITISH FEDERAL COUNCIL OFFICIAL PUBLICATIONS

(K. Marx) Address and Provincial Rules of the Workingmen's
International Association. Established September 28, 1864. At
a public meeting held at St. Martin's Hall, Long Acre, London.
Printed at the *Beehive* Newspaper Office, 1864. Also in Marx-
Engels Selected Works, vol. 1, Moscow, 1950, pp. 342-53. (Also
in *Founding of The First International*)

The Founding of The First International. A Documentary Record
edited by L. E. Mins, New York, International Publishers, 1937

(K. Marx) Rules of the I.W.M.A. founded September 28, 1864.
London, Westminster Printing Co., n.d. (1866)

(K. Marx) Address of the I.W.M.A. to Abraham Lincoln, *Beehive*,
No. 169, January 7, 1865. Reprinted in K. Marx and F. Engels,
The Civil War in the United States, 1939, pp. 279-81

(K. Marx) Address of the I.W.M.A. to President Johnson, *Beehive*,
No. 188, May 20, 1865. Reprinted in K. Marx and F. Engels,
The Civil War in the United States, pp. 235-8

(K. Marx) Agenda for London Conference, 1865, one-page leaflet
(Moscow, I.M.L.) In Russian, *Soc.*, vol. 13/1, p. 394

(K. Marx) Instructions to Delegates of the Provisional Central
Council on Certain Questions. September 1866. *The Working
Man*, March 1, April 6, 1867. In Russian, *Soc.*, vol. 13/1,
pp. 195-204. (The French text, which was published simultaneously with the English text in *Courrier International* was
reprinted in *La Première Internationale*, edited by Jacques Frey-
mond, vol. I, pp. 27-36.) Geneva, 1962

Geneva Congress, September 1866

An Appeal from the British members of the General Council to their
fellow working men of the United Kingdom. E. Bottigelli, Paris
Ier Congrès Ouvrier de l'Association Internationale des Travailleurs
tenu à Genève, du 3 au 8 septembre 1866. Geneva, 1866,
30 pp. (Reprinted in full in *La Première Internationale*, vol. I,
op. cit., pp. 61-84)
Leaflet on Poland, January 22, 1867. Bis.
(K. Marx) Address of the G.C. of I.W.M.A. to members, Local
Organisations and all workers. August 1867. *Beehive*, August
17, 1867. In Russian, *Soc.*, vol. 13/1, pp. 402-4

Lausanne Congress, September 1867

(G. J. Eccarius) Report of G.C. of the I.W.M.A. to the Lausanne
Congress, September 1867. *The Times*, September 6, 1867
Procès-verbaux du Congrès de l'Association Internationale des
Travailleurs réuni à Lausanne du 2 au 8 septembre, 1867.
Chaux-de-Fonds, 1867
Rapports lus au Congrès Ouvrier réuni du 2 au 8 septembre 1867 à
Lausanne. Chaux-de Fonds, 1867. (The two booklets have
been reprinted in *La Première Internationale*, vol. I, *op. cit.*,
pp. 111-236
(K. Marx) The Imprisoned Fenians in Manchester and the I.W.M.A.,
November 20, 1867. One-page leaflet. Original in I.I.S.G. In
Russian, *Soc.*, vol. 13/1, pp. 261-2. Also in *Beehive*, November
23, 1867
(K. Marx) Resolution of G.C. of I.W.M.A., against F. Pyat, July 7,
1868. Printed in *Beehive*, No. 352, July 18, 1868. In Russian,
Soc., vol. 13/1, p. 271
(K. Marx) The Resolution of the G.C. of I.W.M.A., July 14, 1868,
on the Conduct of the English Government in relation to Polish
Emigrants. *Beehive*, No. 352, July 18, 1868. In Russian, *Soc.*,
vol. 13/1, p. 272

Brussels Congress, September 1868

(K. Marx) Report of G.C. of the I.W.M.A. to the Brussels Congress.
The Times, September 9, 1868. In Russian, *Soc.*, vol. 1/1,
pp. 274-8
Troisième Congrès de l'Association Internationale des Travailleurs,
Compte rendu officiel, Brussels, 1868. (The report is printed in
La Première Internationale, *op. cit.*, pp. 239-447)
(K. Marx, Editor) The I.W.M.A. office of General Council, 256
High Holborn, W.C. Resolutions of the Congress of Geneva,
1866, and the Congress of Brussels, 1868. London, n.d., 1868

(K. Marx) The I.W.M.A. and the Alliance of Socialist Democracy, December 22, 1868. In Russian, *Soc.*, vol. 13/1, pp. 290-2. (Written originally in French and signed by all the members of the G.C.) Original in I.I.S.G. Also in *Les Prétendues Scissions dans l'Internationale*, Geneva, 1872, pp. 7-8

The G.C. of the I.W.M.A. to the Central Bureau of the International Alliance of Socialist Democracy, March 9, 1869. In Russian, *Soc.*, vol. 13/1, pp. 295-6 (written originally in French). Original in I.I.S.G. Also in *Les Prétendues Scissions*, pp. 8-9

(F. Engels) Report on the Unions of Miners in Saxony. Abridged in *Beehive*, February 27, 1869. Full text in *Social Demokrat*, No. 33, March 17, 1869. In Russian, *Soc.*, vol. 13/1, pp. 297-303. (Report was delivered by Marx, but was prepared by Engels and translated into German by Marx)

(K. Marx) Belgian Massacres. To the workmen of Europe and United States. London, 1869, I.I.S.G. In Russian, *Soc.*, vol. 13/1, pp. 304. Full text in *Beehive*, May 8, 1869. Abridged in *Social Economist*, No. 28, June 1, 1869

(K. Marx) Address to the National Labour Union of the United States. *Beehive*, May 15, 1869. Four-page leaflet, London, 1869. I.I.S.G. In Russian, *Soc.*, vol. 13/1, pp. 309-11

Basle Congress, September 1869

(K. Marx) Report of the G.C. to the Fourth Annual Congress of the I.W.M.A., held at Basle in Switzerland. London, 1869. In Russian, *Soc.*, vol. 13/1, pp. 322-35

Association Internationale des Travailleurs. Compte-rendu du IVe-Congrès International, tenu à Bâle en septembre 1869. (Reprinted in full in *La Première Internationale*, *op. cit.*, vol. II, Geneva, 1962, pp. 5-131)

(K. Marx, Editor) Report of the Fourth Annual Congress of the International Working Men's Association, held at Basle in Switzerland. From 6 to 11 September 1869. Published by the General Council Office, 256 High Holborn, London, W.C., 1869

Baselski Kongress Pervovo Internationala, 1869, ed. by V. Adoratski. Moscow, 1934

(K. Marx) Resolution of G.C. on the Policy of Gladstone in relation to the imprisoned Irish. *Reynolds's Weekly*, November 21, 1869. In Russian, *Soc.*, vol. 13/1, p. 339

(K. Marx) The General Council to the F.C. of the Swiss Romande in Geneva, January 1, 1870. *In Letters to Kugelmann*, pp. 105-9. Originally written in French. Mimeographed copy in I.I.S.G.

(K. Marx) The G.C. of the I.W.M.A. to members of the Russian Section in Geneva, March 24, 1870. In *Narodnoye Delo*, No. 1, April 1870, Geneva. In Russian, *Soc.*, vol. 13/1, pp. 353-4

K. Marx) Confidential Communication, March 1870. *In Letters to*

Kugelmann, pp. 102-10. (Reprinted in *La Première Internationale*, *op. cit.*, vol. II, pp. 133-8)

(K. Marx) Resolution of the G.C. of the I.W.M.A. of April 26, 1870, against the *Beehive*. In *Volkstaat*, May 11, 1870. In Russian, *Soc.*, vol. 13/1, p. 377

Declaration of the G.C. of the I.W.M.A. London, May 3, 1870. I.I.S.G.

(K. Marx) On the persecutions of the members of the French sections of the I.W.M.A. *La Liberté*, May 8, 1870. In Russian, *Soc.*, vol. 13/1, pp. 378-9

(K. Marx) Resolution of the G.C. of the I.W.M.A., May 10, 1870, against the London French Branch. I.I.S.G. In Russian, *Soc.*, vol. 13/1, p. 380

(K. Marx) Resolution of the G.C. of the I.W.M.A., May 17, 1870, on convening a Congress in Mayence. *Volkstaat*, No. 42, May 25, 1870. In Russian, *Soc.*, vol. 13/1, p. 381

(K. Marx) Letter in *Tagwacht*, Zurich, No. 16, June 4, 1870. Photostat (Bert Andreas, Geneva)

(K. Marx) The Lock-Out of the Building Trades at Geneva. London. July 5, 1870. Signed on behalf of G.C. by B. Lucraft, John Weston and George Eccarius. I.I.S.G. In Russian, *Soc.*, vol. 13/1, pp. 382-4

(K. Marx) Die Aussperrung der Bauarbeiter zu Genf. Leipzig, W. Liebknecht, 1870. In addition to the above signature, also signed by Marx as correspondent for Germany

(K. Marx) The Fifth Annual Congress of the I.W.M.A., London July 12, 1870. One-page leaflet signed by Lucraft, Weston and Eccarius. I.I.S.G. In Russian, *Soc.*, vol. 13/1, p. 385

(K. Marx) The G.C. of the I.W.M.A. on the war. London, July 23, 1870. (In K. Marx, *The Civil War in France*, any edition.) Original in I.I.S.G.

The G.C. of the I.W.M.A. on the war. Second Address of the G.C. on Franco-Prussian War. London, September 9, 1870. (In K. Marx, *The Civil War in France*, any edition.) Original in British Museum. BM

(K. Marx) Resolution of the G.C. of the I.W.M.A. on Tolain's expulsion. *L'Internationale*, May 14, 1871. In Russian, *Soc.*, vol. 13/1, p. 283

(K. Marx) *The Civil War in France*. Ed. R. W. Postgate. London, 1921, p. 49. (The original edition of June 14, 1871, London, went through three editions within three months)

(K. Marx) *The Civil War in France*, with an introduction by F. Engels. London, 1937

John Hales (K. Marx) on behalf of G.C. to the Editor, *The Times*, June 13, 1871. In Russian, *Soc.*, vol. 13/2, p. 341

John Hales (K. Marx) on behalf of the G.C. to the Editor, *Daily News, Eastern Post*, July 1, 1871. In Russian, *Soc.*, vol. 13/2, pp. 345-6

(K. Marx) Mr. Washburne, the American Ambassador in Paris.

London, 256 High Holborn, W.C. July 11, 1871. Marx Memorial Library, London

London Conference, September 1871

Resolutions of the Conference of the International Working Men's Association, held in London, September 1871. London, 1871. Goldsmiths' Library, London

(K. Marx, Editor) General Rules and Administrative Regulations of the I.W.M.A. Official Edition, revised by the G.C. London, 1871. Marx Memorial Library, London

(K. Marx, Editor) Résolutions des délégués de la conférence de l'AIdT. Réunie à Londres, du 17 au 23 septembre, 1871. London, l'Association Internationale, 1871. I.I.S.G.

(K. Marx, Editor) Statuts généraux et règlements administratifs de l'AIdT, London, 1871. (The last two items reprinted in *La Première Internationale*, vol. II, pp. 233-96)

Londonskaya Konferentsia Pervovo Internationala, 1871. Moscow, 1936

(K. Marx) Resolution of the G.C. of the I.W.M.A. to expel Durand. October 6, 1871. In Russian, *Soc.*, vol. 13/2, p. 366

(K. Marx) Resolution of G.C. of the I.W.M.A. of October 19, 1871, on Nechayev. *Eastern Post*, October 21, 1871. *Der Volkstaat*, November 1, 1871. In Russian, *Soc.*, vol. 13/2, p. 367

John Hales (K. Marx) on behalf of the G.C. of the I.W.M.A. to the Editor, the *Eastern Post*, November 11, 1871. In Russian, *Soc.*, vol. 13/2, pp. 321-2

(K. Marx) Les Prétendues Scissions dans l'Internationale. Circulaire privée du Conseil Général de l'AIdT. Geneva, 1872

(K. Marx and F. Engels) Declaration of G.C. of the I.W.M.A. on the search of Outin. *The Eastern Post*, February 27, 1872. In Russian, *Soc.*, vol. 13/2, pp. 387-8

(K. Marx) Resolution of the G.C. of the I.W.M.A. on the split in the federation of the U.S. Passed at the meeting of March 5, and 12, 1872. In Russian, *Soc.*, vol. 13/2, pp. 434-6

(K. Marx, J. P. McDonnell and J. Milner) Police Terrorism in Ireland. London, April 9, 1872. Signed by G.C. members. Original in I.I.S.G. In Russian, *Soc.*, vol. 13/2, pp. 140-1

(K. Marx) An Address of the G.C. of the I.W.M.A. in connection with the speech of Cochrane against the International. *The Eastern Post*, April 20, 1872. Also published as a leaflet. Signed by the members of the G.C. Original in I.I.S.G. In Russian, *Soc.*, vol. 13/2, pp. 442-7

(F. Engels) Report of the Saragossa Congress of the Spanish Section of the International. The *Eastern Post*, May 12, 1872. In Russian, *Soc.*, vol. 13/2, pp. 448-51

(K. Marx) The Declaration of the G.C. of the I.W.M.A. relating to the 'Universal Federalist Council'. *The International Herald*

June 1, 1872. Signed by the members of the G.C. In Russian, *Soc.*, vol. 13/2, pp. 352-4

(F. Engels) Resolution of the G.C. of the I.W.M.A. of June 18, 1872, on the Agenda and Congress Resolutions in the Hague. *International Herald*. In Russian, *Soc.*, vol. 13/2, pp. 458-9

(F. Engels) On the Bakuninist 'Alliance'. *La Emancipación*, August 17, 1872. Signed by the members of the G.C. In Russian, *Soc.*, vol. 13/2, pp. 472-4

(F. Engels) The G.C. A Circular letter to all members of the I.W.M.A. August 1872. In Russian, *Soc.*, vol. 13/2, pp. 475-80

(F. Engels) The G.C. on the Madrid Federation. *La Emancipación*, August 24, 1872. In Russian, *Soc.*, vol. 13/2, pp. 481-2

Hague Congress, September 1872

(K. Marx) The Report of the G.C. to the Fifth Annual Congress of the I.W.M.A. in Hague, meeting from September 2 to September 7, 1872. The *International Herald*, October 5, 12 and 19, 1872. In Russian, *Soc.*, vol. 13/2, pp. 483-91

Offizieller Bericht des Londoner Generalraths, verlesen in der Öffentlichen Sitzung des Internationalen Kongresses, Braunschweig, 1872. I.I.S.G.

(Maltman Barry) Report of the Fifth Annual General Congress of the I.W.M.A. held at the Hague, Holland, September 2-9, 1872. London, 1872. (First printed in the *Standard*)

The First International. Minutes of the Hague Congress of 1872 with related documents. Edited and translated by Hans Gerth, Madison, University of Wisconsin Press, 1958. This contains Sorge's account and Barry's reports. (For the French edition of a report of the Hague, in *La Première Internationale*, vol. II, pp. 317-80)

(F. Engels) Report on behalf of the G.C. to the Hague Congress on the Alliance of Socialist Democracy. In Russian, *Soc.*, vol. 13/2, pp. 492-502

AIdT Résolution du Congrès Général tenu à la Haye du 2 au 7 septembre 1872, Londres, 1872

AIdT Congres de la Haye, 1872. Geneva, 1872

(F. Engels) Report of the G.C. of the I.W.M.A. upon the situation in Spain, Portugal and Italy, October 31, 1872, in *Briefe und Auszüge aus Briefen an F. A. Sorge, und andere*, pp. 66-70

British Federation of the I.W.M.A. Address of the British Federal Council to the Branches, Sections, Affiliated Societies, and Members of the Federation. 1872

Resolutions of London Conference of British Federal Council, 1873. I.I.S.G.

(F. Engels) I.W.M.A. The Manchester Foreign Section to all Sections and Members of the British Federation. Manchester,

December 1872. Photostat, C.A. In Russian, *Soc.*, vol. 13/2, pp. 530-4

(F. Engels) I.W.M.A. Address of the British Federal Council and the Sections, Branches, Affiliated Societies and Members. London, *International Herald*. December 1872, Photostat, CA.

General and British Federative Rules of the I.W.M.A. together with a report of the Second Annual Congress of the British Federation held at Manchester, June 1 and 2, 1872. London, published by the British Federal Council, n.d. (1873)

(K. Marx, F. Engels and P. Lafargue) L'Alliance de la démocratie socialiste et l'Association Internationale des Travailleurs. Londres, 1873. (Reprinted in *La Première Internationale, op. cit.*, vol. II, pp. 381-478)

The Workingman's Voice on the Normal Working Day. From *Das Kapital*, by Karl Marx. London. A Few Citizens of the I.W.M.A., 1872. Leaflet. L.S.E.

(c) NEWSPAPERS AND JOURNALS

Amalgamated Society of Carpenters and Joiners. *Monthly Reports*, 1866
Beehive, 1862
Bookbinders' Trade Circular, 1872
Builders' Trade Circular, 1869
Chelsea News, 1868
Commonweal, 1889
Contemporary Review, 1872
Courrier International, 1867
Daily News, 1865
Daily Telegraph, 1861
Diplomatic Review, 1867
Dublin Review, October 1871
Eastern Morning News, 1869
Eastern Post, 1871
Edinburgh Review, 1859
Evening Star, 1865
Examiner, 1871
Express, 1871. (In Larcom papers, Dublin)
Fortnightly Review, 1867
Fraser's Magazine, 1871
Freeman, Dublin, 1872
Glasgow Sentinel, 1867
Globe, 1869
The Industrial Magazine and Trades' Co-operative Record
Industrial Partnership Record, 1867 (later the *Social Economist*, Rochdale)
International Courier, 1867

International Herald, 1872

Leader, 1859

Lloyds' Weekly London Newspaper, 1869

Manchester Guardian, 1871

Miner and Workman's Advocate, 1864 (later *Workman's Advocate, Advocate,* then *Commonwealth*)

Morning Advertiser, 1868

Morning Post, 1869

Morning Star, 1863

National Reformer, 1869

National Review, 1883

Newcastle Weekly Chronicle, Newcastle-on-Tyne, 1867

New Moral World, 1843

New York Daily Tribune, New York, 1862

Nineteenth Century, 1878

North American Review, Boston, 1872

Northern Star, 1847

Notes to the People, 1851

Observer, 1871

Operative Bricklayers' Society's Trade Circular, 1861

Operative Stone Masons' Friendly Society, Fortnightly Return Sheet, 1865

Pall Mall Gazette, 1869

People's Paper, 1855

Pioneer, 1834

La Presse, Paris, 1865

Progress, 1883

Quarterly Review, 1871

Qui Vive, 1871

Reasoner, 1860

Republican, 1870

Revue Contemporaine, Paris, 1866

Revue des Deux Mondes, Paris, 1866

Reynolds's Weekly Newspaper, 1850

St. Crispin, 1877

Saturday Review, 1868

Scotsman, 1871

Sheffield and Rotherham Independent, 1869

Social Economist, 1869

Spectator, 1871

Standard, 1868

Tablet, 1871

Tailor, 1866 (later *Tailor and Cutter*)

The Times, 1863

The Vanguard, ed. by G. J. Harney. London, 1853 (Goldsmiths' Library)

Der Vorbote, ed. by Joh. Phil Becker. Geneva, 1866–71. (The organ of the German-speaking group of the I.W.M.A.)

Weekly Dispatch, 1862
The Workingman's Advocate. (Chicago, 1869)
Workman's Advocate, 1866 (later *Commonwealth*)
Workman, 1861 (later *Working Man*)
World, New York, 1871

(d) *MARX-ENGELS*

(i) Books and Collections
(ii) Articles on the I.W.M.A. published between 1864–83.
(Original mentioned and if available in English. Otherwise the *Soc.* reference is given.) Individual letters posthumously issued are not classified separately. (See also section : Addresses and Statements of the G.C.)

(i) *Books and Collections*

Aus der Frühzeit des Marxismus. Engels' Briefwechsel mit Kautsky, edited by Karl Kautsky. Prague, 1935
Archiv Marxa i Engelsa, vol. III (VIII). Ed. V. Adoratski, Moscow, 1934. (Contains the early drafts of *The Civil War in France*)
Karl Marx-Friedrich Engels. Briefe an A. Bebel, W. Liebknecht, K. Kautsky *und andere*, vol. I, 1870–1886. Ed. V. Adoratski. Moscow, 1933
Briefe und Auszüge aus Briefen von Joh. Phil. Becker, Jos. Dietzen, Friedrich Engels, Karl Marx, *und andere* an F. Sorge *und andere*. Stuttgart, 1906
Karl Marx and Friedrich Engels. Die Briefe an Danielson (Nicolai-on). Ed. Kurt Mandelbaum. Leipzig, 1929
Karl Marx-Friedrich Engels. Briefwechsel, vols. 3 and 4, 1861–1867, 1868–1883. Berlin, 1950
Karl Marx. Capital, vol. 1, 1946
Karl Marx and Friedrich Engels. The Civil War in the United States, New York, n.d.
Karl Marx. La Commune de Paris, traduction, préface et notes de Charles Longuet. Paris, 1901. (This edition contains useful biographic material of I.W.M.A. members)
Friedrich Engels. Po und Rhein. Hamburg, 1859
Friedrich Engels, Paul et Laura Lafargue. Correspondance 1868–1880, Tome I. Ed. Émile Bottigelli. Paris, 1956
Karl Marx. Critique of the Gotha Programme. Ed. C. P. Dutt, n.d.
F. Engels. On the Death of Karl Marx. March 14, 1883. London, 1933
Marx-Engels-Lenin-Stalin. Facsimiles. Moscow, 1939. (Containing Marx's Nationalisation of the Land ; Letter to President Lincoln)
Karl Marx. La Guerre civile en France, 1871, accompagnée des travaux préliminaires de Karl Marx. Paris, 1953. (This

Y

contains the two preliminary drafts of the Civil War in France and cuttings of newspapers)

Friedrich Engels. Internationales aus dem Volkstaat (1871–7). Berlin, 1954

Karl Marx and Friedrich Engels. Letters to Americans, 1848–1895. New York, 1953

Karl Marx. Letters to Dr. Kugelmann, n.d.

Friedrich Engels. Notes on the War. Sixty articles reprinted from the *Pall Mall Gazette*, 1870–1871. Ed. Friedrich Adler. Vienna, 1923

Karl Marx, F. Engels, V. I. Lenin. O Proletarskom Internationalisme. Moscow, 1957

Karl Marx and Friedrich Engels. Selected Correspondence 1846–1895. Ed. Dona Torr, 1936

Perepiska K. Marxa i F. Engels s Russkimi Politicheskimi Deyateliami. Moscow, 1947

Marx-Engels Selected Correspondence. Moscow, 1956

Marx Engels Selected Works, 2 vols. Moscow, 1948–1950

Marx-Engels. Sochinenia, vols. 13/1, 13/2, 15, 16/1, 16/2, 23-27, 29. Moscow, Marx-Engels-Lenin Institute, 1930–1946

Marx-Engels. Sochinenia, vols. 1-32. Moscow. (Series not yet finished) 1955–1964

Karl Marx. Value, Price and Profit. 1938

Marx-Engels Scritti italiani. Ed. by Bosio. Milan, 1955

Karl Marx. Die Polnische Frage. Ed. Werner Conze and Dieter Hertz-Eichenrode. The Hague, 1961

Karl Marx. A Workers' Enquiry. April 20, 1880. London, 1933

(ii) *Letters and Articles on the I.W.M.A.*

K. Marx, on Proudhon. January 24, 1865. Letter to J. B. Schweitzer in *Social-Demokrat*, No. 16, 17, 18. February 1, 3, 5, 1865. English in Sel. Works, vol. 1. Moscow, 1951, pp. 354-60

F. Engels and K. Marx. February 23, 1865. Letter to Social-Demokrat, in *Social-Demokrat*, No. 29, March 3, 1865. Original in *ibid.*, p. 840. Russian in *Soc.*, vol. 13/1, p. 78

K. Marx. *To the Reform*, No. 78, April 1865. Russian in *Soc.*, vol. 13/1, p. 35

K. Marx. Correction. *Der Weisse Adler*, Geneva, April 22, 1865. Russian in *Soc.*, vol. 13/1, pp. 91-2

H. Marx. Value, Price and Profit. May 1865. London, 1898, S.W., vol. 1, pp. 361-405

H. Jung (K. Marx). Letter to the Editor, *Écho de Verviers*, No. 43, February 20, 1866. Russian in *Soc.*, vol. 13/1, pp. 395-400

F. Engels. What have the Working Classes to do with Poland? In *Commonwealth*, March 24, 31 and May 5, 1866. Reprinted by D. Ryazanoff in Grünberg's *Archiv*, vol. 6, pp. 212-19. Russian in *Soc.*, vol. 13/1, pp. 151-61

F. Engels. Notes on War in Germany. *Manchester Guardian*, Nos. 6190, 6194, 6197, 6214, June 20, 25, 28, July 3 and 6, 1866. Russian in *Soc.*, vol. 13/1, pp. 167-189

Karl Marx. A Warning. May 4, 1866, in *Mitteldeutsche Volkszeitung*, No. 184, August 10, 1866. Russian in *Soc.*, vol. 13/1, pp. 162-3

Karl Marx. Speech on Poland. January 22, 1867. Russian in *Soc.*, vol. 13/1, pp. 190-4. English original has so far not been found

Karl Marx. Letter to *Zeitung fuer Norddeutschland*, February 18, 1867. Russian in *Soc.*, vol. 13/1, p. 205

Karl Marx. Plagiatoren, in *Zukunft*. No. 291, December 12, 1867. Russian in *Soc.*, vol. 13/1, pp. 263-8

Karl Marx. Effects of Machinery. Speech delivered in the G.C. *Beehive*, August 1, 1868. Reprinted in Labour Monthly, 1956, pp. 331-3

Karl Marx, To the President and Board of the German Womens' Union, in *Social-Demokrat*, No. 100, August 28, 1868. Russian in *Soc.*, vol. 13/1, p. 273

F. Engels, on the Dissolution of the Lassallean Womens' Union, in *Demokratisches Wochenblatt*, No. 40, October 3, 1868. Russian in *Soc.*, vol. 13/1, pp. 279-82

F. Engels, on the Dissolution of the Lassallean Union, in *Demokratisches Wochenblatt*, No. 41, October 10, 1868. Russian in *Soc.*, vol. 13/1, p. 283

Karl Marx. Note on M. Hirsch, in *Demokratisches Wochenblatt*, No. 42, October 17, 1868. Russian in *Soc.*, vol. 13/1, pp. 285-6

Karl Marx. How Mr. Gladstone's Bank Letter Procured a Loan for Russia, in *Diplomatic Review*, December 2, 1868. Russian in *Soc.*, vol. 13/1, pp. 287-9

Karl Marx. Preface to the Second Edition of the Eighteenth Brumaire of Louis Bonaparte, June 23, 1869, in the Eighteenth Brumaire, London, 1939, pp. 17-19

F. Engels, Karl Marx, in *Zukunft*, No. 185, August 2, 1869. Russian in *Soc.*, vol. 13/1, pp. 314-21

Karl Marx. Nationalisation of the Land, in Facsimiles—Marx-Engels-Lenin-Stalin, Moscow, 1939. Reprinted in *Labour Monthly*, 1952, pp. 415-17

Karl Marx. The English Government and the Imprisoned Fenians. In *L'Internationale*, No. 59, February 27 and No. 60, March 6, 1870. Russian in *Soc.*, vol. 13/1, pp. 405-11

J. Williams (Jenny Marx). Eight Articles on the Irish Question. *La Marseillaise*, Nos. 71, March 1, 1870; 79, March 9, 1870; 89, March 19, 1870; 91, March 21, 1870; 99, March 29, 1870; 113, April 12, 1870; 118, April 17, 1870 and 125, April 24, 1870. Russian in *Soc.*, vol. 13/1, pp. 412-29

F. Engels. Preface to 'The Peasant war in Germany', April 1870. In *The Peasant War in Germany*

H. Jung. (K. Marx.) The G.C. to Romand F.C. June 29, 1870. In *Le Mirabeau*, No. 53, July 24, 1870. Russian in *Soc.*, vol. 13/1

Karl Marx to *Volkstaat*.   *Der Volkstaat*, No. 26, March 29, 1871.
    Russian in *Soc.*, vol. 13/2, 278-80

Marx to *The Times*.   *The Times*, April 4, 1871.   Russian in *Soc.*, vol.
    13/2, p. 281

Karl Marx to Coenen, Editor of *De Werker*.   *De Werker*, April 8,
    1871.   Russian in *Soc.*, vol. 13/2, p. 280

F. Engels.   On the strike of the Antwerp Cigarmakers.   *Der Volkstaat*,
    April 12, 1871.   Russian in *Soc.*, vol. 13/2, p. 282

F. Engels, once again Herr Vogt.   *Der Volkstaat*, No. 38, May 10,
    1871.   Russian in *Soc.*, vol. 13/2, pp. 284-90

Karl Marx to the Editor, *Pall Mall Gazette*.   *Pall Mall Gazette*,
    June 9, 1871.   Russian in *Soc.*, vol. 13/2, p. 338

Karl Marx to the Editor, *Neue Freie Presse*.   *Neue Freie Presse*,
    Vienna, July 4, 1871.   Russian in *Soc.*, vol. 13/2, p. 344

Marx to the Editor, the *Eastern Post*, July 1, 1871.   Russian in *Soc.*,
    vol. 13/2, p. 387

Karl Marx to the *Pall Mall Gazette*.   *The Eastern Post*, July 8, 1871.
    Russian in *Soc.*, vol. 13/2, p. 348

F. Engels.   Correspondence in *Volkstaat*.   *Der Volkstaat*, July 5, 1871.
    Russian in *Soc.*, vol. 13/2, pp. 349-50

Karl Marx to the Editor, *Morning Advertiser*, July 13, 1871.   Russian
    in *Soc.*, vol. 13/2, p. 356

Marx to the Editor, *Standard*, July 17, 1871.   Russian in *Soc.*, vol.
    13/2, p. 356

Karl Marx to *The Times*, August 7, 1871.   Russian in *Soc.*, vol. 13/2, p. 357

Marx to the Editor, *L'Internationale*.   *Der Volkstaat*, August 23, 1871.
    Russian in *Soc.*, vol. 13/2, p. 359

Karl Marx to the Editor, *Public Opinion*, August 26, 1871.   Russian
    in *Soc.*, vol. 13/2, p. 360

Karl Marx to *Le Gaulois*, August 27, 1871.   Russian in *Soc.*, vol. 13/2,
    p. 361

Karl Marx to the Editor, *La Vérité*, September 3, 1871.   Russian in
    Soc., vol. 13/2, p. 362

Karl Marx to the Editor, *Evening Standard*, September 6, 1871.
    Russian in *Soc.*, vol. 13/2, p. 363

K. Marx.   Speech at the Seventh Anniversary of the I.W.M.A. *The
    World*, New York, October 15, 1871.   Russian in *Soc.*, vol. 13/2,
    pp. 666-8

K. Marx to the Editor, *Woodhull and Claflin's Weekly*, October 21,
    1871.   Russian in *Soc.*, vol. 13/2, p. 365

F. Engels.   Correspondence, *Der Volkstaat*, No. 91, November 10,
    1871.   Russian in *Soc.*, vol. 13/2, pp. 368-70

Marx to the Editor, *Frankfurter Zeitung*, November 28, 1871.   Russian
    in *Soc.*, vol. 13/2, p. 373

F. Engels to the Editor, *La Roma del Popolo*, December 21, 1871.
    Russian in *Soc.*, vol. 13/2, pp. 374-5

K. Marx to the Editor, *The Eastern Post*, December 23, 1871.   Russian
    in *Soc.*, vol. 13/2, p. 376

F. Engels. The Congress in Sonvillier and the International. *Der Volkstaat*, January 10, 1872. Russian in *Soc.*, vol. 13/2, pp. 377-382

K. Marx to the Editor, *The Eastern Post*, January 29, 1872. Russian in *Soc.*, vol. 13/2, p. 383

K. Marx to the Editor, *The Eastern Post*, January 28, 1872. Russian in *Soc.*, vol. 13/2, p. 384

K. Marx to the Editor, *La Liberté*, March 17, 1872. Russian in *Soc.*, vol. 13/2, p. 437

F. Engels to the Citizen Delegates of the Saragossa Congress in Spain. *La Emancipación*, Madrid, April 13, 1872. Russian in *Soc.*, vol. 13/2, pp. 438-9

K. Marx to the Editor of *Gazzettino Rossa*, May 28, 1872. Russian in *Soc.*, vol. 13/2, pp. 455-7

K. Marx and F. Engels. Preface to the Communist Manifesto, June 24, 1872. (In all editions of the C.M.)

F. Engels. The International in America. *Der Volkstaat*, July 17, 1872. Russian in *Soc.*, vol. 13/2, pp. 462-8

K. Marx to the Striking Miners of the Ruhr Province. *Der Volkstaat*, July 27, 1872. Russian in *Soc.*, vol. 13/2, pp. 469-71

K. Marx to the Editor, *Corsaire*, September 15, 1872. Russian in *Soc.*, vol. 13/2, pp. 502-3

K. Marx. Speech at the Meeting in Amsterdam after the Hague Congress, *La Liberté*, Brussels, September 15, 1872. English in Stekloff, *History of the First International*. Pp. 239-42

K. Marx to the Editor, *Daily News*, September 18, 1872. Russian in *Soc.*, vol. 13/2, p. 504

F. Engels to Bignami, *La Plebe*, October 5, 1872. Russian in *Soc.*, vol. 13/2, pp. 511-16

F. Engels. The deciding Mandates at the Hague Congress, *La Emancipación*, October 13, 1872. Russian in *Soc.*, vol. 13/2, pp. 505-10

K. Marx to the Editor, *Der Volkstaat*, October 26, 1872. Russian in *Soc.*, vol. 13/2, pp. 517-18

F. Engels. Report to the G.C. of the I.W.M.A. on the position of the Society in Spain, Portugal and Italy, October 31, 1872. Original in *Briefe an Sorge*, pp. 60-70

F. Engels. Letter from London, *La Plebe*, December 14, 1872. Russian in *Soc.*, vol. 13/2, pp. 524-6

F. Engels and K. Marx. To the Editor, the *International Herald*, December 21, 1872. Russian in *Soc.*, vol. 13/2, pp. 527-9

F. Engels. The Housing Question. S.W., vol. 1, pp. 505-74

F. Engels. On Authority, January-February 1873. *Almanacco Repubblicano per l' Anno 1874*. S.W., vol. 1, pp. 575-8

K. Marx. Political Indifferentism, January 1873. *Almanacco Repubblicano per l' Anno 1874*. Russian in *Soc.*, vol. 15, pp. 85-95

F. Engels. A letter to the Editor, *Der Volkstaat*, No. 37, May 7, 1873. Russian in *Soc.*, vol. 15, pp. 96-8

F. Engels, Die Bakunisten an der Arbeit. *Der Volkstaat*, October 31, November 2 and 5, 1873. In *Internationales aus dem Volkstaat*, Berlin, 1894, pp. 16-33

F. Engels. Notes to Lissagaray's Histoire de la Commune, 1876. Russian in *Soc.*, vol. 15, pp. 360-5

F. Engels. *Karl Marx. Volks-Kalender*, Braunschweig, 1878. S.W., (M), vol. 2, pp. 143-52

K. Marx to the Editor, the *Daily News*, June 13, 1878. On Lothar Bucher. Russian in *Soc.*, vol. 15, pp. 424-5

K. Marx. Mr. George Howell's History of the International Workingmen's Association. *The Secular Chronicle*, Birmingham, August 1878. Reprinted in *Labour Monthly*, vol. 36, No. 9, pp. 417-21. (Slightly abridged)

(e) BOOKS, PAMPHLETS AND LEAFLETS

Appeal to the Workingmen of America, with full text of Preamble and Rules, New York, F. Bolte, May 19, 1872. Wisconsin University Library

AIdT. Protestation contre la guerre. Bruxelles, 1870, p. 2, I.I.S.G.

A.S.E. Monthly Reports, 1867

L'Association Internationale des Travailleurs. Paris, May 1870. 54 pp. (Official Indictment of the French Police on the I.W.M.A.) Goldsmiths' Library

Michael Bakunin. Gesammelte Werke. Ed. Max Nettlau, 3 vols. Berlin, 1921-3-4

Michael Bakunin. Marxism, Freedom and the State. Translated and ed. with Biographical Sketch by K. J. Kenafick. London, Freedom Press, 1950

Michael Bakunin. The Organisation of the International, translated by Freda Cohen. London, Bakunin Press, 1919

M. Bakounine. Œuvres, ed. M. Nettlau (only vol. 1) and G. Guillaume, 6 vols. Paris, 1902–13

Michael Bakunin. The Policy of the International. London, Bakunin Press, 1919

Michael Bakunin's Sozial-politischer Briefwechsel mit Alexander Iw. Herzen und Ogarjow. Ed M. Dragomanov. Stuttgart, 1895

Maltman Barry. To the Electors of Marylebone, 1874. Leaflet. I.I.S.G.

Basle Congress

Volume of English newspaper cuttings on the Basle Congress, September 1869, and kept by Applegarth. Now in L.S.E. The volume contains reports from the following papers:

Sheffield Independent, the report written by Applegarth

The Times, report written by Eccarius
The *Standard*, report written by Onslow Yorke
The *Pall Mall Gazette*
The Sunday Times
The Builder's Trade Circular
The *Eastern Morning News*
The *Morning Star*
The *Saturday Review*
The *Workingman's Advocate*
   In addition, the volume has two leaflets :
(a) Agenda of Congress in English, issued from 256 High Holborn, London, W.C.
(b) Names of delegates in German, published in Basle
G. Mollin. Rapport sur le Congrès de Bâle. Paris, 1870
A. Murat. Chambre Syndicale des Ouvriers mécaniciens de Paris. Paris. Rapport du délégué au Congrès de l'Association Internationale des Travailleurs. Tenu à Bâle (Suisse), Paris, 1869
K. Bürkli. Direct Legislation by the People versus Representative Government. Translated by Eugene Oswald with a preface by W. F. Cowell Stepney. London, 1867
E. S. Beesly. Amalgamated Society of Carpenters in *Fortnightly Review*, London, March 1, 1867
E. S. Beesly. The International Workingmen's Association, in *Fortnightly Review*, November 1870
E. S. Beesly. Letters to the Working Classes, 1870
E. S. Beesly. On the Paris Revolution. *Beehive*, March 25, April 1, 18, 22, 29, May 20, 27, June 3, 10, 17, 1871
E. S. Beesly. The Social Future of the Working Classes
E. S. Beesly. A Word for France : Addressed to the workmen of London. 1870
Martin James Boon. Home Colonisation including a plan showing how all the Unemployed might have profitable Work, and thus prevent want, pauperism, and crime. 1869
Martin James Boon. A Protest against the present emigrationists including remedies for the present stagnation of trade and finally to remove starvation, pauperism and crime. 1869
Martin James Boon. Important to Ratepayers. 1870
Martin James Boon. How to nationalise the Commons and Waste Lands, Railroads, Tramways, Water Works, Gas Works, Public Buildings, and other Works throughout England and the Colonies without the burden of interest. 1873
Bourgeois Republicain (Fiaux ?). Histoire de l'Internationale, 1862–1872. 1873
W. Bracke. Der Braunschweiger Auschuss der Sozial-demokratischen Arbeiterpartei in Loetzen und von dem Gericht. Braunschweig, *Braunschweiger Volksfreund*, 1872
P. Brousse. L'État à Versailles et dans l'Association Intern. des Traveilleurs. Paris, 1873

Resolutions of London Congress of British Federal Council. 1873. I.I.S.G.

Chas. C. Chesney. England and the French Republic. *Fortnightly Review*, November 1871

The Principles and Objects of Communism exposed. The opening of Mission Halls for the Working Classes recommended. 1871. (Originally appeared in the *Record*)

Correspondence between the British and Spanish Governments respecting the International Society: 1872. Presented to both Houses of Parliament by command of Her Majesty, 1872. (C. 502), 1872

S. Crawford. Character of Working Class Association in England and Italy in Transactions of the National Association for Promotion of Social Science, 1862, pp. 629-32

(A. G. Dalseme.) Les Mystères de l'Internationale. Paris, 1871

AIdT. Déclaration de la Section Française Fédéraliste de 1871 siégeant à Londres. 1871. (Thirty-six signatories)

Die Deutschen Schneider in London an ihre Arbeitsgenossen in Deutschland. Leaflet. Ed. K. Marx. London, 1865. Original in I.M.L., Moscow

George J. Eccarius. Eines Arbeiters Widerlegung der National Oekonomischen Lehren, John Stuart Mill's. Hottingen-Zürich, 1888

G. J. Eccarius. The Hours of Labour. A paper read at the Century Club, under the auspices of the Labour Representation League, Thomas Brasey, M.P. in the chair. N.d. (1872)

G. J. Eccarius. The International Workingmen's Association. In *The Times*, October 27, 1871

W. Eichoff. Die Internationale Arbeiter-Association. Berlin, 1868

Charles Ernest. A Word to the Working Classes on the 'Internationale'. 1872

E. E. Fribourg. L'Association Internationale des Travailleurs. Paris, 1871

Congrès Général de l'Association Internationale des Travailleurs (VIe), compte-rendu officiel du Congrès Général de l'Association Internationale des Travailleurs tenu à Genève du 1 au 6 septembre 1873. Le Locle, 1874

Congrès Général de l'Association Internationale des Travailleurs (VIIe), compte-rendu officiel. . . . Bruxelles, septembre 7-13, 1874. Verviers, 1875

Le Grand Chef de l'Internationale. Editorial in *Paris-Journal*, March 17, 1871

William B. Greene. Address of the Internationals, in his book, *Socialistic, Communistic, Mutualistic and Financial Fragments*, Boston, 1875, pp. 225-71

E. Gryzanovski. On the International Workingmen's Association: its origin, doctrine and ethics. *North American Review*, Boston, 1872

Georges Guéroult. Les Théories de l'Internationale. Étude critique. Paris, 1872

N. Domela (Domela Niewenhuis ?). Der Congress der Internationale im Haag, von 2.-7. September, 1872. Translated into German from Dutch. Berlin, 1873

Internationale et révolution à propos du Congrès de la Haye, des réfugiés de la Commune ex-membres du Conseil Général de l'Internationale. 1872

Réponse de quelques internationaux membres de la Fédération à la circulaire privée du Conseil Général de Londres. (Extrait du *Bulletin de la Fédération Jurassienne*.) Neuchâtel, n.d. (1872)

John Hales. To the Electors of the Borough of Hackney. 1874. Leaflet. I.I.S.G.

Hansard, 3rd Series, vols. CCIX-CCX. 1872

Frederic Harrison. The Strike of the Stonemasons in London, 1861–1862, in *Transactions of the N.A.P.S.S.*, London, 1863, pp. 710-22

Lord Hobart. The International and the Manchester School. In the *Fortnightly Review*, 1872, pp. 191-5

G. J. Holyoake. Working Class Representation. 1868

George Howell's Address to the Neapolitan Workers. April 20, 1862. Leaflet in Bis.

L'Internationale, Karl Marx, Mazzini et Bakounine. Brussels, September 1871

Johann Jacoby. The Social Question. A Speech delivered to his constituents on January 20, 1870. London, printed for Private Circulation, 1870

Labour Protection League. June 1877. Leaflet. I.I.S.G.

Lausanne Congress

Reymond. Rapport du Congrès International de Lausanne, 1867. Paris, Mimeographed

Circular of Lessner from *Commonwealth*, August 25, 1866

Congrès Ouvrier Association Internationale des Travailleurs. Paris, M. Fribourg, 1865, reprinted in *La Première Internationale, op. cit.*, vol. I, pp. 16-27

J. M. Ludlow and Lloyd Jones. Progress of the Working Classes, 1832–1867. 1868

Mrs. E. Lynn Linton. The story of Joshua Davidson. 1872

M. B. Zur Geschichte der Internationale. Leipzig. 1872

B. Malon. L'Internationale: son histoire et ses principes. (Extrait de la *République républicaine* de Lyon.) 1872

Mémoire présenté par la Fédération Jurassienne de l'AIdT à toutes les Fédérations de l'Internationale. Sonvillier, 1873

Letters of J. S. Mill. Ed. H. Elliot, 1910. 2 vols.

Charles Murray. A Letter to Mr. George Jacob Holyoake. London. 1855

George Odger. Odger's Monthly, 2 Nos. London, 1871

James Bronterre O'Brien. The Rise, Progress and Phases of Human Slavery, London, 1885. (Originally published as articles in 1850)

The Paris Commune

J. H. Bridges. Why we should stand by France. 1871

Rev. Percival J. Brine. The Revolution and Siege of Paris, with the Elections and entry of the Prussians in 1870–1. 1871

Elliot C. Cowdin. France in 1870–1, New York Cooper Union, 1872

Edinburgh Review, 1871 — article on International

Enquête parlementaire sur l'insurrection du 18 mars. Pièces justificatives. Paris, 1872

W. Pembroke Fetridge. The Rise and Fall of the Paris Commune in 1871. New York, 1871

Fraser's, June and August 1871

A French Positivist. Political Notes on the present situation of France and Paris with a preface by E. S. Beesly. 1871

William Gibson. Paris during the Commune, 1871, being letters from Paris and its neighbourhood. 1872

Le Comte Alfred de la Guéronniere. L'Internationale et la Guerre civile en France. Paris, 1871

Frederic Harrison. The Commune. In the *Fortnightly Review*, August 1871

(Henry Labouchaire) Diary of the Besieged Resident in Paris. 1871

John Leighton. Paris under the Commune: or, the Seventy-three Days of the Second Siege. 1871

G. de Molinari. Le Mouvement socialiste, et les réunions publiques, avant la Révolution du 4 septembre 1870. Paris, 1872

G. de Molinari. Les Clubs Rouges pendant la siège de Paris. Paris, 1871

The Commune and the Internationale. *Quarterly Review*, No. 262, 1871, pp. 549-80

Reviews of :

    Paris sous la Commune, E. Moriac, Paris, 1871

    Le Gouvernement du 4 septembre et la Commune de Paris, 1871

    Les 73 Journées de la Commune, Cartellemandes

    L'Internationale, O. Testut, Paris, 1871

    Le Livre noir de la Commune de Paris, Brussels, 1871

    Civil War in France, London, 1871

    The Programme of the Land Tenure Reform Association. London, 1871

A Resident. Paris during the Siege and a History of the Rise and Fall of the Commune, n.d. (1871)

P. Vésinier. Histoire de la Commune de Paris. London, 1871

P. Vésinier. History of the Commune of Paris. Translated by J. V. Weber, London, 1872

Paris-Journal, Paris, March 10, 1871

    Editorial, Les Scrupules de l'Internationale, *Paris-Journal*, Paris, March 14, 1871

Editorial, Le Grand Chef de l'Internationale, *Paris-Journal*, Paris, March 19, 1871

Lettre du Grand Chef de l'Internationale. (Forgery attributed to Marx)

Letter of Marx to *Paris-Journal*, March 3, 1871

Jacques Populus. Histoire de l'Internationale, Paris, Au Bureau de l'Éclipse. 1871, 128 pp. (The name of the author is a pseudonym)

Police Terrorism in Ireland. Leaflet, McDonnell Papers, 1872

Procès de l'Association Internationale des Travailleurs, Première et Deuxième Commissions du Bureau de Paris. 2nd Ed. Paris, June 1870

Troisième Procès de l'Association Internationale des Travailleurs à Paris. Paris, July 1870

P. J. Proudhon. La Guerre et la paix. 2 vols. Brussels, 1862

P. J. Proudhon. Du principe fédératif. Paris, 1863

P. J. Proudhon. De la capacité politique des classes ouvrières. Paris, 1865

P. J. Proudhon. General Idea of the Revolution in the Nineteenth Century, 1923

Félix Pyat, Besson, A. Talandier. Lettre au Parlement et à la presse. London, 1858

Religion of Humanity. Republic of the West. Papers on the War between France and Germany. 1870

Réponse de quelques membres de la Fédération Jurassienne à la circulaire privée du Conseil Général de Londres, Chaux-de-Fonds, 1872

Proceedings of the First Congress of the American International Workingmen's Association, held in Philadelphia, Pen., July 9 and 10, 1872. Declaration of Principles, Platform and Plan of organisation of the American Confederation of the International Workingmen's Association, New York, 1872

W. H. Riley. Strikes. Their Cause and Remedy. Leeds

W. H. Riley. British Slavery. A Tract dedicated to all Working Men. n.d., *c.* 1873

Les Scrupules de l'Internationale. Editorial on Marx in *Paris-Journal*, March 10, 1871

Proceedings of Separatists and Secessionists of the I.W.M.A. collected by Friedrich Lessner from May 26, 1872 to August 18, 1873. (Newspaper cuttings bound in a volume.) I.I.S.G.

Thomas Smith. Letters on the Commune. The Law of the Revolution: or the Logical Development of Human Society. Reprinted from the *Nottingham Daily Express*, by the Nottingham Branch of the I.W.M.A. March 1872. *Nottingham Daily Express*, 1872

Soho Irish Branch. Leaflet, 1872. I.I.S.G.

Oscar Testut. Die Internationale, ihre Wege and ihre Bestrebungen. Leipzig, 1872

Oscar Testut. L'Internationale. 3rd Ed. Paris, 1871

Oscar Testut. L'Internationale et le jacobinisme au ban de l'Europe. 2 vols. Paris, 1872

Oscar Testut. Le Livre bleu de l'Internationale. Paris, 1871

Organisation and Rules of Trades Unions : First Report. 1867

Trades Societies and Strikes. National Association for the Promotion of Social Science, 1860

Universal Federalist Council of the International Working Men's Association and of Republican and Socialist Societies adhering. 1872

Universal Republican League, April 21, 1871. Leaflet. I.I.S.G.

Edmond Villetard. Histoire de l'Internationale. Paris, 1872

Alfred A. Walton. Co-operative Self-Government Safely and Systematically arranged. N.p., n.d. (1865, Brecon?)

Alfred A. Walton. History of the Landed Tenures. 1865

J. Weston. An Appeal to Edmund Beales to Publicly Renounce or Justify his connection with Sir George Grey, together with Beales's reply. London, n.d. (1870). (Originally appeared in *The Democratic News*, which has not been found)

Thomas Wright. Our New Masters. 1873

Onslow Yorke. The Secret History of the International. 1872

SECONDARY MATERIAL

REFERENCE WORKS AND BIBLIOGRAPHIES

Giuseppe del Bo. La Commune di Parigi. Milan, Istituto Giangiacomo Feltrinelli, 1957, pp. vi, 142

Giuseppe del Bo. La Première Internationale. A Bibliography. 3 vols. Paris, 1958–63

Encyclopédie Socialiste, Syndicale et Coopérative de l'Internationale Ouvrière, 12 vols. Ed. Compère-Morel, Paris, 1912–21

Marx, Karl. Chronik seines Lebens in Einzeldaten. Moscow, 1934

M. Nettlau. Bibliographie de l'Anarchie. Paris, 1897

Maximillian Rubel. Bibliographie des œuvres de K. Marx. Paris, 1956

Josef Stammhammer. Bibliographie des Sozialismus und Kommunismus. 3 vols., Jena. 1893–1909

J. M. Wheeler. A Biographical Dictionary of Freethinkers of all Ages and Nations. The Pioneer Press, 1889

ARTICLES, BOOKS AND PAMPHLETS

Charles Francis Adams. The American Ambassador's Reply to Address of the I.W.M.A. *The Times*, February 6, 1865. Reprinted in K. Marx and F. Engels, *The Civil War in the United States*, pp. 282-3

E. D. Adams. Gt. Britain and the American Civil War. 2 vols. 1925
W. E. Adams. Memoirs of a Social Atom. 2 vols. 1903

Applegarth

A. W. Humphrey. Robert Applegarth: Trade Unionist, Educationist Reformer. 1914
Raymond Postgate. Robert Applegarth, 1834–1924, in Great Democrats, ed. Barratt Brown. London, 1934, pp. 15-25
W. H. G. Armytage. Ruskin as Utopist. (In *Notes and Queries*, May, 1956)
Antony Babel. La Première Internationale: son début et son activité à Genève de 1864 à 1870. In *Mélanges d'Études Économiques et Sociales offerts à William E. Rappard*. Geneva, 1944
L'Association des Ouvriers Anglais, amis de la paix, aux ouvriers de France. 1882. Leaflet. I.I.S.G.
Phillip B. Bagenall. The International. *National Review*, 1883

Bakunin

Fritz Brupbacher. Marx und Bakunin. Ein Beitrag für Geschichte der Internationalen Arbeiterassoziation, Munich. N.d. (1912)
E. H. Carr. Michael Bakunin. 1937
V. Dave. Michel Bakounine et Karl Marx. Brussels, 1900
K. J. Kenafik. Michael Bakunin and Karl Marx. Melbourne, 1948
Max Nettlau. Michael Bakunin. Eine biographische Skizze. Berlin, 1901
Max Nettlau. Bakunin und die Internationale in Italien bis zum Herbst 1872, in Grünberg's *Archiv*, vol. 2. Leipzig, 1912, pp. 275-329
Max Nettlau. Bakunin und die Russische Revolutionaere Bewegung in den Jahren 1868–1873, in Grünberg's *Archiv*, vol. V. Leipzig, 1915, pp. 357-422
Max Nettlau. Bakunin und die Internationale in Spanien 1868–1873, in Grünberg's *Archiv*, vol. 4, Leipzig, 1914, pp. 243-303
N. Rjasanoff. Bakuniana. I. Bakunin und Karl Marx. II. Bakunin und J. Ph. Becker. III. Programm der Allianz, in Grünberg's *Archiv*, vol. V, Leipzig, 1915, pp. 182-99
G. Stekloff, Bakunin. Moscow. 4 vols.

Barry

Maltman Barry. The Labour Day. Aberdeen, 1890
Joseph Burgess. Will Lloyd George supplant Ramsay Macdonald? London, n.d., *c.* 1930. (Contains material against Maltman Barry)
William Collinson. The Apostle of Free Labour told by Himself, 1913. (Contains material favourable to Maltman Barry from an anti-Labour standpoint)
Ernest Balfort Bax. Reminiscences and Reflections of a Mid and Late Victorian. 1918

A. Bebel's Reminiscences. Translated from the First German Edition by Ernest Untermann, New York, 1911

M. Beer. Fifty Years of International Socialism. 1937

M. Beer. A History of British Socialism with an Introduction by R. H. Tawney. 1940

Max Beer. The International: Recollections, in *Socialist Review*, July-September 1914

Paul Bernard. Le Mouvement ouvrier en France pendant les années 1852-1864 d'après les rapports politiques des Procureurs Généraux. Documents inédits. In *International Review of Social History*, Amsterdam, 1939, pp. 289-321

Edward Bernstein. Evolutionary Socialism. A Criticism and Affirmation. 1909

Louis Bertrand. César de Paepe. Sa vie, son œuvre. Brussels, 1909

Louis Bertrand. Histoire de la démocratie et du socialisme en Belgique depuis 1830. 2 vols. Brussels, 1906-7

L. A. Blanqui. Critique sociale. 2 vols. Paris, 1885

Hypatia Bradlaugh Bonner. Charles Bradlaugh. A Record of his life and Work. 2 vols. 1894

Martin James Boon. How to Construct Free State Railways. 1884

Martin James Boon. Malthusian Quackery. 1884

Martin James Boon. National Paper Money. 1885

Georges Bourgin. La Lutte du Gouvernement Français contre la Première Internationale. Contribution à l'histoire de l'Après-Commune. In *International Review of Social History*, 1939, pp. 39-138

Georges Bourgin. Une Entente franco-allemande. In *International Review of Social History*, 1956, pp. 41-53

T. Brassey. On Work and Wages. 1873

T. Brassey. Foreign Work and English Wages. 1879

Asa Briggs. Victorian People. 1954

Peter Brock. Polish Democrats and English Radicals, 1832-62. In *Journal of Modern History*, New York, June 1953

Luigi Brentano. Meine Polemik mit Karl Marx. Berlin, 1890

Martin Buber. Paths in Utopia. 1949

John Burnett. The Nine Hours Movement: A History of the Engineers' Strike in Newcastle and Gateshead, 1872

Giuseppe del Bo. Lo spionaggio intorno alla Internazionale: Oscar Testut, agente segrete 'Numero 47'. *Movimento Operaio*, 1952, No. 6, Milan, Feltrinelli, pp. 954-70

John Francis Bray. A Voyage from Utopia, 1957. Ed. with an introduction by F. Lloyd-Pritchard

Edward Carpenter. Sketches from Life in Town and Country, 1907. (Contains a study of W. H. Riley)

J. H. Clapham. Economic Development of France and Germany. 1815-1914, 1921

G. B. Clark. A Plea for the Nationalization of the Land. N.d.

G. D. H. Cole and A. W. Filson. British Working Class Movements : Select Documents. 1789–1875. 1951

G. D. H. Cole. Marxism and Anarchism. 1850–1890. 1954

G. D. H. Cole. Chartist Portraits. 1941

J. R. Commons and others. A Documentary History of American Industrial Society, 10 vols. Cleveland, 1910–11

John R. Commons and others. History of Labour in the United States, 4 vols. New York, Macmillan. 1918–35

Stephen Coltham. Potter and the *Beehive*. Doctoral Thesis, Oxford University, 1956

Howard Evans. Sir Randal Cremer : His Life and Work. 1909

E. Dupont. Les Ouvriers, histoire populaire illustrée des travailleurs. Paris, 1890

Third Report of the Royal Commission appointed to enquire into the working of the Elementary Education Acts, 1887

Richard T. Ely. French and German Socialism in Modern Times. 1883

Henry Fawcett. State Socialism and the Nationalization of the Land. 1883

The First International and the Paris Commune. Working Class History, No. 4, n.d.

H. A. L. Fisher. The Republican Tradition in Europe. 1911

P. S. Foner. History of the Labour Movement in the United States to the Founding of the American Federation of Labour. New York, 1947

W. Z. Foster. A History of the Three Internationals. New York, 1955

Alan Fox. A History of the National Union of Boot and Shoe Operatives. 1874–1957. 1958

Frances Elma Gillespie. Labor and Politics in England, 1850–1867. North Carolina, 1927

J. H. Gleason. The Genesis of Russophobia in Great Britain. Harvard. 1950

James Guillaume. L'Internationale, documents et souvenirs 1864–1878. 4 Parts, Paris, 1905

Gathorne Hardy. A Memoir, 2 vols. 1910

Frederic Harrison. Autobiographic Memoirs, 1911

Royden Harrison. British Labour and the Confederacy. *The International Review of Social History*, Amsterdam, 1957, pp. 78-105

Royden Harrison. English Positivists and Labour Movements 1859–1885. Doctoral Thesis. Oxford, 1955

Royden Harrison. Land and Labour League. *Bulletin of the International Institute of Social History*, 1953, pp. 169-95

Adolphe S. Headingley. The Biography of Charles Bradlaugh. 1880

A. Herzen. My Past and Thoughts. 6 vols. 1926

A. Herzen. Polnoye Sobranie Sochineni i Pisem, 16 vols. Ed. M. K. Lemke. Leningrad, 1920

R. J. Hinton. English Radical Leaders. New York, 1875

Helmut Hirsch. Denker und Kaempfer. Frankfurt a/Main, Europaeische Verlagsanstalt, 1955

S. Higginbotham. Our Society's History. Manchester, 1939

G. J. Holyoake. Sixty Years of an Agitator's life. 1906

Mark Hovell. The Chartist Movement. 1925

Elic Howe and John Child. The Society of London Bookbinders, 1870–1951. 1952

George Howell. The Conflicts of Capital and Labour. 1878

George Howell. Labour Legislation, Labour Movements and Labour Leaders, 1902

A. W. Humphrey. A History of Labour Representation. 1912

Robert Hunter. Violence and the Labour Movement. New York. 1914

Henry Mayers Hyndman. The Record of an Adventurous Life. 1911

Address and Provisional Rules of the International Labour Union, 1877. I.I.S.G.

Iz. Istorii Borby Marxa i Engelsa za Proletarskuyu Partiu. Ed. I. S. Galkin, Moscow, 1955

G. Hampden Jackson. Marx, Proudhon and European Socialism. 1957

Gustav Jaeckh. Das Ende der Internationale in England. *Neue Zeit*, vol. 23/2, 1904

G. Jaeckh. The International. 1905

Fr. de Jong. Amsterdam Meetings of the First International in 1872. *Bulletin of the International Institute of Social History*, Amsterdam, 1951, No. 1, pp. 1-15

Jordan and Pratt. Europe and the American Civil War. 1931

M. Kaufmann. Karl Marx and the International. In *Leisure Hour*, 1878, pp. 788-92 and 821-5

M. Kaufmann. Utopias; or, Schemes of Social Improvement from Sir Thomas More to Karl Marx. 1879

B. P. Kosmin. Russkaya Sektsia Pervovo Internationala. Moscow, 1957

Labour and Socialist International. The International 1864-1924. Souvenir. 1924

Labour's Formative Years, 1849-1879. Ed. James B. Jeffreys. 1948

Harry W. Laidler. A History of Socialist Thought. 1927

George Lansbury. My Life. 1928

Emile de Laveleye. Socialism of Today. Translated by Goddard H. Orpen. 1884

Pisma P. L. Lavrova k Germanu Jungu, with a preface by B. Nicolaevski in *Letopisi Marxisma*, vol. II (XII), pp. 151-81. Moscow, 1930

H. W Lee and E. Archibold. Social-Democracy in Britain. Fifty Years of the Socialist Movement. 1935

V. I. Lenin. Critical Remarks on the National Question. Moscow, 1951

J. B. Leno. The Aftermath. 1892

Frederick Lessner. Sixty Years in the Social-Democratic Movement. Before 1848 and After. Recollections of an old Communist. 1907

W. J. Linton. Nineteenth Century Slanderers. George Howell and James Knowles. n.d. (New Haven, Conn., U.S.A.) January 1879

(George Tate.) London Trades Council, 1850–1950. A History. Foreword by Julius Jacobs. 1950

Paul Louis. Histoire du mouvement syndical en France. 1789–1910. Paris, 1920

S. Maccoby. English Radicalism, 1853–1886. 1938

B. Malon. Histoire du socialisme. 5 vols. Paris, 1882–1858

Marx and Engels

I. Berlin. Karl Marx. 1939

E. H. Carr. Karl Marx. A Study in Fanaticism. 1934

Giuseppe del Bo. Nuova luce sulla vita di Marx da un carteggio inedito della moglie e della figlia Jenny. Vol. 7, No. 2, Milano, *Movimento Operaio*, 1955, pp. 252-93

James Guillaume. Karl Marx Pangermaniste et l'AIdT de 1864 à 1870. Paris, 1915

Iz. Istorii Borby Marxa i Engelsa za Proletarskuyu Partiu. A miscellany ed. J. S. Galkin. Moscow, 1955

Harold J. Laski. Karl Marx. An Essay. 1934

Edmund Laskine. L'Internationale et le pangermanisme. Paris, 1916

Jean Longuet. La Politique internationale du marxisme, Paris, 1918

A. Lozovsky. Marx and the Trade Unions. 1935

Gustav Mayer. Friedrich Engels. 2 vols. Hague, 1934

Gustav Mayer. Friedrich Engels. A Biography. 1936

Franz Mehring. Karl Marx. The Story of his Life. Translated by E. Fitzgerald. 1939

Franz Mehring. Aus dem literarischen Nachlass von Karl Marx, Friedrich Engels und Ferdinand Lassalle. Stuttgart. 4 vols. 1902

Boris Nicolaievsky and Otto Maenchen Helfen. Karl Marx: Man and Fighter. 1936

Raymond Postgate. Karl Marx. 1933

Karl Marx, Man, Thinker and Revolutionist. A symposium ed. D. Ryazanoff. 1927

D. Riazanov. Karl Marx and Friedrich Engels. n.d. (1927)

D. Riazanov. The Communist Manifesto of Karl Marx and Friedrich Engels. 1930

D. Rjasanoff. Karl Marx und Friedrich Engels ueber die Polenfrage, in Grünberg's *Archiv*, vol. 6, Leipzig, 1916, pp. 175, 221

D. Riazanov. Novye Dannye o Russkich Priyateliach Marxa i Engelsa, in *Letopisi Marxisma*, vol. 6, pp. 41-9. Moscow, 1928

John Spargo. Karl Marx. New York, 1910

Z

A. Wiznitzer. Marx und die Irische Frage, in Grünberg's *Archiv*, vol. 10. Leipzig, 1922, pp. 49-53

G. J. Mazzini. Life and Writings of Mazzini (vols. I-VI). 1846–70

Joseph Mazzini. The Duties of Man, etc., n.d., Everyman Edition

R. Meyer. Der Emancipationskampf des Vierten Standes. 2 vols. Berlin, 1875–82

Rudolfo Mondolfo. Die Anfaenge der Arbeiterbewegung in Italien bis 1872 und der Streit zwischen Mazzini und Bakunin, in Grünberg's *Archiv*, vol. 14, Leipzig, 1929, pp. 339-63

John De Morgan. John De Morgan's Monthly. December 1876– May 1877

Stephen St. Clair. Sketch of the Life and Labours of John De Morgan, Orator, Elocutionist and Tribune of the People. Leeds 1880

A. Mueller Lehning. The International Association 1855–9 in *International Review of Social History*, vol. 3, Leiden, 1938, pp. 185-286

Max Nettlau. Der Anarchisimus von Proudhon zu Kropotkin, seine historische Entwicklung in den Jahren 1859–1880. Berlin, 1927

M. Nettlau. Aus der Geschichte der Sozialismus. Zur Vorgeschichte der Internationale, in Documente des Sozialismus, vol. 5, No. 7, pp. 324-9. No. 8, pp. 373-7. Berlin, 1908

M. Nettlau. Ein verschollener Nachklang der Internationale : The International Labour Union. (London, 1877–8) in Grünberg's *Archiv*, vol. 9, Leipzig, 1921, pp. 134-45

B. Nicolaevsky. Toward a History of 'The Communist League', 1847–1852. In *International Review of Social History*, vol. 1, pp. 234-52, Amsterdam, 1956

Odger

W. H. G. Armytage. George Odger (1820–1877), *University of Toronto Quarterly*, October 1948, pp. 68-75, Toronto, Canada

Eugene Oswald. Reminiscences of a Busy Life. 1911

R. Pankhurst. The Saint-Simonians : Mill and Carlyle, 1957

Paris, Cmte. de. The Trade Unions of England. London, 1869

The Paris Commune

E. Belfort Bax, Victor Dave and William Morris. A Short Account of the Commune of Paris. 1886

Frank Jellinek. The Paris Commune of 1871. 1937

J. Knishnik-Vetrov. Geroina Parishkoi Kommuny 1871, E. L. Toumanovskaya in *Letopisi Marxisma*, vol. 7/8, Moscow, 1928

Melvin Kranzberg. The Siege of Paris. 1870–1871. A Political and Social History. Ithaca, U.S.A., 1950

Lissagaray. History of the Commune of 1871. New York, 1898

A. Y. Lurye. Portrety Deyatelei Parishkoi Kommuny. Moscow, 1956

D. Riazanov. Novye Dannye o Geroine Parishkoi Kommuny. Elizavete Dimitrievoi in *Letopisi Marxisma*, vol. II (XII), pp. 3-9, Moscow, 1930

Max Schachtman. 1871, The Paris Commune. Chicago, n.d., (1922)

Park. The English Reform Bill of 1867. Columbia University, New York

George Plechanoff. Anarchism and Socialism. Translated by Eleanor Marx Aveling, Chicago, n.d.

Raymond Postgate. The Workers' International, 1921

Raymond Postgate. The Builders' History. 1923

Raymond Postgate. Life of George Lansbury. 1956

Raymond Postgate. Papers of the First International. The George Howell Collection in *Marx-Engels Archiv*. Ed. D. Rjazanov, vol. 1, Frankfurt a/M. 1927, pp. 441-7

Proudhon

D. W. Brogan. Proudhon. 1934

J. L. Puech. Le Proudhonisme dans l'Association Internationale des Travailleurs. Paris, 1907

Dore Neill Raymond. Contemporary British opinion during the Franco-Prussian War. In *Studies in History, Economics and Public Law*, vol. 100, Columbia University, New York, 1921

Rectification concerning Amsterdam Meetings 1872. *Bulletin of the International Institute of Social History*, Amsterdam 1951, No. 3. Leiden, 1951, pp. 198-200

Albert Richard. L'Association Internationale des Travailleurs, Neuchâtel, 1879

D. Rjasanov. Ein Beitrag zur Geschichte der Internationale, Zwei unbekannte Artikel von Fr. Engels und Karl Marx. Neue Zeit, 1913, vol. XXXII, 1, pp. 8-16, 37-44

D. Rjazanov. Die Entstehung der Internationalen Arbeiter Association (Zur Geschichte der Ersten Internationale) in *Marx-Engels Archiv*, vol. 1, pp. 119-202. Frankfurt a/M. 1927.

D. Riazanov. The Establishment of the First International. *The Communist International*. Moscow, 1919, No. 6, pp. 827-35

B. C. Roberts. The Trades Union Congress, 1868-1921. 1958

V. J. Romanienko. Mirovozzrenie N. A. Serno-Solovievicha. Moscow, 1954

Aldo Romano, Storia del movimento socialista in Italia. Milan-Rome 1954. 2 vols.

Arthur Rosenberg. Democracy and Socialism. 1939

Th. Rothstein. From Chartism to Labourism. 1929

W. Stephen Sanders. Early Socialist Days. 1927

Emanie Sachs. The Terrible Siren. Victoria Woodhull, 1838-1927. New York, 1928

Hermann Schlüter. Die Internationale in Amerika. Chicago, 1918

A. R. Schoyen. The Chartist Challenge. 1958

Social Democratic Federation. How I became a Socialist. A Series of Biographical Sketches. 1896

The Socialist League. Constitution and Rules adopted at the Farringdon Hall, London, on July 5, 1885. 1885

Henry Solly. These Eighty Years, or The Story of an Unfinished Life. 2 vols. 1893

Francis William Soutter. Recollections of a Labour Pioneer. 1927

Georg. Stieklow, Die Bakunistische Internationale nach dem Haager Kongress, 1872–1881. Ergänzungsheft zur *Neuen Zeit*, No. 18. Stuttgart, 1914

G. M. Stekloff. History of the First International. 1928

J. Stalin. Marxism and the National Question. 1941

W. Tcherkesoff. Pages of Socialist History. New York, 1902

I. Tchernoff. Le Parti Républicain au Coup d'état et sous le Second Empire. Paris, 1906

Dona Torr. Tom Mann and His Times, vol. 1, 1856–1890. 1956

Ernest A. Vizetelly. My Adventures in the Commune. 1914

Alfred H. Walton. An Appeal to all Trade Societies on the necessity for a National Organisation of Trades for the Industrial, Social and Political Emancipation of Labour. 1848

Sidney and Beatrice Webb. The History of Trade Unionism. 1912

G. Weill. Histoire du mouvement social en France, 1852–1902. Paris, 1904

Clifton K. Yearly, Jr. Britons in American Labor: A History of the Influence of the United Kingdom Immigrants on American Labor, 1820–1914. Baltimore, 1957

Dr. Zacher. The Red International. Translated from the 3rd German edition by the Rev. E. M. Goldart. 1885

V. I. Zasulich. Ocherk Istorii Mezhdunarodnovo Obschestva Rabochich. Geneva, 1889. (Also in her Collected Works, in Russian)

INDEX